Clear and Convincing

**MICHAEL FIX AND
RAYMOND J. STRUYK**
Editors

Clear and Convincing Evidence

Measurement of Discrimination in America

THE URBAN INSTITUTE PRESS
Washington, D.C.

THE URBAN INSTITUTE PRESS
2100 M Street, N.W.
Washington, D.C. 20037

Library of Congress Cataloging in Publication Data

Clear and Convincing Evidence: Measurement of Discrimination in America/Michael Fix and Raymond J. Struyk, editors.

1. Discrimination in housing—United States—Auditing.   2. Discrimination in mortgage loans—United States—Auditing.   3. Discrimination in insurance—United States—Auditing.   4. Discrimination in employment—United States.   I.   Fix, Michael.   II.   Struyk, Raymond J.

HD7288.76.U5C54   1992   92-12966
305′.0973—dc20   CIP

ISBN 0-87766-600-8 (alk. paper)
ISBN 0-87766-599-0 (alk. paper; casebound)

(Replaces old ISBN 0-87766-569-9 paper and 0-87766-568-0 casebound.)

Urban Institute books are printed on acid-free paper whenever possible.

Printed in the United States of America.

Distributed by:
          University Press of America
4720 Boston Way   3 Henrietta Street
Lanham, MD 20706   London   WC2E 8LU   ENGLAND

THE URBAN INSTITUTE is a nonprofit policy research and educational organization established in Washington, D.C., in 1968. Its staff investigates the social and economic problems confronting the nation and public and private means to alleviate them. The Institute disseminates significant findings of its research through the publications program of its Press. The goals of the Institute are to sharpen thinking about societal problems and efforts to solve them, improve government decisions and performance, and increase citizen awareness of important policy choices.

Through work that ranges from broad conceptual studies to administrative and technical assistance, Institute researchers contribute to the stock of knowledge available to guide decision making in the public interest.

Conclusions or opinions expressed in Institute publications are those of the authors and do not necessarily reflect the views of staff members, officers or trustees of the Institute, advisory groups, or any organizations that provide financial support to the Institute.

ACKNOWLEDGMENTS

This volume, and much of the work upon which it is based, have been both supported and guided by James Gibson, director of the Equal Opportunity Program of The Rockefeller Foundation through most of the period when the work was being done. Our debts to Jim, who is now at the Urban Institute, are many and we gratefully acknowledge them.

We are also deeply indebted to Sheila Lopez, who coordinated the conference upon which the volume is based, and to Ellen Jacobs who assisted with the conference and this volume.

We would like to thank David Strauss of the University of Chicago Law School and Michael White of the Department of Sociology and the Population Studies Program of Brown University for their incisive comments on a previous version of the manuscript. And we would like to express our appreciation to Representative John Conyers, Chair of the Government Operations Committee of the United States House of Representatives and to his staff, for making available the offices and facilities of the Committee for the conference.

Finally, we would like to thank Felicity Skidmore, Director of the Urban Institute Press and our editor, Michal Keeley, for their expert assistance in the publication of this volume.

CONTENTS

Tables

Figures

FOREWORD

Few issues divide the nation as much as race and civil rights and the questions of distributional justice to which they give rise. Auditing for discrimination can both enhance our ability to measure discrimination and increase the effectiveness of civil rights law and enforcement designed to counteract it. As illustrated by the use of audits to support the Fair Housing Act Amendments of 1988, auditing's link to public policy is especially close. Because of this, documentation of discrimination such as that presented in this volume can influence the terms of the debate over strengthening equal opportunity legislation.

Beyond its value as a tool for measuring discrimination and conducting public policy research, auditing can contribute importantly to efforts to enforce the law. Discrimination against race, ethnicity, or gender is illegal in this country, just as not paying income taxes is illegal. But while the Internal Revenue Service has a carefully drawn, systematic strategy for enforcing the tax code, to date there is no comparable strategy to enforce the laws against discrimination, despite their importance. Auditing the behavior of employers, real estate agents, and bankers for evidence of discrimination in hiring, housing, and credit lending could be an essential part of such a strategy.

This book presents the detailed results of nationwide employment, housing, and credit audits conducted to date, and analyzes the strengths and limits of auditing for discrimination. One important dimension these analysts add to the debate over the use of auditing is an examination of behavior that "diminishes" as well as behavior that "denies" opportunities to certain individuals in society. This distinction is especially useful at a time in this country when discrimination has grown more subtle. It is our hope that this analysis of the auditing technique will help shed light on how we might better discern less visible but no less damaging forms of discrimination.

William Gorham
President

Chapter One

AN OVERVIEW OF AUDITING FOR DISCRIMINATION

Michael Fix, George C. Galster, and Raymond J. Struyk

The concept of auditing for discrimination is straightforward. Two individuals (auditors or testers) are matched for all relevant personal characteristics other than the one that is presumed to lead to discrimination, e.g., race, ethnicity, gender. They then apply for a job, a housing unit, or a mortgage, or begin to negotiate for a good or service. The results they achieve and the treatment they receive in the transaction are closely observed, documented, and analyzed to determine if the outcomes reveal patterns of differential treatment on the basis of the trait studied and/or protected by antidiscrimination laws. The technique of auditing for discrimination was first broadly used in the area of housing (Wienk et al. 1979) and has subsequently been adapted at least experimentally to activities such as seeking employment (Cross 1990; Turner, Fix, and Struyk 1991), applying for a mortgage (Center for Community Change 1989), seeking home owner's insurance (Squires and Velez 1988), negotiating the price of a car (Ayres 1991), seeking taxi services (Ridley 1989) and applying for membership in a health club. Auditing is used for both research and enforcement. When used in the enforcement context it is typically referred to as testing rather than auditing. Research auditing is designed to measure the extent of discrimination in a market, requiring a large number of tests in order to obtain statistical reliability for the findings. Studies of employment discrimination, for example, typically require two hundred or more tests within a metropolitan area to achieve acceptable statistical reliability for differences in treatment of minority and majority auditors. Moreover, the sample of "opportunities" to be audited must be carefully drawn. This involves both defining the sampling frame with precision, i.e., what subset of all opportunities can be or will be included, and randomly selecting the opportunities for testing to insure a representative sample.

Enforcement auditing (testing) in contrast, is designed to develop evidence of discrimination against an individual or firm for use in legal proceedings. In this instance the firm is selected on the basis of a formal complaint or other reason to suspect discriminatory behavior. A single carefully executed test may be sufficient, although the results of several tests are typically presented as evidence. The results of an audit study for a metropolitan area can help establish the context in which the results of individual tests are presented, and can help target individual audits (by neighborhood or industry, for example).

The utility and value of auditing have grown in the current legal and political environment. It is a particularly effective instrument for detecting the more subtle forms of discrimination that have evolved since the civil rights revolution of the 1960s. Auditing can make plain the need for sustained, expanded, or redirected civil rights enforcement activity. Auditing also provides direct evidence of discrimination that may, in some cases, offer an evidentiary alternative or supplement to plaintiffs whose cases would otherwise rest on statistical evidence alone. This chapter provides an overview of past use of auditing, or testing, for discrimination and discusses how it might be applied in the future. We believe that auditing to establish the general incidence of discrimination and testing to support litigation against discriminatory practices have the potential to improve the effectiveness of civil rights law and enforcement.

The chapter is divided into seven sections. The first section sets the context by describing recent trends in public attitudes and expert understanding of the scope and character of discrimination. These trends have been influenced by auditing and, in turn, will shape its future. The second section sketches the strengths and limits of auditing for both research and enforcement purposes, emphasizing ethical issues that have been raised. In the third section we review the major results of the employment, housing, and credit audits conducted to date. The fourth section explores a series of methodological issues raised in this volume and elsewhere relating to the design of audits and interpretation of their results. The fifth section looks at the impact that audit results may have had on the shape of recent civil rights legislation, focusing on the Fair Housing Amendments Act of 1988, a law that expanded existing civil rights protections. We contend that the extensive documentation of housing discrimination, to which audits contributed, was instrumental in this expansion. The sixth section examines the potential role of auditing and testing in a comprehensive enforcement strategy, focusing on the case of housing. We conclude with a discussion of the implications of auditing for civil rights policy.

THE CONTEXT FOR EXPANDING THE USE OF AUDITING

We summarize two strands of related developments in housing, housing credit, and employment rights in recent years to set the stage for the ideas considered later in this chapter and the rest of the volume. First, public attitudes about equal rights and affirmative action have diverged in housing and employment; such divergent attitudes can be expected to affect the extent of discrimination in each area and to influence decisions made by Congress and the courts. Second, important differences among housing, housing credit, and employment exist in the corpus of evidence on discrimination and its reflection in conventional wisdom and expert opinion. A key issue is the extent to which audit findings are consistent with attitudinal differences and variation in expert opinion on different areas.

Trends in the Attitudes of Whites

Congressional legislation and, to a lesser extent, the decisions of the courts are influenced (as they should be) by the attitudes of the nation's citizens. This has indeed been the case for civil rights in recent years.

Table 1.1 presents the responses to questions about the attitudes of whites to equal opportunities in housing and employment for blacks over the 1963–1990 period.[1] Each question included in the table has been asked in the same form over a long period by a prominent national survey organization. Following the lead of Schuman et al. (1985), we assemble the questions in the table into three groups:

Principles. Questions that ask respondents whether they endorse broad principles of nondiscrimination and desegregation in important areas of social life.

Government Role/Implementation. Questions that deal with steps that the government (usually but not always the federal government) might take either to reduce discrimination or segregation or to improve the economic status of blacks.

Social distance. Questions that ask how respondents would react in situations that involve some degree of integration at a personal level. Thus the questions deal with the principle of integration, not in an abstract way or in terms of government enforcement, but rather at the level of the individual's behavior or feelings. (Pp. 72–3)

Table 1.1 TRENDS IN WHITE ATTITUDES TOWARDS BLACKS IN HOUSING AND EMPLOYMENT, 1963–1990

	Year of survey																												Last minus first
	63	64	65	66	67	68	69	70	71	72	73	74	75	76	77	78	79	80	81	82	83	84	85	86	87	88	89	90	
A. Housing																													
1. Questions concerning principles																													
Residential choice, 1 alt. (NORC)[a]																													
% Agree slightly	21	—	—	—	—	25	—	18	—	15	—	—	—	18	21	—	17	—	15	—	—	14	15	—	12	15	14	14	−7
% Disagree slightly	20	—	—	—	—	25	—	19	—	23	—	—	—	26	29	—	29	—	32	—	—	25	28	—	22	24	23	25	+5
% Disagree strongly	19	—	—	—	—	19	—	34	—	40	—	—	—	34	28	—	38	—	39	—	—	48	44	—	56	54	55	53	+34
Residential choice, 2 alt. (ISR)																													
% Blacks have rights	—	—	—	—	—	73	—	—	—	88	—	—	—	—	—	—	—	—	—	—	—	—	—	—	—	—	—	—	+15
2. Implementation questions																													
Open housing (NORC)																													
% No discrimination	—	—	—	—	—	—	—	—	—	—	—	34	—	34	35	—	37	—	40	—	—	46	51	51	52	56	59	55	+21
3. Social distance questions																													
Next door (Gallup)																													
% Might	24	—	23	21	24	—	—	—	—	—	—	—	—	—	—	10	—	—	—	—	—	—	—	—	—	—	—	4	−20
% No	55	—	63	66	63	—	—	—	—	—	—	—	—	—	—	86	—	—	—	—	—	—	—	—	—	—	—	93	+38
Great numbers (Gallup)																													
% Might	28	—	30	31	32	—	—	—	—	—	—	—	—	—	—	33	—	—	—	—	—	—	—	—	—	—	—	18	−10
% No	23	—	28	30	28	—	—	—	—	—	—	—	—	—	—	46	—	—	—	—	—	—	—	—	—	—	—	68	+45
Same block (NORC)																													
% No	63	64	69	71	—	77	—	—	—	85	—	—	—	—	—	—	—	—	—	—	—	—	—	—	—	—	—	—	+22
B. Employment																													
1. Questions concerning principles																													
Equal jobs (NORC)																													
% As good a chance	85	—	—	89	—	—	—	—	—	97	—	—	—	—	—	—	—	—	—	—	—	—	—	—	—	—	—	—	+12

2. Implementation questions

Federal job intervention

1. Gov't see to job and living standard: — — — — — 13 — 12 — 11 — 7 — 10 — 10 — 10 — 10 — 9 — 9   −4
2.   6 — 5 — 5 — 3 — 6 — 7 — 6 — 6 — 6   0
3.   9 — 8 — 8 — 7 — 9 — 9 — 11 — 8 — 9   0
4.   20 — 20 — 17 — 19 — 18 — 20 — 20 — 21 — 18   −2
5.   13 — 12 — 10 — 15 — 13 — 16 — 16 — 16 — 16   +3
6.   8 — 8 — 11 — 12 — 16 — 13 — 13 — 14 — 14   +6
7. Gov't let each person get ahead on his own: 19 — 17 — 18 — 17 — 12 — 12 — 9 — 17 — 13   −6
   13 — 16 — 20 — 21 — 16 — 14 — 14 — 7 — 15   +2

Sources: Data for 1963–83, Schuman et al. (1985), tables 3.1, 3.2, 3.3; 1984–90, NORC General Social Surveys, Gallup and Hujick (1990), and ISR unpublished tabulation.

[a]NORC is the National Opinion Research Center; ISR is the Institute for Social Research at the University of Michigan.

Question wordings and variants:

Residential choice, 1 alternative (NORC): "Here are some opinions other people have expressed in connection with black–white relations. Which statement on the card comes closest to how you yourself feel? White people have a right to keep blacks out of their neighborhoods if they want to, and blacks should respect that right."

1. Agree strongly
2. Agree slightly
3. Disagree slightly
4. Disagree strongly

Residential choice, 2 alternatives (ISR): "Which of these statements would you agree with: White people have a right to keep black people out of their neighborhoods if they want to, or, black people have a right to live wherever they can afford to, just like anybody else?"

1. Keep blacks out
2. Blacks have rights

(Variant: In 1964 replace "anybody else" with "white people.")

continued

Table 1.1 TRENDS IN WHITE ATTITUDES TOWARDS BLACKS IN HOUSING AND EMPLOYMENT, 1963–1990 (continued)

Open housing (NORC): "Suppose there is a community-wide vote on the general issue. There are two possible laws to vote on. One law says that a homeowner can decide for himself who to sell his house to, even if he prefers not to sell to blacks. The second law says that a homeowner cannot refuse to sell to someone because of their race or color. Which law would you vote for?"

1. Homeowner can decide
2. No discrimination

Next door (Gallup): "If black people came to live next door, would you move?"

1. Yes, definitely
2. Might
3. No

Great numbers (Gallup): "Would you move if black people came to live in great numbers in your neighborhood?"

1. Yes, definitely
2. Might
3. No

Same block (NORC): "If a Negro with the same income and education as you have moved into your block, would it make any difference to you?"

1. Yes
2. No

Equal jobs (NORC): "Do you think Negroes should have as good a chance as white people to get any kind of job, or do you think white people should have the first chance at any kind of job?"

1. As good a chance
2. White people first

Federal job intervention (ISR): "Some people feel that the government in Washington should see to it that every person has a job and a good standard of living. Others think the government should just let each person get ahead on his own. And, of course, other people have opinions somewhere in between. Where would you place yourself on this scale, or haven't you thought much about this?" (7-point scale shown to respondents).

1. Government see to job and good standard of living
2.
. . . .
7. Government let each person get ahead on his own.

Turning to the responses to the housing questions first, one sees truly remarkable changes in attitudes of whites in support of the rights of black people over the past quarter century in all three areas—principles, government role/implementation, and social distance. The figures indicate a major increase in racial tolerance. Importantly, these changes continued to evolve during the 1980s. Particularly telling is the response to the government role question, which asks if a home owner should be able to decide whom he is willing to sell his home to: Over the 1980s the percentage of respondents saying he should not be able to discriminate rose by 15 percentage points.

Questions dealing with employment rights indicate a more mixed picture. On the one hand, as early as 1972 nearly all respondents agreed in principle that blacks should have as good a chance at obtaining any kind of job as whites. On the other hand, for the one question on the government's role for which longitudinal data exist throughout the 1980s, the pattern of responses shows little change over the 1972–88 period in the percentage of respondents who believed the government "should see to it that every person has a job and a good standard of living." In the area of employment, then, there is an abiding reluctance to allow government to determine outcomes. This suggests that there are differences in attitudes of whites on issues involving housing versus employment—differences that may inform the formulation of antidiscrimination policy in the two areas.

Current Knowledge about Discrimination

What is the conventional wisdom in the public policy and research communities about the extent of discrimination against blacks in housing availability, employment, and mortgage credit, and upon what is it based?[2]

Before the advent of audits, research findings typically come from studies employing multivariate analyses. In these studies the analyst controls for factors, such as age and education, that could reasonably be expected to account for the outcomes observed for majorities and minorities separately—such as being employed or having a mortgage loan approved. The analyst then identifies a residual difference between the two groups, that is, a difference putatively not associated with attributes included in the analysis. Some unknown share, possibly all, of the residual is suspected of being due to discrimination; but often the share cannot be identified. Moreover, many problems emerge in attempting to fully specify the multivariate models, which introduces uncertainty about whether the magnitude of the residual itself is correct.[3] Further, such studies cannot report the incidence of discrimination, only the magnitude of the resulting impact. In short, a good deal of uncertainty about the level of discrimination is the rule in such studies (Price and Mills 1985).[4]

Employment. In the broadest terms, economists have found that blacks operate at a disadvantage in the labor market relative to comparable whites in terms of earnings, occupations, and employment levels (Jaynes and Williams 1989, 146–7).[5] Most economists would attribute at least some of this difference to discrimination in the market; part of the difference is also due to residential segregation that puts lower-skilled blacks a greater distance from suburban blue-collar jobs than their white counterparts. Residential segregation, in turn, may result at least partially from housing discrimination. Young black men, who appear especially disadvantaged, have received the most intense study (e.g., Freeman and Holzer 1986; Rees 1986; Freeman 1990). Most recently, analysts have been struck by the decline in the employment rates of all black men compared with white men during the 1980s when their relative wages appear to have risen; a similar pattern has not been observed for black women (Jaynes 1990).

Beneath the surface of this general agreement on the existence of employment discrimination, however, there is much controversy. On the basis of standard statistical methods, some analysts have suggested sharp declines in the extent of discrimination; others[6] contend that differences in blacks' outcomes relative to whites' are culture-based and not reasonably attributed to discrimination.[7] Ballen and Freeman (1986), after controlling for differences in factors affecting the probability of employment, such as education and age,[8] identified a large difference in the rates at which white versus inner-city black youth make the transition between unemployment and employment. They suggested that this residual difference may have been due in part to employers' adverse reaction to employment histories involving numerous short-duration positions—a pattern more common among inner-city black youth. But the authors were unable to provide a quantified explanation of the residual, that is, the share attributable to discrimination.

There has been and is a large and continuing controversy about the role suburbanization of blue-collar jobs has played in reducing black employment opportunities.[9] Ihlanfeldt and Sjoquist (1990) have provided convincing econometric evidence that location does matter; after controlling for other factors such as individual characteristics and family background, they found the range of the racial gap in employment rates attributable to job access to be 30 to 50 percent. Note that, again, 50 to 70 percent of the racial gap remains to be explained—some of which is presumably attributable to discrimination. And numerous complaints about discrimination on the basis of race in hiring, but especially wages and promotions, continue to be filed with state and federal administrative agencies and courts (Donohue and Siegelman 1991).

In sum, analyses of discrimination in employment have generated substantial consensus that blatant discrimination in hiring and wages has been largely eliminated (Donohue and Heckman 1990). Moreover, the statistical estimates indicate that there is little, if any, discrimination against black women in comparison with white women (Jaynes and Williams 1989, 146).[10] Yet there remains sharp disagreement about the extent of continuing, more subtle forms of discrimination against minorities; indeed, there is substantial uncertainty about the ability to identify more subtle discriminatory acts (e.g., Strauss 1990). Such controversy is to be expected, given the problems noted earlier in accurately identifying discrimination in hiring and wages from statistical data.

Indeed, congressional hearings on the Civil Rights Acts of 1990 and 1991 focused almost exclusively on the impact of recent Supreme Court decisions on future patterns of litigation. Questions about, or data on, the extent of discrimination were rarely raised.[11] Our understanding of the extent and character of discrimination in mortgage credit markets is even less developed.

Credit. The popular discussion of possible discrimination in lending has been dominated by two simple empirical observations:

- [ ] The rate at which loans are originated per 1,000 owner-occupied dwellings in predominantly white neighborhoods is two to three times greater than the rate in predominantly black neighborhoods.
- [ ] The rejection rate for black mortgage loan applicants is more than twice as high as the rate for white applicants. Moreover, there is a strong suspicion that would-be minority applicants are often discouraged from making an application.[12]

While these findings could result from factors other than discrimination, many in the policy community find this hard to accept. There is a presumption that where there is so much smoke there must be fire (U.S. Senate 1990, 119).

In stark contrast, the responsible supervisory agencies (Federal Reserve Board, Office of the Comptroller of the Currency, etc.) have testified repeatedly that simple tabulations of differences in white-black loan rates and volumes are not meaningful because they fail to control for a host of germane factors influencing the demand for and supply of mortgage loans. Moreover, their examiners have uncovered few, if any, discriminatory actions in mortgage lending by thrifts and banks.[13] Nevertheless the differences in lending rates, buttressed by a number of cases of discrimination documented by private fair-housing groups, have produced an apparently strong disposition in Congress to believe discrimination is occurring in mortgage lending.

Most rigorous statistical analyses of mortgage discrimination have not produced definitive results. Analysts employ the standard methodology described at the beginning of this section. Data on the aggregate number or volume of loans made to neighborhoods or census tracts have been analyzed, as have individual loan applications. Even analyses employing microdata on applicants, however, suffer from having to use indicators of the characteristics of the area in which the property to be purchased is located, rather than information on the specific property. Until recently, the most careful studies employing microdata on mortgage applications yielded mixed results as to the presence of discrimination (Schafer and Ladd 1981; King 1980).[14] However, a recent study (Munnell et al. 1992) conducted by the Federal Reserve Bank in Boston, which examined data from mortgage applications, found that Boston blacks and Hispanics were more frequently denied loans than whites who represented similar credit risks. Given the evidence that there is discrimination at the application stage of mortgage lending, it is reasonable to presume there is also discrimination at the pre-application stage. But little analysis has been done of the extent to which black applicants are discouraged at this preapplication stage—except for the pioneering audit projects reviewed by George Galster (see chapter 7 of this volume).

Housing Availability. Today's conventional wisdom—of widespread discrimination in housing transactions—has been profoundly shaped by the release in 1979 of the results of the Housing Market Practices Survey—the first national audit study of housing availability (Wienk et al. 1979).[15] This study documented that a black home seeker experienced unfavorable treatment in 28 percent of inquiries about the availability of rental units and in 15 percent of those about home owner units advertised in a major metropolitan newspaper. Over a typical housing search in which the minority home seeker contacts several rental or sales agents, the probability of encountering unfavorable treatment at least once thus becomes very large. These national findings have been bolstered by literally dozens of audit studies conducted at the local level and a large number of media stories on their results and the sometimes spectacular awards received by plaintiffs who bring housing discrimination suits (Galster 1990b; 1991a). Scattered audits in several cities conducted between 1978 and 1983 suggest more variable, but similar outcomes for Hispanics.[16] Against this background it is hardly surprising that the presence of discrimination in the housing market is not seriously contested. Indeed, the marshaling of evidence on this score in the congressional report for the Title VIII amendments is striking (U.S. House of Representatives 1988).

ADVANTAGES AND ETHICS OF AUDITING

As we have seen, our knowledge of discrimination is uneven and the tools available to social scientists for measuring it are limited. What, then, are some of the defining strengths and liabilities of auditing in this context?

Among the chief advantages of auditing are the comparative level of confidence its results inspire, the political persuasiveness of those results, its ability to detect subtle forms of discrimination, and its efficiency as an enforcement tool. Critics of auditing point to ethical problems raised by the deception it involves, its invasion of privacy, its use of human subjects without their knowledge or consent, the problem of tester motives and their implications for reliability, difficulties in interpreting the results of audits, and the feasibility of using testing for comparatively complex transactions such as hiring. (In this section we do not go into the statistical issues involved in measuring discrimination on the basis of audit data. These are discussed in the section beginning on p. 25, after we have summarized the audit results.)

Ultimately, the principle guiding judgments on the merits of conducting audits must be whether the benefits that will accrue to society substantially exceed the costs that will be borne by the firms being audited and the costs of actually conducting the audit.

In discussing the comparative advantages and disadvantages of auditing we need to distinguish between the use of audits for research and the use of audits for enforcement. The purpose of research audits is to measure and understand discrimination in order to guide policy—that is, to identify types of transactions that need to be covered by antidiscrimination protections; to identify industries, practices, or regions as targets for enforcement; or to specify effective remedies for discrimination. The deterrent impact of such activities is indirect and differs from that associated with litigation against alleged violators, where the goal is to detect, punish, and deter discrimination. In research studies discriminators do not learn that their practices have been discovered, and there is no direct imperative for them to change their ways. The same, obviously, is not true in the enforcement context.

The Arguments for Auditing

One major advantage of auditing is the comparatively high level of confidence attached to the results, owing to the fact that auditing is usually based on close observation of individuals (e.g., employers, real estate agents) reacting spontaneously to a controlled choice between two or more candidates who are alike except for the presence of a protected trait.[17] With characteristics other than the protected trait controlled for, systematic patterns of differential treatment can be identified.[18] Another value of audits is their ability to present evidence on unequal treatment, while at the same time informing the character of that treatment. That is, audits can detect and distinguish opportunity-denying behavior (e.g., rejection of one job candidate in favor of another) and opportunity-diminishing behaviors such as steering minorities to lower paying jobs. In so doing, well-designed audits can present strong evidence on the incidence, character, and impacts of unequal treatment.

At the same time, it is important to appreciate the limited capacity of other methods of detecting and measuring discrimination. There are basically three alternative research strategies: (1) analysis of statistical imbalances in the distribution of goods, workers, etc; (2) self-reports of possible discriminators (e.g., employers); and (3) victimization studies.

As we have noted, analysts using only statistical data to detect and measure discrimination must control for a host of possibly germane factors before ascribing such unfavorable outcomes as high unemployment rates or higher car payments to the practices of employers, car dealers, and the like. Obviously, the complexity of the analysis and the number of judgments that must be made reduce confidence in the results, as does the heavy reliance on statistical evidence demonstrating "undue coincidence" between race or ethnicity and, say, employment or wage outcomes.

Self-reported results of the incidence and character of discrimination are obtained either through telephone or mail surveys or through face-to-face interviewing. Mail or telephone survey methods can be comparatively effective only when the type of discrimination in question would not constitute an obvious violation of law and when candid responses can be expected. These factors were present in the General Accounting Office's mail survey of employer responses to the employer sanctions provisions of the 1986 Immigration Reform and Control Act (U.S. General Accounting Office 1990). Even here, though, the survey was criticized because some believed its results—which reported widespread discrimination—were due to a mix of misunderstanding and self-interest among the respondents (Bowsher 1990).

Another strategy for exploring discriminatory practices is simply to interview persons in a position to discriminate face to face. This strategy was adopted by two researchers at the University of Chicago, Joleen Kirschenman and Kathryn Neckerman (1991). They found employers in Chicago surprisingly willing to reveal their prejudices vis-à-vis young minority workers. But despite the insights into discrimination this kind of work provides, it has not been used to provide statistical estimates of discrimination.

Finally, victimization surveys draw only on those who believe that they have been discriminated against and who have chosen to come forward. Although such studies are informative, they make no pretense at providing statistically meaningful evidence on the incidence or impact of discrimination.

The limitations that characterize one of more of these approaches—susceptibility to self-interested responses or the inability to generate statistically meaningful results—do not apply to auditing.

The results of auditing are also distinguished by their political legitimacy. This stems not only from confidence in their accuracy, but also from the kind of "story" that auditing tells.[19] The departing premise of audits is a team of candidates who are equivalently qualified (in some cases the minority candidate is slightly better qualified). As a result, any systematic pattern of unfavorable treatment that emerges reveals decisions that are based on factors other than merit. This type of selection violates the most basic notions of fairness and justice. It thus differs from other illegal discriminatory activities that present somewhat more ambiguous moral questions. (An example would be the adoption of neutral practices that are found to have an unfavorable, if unintended, impact on minorities.) The political influence of audits owes in part, then, to the fact they forcefully demonstrate what appears to be patently unfair treatment.

The legitimacy of these controlled tests has a corollary in the enforcement context. Firms whose day-to-day practices are evenhanded will escape detection in audits even when the composition of their work forces or their lending patterns might "look bad on paper." In the case of employment, this might be a desirable policy outcome where a firm's work force is racially imbalanced as a result of historical processes over which the firm had no control. However, it would constitute a less just result where a firm has historically discriminated but has recently changed its policies.

Auditing is useful not only for its scientific and political credibility but also for its sensitivity to otherwise concealed practices. Thus it is especially valuable in an era in which discrimination has grown more subtle and less detectable than was once the case.[20] Discrimination in hiring—an issue that has drawn little analytic attention[21] and represents a constantly declining share of the rising volume of employment discrimination cases[22]—provides a good example of the important policy implications of this ability to detect concealed practices. Contact between the applicant and the employer during the hiring process is typically fleeting, the eventual outcome is unknown to the candidate, and the process itself rarely signals exclusionary intent. As a result few complaints are filed, leading to a general perception that discrimination in hiring is not as important a social problem as discrimination in promotions or terminations, which generate a far larger number of complaints. Public and private enforcement resources are then allocated (and potentially misallocated) on the basis of a possible misperception.

As we have noted, close observation of the comparative outcomes of matched testers as they advance through the hiring process allows one to detect and measure unequal treatment and outcomes, even when they are masked by apparently courteous treatment. But auditing has a further value. And that is its ability to detect and measure opportunity-*diminishing* as well as opportunity-*denying* behaviors. Opportunity denial means that the home or job seeker was refused the possibility of pursuing the home or job advertised or a similar opportunity: The door was closed. For example, a rental agent would tell the minority auditor that no units were available but would tell his white teammate that one or more units were available; or the majority job candidate would be granted an interview or job while his minority counterpart was refused one. Opportunity-diminishing behaviors include those subtle signals of encouragement and discouragement that are hard to detect and that may "save" the discriminator from taking actions that more clearly are violations of the law. The

Urban Institute Employment Discrimination Study, for example, measured differential treatment of black and white job applicants not only in terms of advancement in the process but also in terms of:

—Difficulty in obtaining an application for a job;
—Negative comments;
—Positive comments;
—Interview waiting time;
—Length of the interview;
—Number of interviewers; and
—Quality of job offered (hours, fringe benefits, etc.).

Not only are these behaviors detectable through auditing; in most instances they lend themselves to quantification and even to the development of cumulative measures.

Among such opportunity-diminishing behaviors, audits offer perhaps the best window on the nature and extent of steering. Steering is a process that makes available different, and typically inferior, opportunities to minorities and that sustains existing patterns of segregation and discrimination. Like other opportunity-diminishing behaviors, steering is especially resistant to other forms of detection. In the employment context, take, for example, the case of an audit team responding to an advertisement placed by a car dealer. Both team members apply for and are offered jobs. However, the minority is assigned to the used-car lot, where the commissions are lower and the clientele poorer; the other member of the team is assigned to the new-car lot, where the reverse is the case. In this and similar cases the discrimination involved would escape many statistical assessments.

Another argument that is made for testing is that it can make the enforcement process more efficient. Carefully administered audits are likely to lead to fewer "false positives" or false legal claims than evidence of mere statistical imbalances in neighborhoods or workplaces. In addition, early studies suggest that housing discrimination cases that are based on audits are far more likely to settle before trial and in favor of the plaintiff than are cases brought using other forms of evidence. A more recent study of testing's impact is less conclusive (Turner et al. 1992).[23] By stimulating early settlement, tests reduce costs for the parties, for state and federal court systems, and for administrative agencies and tribunals. Thus adoption of testing by law enforcement agencies could make more efficient use of public enforcement resources.

Beyond these economies, testing provides public and private enforcement agencies with a tool that can help them root out discriminatory practices in a systematic manner rather than simply responding to complaints that might be filed.

The Ethics of Auditing

The use of auditing for both enforcement and research purposes has been criticized on ethical grounds.

One critique, forcefully advanced by Sissela Bok in her book *Lying* (1979, 198–203), condemns the use of deception in social science. A central premise of the book is that the use of deception in all its forms is a "slippery slope" and that its institutionalization will do more harm than good. Deceit for purportedly noble goals will breed deceit for less admirable purposes. Thus Bok would claim that the use of deception in tests for discrimination in housing and employment will only legitimize questionable practices like the use of pseudostudents to monitor the ideological content of college professors' lectures.

Another ethical critique of auditing focuses on the fact that the agent whose behavior is being monitored is effectively used in an experiment without his knowledge or consent, breaching legitimate expectations of privacy. Critics also claim that despite the fact that the researchers may make every effort to limit the intrusiveness of the experiment, some harm is done to the agent in the cost of time lost from other pursuits.

An ethical issue that applies only to testing for enforcement is the issue of entrapment. Critics of auditing who make this argument charge that the purportedly illegal behavior detected was induced by the audit process itself.

Responding to these ethical criticisms requires a balancing of interests and an acknowledgment of the goals and advantages of auditing.[24]

With regard to the critique that testing invades a legitimate privacy interest, the behaviors that have been monitored in the studies documented in this volume all involve public, commercial, or professional acts. In most instances there has been a special invitation issued to the public—via a published ad for a job, apartment, or loan—regarding the transaction that is later monitored. Moreover, the behaviors that have been monitored are all publicly regulated at some level, either by laws barring discrimination or by professional codes of conduct. It could be argued that such activities are similar to the operation of a motor vehicle and, thus, subject to the unannounced monitoring that is accepted practice there. As Christopher Edley argues (chapter 9), such public behavior creates, in effect, an implied consent to this kind of policing that makes it possible.

With regard to enforcement and claims that auditing constitutes entrapment, it is important to distinguish between auditing and other contexts in which this defense is raised. In the audit context no attractive lures (drugs, money) are presented to the discriminator that might tempt or induce him to act in an illegal manner. (Indeed, the reverse could be said to be the case when minority candidates present more favorable credentials than white candidates.) In fact, the purpose of audits is to observe the conventional practices of the monitored firm or individual and not to stimulate exceptional and illegal behaviors.

In the case of auditing for research purposes, it is clear that no real harm, discomfort, or liability attaches to the firm or employee audited. In all cases audits have been structured in a manner to make them as unintrusive as possible, occupying a few moments to an hour of the real estate agent's, employer's, or car salesman's time.[25] Because auditors of hiring practices or housing rentals or sales are instructed to turn down offers soon after they are made, there is no harm to members of the pool of legitimate applicants.

The legitimacy of testing in these separate contexts is reinforced by the fact that there is no good analytic alternative for determining the prevalence and character of discrimination. The courts have led the way in recognizing that testing may provide the only credible way of developing information about discrimination:

> [Because] it is frequently difficult to develop proof in discrimination cases . . . the evidence provided by testers is frequently valuable, if not indispensable.[26]

> [M]any times the evidence gathered by a tester may . . . be the only competent evidence available to prove that the defendant has engaged in unlawful conduct.[27]

Further, there is no alternative to the clandestine character of the test. To request consent would lead to staged (vs. spontaneous) behavior and would defeat the essential purpose of the study.[28]

Audits for both research and enforcement serve an important public purpose: to locate the manifest injustice of discrimination on the basis of race, ethnicity, and gender when it exists, and in doing so, to begin to counteract it. Moreover, as we have noted, the linkage of research to public policy has been unusually close. This has been clearest in the use of audits to support and guide the Fair Housing Act Amendments. Plainly these studies do not constitute exclusively academic inquiries.

On balance, it is our judgment that the costs imposed on the kind of businesses that have been audited to date do not outweigh the benefits that accrue to society from the comparatively precise information these audits provide.

AUDIT FINDINGS IN BRIEF

The results of the most recent and reliable audit studies indicate that substantial levels of unfavorable treatment of blacks and Hispanics remain in America's housing market and in hiring for entry-level jobs.[29] Additionally, it appears that there is some variation in the extent of unfavorable treatment among metropolitan areas, although not between central cities and their suburbs.

Because other chapters in this volume present detailed results of the housing and hiring audits discussed here, this section presents only selected highlights. The results for the housing market are from the recently completed Housing Discrimination Study, in which about 3,800 audits were conducted in the summer of 1989 in 25 metropolitan areas where blacks or Hispanics represented at least 12 percent or 7 percent of the population, respectively (i.e., the same as their shares in the national population). The results are representative for all metropolitan areas with 1980 central-city populations of at least 100,000.[30]

The study's sampling plan was structured so that a few hundred audits were conducted in each of five "in-depth" sites, which yielded statistically reliable results for those individual sites. The study conducted black-white and Hispanic-Anglo audits for both rental and sales units.

The results for hiring are from two pilot studies. The first, carried out in the summer of 1989, tested for unfavorable treatment of accented Hispanics compared with Anglos in San Diego and Chicago (Cross et al. 1990). The second study involved black-white audits in Chicago and Washington, D.C., in the summer of 1990 (Turner, Fix, and Struyk 1991). Both of these studies were deliberately limited in the range of unfavorable treatment covered. First, both tested only for discrimination against young men seeking entry-level jobs—a critical part of the market from the perspective of the career opportunities of minority males.[31] In addition, the audit for Hispanics was conducted as part of a larger study of the potential adverse impact of the employer sanctions provisions of the Immigration Reform and Control Act of 1986 on job attainment by Hispanics (General Accounting Office 1990). The law's framers were concerned that its ban on hiring undocumented aliens would lead to discrimination against foreign-sounding and -looking persons who were legally authorized to work. Consequently, the Hispanic auditors were persons who looked Hispanic and had definite accents.

All three of these audit studies were conducted by the Urban Institute and followed the same sampling methodology and field procedures. In each study the available apartment, home, or job was identified through a random sample of advertisements appearing in the major local newspaper the weekend preceding the audit. The sample was selected exclusively from newspapers and not other, more informal listings (such as jobs posted at plant bulletin boards or apartment rentals on church bulletin boards) or personal recommendations of units for sale or rent or jobs available, because no practical sampling frame for these informal sources could be developed. Without such a frame the representativeness of the opportunities sampled would be unknown. However, this sampling strategy did mean that only limited segments of the labor and housing markets were audited.

Audit teams were assigned qualifications suitable for acquiring each housing unit or filling the job vacancy. They then conducted the audit following carefully defined procedures. The sampling procedure adopted meant that any findings of unfavorable treatment should be interpreted as the unfavorable treatment encountered by a qualified person who identified and pursued a housing or employment opportunity announced in the area's major weekend newspaper.

The procedure followed in these studies is similar in some ways to experimental designs using random assignment. In the experiments with random assignment persons eligible for some type of assistance or other "treatment" (an experimental employment and training program, for example) are randomly assigned to groups receiving different types of assistance or treatment, including, possibly, a "no treatment" control group. The effect of the treatment is inferred from differences in outcomes (changes in housing consumption, work effort, service utilization) among the different groups (Campbell and Stanley 1963).

In audits there are two levels of random assignment: the employment or housing opportunity to be audited can be randomly assigned to an audit team as is the order in which the auditors visit the housing or employment agent. Like analyses done under experimental designs, the outcomes for majority auditors serve as "controls" for the outcomes of the minority auditors. The major difference is that the "treatment" itself (i.e., race) cannot be randomly assigned, although audit studies strive to control for other germane factors affecting the hiring decision through the matching of the audit team members.

The validity of the audit findings hinges on the closeness of the match between the members of each audit pair and the veracity of their reporting. Special care was taken in the hiring audits to ensure similarity. Audit pairs had similar education attainment in real life and were of the same physical appearance and personality type. Careful training included mock interviews in which the pair learned to respond similarly to typical questions asked in real interviews. Biographies presented to would-be employers were synchronized. In brief, extensive effort was devoted to minimizing any systematic differences between the members of each audit team in their qualifications for and approach to obtaining a job.

The figures in tables 1.2 and 1.3 show the percentage of times in which either the minority or the majority auditor received unfavorable treatment. Two types of unfavorable treatment are distinguished: opportunity denying and opportunity diminishing. A discussion of the alternative ways these numbers can be used to measure "discrimination" appears in the following section of this chapter.

The figures show that opportunity denial occurred 20 percent of the time in the black-white hiring audits and 31 percent in the Hispanic-Anglo hiring audits. Stated alternatively, about one time in three a young accented Hispanic applying for a job advertised in the newspaper was denied an application, refused an interview, or not offered a job when his Anglo partner experienced the opposite outcome. In the housing sector, in contrast, this type of treatment occurred about 8 percent of the time when either blacks or Hispanics sought to purchase a home. Black renters were essentially refused any sort of information ("door slamming") 15 percent of the time, while Hispanic renters were treated this way 12 percent of the time. In short, opportunity-denying treatment is more common in hiring transactions involving entry-level positions than in the housing acquisition process.

Opportunity-diminishing behavior includes treatment that lowers the chance of the candidate's obtaining the housing unit or job sought but stops short of eliminating the person from the home or job acquisition process. In renting, for example, opportunity was considered diminished for one auditor if the other was told of more units being available, shown more units, or quoted more favorable rental terms.

Table 1.2 AUDIT ESTIMATES OF UNFAVORABLE TREATMENT IN HOUSING

Characteristic	Coverage	Opp'y deny minority(%)[a]	Opp'y deny White/Anglo(%)[b]	Opp'y deny/ diminish minority(%)[c]	Opp'y deny/diminish White/Anglo(%)[c]
1. Black/White Rental	National	15	5	46	18
2. Black/White Sales	National	8	1	50	20
3. Hispanic/Anglo Rental	National	12	6	43	20
4. Hispanic/Anglo Sales	National	8	3	45	21

[a]The minority rental or home seeker was essentially denied any information while the information was given to the majority.
[b]The majority rental or home seeker was essentially denied any information while the information was given to the minority.
[c]Opportunity diminishing acts are defined as follows: while either the minority or majority auditor was able to learn about the unit requested he was treated less well than his counterpart. In housing, for example, one tester is offered fewer units, or the minority tester is "steered" to neighborhoods with more minorities.

Table 1.3 AUDIT ESTIMATES OF UNFAVORABLE TREATMENT IN EMPLOYMENT

Characteristic	Coverage	Opp'y deny[a] minority(%)	Opp'y deny[b] White/Anglo(%)
Black/White	Chi; D.C.	20	7
Hispanic/Anglo	Chi; S.D.	31	11

Sources: Cross et. al. (1990), figure 5.1: Turner, Fix and Struyk (1991), Table 5, and unpublished tabulations.
[a]The minority auditor was denied the opportunity of advancing as far in the hiring process as his majority counterpart or the majority auditor received a job when his minority partner did not.
[b]The majority auditor was denied the opportunity of advancing as far in the hiring process as his minority counterpart or the minority auditor received a job when his majority partner did not.

For those seeking to purchase a home, such behavior included steering purchasers to different, less desirable neighborhoods and providing less information on potential financing sources. In hiring, opportunity was considered diminished when, for example, one auditor had difficulty in obtaining the employment application, had to wait substantially longer before being interviewed, or was offered a position inferior to that offered to his audit partner.[32] The *combined* incidence of opportunity-denying and opportunity-diminishing treatment for housing is high. On average, blacks encountered unfavorable treatment 46 percent of the time when renting a home and 50 percent of the time when trying to purchase one. For Hispanics the respective rates of unfavorable treatment were almost as high: they encountered unfavorable treatment 43 percent of the time in rentals and 45 percent in sales (see table 1.2). The pervasiveness of opportunity-diminishing treatment is evident by contrasting these figures with those for opportunity denial.

Only one of the pilot hiring audit studies—black-white audits in Chicago and Washington—was structured to capture opportunity-diminishing treatment. The results for these two sites viewed together suggest that such adverse treatment occurs in 36 percent of hiring transactions involving a young black man.

How does one explain the greater overall incidence of unfavorable treatment of minorities in housing in light of the greater incidence of opportunity-denying behavior in hiring? The answer, in part at least, stems from the greater opportunity that housing agents—who often control multiple housing opportunities—have to discourage applicants without denying them some putative assistance. To clarify this point, we discuss the two types of unfavorable treatment further.

Opportunity Denial. The denial of an opportunity to pursue the advertised unit or job or any alternative can occur at any of three distinct stages of the hiring process: obtaining the application, having the interview, or receiving the offer. But in the case of housing the denial occurs typically at the outset, with a refusal to provide information on any unit. The result is the same in both instances: The applicant has no further chance to pursue the job or housing opportunity. However, the opportunities for denial are greater in hiring because the denial can occur at any of a number of stages in the process.

Opportunity Diminishing. In the hiring process, candidates for entry-level positions typically proceed through a fairly well-defined process. There is usually only one available position, and it is controlled by the offeror. The housing transaction is different because the agent controls multiple units, and the process of negotiation between the agent and the home seeker can take many directions. Since many of the units that an agent offers may be inferior to the one advertised (which is the one sought and presumably preferred), the home seeker's opportunity to find *some* acceptable unit is diminished but not completely denied. For example, units other than the one advertised might be offered to the minority home seeker while the advertised unit is shown to his majority partner. The substitute units might be smaller or larger than the one requested or, in the case of sales units, in a different neighborhood. In contrast, in the hiring process, the firm has few if any substitute jobs to offer an applicant. So the opportunity to appear responsive by offering a substitute, even an inferior substitute, is more limited and occurs less frequently in hiring than in housing.

This line of reasoning suggests that comparisons of the incidence of unequal treatment in different types of transactions are complex and should be made with caution. Nevertheless, the basic finding of the audit studies seems valid: Opportunity-denying behavior is more common in hiring, while the combined incidence of opportunity-denying and opportunity-diminishing behavior is higher in housing.

A final question concerns the extent of variation in unfavorable treatment among metropolitan areas.[33] (For simplicity's sake, the table below reports majority-favored outcomes alone as a way of portraying varying patterns of differential treatment across metropolitan areas.) Two rather different patterns appear in the housing audits (table 1.4). There is little variation in the incidence of unfavorable treatment of blacks but a greater dispersion in unfavorable treatment of Hispanics. For example, the lowest incidence in Anglo-Hispanic sales audits is

Table 1.4 VARIATION IN THE LEVEL OF UNFAVORABLE TREATMENT OF
MINORITIES ACROSS METRO AREAS

Site	Black-White (%)		Hispanic-Anglo (%)	
	Rental	Sales	Rental	Sales
Housing[a]				
Chicago	45	39	46	39
New York	40	44	53	61
Los Angeles	44	36	41	38
Atlanta	41	49	NA	NA
San Antonio	NA	NA	31	46
Hiring[b]				
Chicago		17		33
Washington, D.C.		23		NA
San Diego		NA		29

Sources: Housing—unpublished results; Hiring—Cross et al. (1990), tables A.1, A.2; Turner, Fix, and Struyk (1991), table 9.
Note: Each entry is the percentage of audits in which minorities were treated less favorably than their majority group counterparts.
a. Includes both opportunity-diminishing and opportunity-denying behavior. See notes to table 1.2.
b. Opportunity denying only.

39 percent (Los Angeles) and the highest is 61 percent (New York). The results for the hiring audits, limited as they are, suggest a smaller range of unfavorable treatment across metro areas for Hispanics.[34]

No significant differences in the incidence of unfavorable treatment in housing sales and rentals were found between central cities and suburbs within the same metropolitan area.[35] Similarly, no significant differences were detected in the hiring patterns of firms located in central cities versus suburbs. But note that only firms advertising positions were audited (Turner, Fix, and Struyk 1991; Kenney and Wissoker, forthcoming). There may be a difference here in that suburban firms that advertise positions may be less inclined to discriminate compared with all suburban firms than are central-city firms that advertise compared with all central-city firms.

The burden of the evidence, then, is that significant levels of unequal treatment exist in housing markets and in hiring of young workers for entry-level positions; some forms of unequal treatment are worse in some places than in others, but the variation is surprisingly low overall.

Can we claim that the unfavorable treatment just summarized represents discrimination? The straightforward character of auditing and the strength and persuasiveness of its results mask a number of controversial and complex underlying methodological and definitional issues in the translation of unfavorable treatment to discrimination. Some of these are unique to audits, others are shared by studies using experimental designs. These issues are addressed in the next section and appendices 1.A and 1.B, as well as elsewhere in this volume, most notably in chapters 2 and 5.

METHODOLOGICAL ISSUES RELATED TO DESIGNING, INTERPRETING, AND STATISTICALLY EVALUATING AUDITS[36]

How can we be sure that differential treatment is due to race or ethnicity (hereafter referred to simply as race) rather than other factors? What statistical tests are appropriate for interpreting audit findings? Are there flaws in the design of audits themselves that leave the results open to doubt?

This section grapples with these difficult questions. We begin by stressing that different definitions of discrimination imply different interpretations of the differential treatment data provided by audits. We present four alternative definitions of discrimination and demonstrate how the definition chosen governs the statistics analyzed to interpret audit results. The role of random factors related to the behavior of auditors, agents, and the audit process is crucial to this discussion, because how they are treated determines how we assess audit results. (A more detailed discussion is provided in appendix 1.A.) Next, we discuss a number of other methodological concerns raised in this volume and elsewhere about auditing for discrimination. Finally, we show that in the Urban Institute's national housing discrimination study and in three of four employment discrimination sites there is clear and convincing evidence of discrimination, regardless of which definition or statistical test is chosen.

What Do We Mean by Racial Discrimination?

"The unequal treatment of equals on the basis of race" is a straightforward and generally accepted definition of discrimination. This definition is not precise enough, however, to allow us to interpret the results of audits in a world where random factors are mixed up with systematic factors in determining how two persons of different races (but otherwise equal) are treated when they apply for a job, a mortgage, or an apartment for rent. By random events we mean idiosyncratic variations in the behaviors of auditors and agents, and variations in the circumstances facing teammates associated with the audit method itself, that may or may not produce observed differences in treatment between auditor teammates. By systematic differences in treatment we mean differences observed consistently over a large number of audits or in circumstances where random variations are minimal.

"Unequal treatment" in the context of auditing typically refers to an action that is not evenhanded. This is different from evenhanded application of standards or rules that happen to result in more majority than minority applicants being successful. In legal terms, auditing is designed to uncover "differential treatment," not "disparate impact."

Disentangling random from systematic factors produces at least four alternative operational definitions of disparate treatment:

(1) Discriminatory Inclination: When evaluating equally qualified applicants, agents systematically assign penalties on the basis of race, whether those so penalized ultimately are given equal access to the particular market (or opportunity) or not.
(2) Gross Unfavorable Treatment: When confronting equally qualified applicants, agents give greater access to the particular market to majority auditors, whether for random or systematic reasons.
(3) Systematic Unfavorable Treatment: When confronting equally qualified applicants, agents give greater access to the particular market to majority auditors because of a systematically applied penalty based on race.[37] Under this definition, neither penalties that do not result in unequal access nor instances of unequal access that are due to random factors are counted as discriminatory.
(4) Net Market Effects: In a set of comparisons of equally qualified applicants, the number of majority-favored actions (for whatever reason) exceeds the number of minority-favored actions (for whatever reason), thereby creating, on net, reduced access for minorities to the particular market.

Each definition has its strengths and weaknesses. Since subsequent chapters use different definitions, at least implicitly, we discuss differences here to set the stage for interpreting the rest of the volume.

Yinger's "true behavior" (chapter 2) is an application of definition (1). The "discriminatory inclination" notion is based on how economists conventionally model a discrete choice (to favor one auditor or not): by positing that the observed dichotomous choice was produced by some continuous "latent variable" measuring the agent's evaluation of the auditor. The "act" of unequal treatment in this case is imposing a race penalty or bonus. This racial penalty or bonus may, however, be small compared to the effects of randomness, so that minorities are not necessarily provided less access to a particular market even though the agent holds a discriminatory inclination directed against them. This fact suggests a weakness of definition (1): audit data do not distinguish between systematic penalties and random factors, requiring complex statistical techniques to try to distinguish between the two. In addition, some would argue that society's primary concern is with inclinations that result in unequal treatment.

Turner (chapter 3) implicitly employs definition (2), gross unfavorable treatment. Unequal treatment of equals is discrimination, regardless of reason.[38] Being explicitly disfavored is harmful in and of itself. A strength of this definition is that it avoids the need to distinguish systematic from random events. A weakness is its implication that a purely random process that produces differential treatment (like the flipping of a fair coin) discriminates. To avoid this implication, it is typically assumed that differences in treatment observed in audits are infrequently caused by randomness.

Proponents of definition (3), "systematic unfavorable treatment," argue that one must both have an inclination and act systematically in disfavoring minorities before one can be found to have discriminated. It is important to recognize that random factors play an asymmetric role in this definition. Random factors that overcome agents' minority-disfavoring inclinations, thereby resulting in minorities having equal or even greater access, are ignored. But random factors that overcome agents' majority-disfavoring or equal-treatment inclinations, thereby resulting in minorities having less access, must be subtracted from the gross measure of unfavorable minority access. A weakness of this definition, like definition (1), is that it requires one to differentiate the systematic from the random. Furthermore, the appeal of this definition wanes if the size of the racial penalty grows small compared to the influence of randomness on the outcomes. That is, if an agent always assesses a small racial penalty but random influences on treatment overwhelm the effects of the penalties, the agent could end up favoring the minority almost as often as the majority. In this case a court might have difficulty finding discrimination because the evidence would be virtually indistinguishable from that produced by someone who assessed no racial penalty and favored some people over others for purely random reasons.[39]

Heckman and Siegelman (chapter 5) argue for definition (4), the "net market-effects" definition. They argue that the net result of acts that both favor and disfavor minorities is the most relevant concept for policymakers and minorities alike. Take, for instance, a case where minorities are treated less favorably in 30 percent of audits and are treated more favorably in 5 percent of audits (whereupon the net would be 25 percent). The results are dramatically different from the case where both the majority and minority auditors are favored (and disfavored) in 30 percent of the tests (where the net would be 0 percent). This intuitive appeal of the "net" measure is also its weakness, however, because it allows nonrandom acts that may have been systematically favoring majorities to be offset by nonrandom acts that may have been systematically favoring minorities—running the risk of concluding that no discrimination exists, when in fact there may be discrimination against both groups. Put differently, should discrimination against minorities by some be negated by favoritism toward minorities by others?

There is no "best" definition of racial discrimination. But it is important to be clear about one's definitional standpoint, because it can crucially shape one's conclusion about whether discrimination exists in the firm(s) or market(s) being audited.[40]

Each of the four definitions of discrimination employs a different statistical measure.

For ease of notation, let: f represent the proportion of those agents audited who systematically assess a penalty on minorities (i.e., have discriminatory inclinations); P_{maj} the proportion of cases favoring the majority auditor in market access (called "gross majority-favored" in this volume); P_{min} the proportion of cases favoring the minority auditor in market access ("gross minority-favored"); P_{rmaj} the proportion of cases favoring the majority auditor in market access due only to random factors; P_r the proportion of cases where agents have a minority-disfavoring proclivity but minorities do not get less market access because of randomness. The difference $P_{maj} - P_{min}$ is called "net majority-favored." The statistical measures indicating the existence of discrimination corresponding to each definition are as follows:

Definition of Discrimination	Existence Measure
(1) Discriminatory Inclination	$f > 0$
(2) Gross Unfavorable Treatment	$P_{maj} > 0$
(3) Systematic Unfavorable Treatment	$P_{maj} - P_{rmaj} > 0$
(4) Net Market Effects	$P_{maj} - P_{min} > 0$

For assessing whether discrimination exists, each definition looks to see if the particular statistical measure it deems relevant is greater than zero. Note that $f = P_{maj} - P_{rmaj} + P_r$.

Do Audits Provide Data on the Appropriate Statistical Measure?

Audits provide unambiguous measures of gross majority- and minority-favored frequencies; thus, the net majority-favored measure can be easily computed as well. But which of these measures is correct differs according to the definition chosen.

Perhaps the most serious disagreement arises over the test of the existence of discrimination: the so-called "gross versus net debate." All would agree that discrimination exists if the test listed for definition (4) is satisfied, but those employing definition (1) or (2) would argue that the net $P_{maj} - P_{min}$ (and $P_{maj} - P_{rmaj}$ if one were able to obtain it) provides an overly conservative test of the existence of discrimination. Those employing either definition (3) or (4) would reply that the gross P_{maj} (and f, if one were able to obtain it) is not, in itself, convincing. Of course, all would agree that demonstrating discrimination under the $P_{maj} - P_{min} > 0$ test (espoused by definition (4)) would be sufficient to demonstrate it under all definitions.[41]

Debate over the correct measure also has centered on whether and how audit studies account for randomness in their results. The 1977 Housing Market Practices Survey audit study (Wienk et al., 1979), for example, held that the gross minority-favored figure was a good proxy for differential treatment due purely to random factors, i.e., that $P_{min} = P_{rmaj}$. Under this interpretation the net measure becomes an accurate indicator of discrimination from perspectives (3) and (4).[42] Those holding to definition (1) or (2) argue that the $P_{min} = P_{rmaj}$ assumption discounts the possibility of systematic favoritism expressed toward minorities, and overstates P_{rmaj}. On this view, the net measure understates incidence.

New theoretical and empirical work is underway to determine the effects of randomness on audit results. One noteworthy theoretical effort is described by Yinger in chapter 2. Ongoing empirical work centers on audits involving pairs of same-race auditors; "sandwich" audits that involve three auditors, two auditors of one race and a third of another; and repeat audits of the same agents.

Other Methodological Issues

Matching of Auditors. It has been claimed that it is virtually impossible to match auditors on all characteristics that are perceived by the agent as relevant. This criticism is frequently voiced in the field of employment, where a wide variety of personal characteristics are indicative of prospective productivity and auditors may be interviewed more intensively than in the case of a housing audit. Heckman and Siegelman (chapter 5) contend that there may be crucial "unobservable" characteristics of potential workers that hypothetically cannot be matched. They also put forward a theoretical argument that matching auditors on observable characteristics might actually accentuate the differences in unobservables and, under certain conditions, overstate the measured extent of discrimination.

Heckman and Siegelman emphasize a crucial issue, especially for employment audits. More work needs to be done on matching auditor teammates to each other and matching both to prospective jobs being audited. In particular, future audits should seek to quantify (and thereby potentially standardize) dimensions of auditor personality and behaviors. Batteries of psychological and behavioral tests might prove useful in this regard. Matching auditors on bona fide financial and credit history characteristics is especially difficult in the context of mortgage audits (see Galster, chapter 7). Explorations that include teams matched at different skill levels relative to the job requirements might also provide illuminating results, because "overqualified" pairs may face different levels of discrimination from "underqualified" pairs.

Audit Management Approaches. How one recruits, trains, and reimburses auditors raises important questions. James and DelCastillo (1992), for example, have criticized the Urban Institute employment audits for using college-educated youths as auditors, instead of representatives of the minority population that are more representative in demeanor, behavior, speech, and other characteristics. One suggestion is to conduct employment audits involving "clusters" of auditor teams. The auditors in each cluster would be similar in both their actual and fictitious backgrounds, but actual and fictitious backgrounds would differ across clusters. The practical difficulties of recruiting such a diverse stable of auditors may be substantial, however. And using poorly educated auditors may risk compromising the quality of the audit information obtained and recorded.

With regard to auditor training, it has been argued that auditors are likely to be predisposed to find discrimination. In the research context this is referred to as experimenter effects, when the auditors produce the results they intuitively feel are "right." In the enforcement context this predisposition is amplified by the possible recovery of punitive and compensatory damages. As one commentator has written:

> Although substantial efforts have been made in the design of the test
> and the techniques it employs in an attempt to enhance its validity, a

fundamental flaw may remain. This shortcoming relates to the test's dependence on objective sensory impressions in an environment where objectivity is particularly apt to be elusive. . . . [T]he testing process itself demands a formidable psychological and emotional commitment from its participants. At best, this commitment can complicate the testers' ability to distinguish between what he is trained to detect and what is perceived. Arguably, this interest also could create a predisposition that also would attack the objectivity necessary for valid results. Factors such as these taint the process and fuel the contention that the fair housing test is susceptible to fabricating its own evidence and thereby making up its own case. (Millspaugh 1984, 240)

We acknowledge the importance of rigorous auditor training and monitoring, so that the objectivity of the evidence is preserved. Exacting auditor selection and training techniques have been and will continue to be developed as the auditing procedure evolves. In the future these might draw on lessons learned in jury selection to ensure impartial conduct and reporting of results.

A final management issue concerns compensation for auditors. James and DelCastillo claim that the Urban Institute's strategy of paying auditors whether or not they obtained a job application, interview, or offer, encouraged "passive behavior" that was unrepresentative of actual job-seeking behavior. Those authors' Denver employment audits gave bonuses to auditors depending upon the stage in the hiring process they attained, on the assumption that such incentives would stimulate more representative (i.e., "real") job-seeking behavior. We believe such incentives are more likely to distort the audit results. Great care is taken during auditor training to instill behavior that improves comparability between the two members of a team. Differential bonuses hinging on "success" may encourage auditors when confronting agents to draw upon their personal, idiosyncratic resources and thereby disrupt the routinized behaviors learned during training.

Sampling Strategies. How one selects agents to be audited may strongly affect the results. For example, if one samples only agents or firms that have amassed a long record of consumer complaints, the result is likely to be higher measured discrimination than if one took a random sample of all agents or firms. A closely related question is the mechanism through which auditors gain access to an agent.

The audit studies reported in this volume all relied upon metropolitan newspapers as the basis for selecting a random sample of advertisements. This sampling strategy has the shortcoming of covering only a portion of available jobs or dwellings. Most openings are found by bona fide customers through other channels, such as signs, word of mouth, or the community newspaper. We believe, however, that auditing metropolitan newspaper ads is a conservative strategy— probably producing an underestimate of discrimination occurring in an area. This is because those who wish to discriminate are likely to prefer an advertising medium that is more selective in the audience it reaches than the metropolitan newspaper. As Heckman and Siegelman point out in chapter 5, this belief is supported indirectly by survey evidence showing that minorities searching through general newspapers for jobs have a higher rate of success than those using other means. Pilot audits conducted by the Fair Employment Council in Washington, D.C., also indicate lower rates of discrimination against both Hispanics and blacks in jobs advertised in metropolitan newspapers than those advertised in suburban newspapers or in employment agencies (Bendick et al., 1991, 1993). In any event, further research is needed to determine whether other sampling frames are feasible and affordable, and the extent to which audit results using those sampling frames might differ.

A second sampling issue relates not to which agents or firms are audited, but what sorts of jobs or dwellings are focused upon. Does one concentrate on a particular range of housing rents or values, or a particular skill level or industrial category of jobs? In the housing market it is not difficult to audit homes or apartments of any price range; one merely needs to provide the appropriate purchasing power in the auditors' scenario. But in the employment market in-person auditing of any but entry-level jobs may be difficult. Many available higher level positions are listed and, ultimately, filled within the firm. Other professional positions may be advertised externally, but may have such a small pool of potential applicants that in-person auditors might be obvious. Note, however, that McIntyre et al. (1980) and Bendick et al. (1991) have conducted pilot audits using resumes, instead of in-person auditors, to investigate a variety of professional positions. Yet other professional or craft occupations have licensing and technical requirements that would be virtually impossible (and probably illegal) to falsify. It remains an open question, therefore, how wide a spectrum of skills and occupations is amenable to investigations by the in-person auditing technique, and what the potential of audits based on matched resumes is.

Measurement of Unfavorable Treatment. Up to this point we have assumed that we could observe unambiguously whether an auditor was receiving unfavorable treatment in comparison to the teammate. Such might not always be the case in the instance of neighborhood or occupational steering. Minority auditors may, for example, be shown more dwellings than their majority teammates, but these dwellings might all be in neighborhoods occupied predominantly by minorities or with concentrations of low-quality dwellings and inferior public services. Such steering is clearly illegal under fair housing statutes, yet our audits might register instances of "minority-favored" treatment on the criterion of "numbers of dwellings shown." As Yinger points out (chapter 2), such misclassifications of results can have important impacts that would lead us to understate discrimination. If we were to include the cases of inferior housing units to which minorities have been steered, the net white-black difference in homes made available per audit would rise from .48 to .57, and the net Anglo-Hispanic difference from .52 to .66. The analogous case in employment testing is when minority auditors are given more job offers when the jobs in question are menial (as observed by James and DelCastillo, 1992) or do not involve contact with the public.

One might be tempted to score audits on the basis of the "quality" of the dwellings shown or jobs offered, not simply on their number. Operationally, however, quality scoring quickly becomes arbitrary. How should an audit be scored in the hypothetical case where the minority teammate is shown two homes in neighborhoods that are 10 percent minority-occupied and the majority teammate is shown one in a neighborhood that is 7 percent minority-occupied? How does one grade the quality of a job, or devise an index of degree of contact with the public? If one had such grades and indices, how large would the differences between teammates need to be before one judged a result "unfavorable?" Since consensus on such issues is unlikely, researchers using quality scoring should report findings for several alternative scoring schemes, to demonstrate the sensitivity of results to the scoring method used.

Applicability of Auditing Beyond the Housing Market. Audits have been criticized on feasibility grounds. For example, Sen. Alan Simpson (R-Wyo.) has asserted that testing is inappropriate for transactions that are putatively more complex than is the sale or rental of a housing unit, as they introduce a level of subjectivity that complicates judgments about the discriminatory intent and outcomes. Simpson stated on the floor of the Senate on February 22, 1991:

> While the Department of Housing and Urban Development has conducted similar tests of discrimination in public housing [sic], the employer-employee relationship is far more complex than that of landlord-tenant.

There are so many more variables present in deciding whether to hire someone, that I believe that it is necessary for Congress to establish some reasonable ground rules with respect to this sort of "testing."

In response, Senator Simpson introduced legislation that would effectively undermine the use of testing under Title VII of the Civil Rights Act of 1964.[43]

Critics' concerns about the complexity of the hiring process and other similar transactions may be overstated. In the first place, where hiring involves entry-level jobs, the process is usually a summary one, very similar to the rental of a housing unit. Further, audits in the areas of lending, employment, and auto sales all focus on the "front end" of the transaction in question, where records are rarely kept, and practices are often uniform. It is possible to monitor the early phases of these transactions without becoming involved in the kind of complex interpersonal exchanges that would entail outcomes based largely on subjective criteria.

Where discriminatory activities involve more complex transactions—in hiring for a midlevel white-collar position, perhaps—testing may be less useful a tool unless the testers assume their own identities, which raises complicated recruitment and statistical issues. Moreover, in such cases the benefits of the auditing process may not outweigh the cost imposed on the employer, since several interviews involving a significant amount of senior management time could be involved.

Clear and Convincing Evidence?

Taken as a whole, the audit-based data in this volume provide strong evidence that racial-ethnic discrimination, however defined, continues in many American metropolitan housing markets and at least some labor markets, and seriously limits minorities' access to these markets. Even conservative standards of interpretation confirm this conclusion.

Consider first the question of the existence of discrimination. The Housing Discrimination Study (as well as its predecessors, the 1977 Housing Market Practices Survey and dozens of local audits conducted by fair housing organizations) reveals that discrimination against blacks and Hispanics exists in the vast majority of the metropolitan areas audited. This is true regardless of discrimination definition or statistical test employed.

The main challenge has come in the field of employment audits. But recall that a conservative test of the existence of discrimination, regardless of one's definition, is whether the difference between majority-favored and minority-favored audits is significantly greater than zero (i.e., $P_{maj} > P_{min}$). Heckman and Siegelman employ three alternative statistical tests—sign test, large sample chi-squared test, exact small-sample (binomial) test—and find evidence of discrimination in the Urban Institute studies when considering all black-white audits combined, all Hispanic-Anglo audits combined, and all individual employment audits sites except Chicago's black-white audits. These statistical results combining all auditor pairs are permissible, given Heckman and Siegelman's tests for homogeneity.

The evidence from the pilot employment audits to date, therefore, shows that discrimination exists against foreign sounding/looking Hispanic males in San Diego and Chicago and against black males in Washington, D.C.[44] It is not clear in the case of blacks in Chicago (or Denver blacks and Hispanics, based on the James and DelCastillo results, 1992). More employment audits are needed to clarify the geographic extent of racial employment discrimination and test whether racial differentials are similar for men and women.[45]

The differential effect of race on *overall* access to housing and labor markets is not in doubt, however. Regardless of definitional perspective, all analysts would agree that the magnitude of the limitation faced by minorities in a market is given by the net majority-favored measure. The Housing Discrimination Study showed that blacks in the sales market have, on average, 21 percent fewer homes recommended or shown to them than their teammates; in the rental market the comparable figure is 25 percent fewer apartments. Hispanics in the sales market have, on average, 22 percent fewer homes made available to them than their teammates; in the rental market the figure is 11 percent fewer apartments. In the Chicago and Washington black-white employment audits, blacks were offered 23 percent fewer jobs than their teammates. In the Chicago and San Diego Hispanic-Anglo employment audits, Hispanics were offered 34 percent fewer jobs than their teammates.

These racial impacts offer clear and convincing evidence that we have yet to achieve equal opportunity in America.

CONSEQUENCES OF STRONG DOCUMENTATION

Strong documentation of discrimination has two direct results: The frame of reference for debating the strengthening of equal opportunity legislation is altered, and the analysis of differential outcomes by scholars is transformed.

The clearest illustration of the first point comes from comparing passage of congressional amendments to Title VIII of the Fair Housing Act of 1968 with the 1990 defeat of proposed amendments to Title VII of the Civil Rights Act of 1964. The unequivocal documentation of the widespread existence of discriminatory treatment against minority home seekers with audit data from the Housing Market Practices Survey helped change the terms of debate from *whether* to strengthen Title VIII to *how* to strengthen it in a way that would both create an efficient enforcement mechanism and maintain constitutional guarantees of due process. The contrast with the deliberations in 1990 on amending Title VII, where evidence on discrimination was both less central and less definitive, is strong. Mashaw (1990), among others, argued that clear proof of discrimination would be essential for any strengthening of Title VII. However, a law doing so was proposed and enacted in 1991: The Civil Rights Act of 1991.

We recognize, of course, that many other factors were at work in the two cases. Opposition to strengthening housing legislation may be weaker because in a housing sale the buyer and seller do not have a continuing relationship, as do an employer and employee. Additionally, as was pointed out earlier, public opinion gives little support for the idea that the government should intervene in the labor market. Finally, a powerful if unexpected impetus for enacting The Civil Rights Act of 1991 was rising concern with sexual harassment in the workplace—a concern that was dramatized on the eve of the law's passage by sexual harassment allegations against now-Justice Clarence Thomas (Simiscalco and Giansello 1992).

Equally important, the documentation of discrimination in the housing sector has fundamentally changed the way researchers are structuring their analyses of discrimination—a shift that has altered the conventional wisdom. In the 1970s, housing researchers conducted analyses of differences in the prices blacks and whites paid for housing, homeownership rates, the rates at which the two groups consumed various types of housing, and the type of areas in which they lived. In each of these cases the analytic method attempted to control for all factors besides race that might account for the differences, with the residual attributed at least partially to discrimination.[46] In short, the primary effort was given to measuring the presence and extent of discrimination by trying to discern its effects.

Once the presence of discrimination was definitively documented and quantified for 40 metropolitan areas, research gradually shifted to explaining the role of discrimination in observed outcomes. For example, Galster and Keeney (1988) and Galster (1991) analyzed the interrelationships among housing discrimination, interracial occupational disparities, incomes of blacks relative to incomes of whites, and residential segregation across cities. A greater incidence of housing discrimination was found to increase segregation, which in turn produced greater occupational disparities, relatively lower black incomes, and higher poverty rates.

Strikingly, much of the recent research involving discrimination in employment is of the type done in the housing field in the years preceding the documentation of housing discrimination. The following list of "dependent variables" in housing and employment studies illustrates this point:

Housing	Employment
house prices and rents	wages
housing choices and consumption levels	occupation type
residential segregation	workplace segregation

Thus, a similar shift in analysis would be useful in documenting hiring discrimination (particularly for entry-level positions) and in making such measures of discrimination available for a substantial number of metropolitan areas. For example, analysis could be undertaken of the causes of variation in minority relative to white wage rates or minority employment rates across markets using discrimination measures as one explanatory variable. These advances would, in turn, have clear implications both for defining social problems and for the policy interventions that address them.

TESTING AS AN ENFORCEMENT STRATEGY: THE CASE OF HOUSING

This section looks first to the experience in the housing sector to assess the effectiveness of testing in combating discrimination by providing relief for individual complainants; it then examines whether testing can be carried out at high volume. Finally, the section outlines a strategy for the use of testing and auditing in a comprehensive enforcement program.

Effectiveness in Combating Discrimination

The record on the effectiveness of testing programs in combating housing discrimination is based almost exclusively on experience before implementation of the amendments to Title VIII in March 1989. Two gauges of success are relevant: first, the effectiveness of testing in resolving individual cases, and second, the effectiveness of testing in reducing the incidence of discrimination in a local housing market.

Numerous leaders of state and local and public and private fair-housing groups have testified to the effectiveness of careful housing tests in obtaining favorable out-of-court settlements or court decisions involving individual acts of discrimination.[47] The only systematic, statistical evidence on the effectiveness of having testing evidence available comes from the evaluation of the Fair Housing Assistance Program (FHAP) sponsored by the Department of Housing and Urban Development (HUD) in the mid 1980s. Part of this study analyzed case closures in the early 1980s by agencies receiving funding under FHAP. Regression models were estimated of the likelihood of a complainant's obtaining relief with the assistance of the agency. According to that analysis, the likelihood of some form of relief increased by 54 percent when testing evidence was available, after controlling for the agency involved, type of respondent, type of issue, case duration, and other factors (Wallace et al. 1985, table 5.4).

A more recent Urban Institute study of the disposition of fair housing complaints filed by private fair housing groups has generated weaker results. Multivariate and logit analyses revealed that testing played a limited role in determining complaint outcomes after other factors were taken into account. However, the number of cases observed was limited and the controls exerted on the types of cases examined were fewer than was the case in the Wallace study.[48]

Evidence is sparse on the more general question of whether aggressive campaigns of testing can indeed reduce the level of discrimination. Galster (1990) reviewed the experiences of agencies that have mounted ongoing, comprehensive programs of random testing. He concluded:

> Although the evidence is limited, it appears that such collective enforcement techniques can create a potent deterrent. Cleveland Heights, OH, has undertaken a series of random tests in its community since the late 1970s. This program, coupled with efforts to educate the real estate industry about fair housing and well-publicized suits against major real estate brokerage firms, has produced a dramatic decline in the observed incidence of discriminatory acts, as revealed by the tests

themselves. Similar efforts by the Kentucky Commission on Civil Rights have returned comparable dividends. (P. 145)

An important question is whether testing—either in support of developing evidence in response to complaints or on a random basis—can be conducted at a high volume and thus create a "critical mass" of settlements that would collectively change the behavior of rental and real estate agents in larger communities. The answer is clearly affirmative, based on the numbers achieved in the recent housing and hiring audits. About 30 valid audits were completed weekly in each of the five in-depth sites in the Housing Discrimination Study. Similarly, an average of at least 40 valid audit completions were obtained in Washington, D.C., and Chicago in the Employment Discrimination Study.[49] The strains on management of mounting such high numbers of audits were significant in both studies but would likely decline if testing programs of this volume were sustained indefinitely and adjustments were made to manage the work flow. Note that these volumes are probably the upper limits for a program of random audits, since the two studies used most or all of the housing and employment ads for units and positions meeting the audit programs' criteria.

Testing in support of litigation has already reached high aggregate levels in the housing area. One estimate is that in 1990 about 4,500 such tests were conducted by private fair-housing groups—roughly evenly divided between those done in the course of pursuing complaints and those done as part of systematic testing programs.[50]

Finally, what does testing cost? Conducting a test to develop evidence costs from $300 to $600, depending broadly on local wage rates. This is the cost, including overhead and management, of identifying the firm to be audited, briefing the auditors, organizing and conducting the audit, debriefing the auditors, and analyzing the results. It does not include attorney's costs for using this information in legal proceedings.

Testing/Auditing as Part of a Comprehensive Enforcement Effort

Being able to develop strong evidence of discrimination—in this case, through testing—is a crucial element in an enforcement strategy. However, testing must be part of a larger process. Convenient opportunities to file complaints must be available for those who suspect they have been discriminated against, and adequate resources must be devoted to pursuing types of discrimination not amenable to identification or verification through testing.

Development of strong evidence must be coupled with a speedy and effective legal process. One of the most notable features of the 1988 amendments to Title VIII was a strengthened and speedier legal process.[51] Speed was achieved by authorizing hearings before administrative law judges (ALJs) under tight time schedules, while due process was guaranteed by the right of the complainant or respondent to request to have the case heard in a federal district court.[52]

The ALJ process is widely perceived to be notably faster than taking the case to a district court, although precise figures are hard to assemble. In addition, the process benefits the complainant because HUD or the responsible agency in jurisdictions with equivalent laws bears the cost of preparing the case and prosecuting it before the ALJ. Obviously, this arrangement can be more advantageous to aggrieved parties than bringing a private civil suit for alleged discriminatory acts—the common approach in employment discrimination cases. But if the complainant engages a private attorney and prevails, he can then apply to the ALJ for attorney's fees and costs. If HUD files the case and the respondent prevails, HUD may be liable for reasonable attorney's fees.

Importantly, the potentially large costs associated with providing these legal services to an unknown number of complainants appear to be a key factor in making jurisdictions hesitant about revising their laws to conform to the new federal statute and to committing themselves to prosecuting valid complaints.

In summary, the effectiveness of testing in the area of housing has increased because it has been joined with efficient complaint processing and judicial procedures. We now turn to three distinct roles that testing and auditing have to play in a comprehensive enforcement program.

Complaint Processing. Private fair-housing groups, and state and local fair-housing agencies to a lesser extent, have conducted tests in investigating complaints. Conducting the tests immediately after the complaint is filed has been instrumental in obtaining temporary restraining orders in numerous cases and in obtaining more out-of-court settlements favorable to the complainant. Clearly this type of testing is an essential element of a contemporary enforcement strategy. Because HUD has begun to contract for testing as part of its investigations, the use of testing in this context will certainly rise in the years ahead.

Random Testing. A central finding of all the housing audit studies is that discrimination is typically subtle, with the victims seldom realizing that it has occurred. Indeed, one recent HUD estimate is that less than 1 percent of illegal acts of housing discrimination become the subject of a complaint.[53] Consequently, enforcement needs to go beyond responding to complaints. Identifying those who discriminate will require a substantial program of random tests, conducted explicitly to develop evidence of such behavior. Earlier, we noted that a few jurisdictions have conducted these testing programs with considerable effect.

Some assistance with such testing is available to private fair-housing groups under HUD's Fair Housing Initiative Program.[54] A major expansion in the resources available to support programs of random testing is needed for an ongoing, comprehensive program in every metropolitan area. Achieving this objective will require not only additional funding but also support for expanding the coverage of testing organizations to communities lacking active fair-housing programs. Such support could involve assistance in establishing fair-housing groups where they do not now exist, inducing state agencies to fill the void, or, failing these options, having HUD undertake this testing by either contracting with outside groups or managing the process itself.

A Systematic Auditing Program. The results on the extent of housing discrimination for the five in-depth sites in the Housing Discrimination Study underscore the variance in discrimination among areas, although housing discrimination remains a serious problem in all metropolitan areas for which reliable data are available. A program of audits—at both the national and the metropolitan level—is clearly essential for ascertaining the extent to which public policy and changing attitudes are reducing discriminatory behavior. While HUD has been a leader in conducting periodic national audit studies, similar studies should be undertaken at the metropolitan level as well. The metro-specific results could be used in targeting scarce federal enforcement resources.

To date housing audit studies have focused on race and ethnicity. In the future they should be expanded to encompass discrimination based on sex, family status, and age.[55] Having a full inventory of the incidence of discrimination against various groups could be the basis for an efficiently targeted program of random testing.

FUTURE DIRECTIONS FOR AUDITING

Lessons from Housing

The experience with auditing in the housing context makes clear its capacity and its value. First, national, federally funded audits have firmly established the incidence of high levels of both opportunity-denying and opportunity-diminishing behavior disadvantageous to both blacks and Hispanics. The evidence from audits has changed perceptions of opportunity in housing, enabling and guiding policy change. And national studies have demonstrated conclusively that audits can be conducted economically and at high volume.

Second, there is evidence that the use of auditing for enforcement has expedited settlements of legal challenges in favor of plaintiffs, at manageable costs. In addition to the power of audits to help remedy individual cases of discrimination, there is evidence that testing can lead to a decrease in discrimination at the city or county level.

Third, auditing has been an important element in an innovative and generally fruitful collaboration between the federal government (i.e., HUD) and private, nonprofit, and state and local organizations dedicated to fair housing. The government provides limited support for testing, sets basic rules governing its implementation, and now provides a forum for hearing disputes stemming from challenges to which tests have given rise. In return, these nonfederal agencies assume responsibility for field activity and enforcement. In the final analysis, the courts, to which all defendants have recourse, serve to set minimum standards for the fairness and quality of the testing that takes place.

In sum, the coherent approach adopted in the area of housing may represent something of a model for other areas of policy—most notably credit and employment, to which we now turn.

Credit Studies

If housing represents the most fully developed area of activity in terms of scientific methods, institutional commitments, and institutional history, credit is the least developed area covered in this volume.

George Galster's review of early credit-related audits makes clear both the feasibility and the advisability of testing in this area (see chapter 7 of this volume). The studies reviewed indicate that discrimination at the pre-application stage occurred in a small fraction of transactions. Where tests have been concentrated on institutions suspected of discriminating, however, higher levels of discrimination have been found. As Galster points out, these early studies made valiant efforts to pioneer the use of testing within a comparatively complex framework. Galster cautions, though, that the studies tend to "fall short of social-scientific standards of clarity, replicability, and statistical validity."

On the strength of this review it seems clear that a next step will be to develop and implement a pilot study that examines a range of lending and related practices (including home appraisal and mortgage insurance) across several metropolitan areas. The study would draw not only on prior experiments in the credit area but also on advances in housing and employment audits. As Galster notes, such a test, for feasibility purposes, would need to focus on the preapplication stage as the first phase of a broader testing program. But that should not be a problem. Many analysts believe that it is in the preapplication phase that most of the discrimination takes place. Indeed, it is during this phase, prior to development of a traceable paper trail, that individuals and institutions have the greatest incentive to discriminate. Further, the difficulties associated with going beyond the preapplication phase (including operational problems associated with avoiding discovery and issues relating to fraudulent misrepresentation) raise feasibility issues.

Employment Studies

We believe that the employment audits conducted by the Urban Institute not only have established the feasibility of testing in the employment context but have gone some distance toward establishing a workable methodology for fieldwork and analysis.

The results of these early metro-area studies indicate that the incidence of opportunity-denying behavior in hiring is higher than in housing. At the same time, the incidence of opportunity-diminishing behavior is relatively lower in hiring, and overall discrimination in hiring may be more variable across cities than is the case for housing. These initial findings also suggest that discrimination in hiring is worse for accented, foreign-appearing Hispanics than for blacks and is no worse in suburban than in central-city settings.

As in the area of credit, testing in employment may have its greatest power in illuminating that phase of the employment transaction—hiring—about which the least is known, in which employers have the greatest incentive to discriminate, and that may hold the most significant policy implications.

The feasibility of conducting hiring audits may well be limited to entry-level jobs and to the early screening phases (the review of resumes, for example) of more sophisticated jobs. If this is the case, it certainly does not invalidate the conclusions being drawn here. Still, one must be careful not to project these findings to the labor market as a whole.

We mentioned earlier the fact that employment discrimination cases brought under Title VII have grown many times faster than the overall federal civil caseload (Donohue and Siegelman 1991). We also noted that firings account for an increasingly large share of this growing caseload, while hiring cases account for a steadily declining percentage.

These developments have several implications for antidiscrimination efforts and for testing. First, if policymakers look to complaints, they may tend to overlook the abiding problem of discrimination in hiring, focusing attention on other stages of the employment process and thereby misallocating resources. As a result, policies may reflect the interests of minorities who are better off and work in integrated settings. (Both are frequently characteristics of complainants in discharge cases, Donohue and Siegelman point out.)

Second, Donohue and Siegelman contend that the patterns of litigation emerging from Title VII give employers a growing incentive to discriminate against minorities at the hiring stage, where the applicant will be less aware of discrimination, less able to prove it, and less inclined to try. As in the case of credit, it is at the initial hiring stage where the paper record is least complete, enabling and, in some cases, effectively encouraging discriminatory behaviors.

Auditing for research and enforcement can address both of these effects. If further pilot tests continue to affirm the validity of auditing for employment discrimination and its capacity to do so at high volume, it may make sense for the federal government to conduct a national audit of hiring discrimination modeled on HUD's approximately decennial Housing Discrimination Study. Support for the design of early studies has been provided by private foundations, but given that civil rights enforcement is a public responsibility, it makes sense for this larger, more expensive effort to be funded by the federal government.[56] Use of audits in the enforcement context to test for discrimination in hiring makes substantial sense given that hiring discrimination may be underrepresented in Title VII litigation. It also makes sense given the incentives that may be established by Title VII to exclude minorities at the hiring stage.

As chapter 8 in this volume indicates, the legal issues surrounding the use of testing in employment were being litigated in the fall of 1991 in a case brought by the Fair Employment Council of Washington. The case invokes the validity of auditing under both Section 1981 and Title VII. Thus, it is likely to inform the validity of the U.S. Equal Employment Opportunity Commission's (1990) policy guidance announcing that the agency would accept charges based on evidence provided by testers. Expanding the use of testing in employment to the enforcement context raises a number of policy issues. First, to what extent would it be advisable for the federal government to help build an infrastructure of private organizations resembling the fair-housing councils that exist in many metro areas? Second, should the federal government provide direct financial support of testing in employment, as it has in housing? And, if so, should that support be conditioned on conducting tests that conform to certain federally designated procedural standards, as is the case in housing?

Random or targeted testing in the employment area may lend itself to other uses. For example, the Office of Special Counsel of the Department of Justice or the EEOC might consider using random or targeted testing to determine which employers are inadvertently discriminating on the basis of national origin or alienage in response to the 1986 Immigration Reform and Control Act. Findings of discrimination could initially result in guidance on compliance rather than punishment, at the same time providing valuable feedback to the agency on the nature and incidence of discrimination.

In sum, the audit studies discussed in this volume have established the feasibility and advisability of testing in a variety of contexts. It seems to us that audits hold the power to clarify the extent of discrimination, which helps government perform its continuing obligation to counteract it. It makes sense to continue to expand their use for both research and enforcement purposes in the areas of credit and employment.

Notes

Funding to support this work has been provided by The Rockefeller Foundation. The authors thank Larry Pearl, Ron Wienk, Genevieve Kenney, Douglas Wissoker, and Cliff Schrupp for advice and information during the preparation of this chapter.

1. Attention is restricted to white attitudes because comparatively few questions have been asked of blacks consistently over the same period. Schuman et al. (1985, table 4.1) report two questions for this period dealing with housing and employment. As early as 1964—and consistently thereafter—blacks reported essentially unanimous support for the statement of principle that "black people have a right to live wherever they can afford to, just like anybody else." Similarly, in 1964 blacks gave an overwhelmingly positive response (92 percent) to the following question on implementation of the rights of blacks in obtaining jobs: "Should the government in Washington see to it that black people get fair treatment in jobs or leave these matters to the states and local communities?" However, there was some diminution in support for this position by 1974, when 82 percent of blacks still agreed with it.

2. We restrict the discussion to blacks to keep the discussion brief. Analyses similar to those described have been conducted for Hispanics versus Anglos and white women versus white men.

3. Sometimes these studies have employed aggregate data. For example, Bradbury et al. (1989) analyzed the ratio of mortgage loans to structures in Boston neighborhoods as a function of variables measuring the demand for and supply of units and mortgages and the percentage of households in the neighborhood that were black. They interpreted the coefficient of the race variable as suggesting discrimination in lending against blacks.

4. It should be noted that notwithstanding such uncertainty, the courts have been willing to accept evidence of discrimination produced using these methods. See Ashenfelter and Oaxaca (1987) for details.

5. There is substantial inequality in earnings among blacks (even compared with white men), with those with limited education falling further behind (Jaynes and Williams 1989, 275–6).

6. See Shulman (1989) for a summary of the studies and a rebuttal. Heckman (1989) gives greater detail on some of the methodological problems of identifying declines in wage differentials between blacks and whites.

7. Darity (1989) summarizes these studies and argues that other evidence refutes this interpretation.

8. Many more studies have been done attempting to explain differences in wages received by blacks and whites. See, for example, O'Neill (1990) and Haworth et al. (1975).

9. Most recently, for a review of this literature, see Holzer (1991) and Holzer and Vroman (1991). Holzer and Vroman conclude that "the review of the literature indicated widespread support for the idea that labor demand has shifted away from less-educated workers in the past two decades, thus leading to some degree of skill mismatch . . . there is growing evidence that intra-metropolitan movements of firms and population have reduced the demand for black, inner-city residents. But the extent to which these sources of mismatch explain the employment problems of less-educated black males has remained open to question" (p. 36).

10. There is also agreement on the effectiveness of affirmative action programs combined with improved education and other federal action in increasing black employment shares in certain industries during the 1960s and 1970s, although there is far less agreement on the impact on overall employment levels. See, for example, Leonard (1990) and Heckman (1989).

11. U.S. House of Representatives (1990); U.S. Senate (1989).

12. For a summary of these findings, see Fishbein (1989) and Galster (1992).

13. See the testimony of these agencies in U.S. Senate (1990).

14. Beginning in 1990 higher-quality data on mortgage loan applications started being collected from most financial institutions doing such lending under the Home Mortgage Disclosure Act. However, these data do not include detailed information about the specific properties for which mortgage financing is sought. See Wienk (1992).

15. More recent, technically stronger results from another national audit study covering both blacks and Hispanics are discussed later in this chapter, and are presented in greater detail in chapter 2.

16. See Hakken (1979); James et al. (1984); and Galster (1991a).

17. In tests that are carefully administered, comparability is sought by, for example, (a) creating fictional biographies; (b) carefully screening and matching testers so that they

are similar in tangible features such as size, age, and speech, as well as in such intangible features as demeanor and temperament; (c) providing intensive training; and (d) maintaining close oversight of tester performance. See, generally, Turner, Fix, and Struyk (1991).

18. Individual cases of unfavorable treatment may result, however, not from discrimination but from random factors. See the section on methodological issues **(p. 00)** for a detailed discussion.

19. On the need for the social sciences to tell a coherent and compelling story in order to stimulate public action, see Peter Marris (1982).

20. As one scholar has written, "modern forms of both racial prejudice and discrimination have become more subtle, indirect, procedural, and ostensibly non-racial" (Pettigrew 1985, 674).

21. Most studies of discrimination in labor markets focus exclusively on wage versus hiring discrimination. See Donohue and Siegelman (1991).

22. While hiring charges outnumbered termination charges by 50 percent in 1966, the ratio was reversed by more than 6 to 1 by 1985 (Donohue and Siegelman 1991, 8).

23. This result, discussed later in this chapter, was found in a multivariate analysis of outcomes in complaints filed under the Department of Housing and Urban Development's Fair Housing Assistance Program (Wallace et al. 1985). However, later findings from a large-scale Urban Institute research project that systematically compared outcomes in housing discrimination cases brought using audits with those brought without them, produced less conclusive results (Wienk and Simonson 1992).

24. There is substantial precedent for such a balancing of interests. For example, federal policy for the protection of human subjects holds that the following conditions can justify the omission of informed consent:
   An IRB [institutional review board] may . . . waive . . . informed consent provided. . .
   (1) The research involves no more than minimal risk to human subjects;
   (2) The waiver or alteration will not adversely affect the rights and welfare of the subjects;
   (3) The research could not practicably be carried out without the waiver or alteration; and
   (4) Whenever appropriate, the subjects will be provided with additional information after participation.
56 Federal Register 117, p. 28017, June 18, 1991.

25. For example, Ian Ayres (1991) has written regarding the fair-driving testers' efforts to mitigate the process of wasting the salespersons' time: "The study has several features designed to mitigate the problem of wasting the salespersons' time during the negotiation process. Most important, the testers visited the dealerships during the least busy times of the week (from the hours of 9–12 and 1–5 Monday to Friday). During these times few people shop for cars, and there are often several salespeople without customers to serve. In addition, testers were instructed that if all salespeople of a dealership were busy, they should return to the dealership at another time. . . . Steps were also taken to minimize the time that testers spent with the salespeople. The test itself was designed to be completed in 10 to 15 minutes and the testers were instructed to spend no more than an hour at the dealership" (p. 822).

26. *Richardson v. Howard*, 712 F.2d 319, 321 (7th Cir. 1983).

27. *Zuck v. Hussey*, 394 F. Supp. 1028, 1051 (E.D. Mich. 1975), aff'd mem., 547 F.2d 1168 (6th Cir. 1977).

28. Nevertheless, broad knowledge of the existence of such tests might reduce the level of discriminatory behavior that takes place. As a result, broad notice—like that used to make the public aware of tax audits—has some merits.

29. Statistically reliable audit findings are not available for mortgage transactions. See chapter 7 in this volume for details.

30. The results are summarized in Turner, Struyk, and Yinger (1991); also see chapters 2 and 3 of this volume.

31. These studies are summarized in appendix A of this volume. An additional hiring audit study involving both Hispanic-Anglo and black-white tests was conducted in Denver in 1990. The results are not included in the main discussion because the audit procedures followed there were somewhat different from those involved in the other two pilot tests. Details are in James and DelCastillo (1991), and are also discussed in chapters 4 and 5 of this volume.

32. These are only illustrations from much larger lists of the items included in opportunity-diminishing acts. The following rules were applied in the hiring audits to determine which auditor was treated more favorably: (1) If one auditor advanced to a further stage in the hiring process (i.e., obtaining an application, being given an interview, being offered a job) than his partner, he was defined as being treated more favorably; (2) when both auditors advanced to the same stage in the hiring process, if one experienced fewer opportunity-diminishing acts than his partner, then he was defined as being treated more favorably.

33. These data refer to simple differences in unfavorable treatment and make no attempt at disentangling random from systematic behaviors. The estimates in table 1.2 for housing, in contrast, are based on multivariate procedures that purge the random component. Nevertheless, analysis in the Housing Discrimination Study shows that estimates of discrimination and unfavorable treatment are generally quite close. For details, see Yinger (1991b).

34. James and DelCastillo (1991) found no statistically significant levels of hiring discrimination against either blacks or Hispanics in Denver (using somewhat different procedures). Taken at face value, these results indicate a much larger spread for hiring audits than indicated by the other two pilot studies.

35. Yinger (1991a), chap. 6.

36. Craig Coelen, Genevieve Kenney, and Douglas Wissoker made invaluable suggestions that are reflected in this section and in appendix 1.A. Yinger defines systematic as "what would occur if one teammate were able to experience the same circumstances as the other;" see chapter 2.

37. Note that we do not equate systematic with intentional. Differential treatment may be systematic even when it is so habitual, and unconsciously applied, that it may not be conscious.

38. Just as majority-favored audits indicate discrimination against minorities, so do minority-favored audits indicate discrimination against the majority.

39. This case is described in more detail in appendix 1.A.

40. Note that two other questions could be asked here: 1. How much less likely are minorities to receive favorable treatment? 2. How many fewer options (numbers of jobs, dwellings, etc.) are made available to minorities? Regardless of definitional perspective, there is a consensus that the former question is answered by the statistic: proportion majority-favored minus proportion minority-favored, and the latter by a simple difference in the number of total options afforded the group of majority auditors and those afforded the group of minority auditors. These amount to the same thing when the outcomes are simple measures of proportions. Such estimates for housing audits are presented by Yinger (chapter 2), and estimates for hiring audits are presented by Heckman and Siegelman (chapter 5).

41. A related area of disagreement is as follows. Although from the perspective of one holding definition (3) it is clear that P_{maj} will overstate the incidence of discrimination

whenever P_{rmaj} is positive, whether f will be larger or smaller than $P_{maj} - P_{rmaj}$ cannot be determined a priori. (See appendix 1.A for an illustration.)

42. An important qualification is demonstrated in appendix 1.A. The cases of P_{min} are likely to be a poor proxy for P_{rmaj} because P_{rmaj} represents cases of P_{maj} where randomness has overcome minority-favored and equal-favored treatment proclivities. See also chapter 2.

43. Senator Simpson's proposal, which is set out in his own proposed version of the Civil Rights Amendments of 1991, would prohibit employment testers from misrepresenting their education, experience, or other qualifications for the job being offered. This requirement was offered because Senator Simpson viewed it as being "only fair for employers who might be subject to liability under Title VII because of testing programs." Congressional Record S 2259-63, Feb. 22, 1991.

44. When they apply for entry-level jobs advertised in the major metropolitan newspaper. Recently the Washington results were replicated by Bendick et al. (1993).

45. Bendick et al.'s Latino (1991) and black (1993) audits suggested they are not.

46. For a systematic review of these studies, see Yinger et al. (1979), Yinger (1979), and Galster (1992).

47. Such commentary was common, for example, at the 1984 HUD Conference on Fair Housing Testing; for a summary of the proceedings, see Heintz (1985). See also chapter 8 of this volume.

48. The authors themselves conclude:
    This does not necessarily imply that testing does not represent important evidence in individual complaints, or that it is an ineffective mechanism for investigating fair housing complaints. Instead, it seems likely that the most important determinants of both investigative procedures and complaint outcomes are unobserved factors, such as the underlying merits of individual complaints, the quality of testing evidence, and the specific nature of the testing evidence. (Wienk and Simonson, 1992)

49. Data from the Urban Institute work flow logs.

50. See, generally, Wienk and Simonson (1992).

51. In this instance, the case is referred to the Department of Justice for prosecution.

52. Figure in Galster (1990a).

53. Funding for the program in fiscal year 1991 is $5.8 million. HUD's legislative proposals for fiscal year 1992 request expansion of eligibility to state and local agencies whose equivalency status is withdrawn in 1992 because their government does not modify its fair-housing laws to be consistent with the revised federal fair-housing statute.

54. For a further discussion of avenues for expanding the coverage of these studies, see Struyk (1985).

55. There may also be room here for state action. States played a critical role in monitoring discrimination triggered by the Immigration Reform and Control Act's employment discrimination provisions. See California Fair Employment and Housing Commission (1990); New York state Inter-Agency Task Force on Immigration Affairs (1988).

APPENDIX 1.A

INTERPRETING AUDITS USING DIFFERENT DEFINITIONS OF DISCRIMINATION

This appendix provides illustrations of how the implicit definition of discrimination one employs crucially shapes how one statistically evaluates and interprets the results of audits. A closely related issue is how one believes random events affect the audit results.

Because the issues quickly grow complex, we start by considering audits repeatedly conducted on a single agent in an idealized, nonrandom world. We then allow randomness to enter and assess its impact on our audit results. Finally, we expand our hypothetical audits to cover many agents. We employ the same four codes denoting definitions of discrimination and the same symbols as provided in the text. Throughout we consider the questions of the existence and the incidence of discrimination, that is: Does discrimination occur? How often does it occur?

Auditing a Single Agent in a Nonrandom World

Distinctions among the four definitions of discrimination become moot in a world without randomness, i.e., where the single agent being audited behaves consistently, all auditor matches are perfect, and no stochastic events impinge on the audit activities that affect either the agent's or auditors' actions. In such a world, there will be a one-for-one correspondence between the racial penalties agents assess when evaluating applicants and the failure of those so penalized to gain equal access compared to their teammates. The distinction between random and systematic differences in treatment is rendered moot. Finally, the agent will evince favoritism (if any) toward either majority or minority auditors, not both.

As illustration, what if the agent being audited had a discriminating inclination towards minorities, and therefore consistently assessed a race penalty on minority applicants for vacant apartments? We would expect to see that 100 percent of the audits favored the majority (i.e., "gross majority-favored" = 100 percent). This figure would simultaneously provide an indicator of the existence and an accurate estimate of incidence of this agent's discrimination, whether one considers penalty being assessed or explicit acts of differential access, because $f = P_{maj} = 100$ percent.

Thus, in repeated audits of a single agent in a nonrandom world, gross and net measures of favoritism would be identical and equal to both inclinations proclivities and explicit acts of discrimination. Any of the four definitions of discrimination yield the same result regarding the existence and incidence of discrimination.

Auditing a Single Agent When Randomness Occurs

Unfortunately, the above unanimous conclusion evaporates when any one of several potential forms of randomness enter the audit results. First, auditors are unlikely to be matched perfectly on all relevant characteristics, and even if they were in some abstract sense, an agent's evaluations of these matches may not always correspond. Auditors may not behave uniformly in each encounter with an agent, depending on their health, mood, or reaction to the agent. Second, agents are likely to have a random component to their behavior; they may be unable to treat auditors of the same race identically in repeat trials. Finally, external events can intervene to affect agents' behaviors because the auditors do not confront the agent simultaneously. Idiosyncratic events may have immediately preceded the visit by one teammate that were not present during the other's visit: a bona fide applicant appears to take the job or dwelling, the agent receives some upsetting news, etc.

Consider the consequences of any of these sorts of random influences on results of repeated audits of a single agent. We analyze four alternative cases, and show how the veracity of the gross (P_{maj}) and net $(P_{maj} - P_{min})$ measures as tests for the existence and incidence of discrimination varies according to the definition chosen.

Case I. First, suppose we audit an agent who, we assume, never assesses a racial penalty $(f = 0)$. Even though this person tries to be evenhanded, randomness is likely to lead to some audits in which the minority is favored but, on average, just as many in which the majority is favored; let us assume 10 percent each as illustration, i.e., $P_{maj} = P_{min} = 10$ percent. (Eighty percent of the audits would reveal equal treatment.) Thus, the net majority-favored figure would be zero. Now only the gross unfavorable treatment definition (2) of discrimination would claim that the gross majority-favored 10 percent is a correct measure of the incidence of discrimination against minorities; all other definitions would argue that the true incidence was zero, and thus the net measure would be the correct indicator.

Case II. Consider next the results of auditing an agent who tries to assess a penalty against minorities (f = 100 percent), but the penalty is small relative to the effect of inconsistencies in the agent's behavior and/or other randomness generated by the auditors or by external effects. In this case what we would have seen as 100 percent majority-favored in a nonrandom world is obscured: randomness so overwhelms the slight penalty being applied to minorities that we are likely to see many instances of equal treatment and roughly equivalent numbers of minority- and majority-favored outcomes ($P_r \gg P_{min} = P_{maj}$). Indeed, the outcome may be quite indistinguishable from the case described in the previous paragraph. Yet, which definition of discrimination one chooses becomes more important.

In this case, if one adopts the discriminatory inclination definition (1) of discrimination, one would wish for a 100 percent incidence of penalties being assessed against either the black or white auditor; unfortunately, neither the gross (P_{maj}) or net ($P_{maj} - P_{min}$) figure comes close. The gross unfavorable treatment definition (2) would indicate that the gross majority-favored figure accurately gives the incidence of discrimination. The systematic unfavorable treatment definition (3) would agree, because here randomness only serves to push instances of proclivity penalties out of P_{maj}. That is, P_{rmaj} represents those who did not assess a penalty but were erroneously categorized in P_{maj} by the audits; and here $P_{rmaj} = 0$. Definitions (1), (2), and (3) would agree that discrimination exists, however. But definition (4) would, as above, claim that discrimination overall did not exist because the market effect (i.e., net measure) was not significantly different from zero.

Case III. If the agent has an inclination to assess a sizable race penalty that is unlikely to be overwhelmed by random effects, we would expect an audit to reveal more majority-favored than minority-favored cases. For illustration, assume the results were: $P_{maj} = 65$ percent majority-favored, 20 percent equal treatment, $P_{min} = 15$ percent minority-favored. The latter two results must have been produced by random effects that favored minorities ($= P_r$) and thus offset (and, in the case of minority-favored, overwhelmed) the race penalty being exacted 100 percent of the time by the agent.

Definition (1) would say that the gross 65 percent measure badly understates the "true" 100 percent incidence of discriminatory inclination. Definitions (2) and (3) would agree that 65 percent was a correct measure of incidence, as in Case I. Definition (4) would agree with the other three definitions that discrimination exists here because the net figure ($P_{maj} - P_{min} = 50$ percent) is greater than zero.

Case IV. Reverse Case III: the agent has an inclination to assess a sizable race bonus in favor of minorities. The audits reveal: $P_{min} = 65$ percent minority-favored, 20 percent equal treatment, $P_{maj} = 15$ percent majority-favored. Definition (1) would produce a finding of zero discrimination against minorities because f = 0; definition (4) would reject the hypothesis that $P_{maj} - P_{min}$ was greater than zero and so would support this conclusion. Definition (2), as usual, would insist that gross majority-favored $P_{maj} = 15$ percent is an accurate incidence and, presuming it is significantly greater than zero, would conclude that discrimination against minorities exists. (Of course, this definition would also claim that the majority was discriminated against 65 percent of the time.) But (3) would argue for zero incidence of discrimination against minorities, because these 15% were due purely to random reasons: $P_{maj} - P_{rmaj} = 0$. As usual, definition (4) would argue that P_{maj} overstates existence; a net less than zero ($P_{maj} - P_{min} = -50$) obviously would not support the finding of discrimination against minorities.

Summary. Let us summarize the conclusions of the prior cases of single-agent audits. The appropriateness of gross (P_{maj}) and net ($P_{maj} - P_{min}$) majority-favored figures as estimates of the existence and incidence of discrimination against minorities, as seen from the perspective of the various definitions of discrimination, is:

Definition	Case I	Case II	Case III	Case IV
(1) Discriminatory Inclination	gross overst.	gross underst.	gross underst.	gross overst.
(2) Gross Unfavorable Treatment	net correct gross correct	net underst. gross correct	net underst. gross correct	net correct gross correct
(3) Systematic Unfavorable Treatment	net underst. gross overst.	net underst. gross correct	net underst. gross correct	net underst. gross overst.
(4) Net Market Effects	net correct gross overst. net correct	net underst. gross overst. net correct	net underst. gross overst. net correct	net correct gross overst. net correct

The above makes plain that definitional perspective and interpretation of audit results are inextricably linked. In addition, it shows that even if one assumes one definition of discrimination, the accuracy of the simple gross or net measures for investigating existence or incidence of discrimination may be questioned when randomness affects audit results. Only definitions (2) and (4) tautologically finesse this issue: the former by equating discrimination with gross majority-favored incidence and the latter equating discrimination with sizable market effect on net. By contrast, both (1) and (3) must distill the effects of randomness from the observed gross and net audit results in order to estimate the existence and incidence of discrimination within their conceptual framework. This problem is made even more difficult when we consider the scenario typically confronted in audits: a single audit on a large number of agents from many different institutions.

Auditing Many Agents when Randomness Occurs

The difficulty in the straightforward interpretation of audit results is heightened when they represent the composite profile of many agents, their inclinations to assess racial penalties or bonuses, and the degree to which randomness can outweigh such inclinations in shaping the ultimate behavior observed. An additional source of randomness enters the picture here as well: auditor teammates may not always see the same agent. The main point of this subsection is to demonstrate how variations in the distributions of the sizes of race penalties/bonuses assessed, relative to the size of the random effects, crucially influence how those holding to discrimination definitions (1) or (3) evaluate the simple gross and net results from an audit.

We will proceed, as before, by comparing three alternative hypothetical examples involving different assumptions about the relative impacts of race penalties/bonuses vs. randomness. As the basis for each, assume that the sample of 100 agents audited consists of 40 who have proclivities to penalize minorities ($f = 40$ percent), 40 who have proclivities to assess no penalties or bonuses, and 20 who have proclivities to give bonuses to minorities. It is clear, therefore, that the discriminatory inclination definition (1) would like to uncover the "true" incidence of 40 percent with the audits. The "true" incidence as seen from the perspective of the systematic unfavorable treatment definition (3) will vary from case to case, depending on the assumptions made about the impacts of randomness on those holding discriminatory inclinations toward minorities (P_{rmaj}).

Case A. Assume that the distributions of race penalties/bonuses across agents relative to the size of random effects is such that 10 percent of agents starting in any given inclination category end up having behaviors in the audit that place them in the "adjacent" category. That is, 10 percent (i.e., 4) of the majority-favoritists and 10 percent (i.e., 2) of the minority favoritists end up treating both teammates the same; of those with no proclivity for assessing race penalties/bonuses, 10 percent (i.e., 4) end up favoring the majority auditor and 10 percent the minority auditor. This would yield:

Proclivity	Majority-Favored 40	No Difference 40	Minority-Favored 20
Observed Original	36	32	18
Due to Random	4	6	4
Total	40	38	22 (net = 18)

Here, the Majority-Favored lost four to the No Difference group due to random factors ($P_r - 4$), but gained an equal number from the No Difference group for the same reason ($P_{rmaj} = 4$). But fewer Minority Favored were observed in the No Difference group than vice versa, because there were half as many agents in it.

Thus, in this case those using the discriminatory inclination definition (1) would be pleased with the gross majority-favored figure ($P_{maj} = 40$), because it precisely measures the percentage of agents who have a proclivity to assess race penalties. However, those using systematic unfavorable treatment definition (3) would not count the four in the majority-favoritist group who did not end up treating auditors differently, nor those originally in the No Difference group who only favored majority auditors for random reasons ($P_{rmaj} = 4$). Their precise estimate of discrimination incidence would, therefore, only be 36 percent ($= P_{maj} - P_{rmaj}$), which is overstated by the gross measure.

Case B. Assume that those who favor the majority all have an inclination to assess large penalties on minority applicants, such that no random event will lead to anything but majority-favored outcomes being observed in an audit ($P_r = 0$). Now, if all else stayed the same as above, we would observe:

Proclivity	Majority-Favored 40	No Difference 40	Minority-Favored 20
Observed Original	40	32	18
Due to Random	4	2	4
Total	44	34	22 (net = 20)

From the perspective of either definition (1) or (3), the gross majority-favored figure ($P_{maj} = 44$ percent) now overstates the "true" incidence, which in this case equals 40 percent from both perspectives.

Case C. Assume that those with inclinations to favor the majority only penalize minorities a small amount, such that random events end up pushing 50 percent (i.e., 20 agents) into the No Difference audit result category, all else equal ($P_r = 20$). This would yield:

Proclivity	Majority-Favored 40	No Difference 40	Minority-Favored 20
Observed Original	20	32	18
Due to Random	4	22	4
Total	24	54	22 (net = 2)

From the perspective of definition (1), the gross measure ($P_{maj} = 24$ percent) badly understates the "true" value (40 percent), but from the perspective of definition (3) the gross measure continues to overstate the "true" value ($P_{maj} - P_{rand} = 20$ percent).[1]

The above cases should demonstrate sufficiently that the gross incidence of majority-favored audits may (but not necessarily does) badly over- or understate the "true" incidence of those with an inclination to discriminate (definition (1)), depending on the relationship between the sizes of the race penalties these agents assess and the random effects that impinge on the audit process which lead to those with certain inclinations being observed acting differently from their inclinations. Systematic unfavorable acts of discrimination (definition 3) will always be upwardly bounded by the gross measure because P_{rmaj} is non-negative; the gross measure's degree of overstatement will be directly related to P_{maj}: the extent to which random factors result in those who do not have a proclivity to assess penalties against minorities being observed in the majority-favored category nevertheless. Finally, note how those using the market effects perspective of definition (4) would assess the above cases. In the first two, they would agree that discrimination exists because the net figure is significantly greater than zero; in the last case they would not.

Note to Appendix 1.A.

1. Indeed, it should be obvious from these examples that the gross measure will always provide an upper-bound estimate to the incidence of discrimination against minorities from the perspective of definition (3), since randomness can never produce discrimination.

APPENDIX 1.B

LINKING AUDIT METHODOLOGY TO CONVENTIONAL ESTIMATION APPROACHES

This appendix explores how the gross and net measures of discrimination used in audit studies relate to those more familiar to most economists. We first present a simple model that puts the measures from the audit literature in the context of the broader labor economics literature. We then discuss what happens to the interpretation of audit findings when the extent of discrimination varies by employer/auditor characteristics. Finally, we discuss whether it is possible to derive separate estimates of the incidence and severity of discrimination.

Consider first the case of individual, non-paired observations, which is the standard in economics. Here is a conventional formulation: Faced with an individual applying for a job, an employer determines whether to hire $(y = 1)$ or not to hire $(y = 0)$ by the rule

$$y = \begin{matrix} 1 \text{ if } y^* > 0 \\ 0 \text{ if } y^* < 0, \end{matrix} \qquad (1.B.1)$$

where

$$y^* = \beta'x + \alpha z + \epsilon, \qquad (1.B.2)$$

with x = covariate vector, z = race ($z = 1$ for the majority, $z = 0$ for the minority), and the disturbance ϵ is distributed standard normal independent of x and z. The bonus granted to the majority applicant is given by α. The covariate vector includes employer characteristics (e.g., industry), job characteristics (e.g., skill requirements), and applicant characteristics (e.g., productivity or human capital). With y^* unobserved, this is a probit model. It implies that

$$\Pr(y = 1 | x, z) = E(y | x, z) = F(\beta'x + \alpha z), \qquad (1.B.3)$$

where $F(\cdot)$ is the standard normal cumulative distribution function. So for a given x, the difference between the hiring probabilities for a majority and a minority applicant is

$$n(x) = E(y| x, z = 1) - E(y| x, z = 0) \qquad (1.B.4)$$
$$= F(\mu + \alpha) - F(\mu),$$

where $\mu = \beta'x$. On the presumption that α is positive, indicating a preference for the majority, $n(x)$ is positive. If we had repeated observations at a single value of x, and if all employers were following the same rule (1), then we would expect the difference between the proportions of majority and minority applicants hired to be $n(x)$. This is what the net measure based on data from paired audits would pick up in the simplest case.

In practice, of course, there would be variability in x across observations. If we suppose that at each value of x we observed one majority and one minority applicant, the net measure would correspond to the difference in hiring rates:

$$E[n(x)] = E(y| z = 1) - E(y| z = 0)$$
$$= \sum_{x} [E(y| z = 1, x) - E(y| z = 0, x)]\cdot Pr(x) \qquad (1.B.5)$$
$$= \text{average of } n(x) \text{ across the distribution of } x.$$

While α, the bonus given to the majority applicant in the employer's latent evaluation y^*, is measured directly in the probit model, the implied difference in hiring rates, $E[n(x)]$, provides a more intuitive measure of discrimination. Tests for the existence of discrimination take the form $H_0:\alpha = 0$, $H_1:\alpha > 0$ or, equivalently, $H_0:E[n(x)] = 0$, $H_1:E[n(x)] > 0$.

How would the conventional, individual-level formulation carry over to the audit-pair situation, where each employer sees a matched pair of applicants? For the simplest case, we may suppose that the employer makes two independent decisions. In that case, the table of joint probabilities would be

		White	
		$y = 1$	$y = 0$
Black	$y = 1$	$F(\mu+\alpha) F(\mu)$	$[1-F(\mu+\alpha)] F(\mu)$
	$y = 0$	$F(\mu+\alpha) [1-F(\mu)]$	$[1-F(\mu+\alpha)][1-F(\mu)]$

In this table, the gross majority-favored measure corresponds to the probability that the majority applicant is hired and the minority applicant is not, that is, to

$$g(x) = F(\mu + \alpha)[1-F(\mu)].$$

The gross minority-favored measure, which corresponds to the probability that the majority applicant is not hired and the minority is, corresponds to

$$[1-F(\mu + \alpha)] \, F(\mu).$$

These gross measures have no analogue in the economics literature. The net measure corresponds to the difference between the two gross measures, namely

$$F(\mu + \alpha) - F(\mu),$$

which is just the $n(x)$ defined above for individual-level data.

Currently, researchers using the gross measure of discrimination test whether the proportion of times the majority applicant is hired and the minority applicant is not is significantly different from zero (with attendant statistical problems noted in Heckman and Siegelman's chapter 5 of this volume). This assumes that every incident of differential treatment is due to discrimination. However, random factors are very likely to play some role in hiring decisions (as indicated by the specification of a random disturbance term in the hiring model). To obtain an estimate of differential treatment that would occur in the absence of discrimination, same race audit pairs could be used. An appropriate test of discrimination, then, would test whether the proportion of times the majority gets a job and the minority does not is equal to (vs. greater than) the proportion of times one same-race auditor gets a job and the other same-race auditor does not.

When data from audit pairs are used to estimate equation (2), the estimate of the bonus, α, will not depend on x. Since both auditors are matched on observable characteristics and visit the same employers, the measure of the effect of race (α) will be independent of x. The estimate of $E[n(x)]$ can be obtained most simply by subtracting the proportion of audits in which the minority is hired and the majority is not from the proportion of audits in which the majority is hired and the minority is not. This is quite different from the individual-level formulation under which the estimate of α depends on the x's included in the model because the x's differ by race. So, as before, tests for the existence of discrimination take the form $H_0: \alpha = 0$, $H_1: \alpha > 0$ or, equivalently, $H_0: E[n(x)] = 0$, $H_1: E[n(x)] > 0$.

One might also want to allow for dependence of the two decisions made by an employer. Since the auditors went into the hiring process with similar resumes, they could be expected to be comparably suited for the job: in other words they will tend to be over- or underqualified for the same jobs. One way to allow dependence is to introduce an employer-specific effect that correlates the disturbances of the two y^* equations in the context of a bivariate probit model. One recent attempt to estimate such a model produced a very large and statistically significant firm-specific correlation coefficient (Kenney and Wissoker, forthcoming) suggesting that the job hiring probabilities are indeed dependent on one another in audit studies.

Interdependence of Race and Employer/Applicant Characteristics

Until this point, we have assumed that the extent of discrimination is independent of employer and applicant characteristics. However, this assumption may be invalid. First, economic theory suggests that the extent of discrimination differs across employers by the profitability of discrimination and whether an employer is subject to affirmative action regulations. Second, discrimination may vary with the characteristics of applicants, such as skill level, which by construction vary over a very narrow range in audit studies.

These considerations suggest a model in which employer, job, and auditor characteristics (x) are fully interacted with race (z). Such models may yield estimates of how discrimination interacts with employer and job characteristics, but will not provide evidence on how skill level and discrimination relate unless auditors are drawn from many different skill levels. Furthermore, if the extent of discrimination does depend on the skill level of applicants, the audits will yield an estimate of discrimination only for the skill level at which the auditors are matched. In addition, it should be noted that in a model where race and employer/auditor characteristics interact, the correct estimate of the net measure of discrimination is based on an average over the empirical distribution of x.

The dependence of the net measure of discrimination on x makes clear the need to carefully interpret the estimates obtained from the audit studies. Audit studies are based on a set of auditors with a narrow range of applicant characteristics, both real and constructed. The measures of discrimination that result from audit studies are clearly only appropriate for the range of characteristics observed.

Finally, Heckman and Siegelman in chapter 5 of this volume argue that the skill level at which auditors are matched relative to the requirements of the job being sought can systematically affect the rate at which the black and white auditors are hired. In their model, the productivity level of the auditors depends on an observable/matched component and an "unobservable" unmatched component that is observable only to prospective employers. Heckman and Siegelman show that even if the means of the unobservable characteristics are the same for the white and black auditors, the relative hiring rates for the black and white auditors will vary with the skill level of the auditors if the variance of the unobservable characteristic depends on race. Their analysis underscores the need to minimize the extent to which "unobservables" differentiate black and white applicants and to expand audit studies to encompass broader skill levels.

Untangling Incidence and Severity in Audit Studies

This model also provides a context for examining the incidence and severity of discrimination. Incidence refers to the share of employers who discriminate. Severity refers to the intensity of discriminatory preferences and is revealed through consistency of unfavorable differential treatment toward minorities. The formulation above assumes that all employers follow rule (1), that is, have the same α and hire if $y^* > 0$; do not hire if $y^* < 0$. With α positive, one might say that the incidence of discrimination is 100 percent. Given a majority and minority who are identical on x and ϵ, the majority always receives a higher value of y^*, and thus a higher hiring probability. Therefore, one could have a trivially small value of α, manifested in a trivial difference in hiring rates, and nevertheless insist that the incidence of discrimination is 100 percent.

Of course, it is possible to allow for a distribution of rules—in particular of values of α—across employers. In such a case, equation (2) could be modified as

$$y^* = \beta'x + \alpha_i z + \epsilon, \qquad (1.B.2b)$$

where α_i is the bonus applied by firm i. If some α values were positive, others zero, and still others negative, the incidence of discrimination would be less than 100 percent. However, current audit studies (with one audit per employer) lack information on the distribution of α_i across firms. To get a handle on incidence from current audit studies, therefore, one is forced to make strong assumptions about the distribution of α_i and how it relates to observed characteristics (for example, see Yinger's chapter 2 of this volume).

With repeated observations at each firm, α could be estimated for each firm and the proportion of employers with $\alpha_i > 0$ and the average value of α_i could be estimated separately. Clearly, a large number of audits would be required per firm to obtain a precise estimate of the incidence of discrimination. This may not be feasible, because of dangers of detection and because one is constrained by the number of audit pairs. In addition, limited resources force a tradeoff between how many firms can be audited and how many audits can be done per firm. This tradeoff may not favor increasing the number of audits per firm versus the number of firms audited.

Note to appendix 1.B.

This appendix owes its existence to the insights of Arthur S. Goldberger, Douglas Wissoker, and Genevieve Kenney.

References

Amaker, Norman. 1988. *Civil Rights and the Reagan Administration.* Washington, D.C.: The Urban Institute Press.

Ashenfelter, O., and R. Oaxaca. 1987. "The Economics of Discrimination Thirty Years Later: Economists Enter the Courtroom." *American Economic Review* 77(2): 321–5.

Ayres, Ian. 1991. "Fair Driving: Gender and Race Discrimination in Rental Car Negotiations." *Harvard Law Review* 104(4): 817–72.

Ballen, J., and R. B. Freeman. 1986. "Transition between Employment and Nonemployment." In *The Black Youth Employment Crisis,* edited by R. Freeman and H. Holzer, 75–112. Chicago: University of Chicago Press.

Bendick, Marc, Charles Jackson, and Victor Reinoso. 1993. *Measuring Employment Discrimination Through Controlled Experiments.* Washington, DC: Fair Employment Council of Greater Washington.

Bendick, Marc, Charles Jackson, Victor Reinoso, and Laura Hodges. 1991. "Discrimination Against Latino Job Applicants." *Human Resource Management* 30 (4): 469–484.

Bok, Sissela. 1979. *Lying: Moral Choice in Public and Private Life.* New York: Vintage.

Bowsher, C. A. Letter and attached memorandum from Asst. Comptroller Gen. for Program Evaluation and Methodology E. Chelimsky to Sen. Alan K. Simpson (R-Wyo.), June 26, 1990.

Bradbury, K., K. E. Case, and C. R. Dunham. (1989). "Geographic Patterns of Mortgage Lending in Boston, 1982–87." *New England Economic Review* (Sept./Oct.): 3–29.

California Fair Employment and Housing Commission. 1990. "Public Hearings on the Impact and Effectiveness in California of the Employer Sanctions and Anti-Discrimination Provisions of the Immigration Reform and Control Act of 1986," January 11.

Center for Community Change. 1989. "Mortgage Lending Discrimination Testing Project." Unpublished report. Washington, D.C.: U.S. Department of Housing and Urban Development.

Cross, Harry, Genevieve Kenney, Jane Mell, and Wendy Zimmermann. 1990. *Employer Hiring Practices: Differential Treatment of Hispanic and Anglo Job Seekers*. Washington, D.C.: The Urban Institute Press.

Darity, William, Jr. 1989. "What's Left of the Economic Theory of Discrimination?" In *The Question of Discrimination: Racial Inequality in the U.S. Labor Market*, edited by S. Shulman and W. Darity, Jr., 335–76. Middletown, Conn: Wesleyan University Press.

Donohue, J. J., and James J. Heckman. 1990. "Re-evaluating Federal Civil Rights Policy." Paper presented at the Georgetown University Law Center Conference on "The Law & Economics of Racial Discrimination in Employment," November 30.

Donohue, John J., and Peter Siegelman. 1991. "The Changing Nature of Employment Discrimination Litigation." *Stanford Law Review* 43(3): 983–1033.

Duleep, Harriet O., and N. Zalokar. 1991. "The Measurement of Labor Market Discrimination When Minorities Respond to Discrimination." In *New Approaches to Economic and Social Analyses of Discrimination*, edited by R. Cornwall and P. Wannava. New York: Praeger.

Fishbein, A. 1990. "Discrimination in Home Mortgage Lending." Testimony at hearings before the Subcommittee on Consumer and Regulatory Affairs of the Senate, Committee on Banking Housing and Urban Affairs. October 24.

Freeman, R. 1990. "Employment and Earnings of Disadvantaged Young Men in a Labor Short Economy." Working Paper No. 3444. Cambridge, Mass.: National Bureau of Economic Research.

Freeman, R., and H. Holzer. 1986. *The Black Youth Employment Crisis*. Chicago: University of Chicago Press.

Gallup, G. H., Jr., and L. Hujick. 1990. "Racial Tolerance Grows, Progress on Racial Equality Less Evident." *The Gallup Poll News Service* 55(6).

Galster, George. 1990a. "Federal Fair Housing Policy: The Great Misapprehension." In *Building Foundations: Housing and Federal Policy*, edited by D. Dipasquale and L. C. Keyes, 137–56. Philadelphia: University of Pennsylvania Press.

_____. 1990b. "Racial Steering by Real Estate Agents: A Review of the Audit Evidence." *Review of Black Political Economy* 18: 105–129.

————. 1991a. "Racial Discrimination in Metropolitan Housing Markets During the 1980s: A Review of the Audit Evidence." *Journal of Planning Education and Research* 9: 165–75.

————. 1991b. "Housing Discrimination and Poverty of Urban African-Americans." *Journal of Housing Research* 2: 87–122.

————. 1992. "Research on Discrimination in Housing and Mortgage Markets: Assessment and Future Directions." *Housing Policy Debate* 3: 639–684.

Galster, G., and W. M. Keeney. 1988. "Race, Discrimination, and Economic Opportunity: Modeling the Nexus of Urban Racial Phenomena." *Urban Affairs Quarterly* 24: 87–117.

Goering, J. 1986. *Housing Desegregation and Federal Policy.* Chapel Hill: University of North Carolina Press.

Hakken, Jon. 1979. "Discrimination Against Chicanos in the Dallas Rental Housing Market: An Experimental Extension of the Housing Market Practices Survey." Washington, D.C.: U.S. Department of Housing and Urban Development.

Haworth, J. G., J. Gwartney, and C. Haworth. 1975. "Earnings, Productivity, and Changes in Employment Discrimination." *American Economic Review* 65(1): 158–68.

Heckman, J. J. 1989. "The Impact of Government on the Economic Status of Black Americans." In *The Question of Discrimination: Racial Inequality in the U.S. Labor Market,* edited by S. Shulman and W. Darity, Jr., 50–80. Conn.: Wesleyan University Press.

Heintz, K. 1985. "HUD Conference on Fair Housing Testing: Final Summary Report." Washington, D.C.: U.S. Department of Housing and Urban Development.

Holzer, H. 1991. "The Spatial Mismatch Hypothesis: What Has the Evidence Shown?" *Urban Studies* 28(1), 105–22.

Holzer, H., and W. Vroman. 1992. "Mismatches and the Urban Labor Market." In *Urban Labor Markets and Job Opportunity,* eds. George E. Peterson and Wayne Vroman. Washington, D.C.: Urban Institute Press.

Ihlanfeldt, K. R., and D. L. Sjoquist. 1990. "Job Accessibility and Racial Differences in Youth Employment Rates." *American Economic Review* 80(1): 268–76.

James, F. J., B. I. Cummings, and E. A. Tynan. 1984. "Minorities in the Sunbelt." New Brunswick, N.J.: Center for Urban Policy Research, Rutgers University.

James, Franklin J., and Steve W. DelCastillo. 1991. "Measuring Job Discrimination by Private Employers Against Young Black and Hispanic Males Seeking Entry Level Work in the Denver Metropolitan Area." Unpublished Report. Denver: University of Colorado.

Jaynes, G. D. 1990. "The Labor Market Status of Black Americans: 1939–1985." *Journal of Economic Perspectives* 4(fall): 9–24.

Jaynes, G. D., and R. M. Williams, Jr. (1989). *A Common Destiny: Blacks and American Society.* Washington, D.C.: National Academy Press.

Kenney, Genevieve M., and Douglas A. Wissoker. Forthcoming. "An Analysis of the Correlaters of Discrimination Facing Young, Hispanic Jobseekers." *American Economic Review.*

King, Thomas. 1980. "Mortgage Lending, Social Responsibility and Public Policy: Some Perspectives on HMDA and DRA." *American Real Estate and Urban Economics Association Journal* 8: 77–90.

Kirschenman, Joleen, and Kathryn Neckerman. 1991. "We'd Love to Hire Them, But . . . , The Meaning of Race to Employers." In *The Urban Underclass,* edited by C. Jencks, and P. E. Peterson, 203–32. Washington, D.C.: Brookings Institution.

Leonard, Jonathan S. 1990. "The Impact of Affirmative Action Regulation and Equal Employment Law on Black Employment." *Journal of Economic Perspectives* 4(fall): 47–63.

Marris, Peter. 1982. *Meaning and Action.* London: Routledge Kegan and Paul.

Mashaw, J. 1990. "Implementing Quotas." Paper presented at the Georgetown University Law Center Conference on "The Law and Economics of Racial Discrimination in Employment."

McIntyre, S., et al. 1980. "Preferential Treatment in Preselection Decisions According to Race and Sex." *Academy of Management Journal* 23: 738–749.

Millspaugh. 1984. "Fair Housing Testing: Its Legal Status and Policy Implications." *University of Baltimore Law Review* 13: 240.

Munnell, A., L. Browne, J. McEneaney, and G. Tootell. 1992. *Mortgage Lending in Boston: Interpreting the HMDA Data.* Federal Reserve Bank of Boston, paper 92–7.

New York State Inter-Agency Task Force on Immigration Affairs. 1988. "Workplace Discrimination Under the Immigration Reform and Control Act of 1986." November 4.

O'Neill, J. 1990. "The Role of Human Capital in Earnings Differences Between Black and White Men." *Journal of Economic Perspectives* 4(fall): 25–45.

Pettigrew, Thomas F. 1985. "New Patterns of Racism: The Different World of 1984 and 1964." *Rutgers Law Review* 37: 674.

Price, R. and Edwin Mills. 1985. "Race and Residence in Earnings Determination." *Journal of Urban Economics* 17: 1–18.

Rees, A. 1986. "An Essay on Youth Joblessness." *Journal of Economic Literature* 24: 613–28.

Ridley, Stanley E., James A. Bayton, and Janice H. Outtz. 1989. "Taxi Service in the District of Columbia: Is it Influenced by Patron's Race and Destination?" Paper prepared for the Washington, D.C. Lawyer's Committee for Civil Rights.

Schafer, Robert, and Helen Ladd. 1981. *Discrimination in Mortgage Lending.* Cambridge, Mass.: MIT Press.

Schuman, H., C. Steeh, and L. Bobo. 1985. *Racial Attitudes in America.* Cambridge, Mass.: Harvard University Press.

Shulman, S. 1989. "A Critique of the Declining Discrimination Hypothesis." In *The Question of Discrimination: Racial Inequality in the U.S. Labor Market*, edited by S. Shulman and W. Darity, Jr., 126–52. Middletown, Conn.: Wesleyan University Press.

Siniscalco, Gary, and John Giansello. 1992. "An Analysis of the Civil Rights Act of 1991." Papers presented at the American Bar Association 1992 Mid-winter Meeting of the Labor and Employment Law Section, March 4–7. La Quinta, California.

Squires, Gregory, and W. Velez. 1988. "Insurance Redlining and the Process of Discrimination." *Review of Black Political Economy* 16: 63–75.

Strauss, David A. 1990. "The Law and Economics of Race Discrimination in Employment." Paper presented at a conference held at Georgetown University Law Center, on "The Law and Economics of Race Discrimination in Employment: An Agenda for the Next Generation," November 30.

Turner, Margery, Michael Fix, and Raymond Struyk. 1991. *Opportunities Denied, Opportunities Diminished: Discrimination in Hiring*. Washington, D.C.: The Urban Institute Press.

Turner, Margery A., Raymond Struyk, and John Yinger. 1991. "Housing Discrimination in America: Summary of Findings from the Housing Discrimination Study." Washington, D.C.: The Urban Institute.

U.S. Equal Employment Opportunity Commission. 1990. "Policy Guidance on the Use of EEO Testers." *EEOC Compliance Manual* (BNA), Section 405 (November 20): 6899.

U.S. General Accounting Office. 1990. "Immigration Reform: Employer Sanctions and the Question of Discrimination." GAO/GGD 90-62. Washington, D.C.: March.

U.S. House of Representatives, Committee on Education and Labor and Committee on the Judiciary. 1990. Joint Hearing on H.R. 4000, Civil Rights Act of 1990. February 20 and 27, March 13 and 20.

U.S. Senate, Subcommittee on Consumer and Regulatory Affairs of the Committee on Banking, Housing and Urban Affairs. 1990. Hearing on Mortgage Discrimination. May 16.

————. Committee on Labor and Human Resources. 1989. Hearing on S. 2104, Civil Rights Act of 1990. Serial No. 101-649, February 23 and 27, March 1 and 7.

Wallace, J., W. L. Holshouser, T. S. Lane, and J. Williams. 1985. "The Fair Housing Assistance Program Evaluation." Washington, D.C.: U.S. Department of Housing and Urban Development.

Wienk, Ronald, Clifford E. Reid, John C. Simonson, and Frederick J. Eggers. 1979. "Measuring Racial Discrimination in American Housing Markets: The Housing Practices Survey." Washington, D.C.: U.S. Department of Housing and Urban Development.

Wienk, Ron, and John Simonson. 1992. "FHIP: An Evaluation of the Testing Demonstration." The Urban Institute, June.

Yinger, J. 1991a. "Lessons About Discrimination Against Blacks and Hispanics from the Housing Discrimination Study." Washington, D.C.: The Urban Institute.

————. 1991b. "Housing Discrimination Study: Incidence of Discrimination and Variation in Discriminatory Behavior." Washington, D.C.: U.S. Department of Housing and Urban Development.

————. 1979. "Prejudice and Discrimination in the Urban Housing Market." In Current Issues in Urban Economics, edited by P. Mieszkowski and M. Straszheim, Baltimore, Md.: Johns Hopkins University Press.

Yinger, J., G. Galster, B. Smith, and F. Eggers. 1979. "The Status of Research into Racial Discrimination and Segregation in American Housing Markets: A Research Agenda for the Department of Housing and Urban Development." Occasional Papers in Housing and Community Affairs 6: 55–175.

Chapter Two

ACCESS DENIED, ACCESS CONSTRAINED: RESULTS AND IMPLICATIONS OF THE 1989 HOUSING DISCRIMINATION STUDY

John Yinger

INTRODUCTION

This chapter presents some recent evidence concerning a major domestic challenge facing the United States: persistent, widespread racial and ethnic discrimination in housing. This evidence comes from the Housing Discrimination Study (HDS), which was a large, national study sponsored by the U.S. Department of Housing and Urban Development and conducted in 1989.

At one level, the importance of racial and ethnic discrimination is obvious. It violates a fundamental civil right, the right to choose where to live, and is an explicit violation of the 1968 Fair Housing Act. In fact, however, the importance of discrimination in housing is even more profound because of the links between housing market outcomes and many other aspects of social and economic life. Housing market discrimination limits the access of African-Americans and Hispanic-Americans to employment, to education, and to other public services, and it undercuts their ability to accumulate wealth.[1] Thus, discrimination in housing is an important part of the discriminatory system that restricts the opportunities of these groups.[2] Concerned citizens and public officials need to be informed about the nature and extent of this discrimination.

This chapter starts with an overview of the HDS, with a focus on its methodology and the types of discrimination it measures. The most fundamental type of discrimination in housing is a denial of access to information about available housing units. Thus, the next two sections present different aspects of the HDS evidence on this type of discrimination. The subsequent section summarizes some of the key HDS findings on other types of discrimination, and the final section discusses the extent to which housing discrimination constrains the housing opportunities of black and Hispanic households.

THE HOUSING DISCRIMINATION STUDY

A fair housing audit is a refined, and by now widely used, survey technique designed to observe and measure discrimination against minority homeseekers.[3] This section provides a brief overview of the HDS audit methodology and of the types of housing agent behavior that are examined in HDS. For a more detailed discussion of these topics, see Yinger (1991b).

HDS Audit Methodology

Each audit is conducted by a team of two people, one a member of the white majority and the other a member of a minority group. These two people have the same sex and approximately the same age; have been given the same training about how to behave during an audit; and have been assigned similar incomes, occupations, and family characteristics for the purposes of the audit. During the audit they successively visit a landlord or real estate agent to inquire about available housing, and they separately record what they were told on a detailed survey form. For a given sample of audits, discrimination is defined to be systematically less favorable treatment of minority auditors.

The HDS audits were conducted in a sample of metropolitan areas around the country, selected so that valid national estimates of discrimination could be obtained. To be specific, black/white audits were conducted in 20 areas and Hispanic/Anglo audits were conducted in 13 areas (with some overlap between the two sets of areas). Within each site, a random sample of advertised housing units was drawn from the major metropolitan newspaper every weekend. Each advertised unit provided the starting point for one audit; that is, the two teammates began each audit by (separately) inquiring about the availability of one of the sampled units.

Audit teammates were assigned incomes and family characteristics appropriate for the advertised unit assigned to their audit. To help avoid detection, audit teammates' assigned incomes were not identical, and to make certain that income differences did not result in less favorable treatment of minority auditors, the minority teammate was always assigned a slightly higher income.

All these steps are designed to ensure that, to the greatest extent possible, audit teammates are equally qualified for the advertised housing unit. In other words, an audit is set up so that teammates do not differ on any characteristic—except for their minority status— that is known to be relevant to their treatment in the housing market. Thus, any systematic unfavorable treatment of minority auditors can be interpreted as discrimination.

The HDS audits focus on the marketing stages of a transaction for housing that is advertised in a major newspaper. Thus, they cannot observe discrimination that takes place in later stages of a housing market transaction, such as the granting of mortgages and the acceptance of bids in the sales market or credit checks and selection of tenants in the rental market. To the extent that discrimination takes place during these later stages, the audit results understate total discrimination. Moreover, the HDS audits cannot determine how much discrimination takes place in parts of the housing market not served by agents who advertise in major newspapers. Discrimination in these parts of the housing market could be higher or lower than that reported here.

In summary, the HDS sampling procedures imply a precise interpretation for the results presented in this paper. These results measure the discrimination that black and Hispanic homeseekers can expect to encounter if they inquire about housing advertised in a major metropolitan newspaper—and are qualified for that housing. The results do not necessarily measure the discrimination that black and Hispanic homeseekers who cannot afford advertised housing units can expect to encounter, nor do they necessarily measure discrimination against black and Hispanic homeseekers who find housing by means other than newspaper advertisements.

Types of Agent Behavior

The marketing of available housing units, on which the HDS audits focus, can be broken down into three stages. These stages are illustrated in figure 2.1. During the first stage, auditors obtain information from a housing agent about which housing units are available. If information about available units is withheld completely from a minority auditor, she is denied access to the housing market, at least by this agent. If the minority auditor is recommended or shown fewer units

Figure 2.1 THE STAGES OF A HOUSING MARKET TRANSACTION

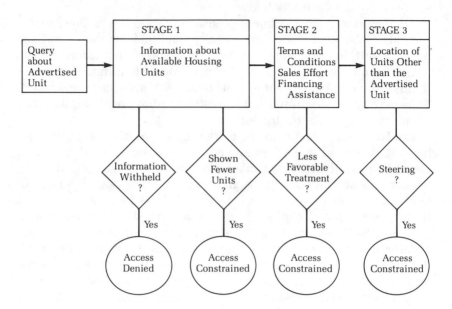

than her audit teammate, then her access to housing is constrained, but not completely closed.

The second stage of a housing market transaction concerns the agent's efforts to complete the housing market transaction. Agent actions in this stage include information provided about the terms and conditions of sale or rental, effort exerted to assist the customer, and, in the sales market, information provided about possible mortgages. Agents constrain minority customers' access to housing by treating them less favorably during this stage. For example, agents may offer information about adjustable-rate mortgages only to Anglo customers or they may quote minority customers a higher rent for the advertised apartment.

The third stage involves the geographic location of advertised housing units. A minority customer's access to housing is also constrained if she is only shown housing in largely black neighborhoods. This type of agent behavior, called steering, is discussed in Turner et al. (1991) and chapter 3, this volume, and is not the focus of this chapter.

This chapter focuses on discrimination in stage 1, but also presents some information on discrimination in the other stages.

THE INCIDENCE OF DISCRIMINATION IN
HOUSING AVAILABILITY

One key indicator of the barriers minorities face in the housing market is the likelihood that a minority homeseeker will encounter a discriminatory act. This indicator is called the **incidence** of discrimination. In this section we discuss alternative ways to measure the incidence of discrimination and present incidence results from the HDS. This discussion begins with two methodological issues—the distinction between net and gross approaches to the study of discrimination, and the problem of accounting for the audit study design. The section concludes with estimates of the net and gross incidence of discrimination using the HDS data. The following section explores an alternative indicator, the **severity** of discrimination.

Net and Gross Approaches to the Incidence of Discrimination

Two approaches to the study of discrimination have appeared in the literature. The first approach, which grew out of the logic of fair housing enforcement, is to say that the incidence of discrimination is the probability that a minority homeseeker will encounter unequal treatment. Although not a legal definition of discrimination, unequal treatment violates the spirit of the Fair Housing Act.[4] This Act, which is Title VIII of the Civil Rights Act of 1968, makes it illegal for a landlord or real estate broker to treat any customer less favorably solely on the basis of her race or ethnicity. Because this approach focuses on cases in which the minority auditor encounters less favorable treatment, without considering cases in which the majority auditor encounters less favorable treatment, it is called the **gross approach**.

The second approach, which is related to studies of wage and housing price discrimination by economists, is to say that the incidence of discrimination is a systematic **difference** in the probability that majority and minority homeseekers will encounter unfavorable treatment. Because this approach focuses on the net or differential impact of agent behavior on minorities, it is called the **net approach**.

At the level of an individual audit, both approaches focus on unfavorable treatment; that is, they both determine whether a minority auditor is treated less favorably than her majority teammate. In a sample of audits, however, the gross approach measures the extent to which minority auditors encounter unfavorable treatment, whereas the net approach determines whether unfavorable treatment of minority auditors is more likely than unfavorable treatment of majority auditors. In other words, the net approach begins with the gross approach and nets out cases in which minority auditors are favored, and therefore inherently yields lower estimates of discrimination than does the gross approach.

Because each approach is valuable for answering certain questions, this chapter presents them both. In effect, the net approach is designed to measure the extent to which agents' actions place minority homeseekers at a disadvantage relative to Anglo homeseekers, and the gross approach is designed to measure the extent to which minorities can expect to encounter actions that violate the notion of equal treatment.

Accounting for the Audit Study Design

Simple gross and net incidence measures of unfavorable treatment are easy to describe and estimate. The simple gross incidence of unfavorable treatment is the share of audits in which the minority auditor was treated less favorably than her majority teammate (for a single type of agent behavior or a set of them).[5] The simple net incidence of unfavorable treatment is the simple gross incidence minus the share of audits in which the majority auditor was treated less favorably than her majority teammate. This net measure was emphasized by Wienk et al. (1979).

Although simple net and gross incidence measures are easy to calculate, they cannot be interpreted as accurate measures of discrimination because they do not account for one key aspect of an audit study design: the fact that audit teammates visit housing agencies at different times and do not encounter exactly the same circumstances.[6]

To understand the importance of this methodological issue, let us begin with a careful definition of discrimination. Discrimination (using either the net or gross approach) exists if blacks or Hispanics are systematically treated less favorably than equally qualified Anglos **under a given set of circumstances**. To help isolate discrimination, audits are, of course, designed to minimize differences in both auditor qualifications and the circumstances they encounter. Even in a well designed audit, however, audit teammates obviously cannot visit an agency at exactly the same time, so the circumstances they encounter are, to some degree, different. Two teammates may encounter different agents with different marketing styles, for example, and housing units may appear or disappear from the market in the interval between teammates' arrivals. Thus, even if an audit study success-fully matches teammates with equal qualifications, directly compar-ing the teammates' treatment does not necessarily yield a measure of discrimination.

Suppose, for example, that the Anglo auditor is the first one to visit a real estate broker's office. Then in the time after the Anglo auditor departs but before the minority auditor arrives, the broker may learn about another house for sale. In this case the minority auditor may be shown one more house than her Anglo teammate—not because the agent is attempting to favor the minority auditor but because of a random event. Another example applies to the rental market. If the minority auditor goes first and the advertised apartment is actually rented to a customer between the two teammates' visits, then the minority auditor may be told that the advertised unit is available whereas the Anglo auditor is told that it is not. As before, this differ-ence in treatment is due solely to random differences in the circum-stances encountered by teammates.

Of course, random differences in circumstances can favor either the minority auditor or the Anglo auditor. Moreover, any treatment of random factors must recognize the role of systematic factors, which also could favor either auditor. What is needed, therefore, is a com-prehensive framework for considering the impact of both systematic and random factors on a housing agent's behavior.

Such a framework was developed for HDS and is presented in figure 2.2. The rows of this chart indicate an agent's behavior based on systematic factors alone; that is, they show the outcome that would occur if random factors were not at work. Audits in which systematic factors lead to discrimination against minority homeseekers, for ex-ample, are in the first row. The effects of random factors associated with differences in teammates' circumstances are shown in the three columns.[7] These factors can work in favor of the majority auditor, the minority auditor, or neither auditor. The entries in the chart indicate what happens when these random factors (the columns) are added to systematic factors (the rows).

Given the audit methodology, the minority may not encounter un-favorable treatment even in the first row, that is, even in audits with systematic factors that lead to discrimination. To be specific, if sys-tematic factors induce an agent to discriminate and random events favor the majority auditor, then the observed outcome is that the ma-jority auditor is favored (cell 2). In contrast, if systematic factors call for discrimination and random events favor the minority auditor, then the observed outcome could be that the majority auditor is favored,

Figure 2.2 TYPOLOGY OF DISCRIMINATION FOR SYSTEMATIC REASONS AND THE EFFECTS OF RANDOM FACTORS

True Behavior	Effect of Random Factors		
	No Effect	Favor Majority	Favor Minority
Favor majority	1 Majority favored	2 Majority favored	3 Majority favored or No difference or Minority favored
No difference	4 No difference	5 Majority favored	6 Minority favored
Favor minority	7 Minority favored	8 Minority favored or No difference or Majority favored	9 Minority favored

Note: The contents of each cell reflect possible observed outcomes for the given combination of true behavior and the effect of random factors.

the minority auditor is favored, or neither auditor is favored, depending on the strength of random factors (cell 3).

The share of audits in which minorities encounter unfavorable treatment, or the "simple gross measure" for short, is sometimes interpreted as a measure of the gross incidence of discrimination; i.e., of systematic attempts to treat minorities less favorably. As shown in figure 2.2, however, this interpretation is not appropriate. The simple gross measure counts the number of majority-favored audits in cells 1, 2, 3, 5, and 8. As explained above, the number of audits involving discrimination is the sum of all audits in cells 1, 2, and 3. Thus, the simple gross measure is the true gross incidence of discrimination plus the majority-favored audits in cells 5 and 8 and minus the audits in cell 3 for which one observes a neutral or minority-favored outcome. It follows that the simple gross measure could either over- or understate discrimination. It overstates discrimination if the majority-favored audits in cells 5 and 8 outnumber the neutral and minority-favored audits in cell 3, and it understates discrimination if the reverse is true. Thus, the greater the true gross incidence of discrimination (and hence, the number of audits that fall into cells 1, 2, and 3), the more likely that the simple gross measure understates the true gross incidence of discrimination.

Similarly, the share of majority-favored audits minus the share of minority-favored audits, or the "simple net measure," is sometimes interpreted as a measure of the net incidence of discrimination.[8] In fact, however, the simple net measure may understate the true net incidence of discrimination. In figure 2.2, the simple net measure counts the majority-favored audits in cells 1, 2, 3, 5, and 8 and subtracts the minority-favored audits in cells 3, 6, 7, 8, and 9. Thus, the simple net measure not only misses the fact that neutral and minority-favored audits in cell 3 involve discrimination, it also subtracts those minority-favored audits. Suppose that all audits fall into the first row, so that the net incidence of discrimination is 100 percent; that one-third of the audits fall into each cell in the row; and that the audits in cell 3 are evenly divided between minority-favored, majority-favored, and neutral. Then the simple net measure is $(33 + 33 + 11 - 11)$ = 66 percent, which is far below the true net incidence of discrimination in this example—namely, 100 percent.

Another problem with the simple net measure arises because housing agent actions in row 3 of figure 2.1, which "favor" the minority auditor, are sometimes difficult to interpret. For example, an agent who shows a house in a largely black neighborhood to a black auditor but not to her white teammate will appear to be, according to the number of houses made available, favoring the black auditor. In fact, however, this behavior is actually an example of steering. This form of agent behavior, which is examined by Turner et al. (1991), limits the options of both minority and Anglo households, and it makes no sense to subtract audits involving steering in determining the relative disadvantage faced by minority auditors.[9]

The problem of interpreting audits in which blacks or Hispanics are "favored" in housing availability is not just hypothetical. For example, 24.0 percent of the sales audits in which blacks are recommended or shown more houses than their Anglo teammates and 25.9 percent of those in which Hispanics are so "favored" involve the steering of the minority auditor to neighborhoods that have a larger minority population or lower-valued houses than those offered to Anglos.[10]

In short, whenever discrimination actually exists, the simple net measure is likely to understate the true net incidence of discrimination. The greater the share of audits in the first row of figure 2.2, the greater this understatement is likely to be. In fact, the only case in which the simple net measure is likely to be an accurate measure of discrimination is when almost all audits fall into the second row. Because random factors associated with different circumstances are likely to have a roughly symmetrical impact on the treatment of minority and majority auditors, this case involves an approximately equal number of audits in cells 5 and 6. Hence, the simple net measure will be close to zero, as is the true net incidence of discrimination. Another way to put this is that the simple net measure can be regarded as a lower bound on the net incidence of discrimination.

Exact solutions to these methodological problems are not yet available, but relatively simple partial solutions provide some perspective on the potential magnitude of the problems. In the case of the net measure, the impact of differences in circumstances can be minimized by focusing on audits in which the circumstances teammates encounter are likely to be relatively similar. For the sales audits, a key indicator of similar circumstances is whether the teammates were served by the same real estate broker. In inquiring about an advertisement, both teammates go to the same real estate firm but may encounter different brokers. Although all the brokers in a firm have access to the same listings, different brokers have different styles and skills and some may decide to show more houses than others. Focusing on audits in which teammates saw the same broker eliminates the impact of random differences in the characteristics of the brokers that teammates encounter.

In addition, the potential impact of steering on the net measure can be seen by eliminating audits in which more units are made available to the minority than to the majority auditor but in which the minority auditor was shown houses in neighborhoods that had a significantly higher minority percentage or significantly lower valued houses.

Thus, to provide a rough indication of the potential problems with the simple net measure in the sales audits, the tables in the next section present not only the simple net measure but also an adjusted net measure that excludes audits in which teammates saw different agents and audits in which steering might explain why minority auditors appear to be favored in number of units available.

On average, fewer housing units are available in the rental audits than in the sales audits, and individual rental agents do not have as much leeway in deciding what to show a customer. Thus, the key difference in circumstances in the rental audits is whether the advertised apartment was rented in the time interval between the teammates' visits. This difference cannot be measured directly, but a rough indication of its potential impact on the net measure can be obtained by not netting out cases in which disappearance of the advertised unit is a possible explanation for favorable treatment of the minority. To be specific, the adjusted net measure for the rental audits does not net out audits in which the minority auditor went first and the advertised unit was shown to the minority auditor but not the majority auditor.

As explained above, the problem of unequal circumstances also affects the simple gross measure. To obtain a rough indication of the magnitude of the problem in this case, the HDS researchers proceeded in three steps (see Yinger 1991c). First, they used a well-known statistical procedure, called multinomial logit analysis, to estimate the impact of systematic factors on housing agent's choices, which are to favor the majority auditor, favor the minority auditor, or favor neither auditor. The probability of each choice is a function of agent characteristics, auditor characteristics, and observable audit circumstances, such as site and timing variables.[11] The logit analysis also controlled for observable differences in teammate characteristics, such as age differences, differences in the number of children assigned for the purposes of the audit, and differences in the timing of their visits to the housing agent.

The second step was to predict each housing agent's choice on the basis of systematic factors (but not observed teammate differences) and the estimated logit coefficients. Specifically, each agent's predicted choice is the choice with the highest predicted probability given that agent's characteristics, as well as the characteristics of the auditors and the audit. This predicted choice is based on systematic factors alone and therefore is not affected by random factors, such as random differences in the circumstances teammates encounter. The third step was to calculate the share of audits in which the agent was predicted to favor the majority auditor. This share is an alternative measure of gross incidence that is not affected by random factors.

Although this alternative measure provides some perspective on the potential role of random factors, it is not an exact solution to the problem of unequal circumstances for teammates. In the first place, this approach cannot distinguish between the impact of randomness associated with differences in teammates' circumstances, which needs to be removed from the gross measure, and the impact of randomness associated with auditor and agent characteristics that we cannot observe, which should not be removed.[12] Second, the ability of a logit model to make accurate predictions depends on the actual probability that a choice is made and on the explanatory power of observed systematic factors; the higher the actual probability and the greater the explanatory power, the greater the accuracy.[13] In the HDS logit regressions, accurate predictions typically cannot be obtained for choices that occur less than 15 or 20 percent of the time. In effect, then, the logit approach tends to break down for types of agent behavior that have a simple gross incidence below about 20 percent. Thus, this approach should be regarded only as a rough correction for the problem of random differences in the circumstances encountered by teammates.

Estimates of the Incidence of Discrimination

The previous section identifies four measures of the incidence of discrimination: the simple net measure, the adjusted net measure, the simple gross measure, and the multivariate gross measure. The four columns of table 2.1 (for black/white audits) and table 2.2 (for Hispanic/Anglo audits) present these four measures for several key indicators of housing availability. In each table, panel A describes results for the sales audits and panel B describes results for the rental audits.

Measures of Housing Availability. The first row in each panel of tables 2.1 and 2.2 concerns the most dramatic form of discrimination—the complete withholding of information about available housing. The next two rows concern information about the availability of the advertised unit. The row labeled "Advertised Unit Available," for example, indicates the share of audits in which the Anglo auditor, but not her minority teammate, was told that the advertised unit was available, and the fourth row indicates when only the Anglo teammate was told that units similar to the advertised unit were available. The fifth through seventh rows present information about discrimination in the number of units made available to minorities. The fifth row focuses on units recommended but not shown, the sixth on units actually shown to an auditor, and the seventh on the total number of units either recommended or shown. Hence, the seventh row provides a comprehensive measure of discrimination in access to housing.

Table 2.1 THE INCIDENCE OF DISCRIMINATION IN HOUSING AVAILABILITY, BLACK/WHITE AUDITS

	Simple Net Measure[a]	Adjusted Net Measure[b]	Simple Gross Measure[c]	Multivariate Gross Measure[d]
Panel A: Sales Audits				
Excluded	6.34*	8.32	7.59	5.07
Advertised unit available	5.45*	6.61	11.09	0.37
Advertised unit inspected	5.63*	8.35	13.35	0.34
Similar units available	9.05*	10.00	19.74	5.53
Number of units recommended	11.09*	11.69	31.34	32.15
Number of units inspected	14.00*	18.99	30.38	27.81
Number of units available	19.44*	25.57	44.07	41.53
Housing availability index	18.96*	23.65	38.35	46.24
Panel B: Rental Audits				
Excluded	10.66*	13.81	15.12	0.50
Advertised unit available	5.48	12.73	17.23	2.84
Advertised unit inspected	12.50*	16.35	23.03	13.12
Similar units available	2.47*	2.90	13.74	18.65
Number of units recommended	11.09*	11.45	22.28	23.22
Number of units inspected	17.16*	20.22	31.72	25.32
Number of units available	23.35*	25.89	41.35	44.55
Housing availability index	21.27*	25.27	40.05	51.19

[a]Entries marked with an asterisk are statistically significant at the 5 percent level or above using the Chamberlain (1980) fixed-effects logit.
[b]The adjusted net measure for the sales audits is restricted to audits in which team-mates encountered the same agent and in which there is no evidence that the minority teammate was "favored" because of steering. For the rental audits it is restricted to audits in which there is no evidence that the minority teammate was "favored" because the advertised unit disappeared after her visit.
[c]All entries in this column are statistically significant at the 5 percent level or above using the weighted t-test described in Yinger (1991b).
[d]The multivariate gross measure is the weighted share of audits in which the agent is predicted to choose to discriminate against the minority based on agent, auditor, and audit characteristics, controlling for observed differences between teammates. See Yinger (1991c).

In addition to measuring discrimination in individual types of agent behavior, it is useful to know whether discriminatory actions tend to cluster, i.e., to occur for many types of behavior in the same audit, or be dispersed, i.e., to occur for one type of behavior in one audit and another type of behavior in another audit. To address this issue, Wienk et al. (1979) devised two types of indexes that summarize unfavorable treatment in a category of agent behavior.

The first type considers an auditor to have encountered unfavorable treatment in the category if she was treated unfavorably on at least

Table 2.2 THE INCIDENCE OF DISCRIMINATION IN HOUSING AVAILABILITY, HISPANIC/ANGLO AUDITS

	Simple Net Measure[a]	Adjusted Net Measure[b]	Simple Gross Measure[c]	Multivariate Gross Measure[d]
Panel A: Sales Audits				
Excluded	4.51*	4.60	7.50	1.54
Advertised unit available	4.20*	3.49	9.53	0.55
Advertised unit inspected	5.35*	5.83	13.23	1.08
Similar units available	6.26*	8.90	17.08	0.21
Number of units recommended	13.12*	14.13	34.40	34.00
Number of units inspected	9.68*	16.25	29.62	18.73
Number of units available	16.50*	24.05	43.59	49.93
Housing availability index	15.55*	23.88	37.12	38.42
Panel B: Rental Audits				
Excluded	6.52*	7.00	12.09	0.00
Advertised unit available	8.37*	11.09	15.51	1.17
Advertised unit inspected	5.09*	6.75	17.64	5.04
Similar units available	1.61	1.22	15.16	18.80
Number of units recommended	5.36	5.00	18.55	20.98
Number of units inspected	7.94	8.92	26.87	18.51
Number of units available	9.76	10.54	34.60	35.27
Housing availability index	11.00	12.84	34.91	31.05

[a]Entries marked with an asterisk are statistically significant at the 5 percent level or above using the Chamberlain (1980) fixed-effects logit.

[b]The adjusted net measure for the sales audits is restricted to audits in which teammates encountered the same agent and in which there is no evidence that the minority teammate was "favored" because of steering. For the rental audits it is restricted to audits in which there is no evidence that the minority teammate was "favored" because the advertised unit disappeared after her visit.

[c]All entries in this column are statistically significant at the 5 percent level or above using the weighted *t*-test described in Yinger (1991b).

[d]The multivariate gross measure is the weighted share of audits in which the agent is predicted to choose to discriminate against the minority based on agent, auditor, and audit characteristics, controlling for observed differences between teammates. See Yinger (1991c).

one of the variables and was not treated favorably on any others. According to this approach, unfavorable treatment in a category exists if and only if there is some unfavorable treatment in that category without any mixed signals about the nature of the treatment.

The second type of index considers an auditor to have encountered unfavorable treatment in the category if she encountered unfavorable treatment on more variables than did her teammate. This approach finds more cases of unfavorable treatment of minorities because it includes cases in which the minority auditor encountered unfavorable treatment in three variables measuring agent behavior, say, but also encountered favorable treatment in one other variable.

In the case of housing availability, these two types of indexes yield similar results, and the results reported in this section are based on the first, more conservative, type of index. To be specific, the housing availability indexes in tables 2.1 and 2.2 are based on four of the variables described above: the availability of the advertised unit, the availability of units similar to the advertised unit, the number of units recommended but not shown, and the number of units shown. The index results are presented in the final row of each panel in these two tables.

The Net Incidence of Discrimination. The first two columns in tables 2.1 and 2.2 present estimates of the net incidence of discrimination.[14] The first column contains the simple net measure and the second column contains the adjusted net measure described earlier. In the sales audits, the simple net measures all fall between 5 and 10 percent for the first four variables and between 10 and 20 percent for the last four variables. In the case of the two most comprehensive variables, namely those in the last two rows, the simple net incidence of discrimination is about 19 percent for the black/white audits and about 16 percent for the Hispanic/Anglo audits. All of these results are statistically significant.[15]

Turning to the rental results, we find that the simple net incidence of discrimination is close to zero for one variable, namely whether units similar to the advertised unit are available, and is lower for the Hispanic/Anglo audits than for the black/white audits for all variables except one, namely whether the advertised unit is available. For the "excluded," "advertised unit inspected," and "number of units recommended" variables, the simple net incidence of discrimination is about 10 percent for the black/white audits and about 5 percent for the Hispanic/Anglo audits. The simple net incidence is considerably higher for the two most comprehensive variables; as shown in the last two rows of panel B, it is over 20 percent for the black/white audits and about 10 percent for the Hispanic/Anglo audits. The results for the number of units inspected fall somewhere in between, at 17 percent and 8 percent for the black/white and Hispanic/Anglo audits, respectively. All of the results for the black/white audits, but only the first three results for the Hispanic/Anglo audits, are statistically significant.[16]

Results for the adjusted measure, which are in the second column of tables 2.1 and 2.2, suggest that the simple net measure is 1 or 2 percentage points below the true net incidence of discrimination for most agent actions but may be as much as 8 percentage points too low.[17] In the case of the "excluded" variable, for example, the adjusted net measure exceeds the simple one by 2 to 3 points in the black/white audits and by 1 point in the Hispanic/Anglo audits; for "advertised unit available," the adjusted measure exceeds the simple measure by over 6 points in all classes of audit except Hispanic/Anglo rental. In only three cases, all of which involve relatively low levels of net discrimination by the simple measure and all of which are in the Hispanic/Anglo audits, is the adjusted net measure below the simple one.

In summary, these results suggest that for the most dramatic form of discriminatory behavior, outright exclusion, the net incidence of discrimination ranges from about 5 percent in the Hispanic/Anglo sales audits to 11 percent (simple measure) or 14 percent (adjusted measure) in the black/white rental audits. Moreover, for the most comprehensive measures of housing agent behavior, namely the total number of units made available and the housing availability index, the net incidence of discrimination is disturbingly high. This incidence is at least 15 to 21 percent (simple measure) and may be as high as 25 percent (adjusted measure) for all classes of audit except Hispanic/Anglo rental, for which the estimates fall in the 11 percent (simple) to 14 percent (adjusted) range.

The Gross Incidence of Discrimination. The third column of tables 2.1 and 2.2 reveals that the simple gross incidence measure is only slightly higher than the simple net measure for "excluded," 5 to 8 percentage points above the simple net measure for variables involving advertised unit, and 10 to 27 points higher for the other five variables. In the case of the number of units inspected, for example, the simple gross measure is about 30 percent for all four classes of audit. For the two most comprehensive measures in the last two rows of each panel, the simple gross measures all fall between 35 and 44 percent. The results for the housing availability index have the striking implication that between one-third and two-fifths of the time, both black and Hispanic customers encounter unfavorable treatment, without any mixed signals, on at least one type of agent behavior concerning housing availability. All of these results are statistically significant.[18]

A few other patterns emerge from these gross incidence results. For "exclusion" and the two variables concerning the advertised unit, the simple gross incidence of discrimination is several percentage points higher in the rental market than in the sales market, but the reverse is true for "similar units available." Moreover, within either the sales or rental market, discrimination against blacks and Hispanics is similar for every variable, although the gross incidence of discrimination tends to be a few percentage points lower against Hispanics, particularly in the rental market.[19]

The last column of tables 2.1 and 2.2 presents the multivariate gross measure.[20] The results in this column suggest that removing random factors (and correcting for observed teammate differences) sometimes increases and sometimes decreases the gross incidence of discrimination. Except for variables with a simple gross measure below about 20 percent, for which the multivariate method usually breaks down, the multivariate gross measure generally is fairly close to the simple gross measure, although it sometimes exceeds it by as much as 11 percentage points or falls short of it by as much as 9 percentage points. These results suggest that correcting for random factors associated with differences in teammates' circumstances is unlikely to alter the basic story told by the simple gross measure but might alter the details of this story. Further research on this topic is needed to provide a more exact solution to this problem.

THE SEVERITY OF DISCRIMINATION IN HOUSING AVAILABILITY

An exclusive focus on incidence misses a key aspect of discrimination because it does not consider the severity of discrimination when it does occur. Incidence measures cannot distinguish, for example, between a situation in which minorities frequently encounter minor acts of discrimination and one in which they frequently encounter severe discrimination. Thus, an analysis of the severity of discrimination in housing, which was introduced by Yinger (1986), complements an analysis of the incidence of discrimination.

Measuring the Severity of Discrimination

The severity of discrimination, which is the magnitude of the difference in treatment between Anglo and minority auditors, cannot be measured for all types of agent behavior. In the case of categorical variables, such as whether or not the advertised unit is available, unfavorable treatment either does or does not exist. But when treatment can vary, as with the number of units inspected, the difference in treatment between minority and majority auditors can differ from one audit to the next. In this section we focus on the severity of discrimination in the number of inspections, recommendations, and total units available.

In addition, a severity measure can be defined for an index of housing agent behavior. In this case severity depends on the number of acts of unfavorable treatment in the types of agent behavior included in the index; the greater the number of acts, the greater the severity of discrimination.[21]

As explained in Yinger (1991b), random factors associated with differences in teammates' circumstances do not create the same problems for interpreting measures of the severity of discrimination that they create for interpreting the incidence of differential treatment. These random factors are, of course, still present, but they have a roughly symmetrical impact on continuous measures of treatment for majority and minority auditors. Random factors sometimes increase the observed difference between the treatment of majority and minority auditors, and they sometimes decrease this difference, but over many audits these effects offset each other. In other words, when one calculates the average difference in the treatment of teammates, the effects of random factors cancel out.

Focusing on the severity of discrimination solves the problem that random factors influence observed audit outcomes, but it does not solve another problem mentioned earlier, namely the difficulty of interpreting audits in which minority auditors are "favored" on housing availability. A procedure that subtracts the average treatment of minority auditors from the average treatment of majority auditors implicitly assumes that minority auditors are indeed favored whenever they are shown more houses, or in other words, that showing a minority customer more houses does not involve steering or some other type of discriminatory behavior. As we have already seen, this assumption is suspect because steering does occur in many of these so-called "minority-favored" audits.

This section presents both gross and net measures of the severity of discrimination, and it shows the potential impact of steering on the net measure. The gross measure indicates the severity of discrimination when the housing agent treats the minority auditor less favorably, and the net measure indicates the severity of discrimination against minority auditors relative to the treatment of Anglo auditors. The relationship between these net and gross measures flows out of a general framework, presented in the next subsection, for analyzing both the incidence and severity of discrimination. After examining estimates based on these two measures, we will also examine another measure that accounts for the fact that housing agents cannot discriminate unless they have the opportunity to do so.

The Relationship between the Incidence and Severity of Discrimination

Analyses of the incidence and severity of discrimination can be integrated by decomposing the standard severity measure. To be specific, the gross severity of discrimination in Anglo-favored audits equals the simple gross incidence of discrimination, which was presented in the previous section, multiplied by the severity of unfavorable treatment given that the audit is Anglo-favored. This relationship is shown in the first three columns of tables 2.3 and 2.4. The first column is the simple gross incidence measure, the second column is the severity of unfavorable treatment for audits classified as Anglo-favored, and the third column is the product of the first two. Similarly, the gross severity of unfavorable treatment in minority-favored audits equals the gross probability that an audit will be minority-favored multiplied by the severity of unfavorable treatment in those audits. This relationship is shown in the second three columns of these tables.

The net severity of discrimination (column 9) is the difference between the gross severity of unfavorable treatment in Anglo-favored audits (column 3) and the gross severity of unfavorable treatment in minority-favored audits (column 6). This net measure indicates the severity of the unfavorable treatment of minority auditors relative to that of Anglo auditors, whereas the gross measure in column 3 indicates the severity of unfavorable treatment minorities can expect without considering minority-favored audits.

The simple net incidence of discrimination also appears in these tables, in column 7. It is the difference between columns 1 and 4. In addition, column 8 is the net difference in the severity of unfavorable treatment between the Anglo-favored and minority-favored audits, which is column 2 minus column 5.

Because of the symmetrical impact of random factors on the treatment of minority and majority auditors, this net measure of the severity of discrimination can be estimated without advanced statistical procedures.[22] It should be remembered, however, that this net measure may understate the true net severity of discrimination if some of the apparently minority-favored audits actually are cases of steering.

Table 2.3 THE INCIDENCE AND SEVERITY OF DISCRIMINATION IN HOUSING AVAILABILITY, BLACK/WHITE AUDITS

Variable	White-Favored Audit (WF)			Black-Favored Audit (BF)			Differences		
	Gross incidence (1)	Severity given WF (2)	Gross severity (3)	Gross incidence (4)	Severity given BF (5)	Gross severity (6)	Net incidence (7)	Net severity given WF or BF (8)	Net severity[a] (9)
Panel A: Sales Audits									
Units recommended	31.34	2.592	0.812	20.25	2.449	0.496	11.09	0.143	0.316*
Units inspected	30.38	1.786	0.543	16.38	1.466	0.240	14.00	0.320	0.294*
Units available	44.06	2.684	1.183	24.62	2.291	0.564	19.44	0.393	0.619*
Housing availability index	38.35	1.718	0.659	19.39	1.423	0.276	18.96	0.295	0.383*
Panel B: Rental Audits									
Units recommended	22.28	1.504	0.335	11.19	1.470	0.165	11.09	0.034	0.170*
Units inspected	31.72	1.301	0.413	14.56	1.233	0.180	17.16	0.068	0.233*
Units available	41.35	1.603	0.663	18.00	1.440	0.259	23.35	0.163	0.404*
Housing availability index	39.01	1.620	0.632	19.65	1.434	0.282	19.36	0.186	0.350*

[a]Entries marked with an asterisk are statistically significant at the 5 percent level or above using a paired, weighted difference-of-means test, as described in Yinger (1991b).

Table 2.4 THE INCIDENCE AND SEVERITY OF DISCRIMINATION IN HOUSING AVAILABILITY, HISPANIC/ANGLO AUDITS

Variable	Anglo-Favored Audit (AF)			Hispanic-Favored Audit (HF)			Differences		
	Gross incidence AF (1)	Severity given AF (2)	Gross severity (3)	Gross incidence HF (4)	Severity given HF (5)	Gross severity (6)	Net incidence (7)	Net severity given AF or HF (8)	Net severity[a] (9)
Panel A: Sales Audits									
Units recommended	34.40	2.980	1.025	21.29	2.309	0.492	13.11	0.671	0.534*
Units inspected	29.62	1.545	0.458	19.94	1.459	0.291	9.68	0.086	0.167*
Units available	43.59	2.921	1.273	27.10	2.114	0.573	16.49	0.807	0.701*
Housing availability index	37.12	1.666	0.619	21.57	1.344	0.290	15.55	0.322	0.329*
Panel B: Rental Audits									
Units recommended	18.55	1.520	0.282	13.19	1.548	0.204	5.36	-0.028	0.078
Units inspected	26.87	1.316	0.354	18.94	1.347	0.255	7.93	-0.031	0.099*
Units available	34.60	1.592	0.551	24.84	1.507	0.374	9.76	0.085	0.177*
Housing availability index	35.50	1.582	0.562	24.26	1.406	0.341	11.24	0.176	0.221*

[a]Entries marked with an asterisk are statistically significant at the 5 percent level or above using a paired, weighted difference-of-means test, as described in Yinger (1991b).

Estimates of the Severity of Discrimination

Tables 2.3 and 2.4 lead to several general results. First, not only is the gross probability that minority auditors encounter unfavorable treatment (column 1) larger than the gross probability that Anglo auditors encounter unfavorable treatment (column 4), it is also true that the severity of the unfavorable treatment in Anglo-favored audits (column 2) is greater than the severity of the unfavorable treatment in minority-favored audits (column 5).[23] In other words, minority customers are more likely to encounter unfavorable treatment than are Anglo customers, and the unfavorable treatment minorities encounter is more severe. This important result cannot be observed with an incidence measure alone.

Second, some of the gross severity results in column 3 are very high. In the sales audits, the gross severity of discrimination for the total number of houses or condominiums available, for example, is 1.18 houses for blacks and 1.27 houses for Hispanics. The comparable figures for black and Hispanic renters are 0.66 and 0.55 apartments. This gross measure therefore implies that minority homeseekers who encounter unfavorable treatment can expect to learn about more than one house (or over one-half an apartment) fewer than their Anglo counterparts, on average.

It is also interesting to note that telling minority customers about fewer housing units has about the same quantitative impact on the number of units they learn about as simply excluding them from all information about available housing. To be specific, the average difference in number of units shown or recommended in audits in which minorities are excluded is between 2.1 and 2.5 for sales audits and about 1.6 for rental audits. Comparing these results to column 2 reveals that, roughly speaking, either outright exclusion or withholding some units denies blacks access to about 2.5 housing units in the sales audits and 1.5 units in the rental audits. Of course, exclusion cuts minorities off from all information about available units, but if minority homeseekers visit several housing agents, a minority homeseeker who encounters exclusion by one agent loses access to approximately the same number of housing units, at least on average, as another minority homeseeker who encounters an agent who withholds some available units.

Third, the net severity of discrimination (column 9) is high in most cases. In the sales audits, this measure implies that minorities systematically learn about over 0.6 fewer houses than do their Anglo teammates each time they visit a real estate broker. The comparable rental figures are 0.40 apartments for the black/white audits and 0.18 apartments for the Hispanic/Anglo rental audits. With one exception, namely the number of units recommended in the Hispanic/Anglo rental audits, these net severity results are all statistically significant.[24]

As explained earlier, the net severity measure in tables 2.4 and 2.5 may understate the true net severity of discrimination because it ignores the possibility that some minorities are shown more houses only because they are being steered to largely minority neighborhoods. If the minority-favored audits in which there is evidence of steering are netted out, the net severity of discrimination in the total number of units available increases by 19.6 percent for blacks (to 0.74 houses) and by 15.4 percent for Hispanics (to 0.81 houses).

No matter which measure is used, however, it is safe to conclude that considerable discrimination still exists in American urban housing markets. Even with the most conservative measure, the unadjusted net, the severity of discrimination for the number of housing units made available is over 0.62 houses in the black/white sales audits, 0.70 houses in the Anglo/Hispanic sales audits, 0.40 apartments in the black/white rental audits, and almost 0.18 apartments in the Hispanic/Anglo rental audits. Expressed as a percentage of the number of units seen by Anglos, these results are, respectively, 21.4, 23.6, 24.5, and 10.9.[25] On average, therefore, blacks in both markets and Hispanics in the sales market learn about fewer than 4 units for every 5 made available to Anglos, and Hispanic renters learn about fewer than 9 for every 10 made available to Anglos. With the adjusted net measure or the gross measure, the results are even more dramatic.

The Opportunity to Discriminate and Marginal Discrimination

The estimates in tables 2.3 and 2.4 present the average severity of discrimination but ignore the fact that housing agents do not always have the opportunity to discriminate against minority customers. An agent with no houses to show, for example, cannot show fewer units to a minority customer than to an Anglo customer. Moreover, the severity of an agent's discriminatory behavior is limited by his opportunity to discriminate. For example, the severity of discrimination by an agent with only one housing unit to show cannot exceed one unit.

In the case of housing availability, the opportunity to discriminate can be measured by the number of housing units available to be recommended or shown. Moreover, the number of housing units available equals the number of units shown to either the minority or majority auditor. This total is not the same as the number shown to the majority auditor plus the number shown to the minority auditor, because some units are shown to both auditors. Using the address information in the HDS data set, the units made available to both auditors can be identified, but only for the sales audits.[26] Thus, we can examine the hypothesis that sales agents take advantage of the opportunity to discriminate by determining whether the severity of discrimination increases with the total number of housing units available for a given audit.

One simple way to examine the relationship between the severity of discrimination and the opportunity to discriminate is with a simple bivariate regression analysis. This is a statistical procedure that determines the extent to which an increase in the opportunity to discriminate, as measured by the number of housing units available to be shown or recommended (or both), is associated with an increase in the severity of discrimination, as measured by the difference in the number of units shown to Anglo and minority auditors.

This approach leads to the concept of **marginal** discrimination, which is the increase in the severity of discrimination that occurs when the opportunity to discriminate goes up by one unit.[27] Consider the severity of discrimination in the number of houses inspected. If the severity of discrimination goes up by 0.15 houses whenever another house becomes available, then marginal discrimination equals 0.15.

The notion of marginal discrimination can be refined to account for the possibility that agents may be either more or less likely to take advantage of the opportunity to discriminate for the advertised housing unit (or units), which presumably is the first one shown, than for other housing units. (It is not uncommon, particularly for condominiums, for an advertisement to refer to several available units in a complex; hence there can be more than one advertised unit.) An agent knows that minority auditors are aware of the existence of advertised units and he may be more reluctant to deny them access to these units than to other, less-publicized units; alternatively, the advertised units may be the agent's hottest properties, which he wants to reserve for Anglo customers.

The net measure for the severity of discrimination presented earlier measures average, as opposed to marginal, discrimination. The average severity of discrimination is the average difference in the number of housing units made available to majority and minority auditors, whereas the marginal severity of discrimination is the difference that arises when one more housing unit becomes available. These two measures provide different information and need not be the same, although, as shown below, they are related.

Estimates of Marginal Discrimination

Estimates of marginal discrimination for the number of houses inspected are presented in table 2.5.[28] These estimates indicate the increase in the severity of discrimination in inspections when an

Table 2.5 MARGINAL DISCRIMINATION IN HOUSING INSPECTIONS

	Black/White Sales Audits	Hispanic/Anglo Sales Audits
Panel A: Marginal discrimination[a]		
Estimated without controls		
Units other than advertised unit	0.1657	0.0987
	(7.127)	(4.480)
Advertised unit	0.0231	−0.1240
	(0.390)	(1.609)
Estimated with controls[b]		
Units other than advertised unit	0.1439	0.0730
	(5.610)	(2.969)
Advertised unit	−0.0125	−0.2229
	(0.020)	(2.769)
Panel B: Expected severity of discrimination at various levels of availability (number of housing units)[c]		
Only advertised unit open for inspection	0.1065	0.1367
Only one unit other than the advertised unit open for inspection	0.2629	0.4325
Advertised unit and one other open for inspection	0.2503	0.2096
Advertised unit and 5 others open for inspection	0.8259	0.5016
Advertised unit and 10 others open for inspection	1.5454	0.8665
Advertised unit and 15 others open for inspection	2.2648	1.2315

[a]Absolute values of *t*-statistics are in parentheses. The one-tailed (two-tailed) 5 percent confidence level is 1.65 (1.96).
[b]The control variables are the agent's age, race or ethnicity, and sex; the auditor's age and sex, and (for Hispanic audits only) whether the minority auditor had dark skin or a heavy accent; the assigned family characteristics (married, number of children), family income, and family income relative to value of advertised unit; the percentage black or Hispanic in neighborhood of both the advertised unit and the agent's office; whether the advertised unit was a condominium or was in a central city; and site dummies, month dummies, and a dummy for afternoon visits. In addition, the regressions control for teammate differences on any of these variables.
[c]The results in this panel are calculated using the regression with controls.

additional house becomes available for inspection. The severity of discrimination may be influenced, of course, by many variables in addition to the opportunity to discriminate. More accurate estimates of marginal discrimination can be obtained, therefore, in a regression that controls for other factors, such as agent characteristics, auditor characteristics, and the site and timing of an audit. Table 2.5 presents estimate of marginal discrimination both with and without control variables.

According to the regressions with controls, marginal discrimination in inspections is 0.144 houses in the black/white audits and 0.073 houses in the Anglo/Hispanic audits. That is, when another house becomes available for inspection, the severity of discrimination increases by 0.144 houses for blacks and by 0.073 houses for Hispanics. Moreover, these results are highly significant statistically. The estimates without control variables are about 2 percentage points higher.

This table also shows that advertised units are treated very differently from other units; when another advertised unit becomes available for inspection, the severity of discrimination does not increase at all for blacks and actually declines for Hispanics. In other words, real estate brokers do not in general take advantage of the opportunity to discriminate in showing housing units they have advertised in the newspaper.

The estimated relationship between the severity of discrimination and the opportunity to discriminate can be used to predict the severity of discrimination when various numbers of housing units are available for inspection. The bottom panel of table 2.5 indicates the severity of discrimination, measured in numbers of houses, for various levels of housing availability. With only the advertised unit open for inspection, for example, the predicted discrimination is 0.11 for the black/white audits and 0.14 for the Hispanic/Anglo audits.[29] Because marginal discrimination equals zero for advertised units, predicted discrimination does not increase when additional advertised units can be inspected.[30] When an advertised unit and 10 others are available to be inspected, however, the predicted severity of discrimination jumps to 1.55 houses for the black/white audits and 0.87 houses for the Hispanic/Anglo audits.

These results for the severity of discrimination also can be expressed relative to the number of units inspected by whites. These calculations require information about the proportion of available units that are shared between audit teammates. If five units are available, for example, three of them are shown to the Anglo auditor and two of them are shown to the minority auditor, then the severity of discrimination is one unit, which is 33 percent of the number shown to the Anglo. In contrast, if all five available units are shown to the Anglo auditor and four are shown to the minority auditor, the severity of discrimination is still one unit, but now this is only 20 percent of the Anglo base.[31]

Under the assumption that there is a single advertised unit and that it is available for inspection, figure 2.3 shows how the severity of discrimination, expressed as a percentage of the number of units inspected by whites, increases as the number of units available increases. Because one advertised unit is available for inspection in most audits and because approximately one unit other than the advertised unit is available for inspection, on average, the average severity of discrimination, now expressed as a percentage of the number of white inspections, is approximated in this figure where one unit other than the advertised unit is available for inspection.[32] In the black/white audits, the predicted severity of discrimination is 17 percent when one unit other than the advertised unit is available, but it increases to about 25 percent of the number of houses seen by whites when 10 or more units are available. In other words, if 10 or more houses are available to be inspected, a black can expect to inspect only three of every four houses inspected by a white. In the Hispanic/

Figure 2.3 THE SEVERITY OF DISCRIMINATION IN HOUSE INSPECTIONS

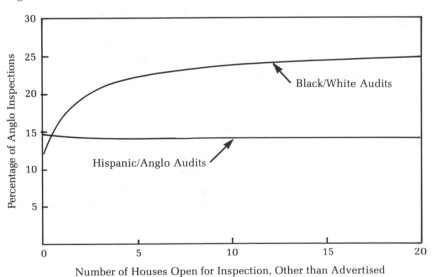

Number of Houses Open for Inspection, Other than Advertised

Anglo audits, however, the severity of discrimination remains constant at about 14 percent of the units seen by whites, regardless of the number of units open for inspection.

OTHER FORMS OF DISCRIMINATION

This section provides a brief overview of the incidence and severity of unfavorable treatment in stage 2 of a housing market transaction. As indicated in figure 2.1, this stage consists of the terms and conditions of sale or rental, sales effort by the housing agent, and credit assistance in the sales audits. In part because the relevant information was not available for many audits, HDS found virtually no differences in the terms and conditions offered to minority and Anglo auditors in the sales market. As a result, this section presents results for terms and conditions in the rental market, credit assistance in the sales market, and sales effort in both markets.

Indexes for Other Forms of Discrimination

To keep the presentation simple, let us focus on indexes of unfavorable treatment. For a more detailed discussion of these indexes, see Yinger (1991b).

The credit assistance index is based on four types of agent behavior: whether the agent offered to help the auditor find financing, whether the agent indicated that the auditor was not qualified for a mortgage, whether the agent told the auditor about conventional fixed-rate financing, and whether the agent told the auditor about adjustable rate mortgages. An auditor was considered to be treated unfavorably on the first variable, for example, if the agent offered to help her teammate find financing but did not offer to help her.

The terms and conditions index is based on five variables. These are whether an application fee was required, whether special rental incentives were offered, the quoted rent for the advertised housing unit, whether the rent of inspected units included extras other than utilities, and the size of the security deposit. To rule out the possibility that a higher rent is offered to some auditors in exchange for a longer lease, an auditor is considered to be disfavored in information about the rent of the advertised unit only if she is quoted a higher rent than is her teammate and is not offered a longer lease.

Finally, the sales effort index is based on the agent's queries about an auditor's income and housing needs, whether the auditor was invited to call back, and the amount of time the agent spent with the auditor. In the sales audits, this index also reflects whether the auditor received a follow-up call from the agent. Note that an auditor was considered to be disfavored if she, but not her teammate, was asked about her income or if her teammate, but not she, was asked about her housing needs. In addition, differences in the amount of time the agent spent with the two auditors were not considered unless they were greater than twenty minutes in the sales audits and five minutes in the rental audits.

A variety of overall indexes can be defined by combining the information in the housing availability, credit assistance, and sales effort for the sales audits and the housing availability, terms and conditions, and sales effort indexes for the rental audits. In the relevant HDS reports (Yinger 1991b and 1991c), overall indexes were formed by treating each of these underlying indexes as a type of treatment. Thus, the overall index would count a minority auditor as disfavored if she was disfavored on at least one of the underlying indexes and not favored on any of them.

To help combine the incidence and severity measures, the overall indexes in this chapter are defined in a somewhat different manner. Instead of treating each underlying index as a type of treatment, I build overall indexes based on each of the underlying types of agent behavior. An overall index combining housing availability and credit assistance, for example, involves eight types of agent behavior, four each from housing availability and credit assistance. Thus, an auditor is considered to be disfavored in this overall index if she is disfavored on at least one of the eight types of agent behavior and not favored on any one of them.

This approach is very conservative; favorable treatment of the minority auditor on a single type of agent behavior ensures that the audit will not be classified as Anglo-favored, even if the Anglo is favored on every other variable in the index. In other words, these indexes consider an auditor to be disfavored only if the evidence is completely unambiguous. These indexes are complemented, therefore, with indexes that use the second approach defined by Wienk et al. (1979). As noted earlier, this second type of index considers an auditor to be disfavored if she is disfavored on more of the items in the index than is her teammate.

Estimates of Discrimination

Results are presented in tables 2.6 to 2.9. These tables provide the complete decomposition developed in the previous section, but I will

Table 2.6 OVERALL INCIDENCE AND SEVERITY OF DISCRIMINATION, BLACK/WHITE SALES AUDITS

Indexes	White-Favored Audit (WF)			Black-Favored Audit (BF)			Differences		
	Gross incidence (1)	Severity given WF (2)	Gross severity (3)	Gross incidence (4)	Severity given BF (5)	Gross severity (6)	Net incidence (7)	Net severity given WF or BF (8)	Net severity[a] (9)
Panel A: first type of index									
Credit assistance	39.13	1.783	0.698	17.96	1.339	0.240	21.17	0.444	0.458
Sales effort	30.52	1.647	0.503	19.45	1.665	0.324	11.07	-0.018	0.179
Stage 2 total	27.27	2.704	0.737	14.30	2.142	0.306	12.97	0.562	0.431
Stage 1 and credit	43.17	2.556	1.104	18.25	1.799	0.328	24.92	0.757	0.776
Stage 1 and 2	24.79	3.608	0.895	11.52	2.724	0.314	13.27	0.884	0.581
Stage 1, 2, and 3	24.21	3.716	0.900	10.15	2.760	0.280	14.06	0.956	0.620
Panel B: second type of index									
Credit assistance	41.61	1.738	0.723	19.07	1.320	0.251	22.54	0.418	0.472
Sales effort	41.83	1.511	0.632	29.24	1.492	0.436	12.59	0.019	0.196
Stage 2 total	51.27	2.294	1.176	27.71	1.834	0.508	23.56	0.460	0.668
Stage 1 and credit	53.90	2.373	1.279	24.40	1.679	0.410	29.50	0.694	0.869
Stage 1 and 2	58.96	2.946	1.737	29.90	2.274	0.680	29.06	0.672	1.057
Stage 1, 2, and 3	57.73	3.090	1.784	29.33	2.259	0.663	28.40	0.831	1.121

[a]All entries in this column are statistically significant at the 5 percent confidence level or above using the paired, weighted difference-of-means test described in Yinger (1991b).

Table 2.7 OVERALL INCIDENCE AND SEVERITY OF DISCRIMINATION, BLACK/WHITE RENTAL AUDITS

Indexes	White-Favored Audit (WF)			Black-Favored Audit (BF)				Differences	
	Gross incidence (1)	Severity given WF (2)	Gross severity (3)	Gross incidence (4)	Severity given BF (5)	Gross severity (6)	Net incidence (7)	Net severity given WF or BF (8)	Net severity[a] (9)
Panel A: First type of index									
Terms and conditions	21.64	1.138	0.246	13.38	1.012	0.135	8.26	0.126	0.111
Sales effort	41.13	1.611	0.663	23.61	1.428	0.337	17.52	0.183	0.326
Stage 2 total	39.23	1.895	0.744	20.53	1.605	0.329	18.70	0.290	0.415
Stage 1 and credit	39.05	1.859	0.726	18.57	1.502	0.279	20.48	0.357	0.447
Stage 1 and 2	30.17	3.105	0.937	12.95	2.208	0.286	17.22	0.897	0.651
Panel B: Second type of index									
Terms and conditions	21.68	1.138	0.247	13.38	1.012	0.135	8.30	0.126	0.112
Sales effort	46.35	1.564	0.725	26.61	1.382	0.368	19.74	0.182	0.357
Stage 2 total	49.21	1.774	0.873	27.19	1.488	0.405	22.02	0.286	0.468
Stage 1 and credit	46.79	1.757	0.822	24.48	1.442	0.353	22.31	0.315	0.469
Stage 1 and 2	53.32	2.532	1.350	27.59	1.897	0.523	25.73	0.635	0.827

[a]All entries in this column are statistically significant at the 5 percent confidence level or above using the paired, weighted difference-of-means test described in Yinger (1991b).

Table 2.8 OVERALL INCIDENCE AND SEVERITY OF DISCRIMINATION, HISPANIC/ANGLO SALES AUDITS

	Anglo-Favored Audit (AF)			Hispanic-Favored Audit (HF)				Differences	
Indexes	Gross incidence (1)	Severity given AF (2)	Gross severity (3)	Gross incidence (4)	Severity given HF (5)	Gross severity (6)	Net incidence (7)	Net severity given AF or HF (8)	Net severity[a] (9)
Panel A: First type of index									
Credit assistance	37.33	1.634	0.610	23.00	1.335	0.307	14.33	0.299	0.303
Sales effort	33.20	1.698	0.564	20.31	1.623	0.330	12.89	0.075	0.234
Stage 2 total	28.39	2.503	0.711	14.75	2.263	0.334	13.64	0.240	0.377
Stage 1 and credit	38.60	2.449	0.945	22.44	1.734	0.389	16.16	0.715	0.556
Stage 1 and 2	22.67	3.765	0.853	11.22	3.090	0.347	11.45	0.675	0.506
Stage 1, 2, and 3	20.06	3.867	0.776	10.20	3.232	0.330	9.86	0.635	0.446
Panel B: Second type of index									
Credit assistance	39.33	1.602	0.630	23.49	1.328	0.312	15.84	0.274	0.318
Sales effort	43.44	1.594	0.693	27.81	1.492	0.415	15.63	0.102	0.278
Stage 2 total	53.29	2.163	1.153	30.16	1.845	0.557	23.13	0.318	0.596
Stage 1 and credit	49.52	2.210	1.094	27.81	1.629	0.453	21.71	0.581	0.641
Stage 1 and 2	54.18	2.899	1.571	30.22	2.225	0.672	23.96	0.674	0.899
Stage 1, 2, and 3	54.92	2.946	1.618	30.84	2.240	0.691	24.08	0.706	0.927

[a]All entries in this column are statistically significant at the 5 percent confidence level or above using the paired, weighted difference-of-means test described in Yinger (1991b).

Table 2.9 OVERALL INCIDENCE AND SEVERITY OF DISCRIMINATION, HISPANIC/ANGLO RENTAL AUDITS

Indexes	Anglo-Favored Audit (AF)			Hispanic-Favored Audit (HF)				Differences	
	Gross incidence (1)	Severity given AF (2)	Gross severit (3)	Gross incidence (4)	Severity given HF (5)	Gross severity (6)	Net incidence (7)	Net severity given AF or HF (8)	Net severity[a] (9)
Panel A: First type of index									
Terms and conditions	22.74	1.074	0.244	12.49	1.135	0.142	10.25	−0.061	0.102
Sales effort	36.38	1.639	0.596	26.00	1.446	0.376	10.38	0.193	0.220
Stage 2 total	34.93	1.822	0.637	20.76	1.715	0.356	14.18	0.107	0.281
Stage 1 and credit	34.44	1.796	0.619	19.70	1.661	0.327	14.74	0.135	0.292
Stage 1 and 2	28.02	2.926	0.820	15.73	2.224	0.350	12.29	0.702	0.470
Panel B: Second type of index									
Terms and conditions	23.38	1.072	0.251	12.70	1.133	0.144	10.68	−0.061	0.107
Sales effort	42.19	1.559	0.658	29.17	1.404	0.410	13.02	0.155	0.248
Stage 2 total	47.19	1.699	0.802	28.42	1.573	0.447	18.77	0.126	0.355
Stage 1 and credit	43.90	1.709	0.750	26.30	1.580	0.415	17.60	0.129	0.335
Stage 1 and 2	51.34	2.442	1.253	33.12	2.025	0.671	18.22	0.417	0.582

[a]All entries in this column are statistically significant at the 5 percent confidence level or above using the paired, weighted difference-of-means test described in Yinger (1991b).

focus on column (9), which is the net severity of discrimination as defined earlier. As noted above, each table presents results for the two types of indexes developed by Wienk et al. (1979).

Let us begin with the indexes for credit assistance in the first row of panel (a) in tables 2.6 and 2.8. These indexes reveal that the net severity of discrimination is 0.458 acts per visit in the black/white audits and 0.303 acts per visit in the Hispanic/Anglo audits. The estimates are only slightly higher in panel (b). Thus, blacks can expect to encounter an act of discrimination in one of the agent actions covered by the credit assistance index about every other visit to a real estate broker, and Hispanics can expect to encounter such an act of discrimination about every third visit.[33]

Discrimination is not so severe in the terms and conditions of rental. In the second row, panel (a), of tables 2.7 and 2.9, we find that net severity is about 0.10 acts for both the black/white and Hispanic/Anglo audits. In other words, both blacks and Hispanics can expect to encounter one act of discrimination in these terms and conditions in 10 visits to a rental agent. As with credit assistance, these estimates are about the same for the second type of index in panel (b).

The severity of discrimination in sales efforts is given in the third row of all four tables. The net measure equals about 0.20 acts for all classes of audit except black/white rental, for which it is 0.33 acts. Thus, blacks and Hispanics can expect to encounter an act of discrimination in sales efforts once during every five visits to housing agents (or every three visits for black renters). The estimates in panel (b) are only slightly higher.

The remaining rows in these tables provide information on the overall indexes. Consider first the index that combines housing availability (stage 1) and either credit assistance (for the sales audits) and terms and conditions (for the rental audits). In panel (a) the net severity of discrimination for this index ranges from 0.29 acts in the Hispanic/Anglo rental audits to 0.73 acts in the black/white sales audits. Thus, black home buyers can expect to encounter 0.73 acts of discrimination in these two categories of agent behavior, on average, each time they visit a real estate broker, whereas Hispanic renters can expect to encounter 0.29 acts, on average. For this index, the estimates in panel (b) are moderately higher, especially in the sales audits.

Finally, consider the final index in each table, which combines stages 1 and 2. In the sales audits, this index also includes stage 3, which is racial or ethnic steering. In panel (a) the net results for this index are about 0.47 acts in both types of Hispanic/Anglo audit and about 0.6 acts for both types of black/white audit. As a rough approximation, therefore, black and Hispanics in both sales and rental markets encounter one act of discrimination every other time they visit a housing agent. The estimates in panel (b) are considerably higher. For both types of sales audits, the estimate is now about 1.0 act; that is, blacks and Hispanic house buyers can expect to encounter one act of discrimination **every time** they visit a real estate broker. The estimate is not much smaller for the black/white rental audits (0.83 acts), but it is considerably smaller for the Hispanic/Anglo rental audits (0.58 acts).

As a reminder, the difference between these two panels is that the indexes in panel (a) treat an audit as neutral if the minority auditor is favored on even a single item in the index, whereas those in panel (b) do not treat an audit as neutral unless both auditors are favored on the same number of items. Because random factors are likely to influence agent behavior in many cases, I find the first approach unnecessarily conservative for an overall index that encompasses many different types of agent behavior. Even with that conservative index, however, the results for all classes of audit indicate that black and Hispanic homeseekers can expect to encounter an act of discrimination every other time they visit a housing agent.

CONCLUSION: TO WHAT EXTENT DOES HOUSING DISCRIMINATION CONSTRAIN MINORITY HOMESEEKERS' ACCESS TO HOUSING?

The most conservative measure of discrimination, simple net incidence, for the most dramatic discriminatory act, outright exclusion, suggests that discrimination against black and Hispanic homeseekers is statistically significant but is not widespread. To be specific, the simple net incidence of exclusion ranges from 4.5 percent for Hispanic home buyers, to about 6.5 percent for black home buyers and Hispanic renters, to 10.7 percent for black renters.

For six reasons, however, the overall impact of discrimination on minorities is far more severe than these results suggest. First, most homeseekers do not visit a single housing agent. A diligent minority family that responds to several advertisements has a much higher chance of encountering exclusion from at least one agent. In fact, black home buyers and Hispanic renters who visit five housing agents can expect to be totally excluded from all available housing by at least one agent about 28 percent of the time.[34] The comparable figure for

Hispanic home buyers and black renters are 20.6 percent and 43.2 percent, respectively. Thus, outright exclusion is not an uncommon occurrence for minority homeseekers—at least not for diligent ones.

Second, minority homeseekers are recommended or shown fewer housing units than their Anglo counterparts far more often than they are excluded from all units. Moreover, our analysis of the severity of discrimination indicates that this withholding of units has about the same quantitative impact on the availability of housing for minorities as does outright exclusion. The simple net incidence of discrimination for the total number of units available ranges from 9.8 percent for Hispanic renters, to 16.5 percent for Hispanic home buyers, to 19.4 percent for black home buyers, and to 23.4 percent for black renters. For minority homeseekers who visit five agents, the net probability of encountering at least one agent who withholds units from them is above 60 percent, except in the case of Hispanic renters where it is 40 percent. In other words, some available housing units will be withheld from most diligent minority homeseekers.

Third, the simple net measure probably understates the true net incidence of discrimination because it does not account for random differences in the circumstances teammates encounter and because it ignores the possibility of steering. Exact solutions to these problems are not possible with the HDS data, but the rough adjustments presented here suggest that the understatement is at least one or two percentage points and may be as high as eight percentage points for some variables.

Fourth, the opportunity to discriminate is low or nonexistent in many audits, but the evidence presented here indicates that many housing agents take advantage of the opportunity to discriminate when it arises. To be specific, for both black and Hispanic home buyers the severity of discrimination in house inspections goes up as the number of houses available for inspection increases. Expressed relative to the number of inspections by Anglos, the severity of discrimination in inspections is about 14 percent for Hispanics, regardless of the number of houses available for inspection. In the case of black homeseekers, however, this severity measure is 17 percent when one house other than the advertised house is available for inspection and increases to 25 percent when ten houses are available. The more houses are available, therefore, the more discrimination blacks can expect to face, even relative to the treatment of Anglos.

Fifth, the net approach on which all these results are based does not correspond to a legal notion of discrimination. Courts are interested in an individual housing agent's discriminatory acts against blacks and Hispanics, not in the net impact of agent behavior on minorities over a sample of agents. A single housing agent who has denied a black or Hispanic customer access to the same housing made available to an Anglo customer has violated the Fair Housing Act, regardless of whether or not another broker on the other side of town has treated a minority customer more favorably than an Anglo customer—for whatever reasons. Hence the extent of behavior that violates the Fair Housing Act, at least in spirit, is more accurately reflected by the simple gross measure than by the simple net measure. For the total number of units made available, the simple gross incidence of discrimination is over twice as high as the simple net incidence in the sales audits, almost twice as high in the black/white rental audits, and over three times as high in the Hispanic/Anglo rental audits. In fact, these gross incidence results imply that a minority household who visits at least five agents can expect to encounter at least one agent who withholds available housing with a probability of 88 percent or more.

Finally, discrimination in housing availability often is accompanied by discrimination in later stages of a housing market transaction, and other forms of discrimination occur even when discrimination in housing availability does not. According to one of the severity calculations presented earlier, black and Hispanic homeseekers can expect to encounter one act of discrimination each time they visit a real estate broker and approximately every other time they visit a rental agent. In the sales market, for example, discrimination in credit assistance is quite common; black home buyers can expect to encounter one act of discrimination in credit assistance if they visit two real estate brokers and Hispanic buyers if they visit three brokers.

These results do not indicate that discrimination forms an impenetrable barrier to minority access to housing, but they do reveal that discrimination in housing remains common, and indeed that the vast majority of black and Hispanic households can expect to encounter housing discrimination at one time or another. Although the most blatant forms of housing discrimination are relatively rare, more subtle actions to discourage minority homeseekers or to limit their housing options are disturbingly frequent. Thus, minority homeseekers have higher search costs, sometimes considerably higher, than Anglo homeseekers. Minority households may be able to gain access to information about some or even most available housing if they are willing to put forth extra effort, but even then some housing will be withheld from them without their knowledge. Although the exact impact of existing discrimination on minority households is difficult to measure, it is clear that minority households face significant discriminatory barriers in finding housing that is best suited for their needs. Hence minority homeseekers must either pay considerably more in search costs than do Anglo households or else settle for housing that does not match their demand as well as the housing Anglos find, or both. This situation is a profound deviation from the equal treatment required by the Fair Housing Act.

These results clearly indicate that as of 1989, when the HDS data were collected, fair housing laws and enforcement procedures had by no means eliminated racial and ethnic discrimination in housing. For two reasons, however, it is difficult to translate this finding into concrete policy recommendations.[35]

The first reason is that the HDS does not reveal how discrimination has changed over time. Although another major study, Wienk et al. (1979), collected audit data in 1977, it did not calculate any measures of the severity of discrimination. Moreover, the two studies differ on a few key aspects of methodology so that their estimates of the incidence of discrimination are difficult to compare. In addition, some of the incidence estimates are higher in the earlier study and some are higher in HDS.[36] My own view is that a comparison of these two studies that accounts, to the extent possible, for methodological differences reveals no clear sign of a change in the incidence of discrimination between 1977 and 1989. Thus, it does not appear that fair housing laws and enforcement procedures had much impact on discrimination during the 1980s, but the evidence is hardly conclusive.

The second reason that the HDS results do not yield clear policy implications is that the Fair Housing Act was amended in 1988 to give the federal government more enforcement power. These amendments were implemented during 1989, when the HDS data were collected. Thus, the HDS study provides a baseline for the future analysis of the effectiveness of the 1988 amendments, but it cannot be used to determine whether those amendments have been effective in eliminating racial and ethnic discrimination in housing. Another audit study needs to be conducted during the 1990s.

At the very least, the HDS results indicate that the 1988 amendments to the Fair Housing Act need to be adequately funded and vigorously enforced. Although the Fair Housing Act was originally passed over 20 years ago, the evidence collected by the HDS indicates that racial and ethnic discrimination in housing has by no means been eradicated. Even the most conservative measures reveal that discrimination in housing is still a significant problem, and more balanced measures show that it continues to be a major obstacle confronting black and Hispanic households in search of housing.

Notes

The Housing Discrimination Study was a major research project sponsored by the U.S. Department of Housing and Urban Development, and I am grateful to the hundreds of people who contributed to it. My job as research director would not have been possible without their efforts. I would particularly like to thank Raymond Struyk, the project director, Margery Turner, the deputy research director, Cliff Schrupp, the director of field operations, and Lauria Grant, Nigel M. Grant, and Stephen Ross, my research assistants. I also received valuable methodological assistance from Axel Boersch-Supan, Edward Bryant, George Galster, Genevieve Kenney, Edgar Olsen, Jan Ondrich, and an anonymous referee. The opinions expressed in this chapter are my own.

1. The link between housing discrimination and access to employment has been extensively studied. See, for example, Ellwood (1986), Holtzer (1991), Jencks and Mayer (1990), and Kain (1992).

2. For an excellent analysis of the system of discrimination, see Galster (1987 or 1991).

3. Other audit studies include Hakken (1979), Feins et al. (1981), and Yinger (1986). For a review of many audit studies, see Galster (1990a).

4. It should be noted that a gross measure does not literally correspond to the share of audits in which legal action is warranted. A court must consider many factors, such as the credibility of the witnesses and the importance of the discriminatory behavior, that are beyond the scope of a research study.

5. Because of the sampling design, the results must be weighted. Specifically, the result for each audit is multiplied by a weight that indicates the share of advertised units in the nation that the audit represents. For details, see Yinger (1991b).

6. It should be pointed out that this problem is less pronounced in an audit, where the time between teammate visits can be kept as small as practical, than in alternative methodologies for studying discrimination.

7. Differences in teammates' circumstances are not the only source of randomness in a model of housing agent behavior. Unobserved variables, such as agent prejudice, show up in the random error term. For the purposes of this discussion, however, these unobserved variables are part of the true behavior that a minority homeseeker can expect to encounter and therefore belong in the rows, not the columns, of figure 2. True randomness in agent behavior could be included in either the columns or the rows, depending on one's definition of discrimination. If discrimination is defined to be systematic unfavorable treatment, then this true randomness belongs in the columns.

8. Some studies assume that the share of audits in which the minority auditor is favored measures random behavior by agents. These studies conclude that the simple net measure, which nets out this share, indicates the extent to which minority auditors encounter unfavorable treatment for systematic reasons. This conclusion is incorrect for two reasons discussed below: random factors may not have the same impact on the probabilities that minority and majority auditors are favored, and minorities are sometimes favored for systematic reasons.

9. In principle, the simple gross measure also could be adjusted to account for steering. For example, the share of audits in which teammates saw the same number of units but in which black were steered to black neighborhoods could be added to the simple gross measure for units shown. I am grateful to George Galster for pointing this out to me. No such adjustments are attempted here.

10. These results are based on the steering index presented in Turner et al. (1991).

11. This logit analysis also can be used to determine whether the probability of discrimination depends on agent, auditor, or audit characteristics. See Yinger (1991c).

12. In effect, the simple gross measure errs by including the impact of random factors associated with differences in teammate circumstances, but the multivariate measure errs by excluding the impact of systematic factors that cannot be observed. Because of these essentially opposite errors, the HDS researchers used the average of the simple gross measure and the logit measure as their final estimate of the gross incidence of discrimination. See Yinger (1991c).

13. Strictly speaking, if a multinomial logit model has no explanatory power, the most common choice will be predicted for every observation. Similarly, if a multinomial logit model has relatively little explanatory power, then the systematic factors that lead to relatively rare choices cannot be identified, and those choices will virtually never be the predicted ones. Unfortunately, the HDS logit equations typically do not have enough explanatory power to reliably predict relatively uncommon choices.

14. The sales results for the housing availability variables involving numbers of units and for the housing availability index differ slightly from the results in Yinger (1991b) because of data revisions. The construction of a data set in which individual houses are the unit of observation, discussed in note 26, uncovered a few houses with incomplete address information, both recommended and shown, that had been missed in the original reports. These revisions affect the net measure, the gross measures, and the severity measures in the next section.

15. Although the simple net measure is just that—simple—the appropriate hypothesis test is not. The test used here employs the logit model with fixed effects developed by Chamberlain (1980). In this model an agent makes a discrete choice about whether to undertake a certain action (e.g., show the advertised unit) for each customer. Audit teammates share an unobserved fixed effect, of the type discussed by Yinger (1986). By differencing the logit equations for teammates, Chamberlain shows that the model reduces to one in which observations involving equal treatment drop out, the dependent variable is whether the Anglo auditor was favored, and the explanatory variables are differences in observed teammate characteristics. The t-test for the constant term is a test of the hypothesis that the net measure is significantly different from zero. In many logit applications, the estimated coefficients can be translated into probability statements, and in principle, this model could be used to provide an incidence measure that improves on the simple net measure. Because the fixed effects are differenced out, not estimated, however, Chamberlain's procedure cannot be used to estimate probabilities. I am grateful to Charles Manski for pointing this out to me.

16. The t-statistic for the housing availability index in the Hispanic/Anglo rental audits is 1.63, which falls just short of statistical significance at the one-tailed, 5 percent level.

17. The two steps built into the adjusted sales index, the restriction to same-agent audits and the elimination of cases with steering, have approximately equal impacts on the outcome. For example, an adjusted index based on the same-agent restriction alone leads to a higher net measure for seven of the eight housing availability results in both the black/white and Hispanic/Anglo audits. The audits in which teammates saw the same agent differed more dramatically from other agents in the HMPS audits, probably because the HMPS auditors asked about a particular type of housing, based on an advertisement, but not about a specific advertised unit. For example, the HMPS housing

availability index, which is similar to the one presented here, was 6 points higher in the sales audits and 9 points higher in the rental audits for the subset of audits in which teammates saw the same agent than for the sample as a whole. See Wienk et al. (1979, pp. 107 and 168). Thus the HMPS simple net incidence calculations may understate the true net incidence of discrimination by considerably more than the simple net results for HDS. These findings emphasize the need to keep teammate circumstances as similar as possible in an audit study.

18. Strictly speaking, standard statistical tests cannot be applied to the simple gross measure because one case of unfavorable treatment is sufficient to reject the null hypothesis that the probability of unfavorable treatment is zero. However, a weighted *t*-test can be interpreted as a rough indication of the likelihood that a particular estimate could arise by chance when the underlying probability is close to zero. Under this interpretation, all of the simple gross measures in this chapter are statistically significant at the 5 percent confidence level. See Yinger (1991b).

19. The only exceptions are for the number of units recommended but not shown in the sales audits and for information about units similar to the advertised unit in the rental audits; in both of these cases the gross incidence of discrimination is slightly higher against Hispanics than against blacks.

20. The multivariate sales results differ from those in the HDS report (Yinger 1991c) because of three revisions: (1) the dependent variables measuring discrimination in the number of units recommended but not shown, shown, and made available were revised (as discussed in note 14); (2) new variables to measure the total number of units shown or recommended but not shown (which are discussed in note 26) were used as explanatory variables in place of white treatment; and (3) the procedures for filling in missing data for a few explanatory variables were revised.

21. In this usage, an act of discrimination is unfavorable treatment on a single type of housing agent behavior. The number of acts of discrimination was not examined in any of the HDS reports. For more on this topic, see Yinger (1991a).

22. The net measure is simply the difference in the average treatment of Anglo and minority auditors. The statistical significance of this measure can be found using a **paired** difference-of-means test. The importance of pairing is discussed in Yinger (1986). As explained in Yinger (1991b), both the difference and the standard error for this test need to be weighted to account for the HDS sampling plan. Note that only the first and last columns of tables 2.3 and 2.4 are presented in the relevant HDS report (Yinger 1991b).

23. The only exceptions are the sales effort index for the black/white sales audits and the terms and conditions index for the Hispanic/Anglo rental audits.

24. The data revisions discussed in note 14 do not alter the statistical significance of the sales results; that is, the significance results in Yinger (1991b) still hold.

25. The comparable numbers for the number of inspections, in the same order, are 18.5, 10.4, 18.0, and 7.6 percent.

26. The total number of units available (or inspected) is found from a data set in which each housing unit encountered by any auditor is the unit of observation. This data set was assembled with the help of Jan Ondrich and Steve Ross. By matching addresses and developing fill-in procedures for units with incomplete address information, we decided which units were seen by both teammates. We were unable to create an analogous data set for the rental audits because the address information for many rental units was missing or very incomplete.

27. It should be noted that this is a different approach to marginal discrimination than the one in the HDS report (Yinger 1991c), which measured the opportunity to discriminate by the number of units made available to the white auditor. The estimates of

marginal discrimination in that report are not comparable to those presented here. As pointed out in that report, using white treatment as the explanatory variable causes some statistical problems that cannot be resolved with audit data. The new approach presented here avoids those problems.

28. Marginal discrimination also can be estimated for the number of units recommended but not shown and for the total number of units made available. For these two variables, however, the relationship between the severity of discrimination and the number of units available is very nonlinear and difficult to summarize, so it is not discussed here.

29. The marginal discrimination results indicate that the severity of discrimination does not increase when another advertised unit becomes available. However, because there is a positive constant term in the regression used for prediction, the severity of discrimination is still positive even when the only unit available is an advertised unit.

30. Note that this result does not imply that the advertised unit always is shown to minority customers—only that the overall severity of discrimination does not increase when another advertised unit becomes available. According to the incidence results presented in the previous section, minority customers are significantly less likely than Anglo customers to see the advertised unit. Thus, when the number of units other than advertised units increases, agents are more likely to withhold units, including advertised units, from minority customers.

31. Mechanically, the severity of discrimination as a share of white inspections is calculated by predicting both the severity of discrimination and the number of white inspections as functions of the total number of units available for inspection. This procedure simply scales the predicted severity of discrimination and does not indicate the expected value of the ratio of severity to white inspections.

32. Remember from note 25 that the average severity of discrimination in sales inspections relative to white treatment is 18.5 percent for blacks and 10.4 percent for Hispanics. The approximations for these results based on figure 3 are 17 percent and 14 percent. These results are not exactly the same because an advertised unit is not available for inspection in some audits and the average number of units open for inspection other than the advertised unit is not exactly equal to one.

33. In principle, some of the audits in which minority auditors were more likely to hear about mortgages could involve steering. In this case an adjusted net measure, similar to those presented earlier, is appropriate.

34. The probability of encountering discrimination in several visits to a housing agent was first calculated by Wienk et al. (1979). As they point out, the formula for the probability of encountering unfavorable treatment at least once in n visits, P_n, given the fixed and independent probability P_i of encountering unfavorable treatment each visit, is given by $P_n = 1 - (1 - P_i)^n$.

35. For a detailed discussion of federal fair housing policy, see Galster (1990b).

36. For a detailed comparison of the HDS results and those in Wienk et al. (1979), see Elmi and Mickelsons (1991).

References

Chamberlain, Gary. 1980. "Analysis of Covariance with Qualitative Data." *Review of Economic Studies* 47 (January): 225–238.

Ellwood, David. 1986. "The Spatial Mismatch Hypothesis: Are There Jobs Missing in the Ghetto?" In R. Freedman and H. Holtzer, eds., *The Black Youth Employment Crisis*. Chicago: University of Chicago Press.

Elmi, Amina, and Maris Mickelsons. 1991. *Housing Discrimination Study: Replication of 1977 Study Measures with Current Data*. Washington, D.C.: U.S. Department of Housing and Urban Development.

Feins, Judith D., Rachael G. Bratt, and Robert Hollister. 1981. *Final Report of a Study of Racial Discrimination in the Boston Housing Market*. Cambridge, Mass.: Abt Associates.

Galster, George. 1991. "Housing Discrimination and Urban Poverty of African-Americans." *Journal of Housing Research* 2 (2): 87–124.

————. 1990a. "Racial Discrimination in Housing Markets during the 1980s: A Review of the Audit Evidence." *Journal of Planning Education and Research* 9 (3): 165–175.

————. 1990b. "Federal Fair Housing Policy: The Great Misapprehension." In D. DiPasquale and L.C. Keyes, eds., *Building Foundations*. Philadelphia: University of Pennsylvania Press, 137–156.

————. 1987. "Residential Segregation and Interracial Economic Disparities: A Simultaneous-Equations Approach." *Journal of Urban Economics*. January, 22–44.

Hakken, Jon. 1979. *Discrimination Against Chicanos in the Dallas Rental Housing Market: An Experimental Extension of the Housing Market Practices Survey*. Washington, D.C.: U.S. Department of Housing and Urban Development.

Holzer, Harry J. 1991. "The Spatial Mismatch Hypothesis: What Has the Evidence Shown?" *Urban Studies* 28 (1): 105–122.

Jencks, Christopher and Susan E. Mayer. 1990. "Residential Segregation, Job Proximity, and Black Job Opportunities." In L.E. Lynn, Jr., and M.G.H. McGeary, eds., *Inner-City Poverty in the United States*. Washington, D.C.: National Academy Press, pp. 187–222.

Kain, John F. 1992. "The Spatial Mismatch Hypothesis: Three Decades later." *Journal of Housing Research* 3 (2): 371–460.

Turner, M.A., M. Mickelsons, and J.G. Edwards. 1991. *Housing Discrimination Study: Analyzing Racial and Ethnic Steering*. Washington, D.C.: U.S. Department of Housing and Urban Development.

Wienk, Ronald E., Clifford E. Reid, John C. Simonson, and Frederick J. Eggers. 1979. *Measuring Discrimination in American Housing Markets: The Housing Market Practices Survey*. Washington, D.C.: U.S. Department of Housing and Urban Development.

Yinger, John. 1991a. "Acts of Discrimination: Evidence from the 1989 Housing Discrimination Study." *Journal of Housing Economics* 1 (December): 318–346.

Yinger, John. 1991b. *Housing Discrimination Study: Incidence and Severity of Unfavorable Treatment*. Washington, D.C.: U.S. Department of Housing and Urban Development.

Yinger, John. 1991c. *Housing Discrimination Study: Incidence of Discrimination and Variation in Discriminatory Behavior.* Washington, D.C.: U.S. Department of Housing and Urban Development.

Yinger, John. 1986. "Measuring Discrimination with Fair Housing Audits: Caught in the Act." *American Economics Review* 76 (December): 881–893.

GOING BEYOND THE HOUSING
DISCRIMINATION STUDY: COMMENTS

William R. Tisdale

In these remarks on the Housing Discrimination Study (HDS), discussed by John Yinger in chapter 2, I focus on the impact such social science research can have on public policymakers, future research approaches, the civil rights community, and the general public.

The implementation of a nationwide, systematic study of the incidence of housing discrimination was an important endeavor for a couple of reasons. First, like the 1977 Housing Market Practices Survey (HMPS), it focused needed attention on civil rights violations that contemporary America is all too eager to dismiss as isolated or economically determined. This type of study provides critical documentation for the argument that patterns of racial segregation are created and maintained by deliberate acts of members of the housing industry. Second, contrary to the alleged dawn of a "color-blind society," race and color still are the predominant factors in accessibility to housing choice. As Yinger notes in chapter 2 when comparing the HDS with the HMPS, "a comparison of these two studies that accounts, to the extent possible, for methodological differences reveals no clear sign of a change in the incidence of unfavorable treatment between 1977 and 1989."

Yet, I believe that we must evaluate the HDS results with a critical eye, toward both their accuracy and their effectiveness. In terms of accuracy, I am most concerned about the method of test site selection, namely random selection of newspaper advertisements. The anchoring of audits to newspaper ads contained only in the sampled metropolitan areas' major newspapers predetermined that steering would be difficult to detect. In 1986 a study of advertising practices by the largest real estate firm in the metropolitan Milwaukee area found that the houses it advertised in *The Milwaukee Journal* were disproportionately located in all-white neighborhoods. The placement of fewer advertisements of homes for sale in predominantly minority or integrated neighborhoods is a common practice within the real estate industry. Therefore, testers responding to advertised homes in the HDS were responding almost exclusively to housing in predominantly white neighborhoods. Moreover, some of the most blatant forms of racial steering uncovered in Milwaukee occurred when test teams requested housing in integrated neighborhoods. This type of steering cannot be detected through anchored testing. The use of major-newspaper advertisements also hindered the accuracy of the HDS rental audits. It is a common practice for landlords who discriminate to limit minorities' access to their housing by *not* advertising in generally distributed media. These landlords frequently seek more selective access to their units by placing advertisements in community or neighborhood newspapers with a predominantly white readership.

For these reasons, the reliance on generally distributed newspapers has created a conservative bias in the HDS that underestimates the level of actual discrimination.

Yinger acknowledges this conservative bias in his discussion of the random factors that influence agent behavior. He states, "Even with that conservative index [of housing agent behavior], however, the results for all classes of audit indicate that black and Hispanic home seekers can expect to encounter an act of discrimination every other time they visit a housing agent." Yinger also states that the results of this particular survey indicate that black and Hispanic home seekers can expect to encounter unfavorable treatment in housing availability about 40 percent of the time they seek housing. It is apparent, based on the results of this survey, that discrimination has become more subtle. Overt, blatant forms of discrimination have, for the most part, taken a back seat to a variety of sophisticated subtleties. These unlawful activities are taking place at this very moment, discouraging and/ or severely limiting the housing choices of minority home seekers. Given these accounts of disparate treatment (especially in view of the great likelihood of undercounting the incidence of discrimination), it is unfathomable that we, as a society, would merely quietly (and academically) accept such behavior—behavior that some 125 years ago was prohibited with the passage of the Civil Rights Act of 1866 (the federal law prohibiting racial discrimination in the sale and rental of housing).

Social science can be important in developing a blueprint for public policy. Despite its articulated benefits, however, social science research can just as easily become an obstacle when its design and implementation interferes with the resolution of the problem it is studying. The contractual provisions of the HDS that prevented its use as an enforcement tool, are, in my opinion, an example of such

an impediment. I believe it is socially irresponsible to identify violations of fair-housing laws and fail to take measures to address them.
I am concerned that the U.S. Department of Housing and Urban Development (HUD) set contractual requirements with the Urban Institute that forbade any further investigation of the violations of federal
law that were uncovered as a result of documentation gathered in the
HDS. How many minority citizens have continued to suffer discrimination at the hands of those same housing providers identified back
in 1989? How many acts of housing discrimination are occurring as a
result of our failure to take action on these known violations of the
law? Civil rights must never be sacrificed for the sake of research.

Despite its flaws, two important points were reconfirmed by the
HDS:

1. The problem of housing discrimination is still alive and well in
   the United States, and
2. Title VIII violations can be effectively uncovered through systemic
   testing.

Three policy interventions are readily obvious. The first is that testing
for systemic fair-housing violations continues to prove its effectiveness as an invaluable tool for uncovering illegal acts of housing discrimination. This study demonstrates that random selection of housing providers does uncover some of the more insidious forms of
discrimination and suggests that future initiatives funded by HUD or
private foundations should not be limited to complaint-generated testing as a means to effectuate the purposes of the fair-housing laws.
Second, sustained, direct funding, from both the public (government)
and private sectors (foundations and citizen support) must be committed at sufficient levels—not only to maintain existing private enforcement activities but also to establish new fair-housing organizations in areas of the country where such activity is absent. Third, we
must not be so singularly focused as to identify enforcement activities
as the only necessary mechanism to achieve equal access to housing
opportunities for minority citizens. Affirmative housing programs
such as the Gautreaux Program in Chicago, the Center for Integrated
Living in Milwaukee, and the Section 8 Mobility Program in Cincinnati are examples of successful integration programs that complement
enforcement efforts in opening communities to all citizens. Only
through the combination of these efforts will minority citizens in this
country have the true freedom of choice guaranteed them by federal
law.

Chapter Three

LIMITS ON NEIGHBORHOOD CHOICE: EVIDENCE OF RACIAL AND ETHNIC STEERING IN URBAN HOUSING MARKETS

Margery Austin Turner

INTRODUCTION

One of the many forms that housing market discrimination can take is the practice of steering, whereby minorities are shown or recommended housing units, but are "steered" away from predominantly white or Anglo neighborhoods toward neighborhoods that are already integrated or are predominantly black or Hispanic. Steering can be particularly difficult for individual home seekers to detect because they are likely to be shown houses that meet their specifications and have few opportunities to find out about the houses and neighborhoods they are not shown. But if minorities are systematically steered away from predominantly white neighborhoods—and vice versa— this form of discrimination clearly limits housing and neighborhood choice for both majority and minority home seekers, and may play an important role in perpetuating patterns of residential segregation.

This chapter presents data on racial and ethnic steering in urban housing markets. It draws primarily upon the analysis of steering conducted as part of the Housing Discrimination Study (HDS), sponsored by the U.S. Department of Housing and Urban Development (HUD), and conducted by The Urban Institute and Syracuse University.[1] Also presented are the findings of an ongoing exploratory study of real estate marketing practices being conducted by The Urban Institute.

Both black and Hispanic auditors experienced steering of one form or another about one out of five times that they were shown or recommended addresses in the Housing Discrimination Study. In effect, when black or Hispanic home seekers respond to advertisements in major metropolitan newspapers, those who are shown or recommended houses face a 21 percent chance of being steered to neighborhoods that are lower percentage white or Anglo, lower income, or lower value than those shown and recommended to comparable white home seekers.

Although the incidence of steering is significant, its severity is low because the magnitude of differences between neighborhoods shown and recommended to minority versus majority home buyers is small. The average percentage of whites in neighborhoods shown and recommended to black versus white auditors differed by only 3 percentage points, and the median house values differed by only $1,700. For Hispanics and Anglos, the average percentage of Anglos in neighborhoods shown and recommended differed by only 1 percentage point, and the median house values by less than $1,000.

One of the primary reasons differences in neighborhood characteristics were so small is that the vast majority of addresses advertised, recommended, and shown by audited agents in the HDS were located in predominantly white, middle-income neighborhoods. Indeed, a random sample of homes advertised in major metropolitan newspapers yields very few addresses in minority or integrated neighborhoods, and the agents encompassed by this sample did not show or recommend many addresses in minority or integrated neighborhoods. Even after controlling for the size and value of the owner-occupied stock, houses in black and Hispanic neighborhoods are less likely to be advertised in major metropolitan newspapers or marketed by agents in the HDS sample than predominantly white or Anglo neighborhoods.

Thus, minority and majority home buyers are limited in their neighborhood choices in two important ways. First, black and Hispanic home buyers who are shown and recommended addresses are likely to be steered to neighborhoods that have fewer whites and are less affluent than those shown and recommended to comparable white or Anglo home buyers. Second, all home buyers who start their search by inquiring about units advertised in major metropolitan newspapers are likely to be shown and recommended houses in predominantly white or Anglo neighborhoods rather than in integrated or minority neighborhoods.

Supplemental analysis of real estate marketing practices confirms that houses for sale in minority and integrated neighborhoods are less likely to be advertised than are those in white neighborhoods. Because white home buyers rely primarily on sources that exclude information about racially or ethnically diverse neighborhoods, they may never find out about housing opportunities in those neighborhoods. This form of differential treatment may play an important role in the perpetuation of residential segregation and may help explain why neighborhoods that receive an influx of minorities often become predominantly minority rather than remaining integrated.

ANALYZING STEERING WITH AUDIT DATA

One of the primary objectives of the Housing Discrimination Study was to measure the national incidence of racial and ethnic steering. Previous researchers had explored this issue. But HUD's previous national fair-housing audit study, the Housing Market Practices Survey, did not report measures of racial steering. And other audit studies of steering focused on individual metropolitan areas. Therefore, the results presented here constitute the first nationwide analysis of racial and ethnic steering in urban housing markets.

This section briefly reviews findings from three previous audit studies of steering, outlines the audit procedures employed in the Housing Discrimination Study, and describes the methodology used to analyze racial and ethnic steering on the basis of HDS audit data.

Previous Audit Studies of Steering

Many analysts of housing market discrimination have considered the issue of steering and its potential role in perpetuating racial segregation.[2] However, only a few audit studies of housing discrimination have incorporated measures of steering. The most prominent examples are those by Newburger (1981), Feins and Bratt (1981), and Pearce (1979). Key findings of these studies—all of which focused exclusively on black/white differences—are briefly reviewed here.

Newburger's study relied on data from the sales audits conducted in HUD's 1977 Housing Market Practices Survey. Matched pairs of black and white auditors visited real estate agents in 40 metropolitan areas for a total of 1,655 sales audits. Audits were based on a random sample of advertised units from each area's major newspaper. Auditors were instructed not to ask for the specific advertised unit, but rather for housing in the designated price range, size category, and location.

Newburger's results showed that blacks were more likely to be shown houses in neighborhoods with a higher percentage of black residents, lower income levels, and lower house values. Specifically, in 47 percent of the audits, blacks were shown houses in neighborhoods with a higher percentage of blacks than the neighborhoods shown to their white partners, while whites were shown houses in higher-percent-black neighborhoods in only 26 percent of the audits. Correspondingly, whites were shown houses in higher income neighborhoods than those shown their black partners in 45 percent of the audits, while blacks were shown houses in higher income neighborhoods only 31 percent of the time. Newburger's results also suggested that differences in neighborhood characteristics may be more likely for houses recommended for future inspection than for houses actually shown to white and black auditors.

However, the magnitude of the differences in neighborhood racial composition for houses shown or recommended to whites versus blacks was very small. For example, of the 432 audits in which blacks were shown houses in higher-percent-black neighborhoods than the neighborhoods shown to their white counterparts, in 327 (76 percent) the difference in percentage of blacks between the two auditors was less than 2.5 percentage points. Moreover, in 72 percent of all cases, both the black and the white auditor were shown houses in neighborhoods that were less than 2.5 percent black. In other words, although the incidence of differential treatment was statistically significant, the size of the differences was extremely small.

The Feins and Bratt study of housing discrimination in Boston focused primarily on differences in housing availability in seven racially mixed neighborhoods. Two all-black and four predominantly white neighborhoods were excluded from the study. The audit sample was randomly drawn from advertisements for rentals and sales in the *Boston Globe* and in local neighborhood papers. Auditors were instructed to ask for a specific advertised housing unit. This "anchored" the audits, ensuring that both minority and white house seekers made the same initial request of the real estate agent. Auditors were subsequently instructed to request other units similar in price and size and in the same broadly defined neighborhood.

Although the measurement and analysis of steering were only a secondary goal of the Boston study, an attempt was made to associate the locations of houses shown to blacks and whites with the racial composition of the neighborhood. The results showed no strong significant differences in the racial composition of neighborhoods in which the white and black auditors were shown houses.

Pearce (1979) focused more explicitly on steering in her audit study of the Detroit metropolitan area. Audits were conducted at a random sample of agents' offices. They were not related to specific advertised units, and the visits by white and minority auditors were sometimes months apart. By design, all auditor teams posed as professionals with above-average incomes who were new to home buying.

Using these audit data, Pearce explored differences in (1) neighborhood racial composition; (2) the average house value of the city where the house shown was located; and (3) the distance of the house shown from black population areas. The results indicated that blacks were shown houses in higher-percent-black neighborhoods and in cities with lower house values. Specifically, the neighborhoods where blacks were shown houses had an average black population of 4 percent and an average house value of $21,500, compared with an average black population of 1 percent and an average house value of $22,500 for neighborhoods shown to whites.

To complement these statistical results, Pearce mapped metropolitan Detroit, showing both Census tract and city boundaries. She then plotted the point pattern of houses shown to black and white auditors. The geographic distribution of the two point patterns demonstrated visually that blacks were systematically shown houses in areas closer to black population centers. On average, houses shown to blacks were approximately one mile closer to predominantly black tracts than were houses shown to whites.

Taken together, the three past audit studies suggest that steering occurs, with blacks shown or recommended housing units in neighborhoods that have a higher percentage of blacks than those shown or recommended to comparable white home buyers. But the differences in neighborhood characteristics for white and black home seekers are typically quite small. However, two of these studies focused on individual cities, and the one national analysis of steering is limited by serious data constraints. Therefore, a primary objective of the HDS was to conduct a systematic and comprehensive analysis of steering for both black and Hispanic home buyers in large urban areas throughout the United States.[3]

Housing Discrimination Study

The Housing Discrimination Study implemented essentially the same audit methodology as that developed in HUD's Housing Market Practices Survey. A sample of 25 metropolitan areas was selected to yield nationally representative estimates of differential treatment experienced by minority home seekers in major urban areas.[4] In each sampled metropolitan area, advertisements were randomly selected from the major metropolitan newspaper, and teams of minority and majority auditors visited sampled sales and rental agents to inquire about the availability of housing units. Income and other household characteristics of the auditor pairs were assigned to be the same and to qualify both team members for the advertised housing unit.

To ensure that both members of each audit team made identical opening requests for housing, each HDS audit began with a request for a specific unit selected from the most recent Sunday newspaper. This research design decision may have limited the extent to which audited agents could have engaged in steering, since both minority and majority auditors started out by asking for housing in the same location. Nevertheless, agents were given ample opportunities to engage in steering because auditors were instructed to ask about other housing units of similar size and price, whether or not the advertised unit was available. If asked by the agent for neighborhood or community preferences, the auditors were noncommittal, indicating only that they were looking for the right-size house in their price range.

It is time-consuming and expensive for auditors to visit a large number of houses with real estate agents. Therefore, for analysis of steering to be effective, it is essential that auditors obtain a complete address for every house that the agent recommends and would be willing to show to the auditor. HDS auditors were instructed to inspect as many houses as possible and to obtain the addresses of other houses by asking the agent to recommend houses that they might visit together at another time or that the auditor might drive by to determine their suitability. This enabled the HDS steering analysis to extend beyond houses that the agent and auditor actually visited, including addresses that the agent identified as available and recommended for inspection by the auditor.

Analysis of racial and ethnic steering requires a linkage between addresses identified as available to minority and majority home seekers and the characteristics of surrounding neighborhoods. For each metropolitan area in which audits were conducted, data were assembled on the socioeconomic characteristics of census tracts within the urban area. At the time the analysis was conducted, 1990 census data were not yet available, and 1980 census data would have been of limited value for this analysis, since racial and ethnic change could be expected to have occurred in many tracts. Therefore, projected values for 1988 census tract population, racial and ethnic composition, and incomes were obtained for each of the 25 audit sites from National Decision Systems, one of several firms that offer estimates of changes in tract characteristics.[5] Addresses of all for-sale houses and condominiums inspected by or recommended for inspection to HDS auditors were linked to their census tract identifiers, using a process known as "geo-coding." Overall, 85 percent of the sales addresses were successfully geo-coded, providing a total of 8,588 addresses for statistical steering analysis (see appendix 3.A).

Measurement Issues

Analysis of racial and ethnic steering focuses on differences in treatment between minority and majority home buyers with respect to neighborhood attributes. Specifically, the following hypothesis is tested:

> When minority home seekers are shown or recommended housing units, the addresses are in neighborhoods that have a higher percentage of minority residents or are less affluent than the neighborhoods shown or recommended to comparable majority home seekers.

Results are based on audit-by-audit measures of differences between the treatment of the majority home seeker and the treatment of the minority partner. Specifically, for each audit the average neighborhood attributes of houses shown or recommended were computed for each auditor. Then differences in average values for the minority and majority team members were analyzed.[6]

Steering is a form of discrimination that is contingent upon treatment received by auditors at early stages in the housing market transaction. Specifically, steering can occur only if both auditors are told that at least one housing unit is available. Thus, analysis of racial and ethnic steering in the HDS was conducted only for those sales audits in which both minority and majority auditors were told about at least one housing unit.

The study also tested a more stringent definition of the circumstances in which steering might occur, limiting analysis to cases in which both auditors were shown at least one unit other than the anchoring, advertised unit. This stringent definition reflects the view that steering cannot occur until an agent goes beyond the advertised unit that was initially requested and shows or recommends other units that may differ for minority and majority customers. Results reported here, however, include the anchoring units in the statistical analysis because it is possible to envision circumstances in which steering occurred even though one of the two auditors was shown only the advertised unit. For example, suppose the advertised unit is in a neighborhood with a low percentage of minorities. An agent seeking to steer minority customers away from this unit might show the advertised unit to the majority auditor, while showing a unit in some other neighborhood to the minority auditor. Or the agent might show both auditors the advertised unit but also show the minority auditor additional houses in other neighborhoods.

Both continuous and categorical measures of differences in treatment were constructed to quantify steering. The categorical measures reflect the *incidence* of steering—the probability is that steering will occur. Continuous measures, on the other hand, reflect the *severity* of differential treatment—the magnitude of differences, on average, between neighborhoods shown or recommended to minority versus majority home seekers. Together, incidence and severity measures provide a comprehensive picture of patterns of racial and ethnic steering, indicating not only how often steering occurs but how big a difference it makes with regard to the neighborhood characteristics of houses shown and recommended to minority and majority home buyers.

The incidence of racial and ethnic steering is defined as the share of cases in which a majority auditor is shown or recommended houses in neighborhoods that have a higher-percent-majority population, higher per capita incomes, or higher median house values than neighborhoods shown or recommended to the minority partner. To construct this measure, each audit was classified as "majority higher," "minority higher," or "no difference" for each of the following neighborhood attributes: (1) estimated percentage of white or Anglo residents, (2) 1988 estimated per capita income, and (3) 1980 median house value.

For each of these neighborhood attributes, a threshold value was defined beyond which the two members of an audit team are deemed to have received differential treatment.[7] These thresholds, which are necessarily arbitrary, were selected to capture meaningful differences in neighborhood characteristics. In other words, differences in percentage if whites of less than 5 percentage points, in per capita income of less than $2,500, and in median house value of less than $5,000 were not considered meaningful differences in treatment between minority and majority auditors, and were not classified as steering.

The share of audits in which the majority was offered houses in neighborhoods with higher values (beyond the threshold) for one of these attributes represents the incidence of steering—or the probability that steering will occur when minority and majority home seekers search for housing by responding to advertisements in their metropolitan newspapers. Also reported here is the share of cases in which minority auditors were shown or recommended houses in neighborhoods with higher-percent-white (or Anglo) populations or higher incomes and house values.[8]

To summarize the incidence of differential treatment with respect to neighborhood attributes, a composite index was developed based on neighborhood percentage of blacks, per capita income, and median house value. The following rules were employed for construction of this summary index:

☐ An audit was classified as "majority higher" if the majority auditor had higher values for percent white or Anglo, income, or house value, while the minority auditor did not have higher values on any attribute.

☐ An audit was classified as "minority higher " if the minority auditor had higher values for percent white or Anglo, income, or house value, while the majority auditor did not have higher values on any attribute.

☐ An audit was classified as "no difference" if neither auditor had higher values for any neighborhood attribute, or if both had higher values on one or more.[9]

The severity of steering is defined as the magnitude of the difference in neighborhood characteristics between addresses shown and recommended to minority versus majority home seekers. Specifically, it is computed as the average value for all white or Anglo auditors minus the average value for all black or Hispanic auditors. Audits in which steering occurred as well as audits in which no steering occurred are incorporated into these calculations, so that the resulting severity measures reflect the overall difference between neighborhoods shown and recommended to white or Anglo home buyers and those shown and recommended to their minority counterparts.

INCIDENCE AND SEVERITY OF STEERING IN THE HOUSING DISCRIMINATION STUDY

This section presents the findings from the HDS steering analysis, using data for urban housing markets across the nation. The first part focuses on the incidence and severity of steering, comparing the experience of black and white home buyers, as well as that of Hispanic and Anglo home buyers. The next part analyzes the neighborhood characteristics of houses included in the Housing Discrimination Study sample and assesses differences in the attributes of houses advertised, shown, and recommended.

Incidence and Severity of Steering

Table 3.1 reports the incidence of differences in neighborhood attributes beyond threshold values for all units shown and recommended to white and black home seekers. For audits in which both partners were either shown or recommended at least one address, the table reports the percentage of audits in which neighborhood values were higher for whites, the percentage in which values were higher for blacks, and the percentage in which both auditors received the same treatment (within threshold ranges). In addition, the standard error term for each of these percentages is reported, indicating that all reported incidence measures are significantly different from zero at a 95 percent confidence interval.[10]

These results indicate that for cases in which agents identified available addresses, neighborhoods shown and recommended to whites had a higher percentage of whites in 12 percent of the audits, higher incomes in 11 percent, and higher values in 17 percent. Overall, blacks face a 21 percent chance of being steered to neighborhoods that are

Table 3.1 INCIDENCE OF STEERING FOR BLACK AND WHITE HOME BUYERS

Neighborhood attribute	Percentage of audits	Standard error
Percent white (1988)		
No difference	82.7	4.21
Majority higher	11.8	3.45
Minority higher	5.6	1.24
Per capita income (1988)		
No difference	82.5	1.96
Majority higher	10.6	1.61
Minority higher	6.9	0.81
Median house value (1980)		
No difference	70.7	2.75
Majority higher	17.2	1.83
Minority higher	12.1	1.43
Composite index		
No difference	67.5	2.91
Majority higher	20.9	2.57
Minority higher	11.6	1.18

Note: Results are based on a total of 828 sales audits in which both auditors were shown or recommended at least one house. Incidences of higher outcomes for majority and minority auditors are all statistically significant at a 95 percent confidence level. Incidences with no difference are all significantly different from 100 percent at a 95 percent confidence level.

either less white or less affluent. Thus, black home buyers for whom houses are made available face a significant chance of being steered toward neighborhoods that are more black or less affluent than the neighborhoods where their white counterparts are shown and recommended houses.[11]

Not surprisingly, the incidence of differential treatment observed varies with the definition of threshold differences in neighborhood characteristics. As discussed earlier, audits were classified as "no difference" if differences between the attributes of neighborhoods shown and recommended to blacks versus whites did not exceed threshold values. Table 3.2 presents the share of audits with small, moderate, and large differences in neighborhood attributes. To illustrate, a "small" difference in neighborhood percent white is defined as less than 5 percentage points, a "moderate" difference is between 5 and 10 percentage points, and a "large" difference is greater than 10 percentage points. Comparable ranges are defined for the other neighborhood attributes as well, as indicated in the table.

Most of the differential treatment that occurred is of a relatively low degree. Because most of the units advertised, shown, and recommended to HDS auditors were in predominantly white, middle-class neighborhoods, few home seekers encountered large differences in treatment. When they did, however, blacks were likely to be shown and recommended neighborhoods that were lower percent white,

Table 3.2 DEGREE OF STEERING FOR BLACK AND WHITE HOME BUYERS

	Majority higher		Minority higher	
Neighborhood attribute	Percentage of audits	Standard error	Percentage of audits	Standard error
Percent white (1988)				
Small difference (<5%)	18.7	2.44	21.2	2.38
Moderate difference (5%–10%)	4.1	1.25	2.9	0.65
Large difference (>10%)	7.6	2.47	2.6	0.69
Per capita income (1988)				
Small difference (<$2,500)	18.2	1.97	20.9	2.18
Moderate difference ($2,500–$5,000)	5.5	1.03	4.5	0.66
Large difference (>$5,000)	5.1	1.56	2.5	0.50
Median house value (1980)				
Small difference (<$5,000)	14.8	1.87	12.3	1.92
Moderate difference ($5,000–$10,000)	5.6	0.63	5.7	0.83
Large difference (>$10,000)	11.7	1.58	6.4	0.91

Note: Results are based on a total of 828 sales audits in which both auditors were shown or recommended at least one house.

were lower income, and had lower house values. Specifically, blacks were steered to substantially less-white neighborhoods in 8 percent of the audits, to substantially lower-income neighborhoods in 5 percent of the audits, and to substantially lower-value neighborhoods in 12 percent of the audits.

The incidence measures presented earlier reflect the probability that blacks will encounter steering but not the magnitude of differences in neighborhood characteristics. Table 3.3 reports the severity of differences in steering between blacks and whites by comparing average values of neighborhood attributes across audits.[12] The first column in the table applies to units shown and recommended and the second applies to units shown and recommended, other than the advertised unit. The third column applies only to units, other than the advertised unit, that the agent actually showed to an auditor, and the fourth column refers to units recommended for further inspection.[13] These last two columns were included to test the hypothesis that the behavior of agents may differ for houses they go to the trouble of showing relative to those they recommend for future inspection.

These results show that differences in neighborhood attributes for black and white home seekers are very small. When the advertised unit is included in the comparison, the average percentage of whites in the neighborhoods shown and recommended is less than 2 points

Table 3.3 SEVERITY OF STEERING FOR BLACK AND WHITE HOME BUYERS

Neighborhood attribute	All units	Excluding the advertised unit		
		Shown & rec.	Units shown	Units rec.
Percent white (1988)				
Majority average	91.5	90.5	91.8	87.9
Minority average	90.1	87.7	90.6	84.0
T-statistic	3.11**	4.78**	3.25**	3.29**
Per capita income (1988)				
Majority average	17,020	16,824	17,471	15,527
Minority average	16,863	16,696	17,401	16,246
T-statistic	2.16*	0.97	0.49	−2.23*
Median house value (1980)				
Majority Average	69,708	68,383	70,690	63,466
Minority Average	68,485	66,728	68,796	65,341
T-statistic	4.60**	3.04**	3.04**	−1.51

**Difference between the means is statistically significant at a 99 percent confidence level using a paired t-test.
*Difference between the means is statistically significant at a 95 percent confidence level using a paired t-test.

lower for black auditors than for white auditors, and the median house value is less than $1,300 lower. Differences in per capita income are not statistically significant. Once beyond the advertised unit, blacks were shown and recommended houses in neighborhoods that were only 3 percentage points less white, with $1,700 lower median house values, than those of their white teammates.

Differential treatment is more severe for houses recommended for future inspection than for those actually inspected. In fact, for addresses recommended (but not advertised or shown), the average neighborhood is 4 percentage points less white for black auditors than for white auditors. For units actually inspected, on the other hand, the difference is only 1 percentage point. In addition, for both blacks and whites, the neighborhoods recommended for future inspection are higher percent black than neighborhoods actually shown. These results suggest that agents advertise and show houses in neighborhoods with a very low percentage of blacks, and that, given the narrow range of variation in these neighborhoods, the severity of any steering that may occur is necessarily low. Agents recommend a wider range of neighborhoods for future inspection, and consequently the magnitude of differences in treatment between white and black customers on this characteristic is greater.

The next set of tables presents a national analysis of differences in treatment between Hispanic and Anglo home seekers. Table 3.4 reports the incidence of steering for audits in which both Anglo and Hispanic auditors were shown or recommended at least one address. In general, Hispanics appear just as likely as blacks to be steered to minority neighborhoods and to less affluent neighborhoods. Specifically, neighborhoods shown and recommended to Anglos had a higher percentage of Anglos in 12 percent of the audits, higher incomes in 11 percent, and higher values in 17 percent. Overall, the incidence of steering experienced by Anglos and Hispanics is 21 percent.

As was observed for blacks, the incidence of differential treatment varies with the definitions of threshold differences in neighborhood characteristics. Table 3.5 reports the share of audits with small, moderate, and large differences in neighborhood attributes. Because most of the units advertised, shown, and recommended to HDS auditors were in predominantly Anglo neighborhoods, few home seekers encountered large differences in treatment. When they did, however, Hispanics (like blacks) were likely to be shown and recommended neighborhoods that were lower percent Anglo, were lower income levels, and had lower house values. Specifically, Hispanics were steered to substantially less-Anglo neighborhoods in 8 percent of the

Table 3.4 INCIDENCE OF STEERING FOR HISPANIC AND ANGLO HOME BUYERS

Neighborhood attribute	Percentage of audits	Standard error
Percent Anglo (1988)		
No difference	80.0	4.94
Anglo higher	12.4	2.97
Hispanic higher	7.6	2.20
Per capita income (1988)		
No difference	81.9	2.83
Anglo higher	10.8	2.01
Hispanic higher	7.3	1.13
Median house value (1980)		
No difference	67.7	3.35
Anglo higher	16.8	2.11
Hispanic higher	15.5	1.73
Composite index		
No difference	62.1	3.44
Anglo higher	21.3	2.14
Hispanic higher	16.7	1.77

Note: Results are based on a total of 847 sales audits in which both auditors were shown or recommended at least one house. Incidences of higher outcomes for majority and minority auditors are all statistically significant at a 95 percent confidence level. Incidences with no difference are all significantly different from 100 percent at a 95 percent confidence level.

audits, to substantially lower income neighborhoods in 4 percent of the audits, and to substantially lower value neighborhoods in 10 percent of the audits.

As for blacks and whites, the severity of differences in neighborhood attributes for houses shown and recommended to Hispanic and Anglo auditors is small but statistically significant. Table 3.6 presents average values across audits of neighborhood attributes for houses shown and recommended to Hispanics compared with those shown and recommended to their Anglo counterparts. Across all audits in which both Hispanics and Anglos were shown or recommended at least one unit, the average percent Anglo is only 1 point lower for Hispanics, per capita income is less than $300 lower, and the median house value is about $500 lower. Differential treatment is no more severe for houses recommended for future inspection than for those actually inspected. In fact, for Hispanics and Anglos, there are no statistically significant differences in neighborhood characteristics for addresses recommended for future inspection. This pattern differs from that observed for blacks and whites, in which blacks are more

Table 3.5 DEGREE OF STEERING FOR HISPANIC AND ANGLO HOME BUYERS

	Anglo higher		Hispanic higher	
Neighborhood attribute	Percentage of audits	Standard error	Percentage of audits	Standard error
Percent Anglo (1988)				
Small difference (<5%)	22.3	2.26	21.8	3.17
Moderate difference (5%–10%)	4.6	1.13	3.2	1.11
Large difference (>10%)	7.9	2.15	4.4	1.38
Per capita income (1988)				
Small difference (<$2,500)	24.3	2.05	21.1	2.75
Moderate difference ($2,500–$5,000)	7.0	1.22	4.8	0.83
Large difference (>$5,000)	3.8	1.11	2.4	0.71
Median house value (1980)				
Small difference (<$5,000)	18.6	2.23	12.5	1.17
Moderate difference ($5,000–$10,000)	7.1	1.02	7.7	1.49
Large difference (>$10,000)	9.7	1.61	7.9	1.04

Note: Results are based on a total of 828 sales audits in which both auditors were shown or recommended at least one house.

Table 3.6 SEVERITY OF STEERING FOR HISPANIC AND ANGLO HOME BUYERS

		Excluding the advertised unit		
Neighborhood attribute	All units	Shown & rec.	Units shown	Units rec.
Percent anglo (1988)				
Anglo average	85.3	87.4	89.0	82.5
Hispanic average	84.4	86.6	87.8	83.5
T-statistic	5.26**	3.23**	2.53*	−1.58
Per capita income (1988)				
Anglo average	16,397	17,214	17,448	16,238
Hispanic average	16,128	16,576	16,776	15,397
T-statistic	3.04**	3.41**	5.40**	2.74*
Median house value (1980)				
Anglo Average	74,873	77,163	79,376	69,992
Hispanic Average	74,353	76,236	77,702	68,702
T-statistic	2.29*	2.37*	2.80**	1.31

**Difference between the means is statistically significant at a 99 percent confidence level using a paired t-test.
*Difference between the means is statistically significant at a 95 percent confidence level using a paired t-test.

likely to encounter differential treatment for units recommended for future inspection and less likely to encounter it for units actually inspected.

Neighborhood Characteristics of Audited Addresses

As explained earlier, the HDS audits were anchored to a random sample of addresses advertised in major newspapers of 25 metropolitan sites. Thus, the agents who were audited, the locations in which audits were initiated, and the locational cues initially provided by auditors were all constrained by the spatial distribution of advertised addresses. This section focuses on the neighborhood attributes of the sample of advertised units, as well as the locational characteristics of agents' offices and of other houses shown and recommended to auditors.

The typical for-sale house advertised in a major metropolitan newspaper is located in a predominantly white, middle- to upper-income neighborhood. Table 3.7 presents average values of census tract characteristics for advertised addresses, for other addresses shown to auditors, for addresses that were recommended for future inspection, and for the offices of audited sales agents.[14] Data from both the black/white and the Hispanic/Anglo audits are presented in this table.

Across the black/white audits, the average advertised unit was in a neighborhood with an 8 percent black population, a per capita income of $17,000, and a median 1980 house value of $69,000. Fewer than 20 percent of the housing units in these neighborhoods dated to the prewar era, and two-thirds of neighborhood households owned their homes. In contrast, the average census tract in the black/white audit sites was 20 percent black, with a per capita income of about $13,000, and a median 1980 house value of $57,000. Almost one-third of the housing stock was built before 1940, and the homeownership rate was about 55 percent.

The average neighborhood income and housing characteristics for advertised units in the Hispanic/Anglo sample were essentially the same as those in the black/white sample. The Hispanic population in neighborhoods surrounding advertised units averaged 16 percent, compared with an average of 24 percent across all tracts in the Hispanic/Anglo audit sites.

Addresses other than the advertised unit shown to auditors were in even more predominantly white and affluent neighborhoods. However, as suggested earlier, agents appear to recommend addresses for future inspection in more diverse locations. For example, among His-

Table 3.7 AVERAGE NEIGHBORHOOD CHARACTERISTICS FOR SALES AUDIT ADDRESSES (National Sample)

Neighborhood attribute	All units shown and rec.	Advertised units	Other units shown	Other units rec.	Agent office	All census tracts in sampled metro areas
Black/white audits						
Percent black (1988)	8.75	7.91	7.29	10.10	7.17	19.87
Per capita income (1988)	16,882	17,002	17,282	16,039	18,261	13,410
Median house value (1980)	69,154	68,690	70,254	64,567	75,645	56,913
Percentage of old housing (1980)	17.89	17.87	16.78	17.78	20.60	31.32
Percentage of home owners (1980)	67.19	66.93	68.90	66.28	62.92	54.85
Total audits	988	798	524	458	918	—
Hispanic/Anglo audits						
Percent Hispanic (1988)	15.64	15.76	11.91	16.04	15.29	23.78
Per capita income (1988)	16,279	16,159	17,337	15,516	17,888	13,134
Median house value (1980)	74,841	74,389	78,413	71,130	82,795	63,474
Percentage of old housing (1980)	16.07	16.36	16.62	15.59	20.30	30.35
Percentage of home owners (1980)	69.64	70.28	69.70	69.88	61.47	48.98
Total audits	1009	827	565	455	919	—

Note: The sample of metropolitan areas in which black/white audits were conducted overlaps with, but is not identical to, the sample of metropolitan areas in which Hispanic/Anglo audits were conducted. Average values of tract characteristics for various groups of addresses are calculated by averaging across units in each audit, and then averaging across audits, applying the applicable sampling weights. All differences between average neighborhood characteristics of audit addresses and average neighborhood characteristics for the sampled metro areas are statistically significant at the 95 percent confidence level.

panic/Anglo audits the average unit recommended (but not shown) was in a 16 percent Hispanic neighborhood, while the average unit actually inspected was in a 12 percent Hispanic neighborhood. The differential is smaller with regard to the black/white audits, however. Even among recommended units, the average unit was in only a 10 percent black neighborhood, half the average percentage across all census tracts in the black/white audit sites.

The offices of audited real estate agents were also in predominantly white neighborhoods, indicating agents who advertise in major metropolitan newspapers have offices in predominantly white, affluent neighborhoods and do most of their business in these neighborhoods. In fact, the racial or ethnic composition of the neighborhood surrounding an agent's office is an excellent predictor of the composition of the addresses he advertises, shows, and recommends. A simple ordinary least squares regression relating racial or ethnic composition for addresses shown or recommended in an audit to the racial or ethnic composition of the agent's office indicates a strong, positive relationship (see table 3.8).

Thus, a random sample of advertisements in major metropolitan newspapers yields very few addresses in minority or integrated neighborhoods. And when home seekers inquire about the availability of units other than those advertised, most of the addresses shown or recommended are in predominantly white or Anglo neighborhoods. Agents tend to show houses in the most white and affluent neighbor-

Table 3.8 AGENT'S OFFICE LOCATION AND CHARACTERISTICS OF ADDRESSES SHOWN AND RECOMMENDED

Statistic	Coefficient	Standard error
Black/white audits		
Average percent black for neighborhoods of houses shown and recommended		
Intercept	6.12	0.53
Percent black for neighborhood of agent's office	0.37	0.03
R^2	12.2%	
Hispanic/Anglo audits		
Average percent Hispanic for neighborhoods of houses shown and recommended		
Intercept	7.58	0.52
Percent Hispanic for neighborhood of agent's office	0.50	0.02
R^2	38.9%	

hoods, while recommending addresses in neighborhoods with a slightly more diverse range of attributes.

One possible explanation for the characteristics of neighborhoods included in the audit sample may be that the anchoring procedure employed in the Housing Discrimination Study limited the range of neighborhoods shown and recommended. If agents tend to advertise addresses that are in white neighborhoods, an auditor's initial request for the advertised unit may send such strong locational signals that all other addresses shown and recommended tend to be in the same vicinity. Yet HDS auditors gave agents ample opportunity to steer by asking for information about additional homes for sale in any neighborhood. Moreover, the neighborhood attributes of houses shown and recommended in the HDS are essentially the same as in the 1977 Housing Market Practices Survey (HMPS), in which auditors did not explicitly ask for the advertised unit. For example, in 89 percent of the HMPS audits in which both auditors saw houses, the houses were all in neighborhoods that were less than 10 percent black. Thus, it does not appear that the differential treatment of minority neighborhoods observed in the HDS is a function of the anchoring procedures.

To explore these patterns further, the focus of the statistical analysis was shifted to the full set of census tracts in the 25 metropolitan areas audited, recording for each tract, whether any addresses within the tract were shown or recommended to one of the HDS auditors. This made it possible to compare the neighborhoods where audited real estate agents were advertising and marketing houses with those in which houses were not advertised, recommended, or shown. Neighborhoods not shown averaged more than 21 percent black versus only about 7 percent black in the neighborhoods where houses were shown or recommended. The percentage of Hispanics was also higher in the neighborhoods not shown, although the differential was much smaller than for the percentage of blacks. Neighborhoods not shown or recommended also had fewer home owners, lower incomes, more older housing, and lower house values.

What is the cause of these differences? Black and Hispanic neighborhoods tend to have more rental units, and to be older, and less affluent than white or Anglo neighborhoods. Thus minority neighborhoods may be underrepresented in the HDS sample simply because they do not offer as many attractive sales opportunities. To test this hypothesis, table 3.9 presents a multivariate model estimating the independent effects of neighborhood race and ethnicity after controlling for the size of the owner-occupied housing stock, the age of the stock, income levels, and owner-occupied house values. The depen-

Table 3.9 DETERMINANTS OF NEIGHBORHOOD MARKETING

Logit	Total national sample
Intercept	$-2.557**$
	(0.09)
1988 percent black	$-1.47*$
1988 percent Hispanic	$-3.64*$
	(0.383)
1988 percent Hispanic squared	$-5.29**$
	(0.522)
1988 per capita income	$0.249**$
	(0.042)
Percentage of 1980 housing stock built by 1940	$-0.308**$
	(0.103)
1980 median house value	$0.028**$
	(0.009)
Number of owner-occupant households	$0.048**$
	(0.003)
R^2	0.332

Note: Based on logistic estimation. Dependent variable is whether a tract had houses advertised, recommended, or shown in the HDS audit sample. Numbers in parentheses are standard errors.
**Significant at the 99 percent level.
*Significant at the 95 percent level.

dent variable is whether any addresses in a census tract were shown or recommended. Since this dependent variable is a dichotomous (yes or no) outcome, maximum-likelihood estimates were employed, and a logistic multiple regression model was fitted to the data for the national sample and for the five in-depth sites.[15]

As anticipated, higher per capita incomes and house values, as well as a larger and newer owner-occupied stock, all increase the probability that addresses in a particular neighborhood will be shown or recommended. However, even after controlling for income levels, house values, owner-occupancy rates, and age of the housing stock, higher percentages of blacks substantially reduce the probability that addresses in that neighborhood will be shown or recommended. Similarly, the size of the Hispanic population has a significant independent impact on the probability that addresses will be shown or recommended. The impact of the Hispanic variable is nonlinear. Specifically, the probability of market activity declines more gradually at low levels of Hispanic population than at higher levels.[16]

NEIGHBORHOOD MARKETING PRACTICES

Analysis of neighborhood characteristics for houses shown and recommended in the HDS reveals that both minority and majority home buyers are limited in their neighborhood choices in two ways. Black and Hispanic home buyers who are shown and recommended addresses are likely to be steered to neighborhoods that are less white and less affluent than those shown and recommended to comparable white or Anglo home buyers. However, the differences in racial or ethnic composition of neighborhoods shown and recommended to whites and Anglos versus those shown and recommended to blacks and Hispanics are small. More important, all home buyers who start their search by inquiring about the availability of units advertised in major metropolitan newspapers are likely to be shown and recommended houses in predominantly white or Anglo neighborhoods rather than in integrated or minority neighborhoods. Even after controlling for the size and value of a neighborhood's owner-occupied stock, minority and integrated neighborhoods are significantly less likely to be advertised, shown, or recommended than comparable white or Anglo neighborhoods.

These findings raise several key questions about how houses in minority and integrated neighborhoods are marketed and about how minority households search for housing:

☐ Are houses in minority and integrated neighborhoods less likely to be advertised in major metropolitan newspapers than houses in comparable neighborhoods that are predominantly white?

☐ Are houses in minority and integrated neighborhoods advertised in other newspapers or through some other mechanisms?

☐ Do agents who advertise and market houses in predominantly white or Anglo neighborhoods also list and sell houses in minority neighborhoods, or does a different group of agents dominate the minority market?

☐ Do minority home seekers use different sources of information from those used by comparable whites to search for housing?

In an effort to address these questions, Urban Institute researchers conducted an exploratory study of neighborhood marketing and housing search behavior in the Washington, D.C., metropolitan area, which is described below.

Patterns of Newspaper Advertising

Four sets of census tracts were selected for study in the Washington, D.C., metropolitan area. Each set consists of three tracts—one predominantly black, one integrated, and one predominantly white—that are comparable with respect to house values, income levels, and homeownership rates.[17] Appendix C summarizes the characteristics of each set. Two sets of tracts are located within the District of Columbia, and two sets are located in Prince George's County, a moderately priced suburban jurisdiction that has experienced rapid growth in black population over the 1980s. All the selected tracts are middle- to upper-income neighborhoods, in which the majority of households are owner-occupants.

A "windshield" survey was conducted in each study tract to inventory all addresses with a for-sale sign displayed on a given weekend.[18] This inventory represented the best approximation of the pool of houses on the market in the study neighborhoods at a given point in time. Researchers then tabulated the share of those addresses advertised in The Washington Post on the same weekend or any of the preceding three weekends and the share advertised as open houses.[19] In addition, researchers conducted an exhaustive review of neighborhood and community newspapers that might be used to advertise housing opportunities in the Washington metropolitan area. Surprisingly, there does not appear to be any significant volume of real estate advertising in black newspapers, nor was any important advertising vehicle other than The Washington Post identified for the District of Columbia. One of the predominantly white study tracts in Prince George's County is served by a community newspaper with a substantial real estate advertising section—The Bowie Blade—and advertisements in this newspaper were considered separately.

The results of this exploratory analysis support the hypothesis that black and integrated neighborhoods are marketed differently than predominantly white neighborhoods, even after controlling for differences in house values and income levels. Table 3.10 presents the share of for-sale houses in each neighborhood that was advertised in The Washington Post and the share advertised as open houses. Overall, only 14 percent of the houses for sale in predominantly black neighborhoods were advertised in The Washington Post, compared with 32 percent of the houses in integrated neighborhoods, and 46 percent of the houses in predominantly white neighborhoods. Open houses were advertised for 14 percent of the houses for sale in black neighbor-

Table 3.10 HOUSES FOR SALE, ADVERTISED, AND ADVERTISED AS OPEN HOUSE IN WASHINGTON, D.C., AREA NEIGHBORHOODS

Neighborhoods	Number for sale	Percentage advertised	Percentage advertised as open house
Washington, D.C.			
Set A			
White	45	73.3	71.1
Integrated	42	35.7	33.3
Black	8	0.0	0.0
Set B			
White	24	41.7	41.7
Integrated	31	38.7	38.7
Black	14	42.9	42.9
Prince George's County			
Set A			
White	31	38.7	9.7
Integrated	21	33.3	9.5
Black	5	0.0	0.0
Set B			
White	20	40.0	15.0
Integrated	12	0.0	0.0
Black	15	0.0	0.0

hoods, 26 percent of those in integrated neighborhoods, and 41 percent of those in predominantly white neighborhoods.

In one set of D.C. tracts, all three neighborhoods received the same level of advertising. In the remaining three sets, none of the houses for sale in the predominantly black neighborhoods were advertised. And in two sets (one in Prince George's County and one in D.C.) the houses for sale in the integrated tract were advertised at a lower rate than the houses in the predominantly white tract. When advertisements in *The Bowie Blade* are added to the tally for the predominantly white tract in Prince George's set A, the share of advertised units for this neighborhood increases to 52 percent, and the share advertised as open houses increases to 16 percent.

Two exploratory studies by other researchers yielded similar results. In Milwaukee, as a result of a court settlement, the local fair-housing group had access to information on all the listings of a major real estate company active in a racially changing area. This area included a predominantly white section, an integrated section, and a section (adjacent to Milwaukee's central black neighborhood) that was becoming increasingly black. House values did not vary significantly across the three neighborhoods. Over a three-year period, researchers monitored the firm's advertising in Milwaukee's major newspaper, in suburban weekly newspapers, and in two black-owned newspapers. They found that houses for sale in integrated or black neighborhoods were advertised in the *Milwaukee Journal* at half the rate of comparable houses in white neighborhoods and were one-fourth as likely to have an open house.[20]

In conjunction with the work Urban Institute researchers have been conducting in Washington, Harriet Newburger analyzed real estate marketing practices in an area of Boston that includes white, integrated, and predominantly black neighborhoods and in which house values do not appear to vary significantly among neighborhoods. She finds that there are substantially fewer open houses in the black and integrated sections of the area, relative to the number of for-sale signs. Moreover, the mix of brokers active in these areas is somewhat different in the black and integrated sections than in the predominantly white sections, and the agents active in the predominantly black section are less likely to participate in a multiple listing service.

Taken together, the exploratory studies in Washington, Milwaukee, and Boston strongly support the hypothesis that black and integrated neighborhoods are marketed differently than predominantly white neighborhoods and that black and integrated neighborhoods are less likely to be advertised in the newspaper and less likely to be marketed through open houses. This finding appears to apply across quite different housing markets and to hold whether the focus is on all the listings and advertisements of a single firm or on the advertisements of all firms with listings in selected neighborhoods. Moreover, there is no support for an argument that houses in integrated and black neighborhoods are heavily advertised in black newspapers. Nevertheless, findings on this question may differ substantially from one metropolitan area to another.

Patterns of Housing Search

The finding that houses for sale in minority and integrated neighborhoods are unlikely to be advertised in major metropolitan newspapers raises questions about how minority households find out about the housing units they buy and whether they search for housing differently than do comparable white households. One plausible hypothesis is that minority home buyers are aware of the costs imposed by discrimination in housing availability practiced by agents who advertise through major metropolitan newspapers and that they attempt to min-imize these costs by using other search mechanisms. A related hy-pothesis is that many black and Hispanic households may prefer in-tegrated or minority neighborhoods to predominantly white or Anglo neighborhoods and that they therefore use search strategies that max-imize information about housing opportunities in those neighbor-hoods. If minority households do rely upon different search strategies than white households, then that might help explain why houses in minority and integrated neighborhoods are not advertised in major metropolitan newspapers, since real estate agents would know that the primary buyers of houses in these neighborhoods do not use this information source.

To provide preliminary insights on possible differences in search behavior between white and black home buyers, Urban Institute re-searchers conducted a survey of recent home buyers in Washington, D.C., and Prince George's County, focusing on a limited number of middle- to high-income census tracts that include the four sets of tracts discussed earlier. Households that purchased homes during the last two quarters of 1990 were sent a brief mail questionnaire asking about the sources of information they used and the extent of their reliance upon real estate agents. A total of 575 questionnaires were mailed, and 193 (or 34 percent) were completed and returned. Al-though this sample is small, it provides suggestive insights into hous-ing search behavior by black and white households in the Washington metropolitan area.

In general, blacks and whites appear to use very similar search strategies, with only modest differences. As shown in table 3.11, blacks are somewhat less likely than whites to use *The Washington Post*, but no more likely to use other newspapers. Interestingly, blacks are substantially less likely to use open houses in their search than are whites, and this result dovetails with the earlier finding that open houses are more likely to be held in predominantly white neighbor-hoods than in black or integrated neighborhoods. Blacks appear more likely than whites to rely upon agents to identify homes, and, inter-estingly, blacks are more likely than whites to find an agent through newspaper ads and less likely to select an agent on the basis of a personal referral.

Although these results suggest that blacks and whites may employ somewhat different search strategies, they do not provide convincing support for the initial hypothesis that blacks avoid major metropolitan newspapers and rely primarily on alternative information sources. The majority of black home buyers in this sample used *The Washing-*

Table 3.11 METHODS OF HOUSING SEARCH

Information sources	Percentage of blacks	Percentage of whites
Possible search methods used		
Real estate agents	97	89
Washington Post	61	71
Other papers	44	43
Open houses	53	80
For-sale signs	72	70
Other	14	13
Initial source of information about home purchased		
Real estate agents	50	54
Newspaper ads	14	13
Open houses	0	6
For-sale signs	17	16
Other	19	10
Source of information about agent used		
Newspaper ads	13	6
For-sale signs	10	7
Open houses	16	19
Walk-ins	10	1
Previous use	3	13
Personal referral	23	34
Other	26	16

Note: Based on a sample of home buyers who purchased homes in Washington, D.C., and Prince George's County neighborhoods during the third and fourth quarters of 1990.

ton *Post,* and the share using other papers was no higher for blacks than for whites. Thus, there is no convincing evidence that black home buyers ignore major metropolitan newspapers as an information source, and it remains difficult to explain why agents who market houses in integrated and black neighborhoods would not use this medium.

IMPLICATIONS FOR NEIGHBORHOOD CHOICE AND PUBLIC POLICY

The Persistence of Residential Segregation

The potential implications of these differences in neighborhood marketing practices are significant. If minority and integrated neighborhoods are not marketed as intensively as are predominantly white neighborhoods, white home seekers may not find out about housing opportunities in integrated or predominantly black neighborhoods. These practices could contribute significantly to the persistence of residential segregation, since the vast majority of white home buyers will simply continue to purchase homes in the predominantly white neighborhoods that they find out about through the newspaper and through real estate agents who advertise in the newspaper. Moreover, the HDS provides little information about the incidence of steering in integrated and minority neighborhoods, and it is possible that white home seekers are systematically steered away from any minority and integrated neighborhoods that they encounter in their housing searches.[21]

In addition to its impact on residential segregation, lack of white demand for housing in integrated and minority neighborhoods (resulting in part from differential marketing practices) may contribute to lower rates of house price appreciation, since competition for housing in these neighborhoods is largely limited to minority home buyers. Finally, if the level of advertising for a neighborhood declines as the neighborhood changes from predominantly white to racially integrated, and if this decline in advertising reduces the level of white awareness of and demand for housing in the neighborhood, marketing practices could help explain the paucity of stable, integrated neighborhoods in American cities as well as the tendency for neighborhoods to become predominantly black once they begin to integrate.

Policy Interventions and Research Issues

The study findings reported here indicate that several different housing market practices work in combination to discourage racial and ethnic integration of residential communities. Some of these practices involve differential treatment of individual home seekers, but others appear to involve differential treatment of neighborhoods based on their racial or ethnic composition. Thus, policy interventions are needed not only to influence agent behavior toward individual home seekers but also to influence agent and firm decisions about how to market housing in different neighborhoods. In addition, there appears to be a meaningful role for public policy initiatives that seek to expand the availability of information about housing opportunities in the widest possible range of neighborhoods to both minority and majority home seekers.

Fair-housing enforcement has traditionally focused on the treatment of individual home seekers by real estate agents, seeking to ensure that minorities receive the same treatment as comparable whites. The results of the HDS clearly indicate that this type of enforcement needs to be sustained and expanded. Both blacks and Hispanics are systematically denied information about available housing units; they are not provided with the same level of information and assistance in completing a housing transaction as are white home seekers; and when minorities are shown or recommended houses, there is a one-in-five chance that these houses will be in neighborhoods that are less white or less affluent than those shown and recommended to comparable white or Anglo home seekers.

In conjunction with traditional fair-housing enforcement efforts, more information is needed regarding the treatment of both minority and majority home seekers when they attempt to find housing in integrated or minority neighborhoods. It may be that whites are denied information about available housing in these neighborhoods or are encouraged to look in predominantly white neighborhoods. This form of discrimination has received less attention than the denial of equal treatment to minority home seekers, but it may play an important role in perpetuating residential segregation.

One strategy for assembling more information on patterns of discrimination in integrated and minority neighborhoods would be to conduct an audit study targeted to these neighborhoods. Newspaper advertisements would not be used to select agents for auditing. Other marketing mechanisms, such as for-sale signs or possibly a multiple listing service, would have to be used to generate a representative sample of agents or available housing units. The audit would be designed to record any comments discouraging whites from considering minority or integrated neighborhoods or encouraging them to consider other locations or to contact other agents.

In addition to sustained efforts to equalize treatment of individual minority and majority home seekers, the results presented here argue for attention to the treatment of minority, integrated, and majority neighborhoods by real estate agents. Investigation and enforcement techniques should be developed to determine whether individual real estate firms or offices are marketing listings from minority and integrated neighborhoods differently than listings in predominantly white neighborhoods, establishing offices only in predominantly white neighborhoods, turning down listings in minority and integrated neighborhoods, or referring these listings to smaller, localized firms with fewer marketing resources.

One promising strategy for investigating these forms of differential treatment would be audits in which testers posed as home sellers rather than home buyers. This type of testing has been employed on a small scale by private fair-housing groups but has not been systematically implemented for research purposes.[22] The costs and logistical hurdles associated with this type of testing could be high, since each audit team would have to have comparable houses in different types of neighborhoods to pretend to put on the market. However, these audits might yield valuable insights into differential marketing practices for houses for sale in minority, integrated, and majority neighborhoods.

In conjunction with investigative and enforcement initiatives focused on differential treatment of home seekers and residential neighborhoods, public sector interventions could be designed to expand the general availability of information about housing opportunities in all types of neighborhoods. In particular, housing opportunities in integrated or racially changing neighborhoods could be publicized to all types of households so that majority as well as minority households would be informed about these communities. Information strategies should be designed to widen and facilitate housing searches by both minority and majority households, and to promote all types of neighborhoods.

Notes

Many researchers at The Urban Institute and elsewhere have contributed to the research and analysis presented in this chapter. In particular, I am grateful for the assistance of John Edwards, Ron Wienk, Amina Elmi, Fred Freiberg, Amy Bogdon, and Carla Herbig. In addition, Raymond Struyk and John Yinger provided invaluable guidance and review throughout the course of the research efforts.

1. Overall findings from the HDS are summarized in Turner et al. (1991b). Complete results of the steering component of the HDS are reported in Turner et al. (1991a).

2. See, for example, Simonson and Wienk (1984); Newburger (1989).

3. Analysis of steering in the HDS was limited to the sales market. Conceivably, steering also occurs in rental markets, but it seems likely that the racial composition of a rental building rather than of the surrounding neighborhood would be the determining factor in rental steering.

4. Metropolitan areas were included in the universe for selection if they had central-city populations greater than 100,000 and were more than 12 percent black or more than 7 percent Hispanic—the average share of blacks and Hispanics in the United States as a whole.

5. Estimates are obtained using proprietary forecasting algorithms, combined with supplemental data gathered by state, regional, county, and municipal planning departments as well as test surveys conducted by the Census Bureau. Note that these estimates may be inaccurate in rapidly changing areas, including large new developments.

6. In conjunction with this statistical analysis of racial and ethnic steering for the national sample of audit data, mapping analysis was conducted for five "in-depth" audit sites—Chicago, Los Angeles, New York, Atlanta, and San Antonio. Results of the mapping analysis are reported in Turner and Mikelsons (1991).

7. Additional neighborhood characteristics tested included percentage of the housing stock built after 1940 and the owner-occupancy rate. However, results for these variables were statistically insignificant and are not reported here.

Treatment	*Threshold*
Average percent white or Anglo for addresses shown and recommended to the majority auditor minus average percent white or Anglo for addresses shown and recommended to the minority.	A value of plus or minus 5 percentage points is classified as no difference; more than 5 points is classified as majority higher; less than -5 points is classified as minority higher.
Average per capita income for addresses shown and recommended to the majority auditor minus average per capita income for addresses shown and recommended to the minority.	A value of plus or minus $2,500 is classified as no difference; less than $-$2,500$ is classified as minority higher; more than $2,500 is classified as majority higher.
Average house value for addresses shown and recommended to the majority auditor minus average house value for addresses shown and recommended to the minority.	A value of plus or minus $5,000 is classified as no difference; less than $-$5,000$ is classified as minority higher, more than $5,000 is classified as majority higher.

8. For extensive consideration of the interpretation of "minority-favored" outcomes, see Yinger (1991).

9. An alternate version of the summary index was also constructed. In this version, an audit was classified as "majority higher" as long as the majority auditor had higher values on more items than did the minority auditor. No significant differences in results were found when the two index versions were compared.

10. For details on procedures for testing statistical significance in the HDS, see Yinger (1991).

11. Since blacks were shown houses in predominantly white neighborhoods in a significant share of the audits, the hypothesis was tested that agents use favorable and unfavorable comments about neighborhood attributes to steer blacks away from these neighborhoods, or to steer whites away from racially mixed areas. The results suggest that the number of favorable comments may be lower for houses in predominantly black neighborhoods, but there is no evidence that comments vary with the race of the auditor. Moreover, so few neighborhood-related comments were made by agents under any circumstances that differential patterns cannot be discerned with any reasonable degree of statistical certainty.

12. The statistical significance of differences between black and white averages is estimated by a paired means *t*-test, which adjusts for the covariance between the two samples. This test is explained fully in Yinger (1991).

13. The number of audits for the "shown" and "recommended" columns do not add up to the number in the "shown and recommended" column because averages in these columns are based on audits in which *both* auditors were shown at least one address

beyond the advertised unit and those in which *both* auditors were recommended at least one unit for future inspection. Audits in which one partner was shown a unit and the other was recommended a unit would be included in the "shown and recommended" column but not in either of the other two.

14. Average characteristics for each subset of addresses were computed by first averaging the characteristics of addresses for each audit and then averaging across audits, applying normalized sampling weights.

15. An ordinary least squares regression equation predicting the *number* of houses recommended or shown in those tracts where the number was greater than zero did not contribute any additional insights to the results presented here.

16. A test for a nonlinear relationship between percent black and the probability of market activity found that when the squared percent-black term was introduced to the list of explanatory variables, the coefficient on the linear term became insignificant.

17. This exploratory analysis focused exclusively on black and racially integrated neighborhoods because blacks are the predominant minority group in the Washington metropolitan area. The same methodology could certainly be applied to Hispanic neighborhoods as well.

18. Researchers were not able to survey all the tracts on the same weekend. However, all three tracts in a given set were surveyed on the same weekend (or within one or two days of one another).

19. For advertisements that did not include the property address, houses with for sale signs were matched to advertisements on the basis of community name, real estate company name, agent name and telephone number, and (if necessary) a telephone call to the listed agent.

20. See Galster et al. (1987).

21. Note, however, that the audit study conducted in Boston by Feins and Bratt (1981) focused explicitly on racially mixed neighborhoods and found no evidence of steering.

22. The Leadership Council in Chicago has conducted a limited number of audits of this type.

APPENDIX 3.A: MATCHING AUDITED ADDRESSES TO CENSUS TRACTS

To match the addresses of houses shown and recommended to their census tracts, a machine-readable file of addresses was sent to Harte-Hanks Data Technologies, which used its in-house geo-coding system to provide the census tract identifier for each address. After completing one full pass through these data, Harte-Hanks returned the file of addresses to The Urban Institute, where researchers corrected or supplemented addresses that had not been successfully matched to census tract identifiers by using the original data collection instruments, local zip code directories, and detailed maps of the 25 metropolitan areas. Addresses were then returned to Harte-Hanks for a second pass through the geo-coding process. This procedure resulted in a significant improvement in the share of addresses matched to census tract identifiers.

Table 3.A.1 GEO-CODING SUCCESS RATES: SALES AND AGENT OFFICE ADDRESSES

	Black	White	Hispanic	Anglo
Sales addresses				
Total addresses	2,307	2,757	2,190	2,886
Geo-coded addresses	1,907	2,304	1,862	2,515
Percent geo-coded	82.7	83.6	85.0	87.1
Without advertised unit				
Total addresses	1,512	1,888	1,415	2,042
Geo-coded addresses	1,230	1,553	1,175	1,768
Percent geo-coded	81.3	82.3	83.0	86.6
Office addresses				
Total addresses		1,910		1,878
Geo-coded addresses		1,751		1,741
Percent geo-coded		91.7		92.7

As illustrated in table 3.A.1, the overall success rate for address matching was 85 percent, providing a total of 8,588 addresses for statistical analysis. Addresses shown and recommended to minority auditors were geo-coded just as successfully as those shown and recommended to their majority teammates. Advertised units—the "anchors" for each of the HDS audits—were geo-coded more successfully than the remainder of the addresses shown and recommended to minority and majority auditors. The addresses of agents' offices were also recorded by the auditors, and geo-coded to census tract identifiers. Office addresses were even more successfully geo-coded than house addresses. Overall, 92 percent of all office addresses were matched to tract identifiers.

APPENDIX 3.B: SELECTED CENSUS TRACTS IN WASHINGTON, D.C., AND PRINCE GEORGE'S COUNTY

Table 3.B.1 summarizes key 1980 and 1990 characteristics of the Washington, D.C., and Prince George's County census tracts selected for the Urban Institute survey of neighborhood marketing practices. These tracts were selected on the basis of 1980 characteristics, with data for 1990 becoming available later. Racial composition and owner-occupancy rates have remained relatively stable, although most of the integrated tracts became increasingly black over the decade. House values are less well matched for 1990 than they are for 1980 in three of the four sets. White neighborhoods experienced substantially greater growth in median house values than did integrated or black neighborhoods.

Table 3.B.1 1980 AND 1990 CENSUS CHARACTERISTICS OF WASHINGTON, D.C., AND PRINCE GEORGE'S (P.G.) COUNTY STUDY NEIGHBORHOODS

Set	Tract	% black		% owner		Med. house value		Med. income	
		1980	1990	1980	1990	1980	1990	1980	1990
D.C.									
Set A	15	9	11	83	82	142,800	367,900	41,441	
	16	66	72	87	88	132,000	292,000	43,248	
	99.01	84	91	85	83	80,000	144,500	28,471	
Set B	14	6	8	53	54	130,000	337,450	25,474	
	67*67.1	43	30	52	51	111,500	236,400	26,005	
	26	71	66	71	69	139,300	347,500	30,200	
P.G.									
Set A	8004.02	2	3	84	84	66,100	142,700	31,871	
	8036.08	46	58	76	79	63,900	117,300	27,927	
	8028.05	97	97	79	79	63,500	97,300	29,319	
Set B	8070	9	12	65	51	60,400	116,300	21,972	
	8014.04	28	56	71	61	65,800	116,300	25,716	
	8028.04	91	95	60	58	63,730	104,300	21,667	

Note: Figures for 1990 median income not available.

References

Feins, Judith, and Rachel Bratt. 1981. "Barred in Boston: Racial Discrimination in Housing." *Journal of the American Planning Association* 49: 544–55.

Galster, G., F. Freiberg, and D. Houk. 1987. "Racial Differences in Real Estate Advertising Practices: An Explanatory Case Study." *Journal of Urban Affairs* 9(3): 199–215.

Newburger, Harriet. 1989. "Discrimination by a Profit-Maximizing Real Estate Broker in Response to White Prejudice." *Journal of Urban Economics* 26: 2–19.

Newburger, Harriet. 1981. "The Nature and Extent of Racial Steering Practices in U.S. Housing Markets." Unpublished manuscript.

Pearce, Diana. 1979. "Gatekeepers and Homeseekers: Institutional Patterns in Racial Steering." *Social Problems* 3: 325–342.

Simonson, John, and Ronald Wienk. 1984. "Racial Discrimination in Housing Sales: An Empirical Test of Alternative Models of Broker Behavior." Unpublished manuscript.

Turner, M.A., and M. Mickelsons. 1991. "Housing Discrimination Study: Mapping Patterns of Steering for Five Metropolitan Areas." Washington, D.C.: U.S. Department of Housing and Urban Development.

Turner, M.A., J.G. Edwards, and M. Mickelsons. 1991a. "Housing Discrimination Study: Analyzing Racial and Ethnic Steering." Washington, D.C.: U.S. Department of Housing and Urban Development.

Turner, M.A., R. Struyk, and J. Yinger. 1991b. "Housing Discrimination Study: Synthesis." Washington, D.C.: U.S. Department of Housing and Urban Development.

Yinger, John. 1991. "Housing Discrimination Study: Incidence and Severity of Unfavorable Treatment." Washington, D.C.: U.S. Department of Housing and Urban Development.

THE REAL ESTATE INDUSTRY'S VIEW OF AUDIT RESULTS: COMMENTS

Robert D. Butters

The federal fair-housing laws have been largely successful in reducing the incidence of real estate professionals' refusing outright to sell or rent a dwelling to an otherwise qualified person because of that person's race or other protected characteristic. As a result, the focus of public and private fair-housing enforcement has shifted to so-called subtle forms of discrimination that are manifested in differences in the treatment of minority and nonminority persons in their search for housing. Racial steering is one of the ways in which minority and nonminority home seekers can be treated differently in the housing search process.

RACIAL STEERING AS A FORM OF DISPARATE TREATMENT

Racial steering is defined, in its simplest terms, as actions by a real estate agent, or other housing provider, that result in minority and nonminority home seekers who have the same housing needs and financial qualifications being shown different housing options. In the typical racial steering case, it is alleged that minority home seekers are offered, or "steered" toward, housing choices in neighborhoods with relatively higher minority populations, while nonminority home seekers are offered choices in neighborhoods with few, if any, minority residents.

Since racial steering is fundamentally a form of disparate treatment, it is necessary, when prosecuting a racial steering case, for the plaintiff to show that the only variable that can explain the difference in treatment between the minority and nonminority home seekers is their race. Not surprisingly, testing or auditing is the investigatory technique most often used to determine whether a housing provider or real estate agent is engaging in racial steering.

Testers are "matched" such that each presents the same financial qualifications and asks to see the same type or style of housing in the relevant market. If properly matched, the only difference between the testers is their race, or other protected characteristic. The testers then record the properties they are shown and the manner in which the agent or provider attempts to satisfy their housing needs. If the testers are shown properties in neighborhoods with different racial compositions, this is evidence that they were steered to these particular neighborhoods because of their race.

Because racial steering can be detected only by comparing the experience of two prospective home seekers matched in all material respects except for race, it is extremely rare for a racial steering case to involve a bona fide housing seeker. A bona fide home seeker has no way of knowing whether he is being steered unless he is aware of how similarly situated home seekers of different races are being treated. As a result, almost all litigated cases involving racial steering are brought by fair-housing organizations or municipalities and the testers they employ to develop evidence of racial steering.

THE VARIABLE NATURE OF THE HOME-BUYING PROCESS

Notwithstanding the relative simplicity with which racial steering can be described, the practical realities of the home-buying and -selling process make racial steering a very difficult phenomenon to prove based simply upon comparisons between the experiences of testers who visit a particular real estate office. Single-family homes are basically unique commodities. They always vary by location, as well as by style, square footage, amenities, and size and shape of the lot. They also vary in terms of the seller's motivation to sell and the contract terms the seller is willing to accept beyond simply the asking price. Likewise, buyers are rarely the same in terms of financial capabilities, motivation to buy, or preferences in housing style, amenities, and location.

Just as buyers, sellers, and individual properties are all quite different, real estate agents are also unique as individuals. The real estate industry is a highly deconcentrated industry. It is very unusual for the largest firm in a particular market to control more than 10 percent of the listings or account for more than 10 percent of the sales. Therefore, most real estate markets include a dozen or more real estate firms competing for the patronage of buyers and sellers. Each of these firms has its own style and philosophy of marketing.

Effect of Commissions on Agents' Actions

Not only are real estate markets characterized by a large number of competing firms, but each real estate agency is composed of one or more principal brokers, who are often owners of the firm, and a larger number of individual sales agents who are affiliated with the firm, usually as independent contractors. As independent contractors, real estate sales agents are compensated almost exclusively through sales commissions. Therefore, an agent, like the firm itself, is paid if and only if the agent is successful in procuring a ready, willing, and able buyer for a listed property. This commission-based compensation system rewards agents and firms that achieve results. The manner in which the results are achieved is entirely secondary, since extra effort does not produce additional compensation unless it produces additional sales.

This results-based compensation system encourages agents to maximize the number of successful transactions they can arrange in a given period of time. Real estate agents, therefore, have an incentive to treat buyers differently if differences in treatment will result in more successful transactions with an equivalent investment of time and resources.

Differentiation among Buyers as the Key to Agents' Success

Differences in treatment that stem from a compensation system that rewards results, not degree of effort, are generally based on factors having nothing to do with race or any other protected criteria. For example, one of the valuable services real estate agents perform for buyers is to reduce their "search costs" in locating the specific home they wish to purchase from the scores or hundreds that may be on the market at any given time. This function is performed by differentiating the housing needs and wants of one buyer from those of other buyers in the market and matching those needs and wants with houses available for sale.

Real estate agents differentiate among buyers by gathering information from them about their financial capabilities and needs and their preferences for housing of a particular style, location, or other distinguishing features. Having gathered such information, an agent then evaluates it and compares it against the inventory of homes for sale that is available to the agent, which is usually found in a multiple listing service in which the agent's firm participates. The agent then makes a judgment about several houses to show to the prospective purchaser from literally scores that may be available in the multiple listing service.

As these showings occur, the agent notes how the buyer reacts when presented with certain styles of housing and with certain neighborhoods in the market area. Because the agent is paid only if he arranges a successful transaction, he constantly processes information received from the buyer through the buyer's statements, demeanor, and body language, with the paramount objective of matching this particular buyer with the one house presently on the market that will prompt that buyer to make an offer to purchase that has a reasonable chance of being accepted by the seller.

The range of nonracial variables that can enter into this process is enormous. Just as no two agents are identical in how they gather, evaluate, and respond to information from a buyer about his housing needs and wants, no two buyers will have exactly the same experience with an individual agent. The agent may have significant time to spend with one buyer but be short of time to spend with another buyer. Also, the buyer who visits the agent immediately after the agent has returned from a tour of homes recently listed for sale may be presented with a much different range of options than the buyer who visited the agent the day before the tour.

In addition, agents may simply relate differently to different buyers. Agents develop rapport with some buyers more easily than with others. An agent may quickly and accurately perceive one buyer's needs and wants and identify an appropriate home in short order. With another buyer, the agent may misread the buyer's statements about his needs and wants, or the buyer's priorities may shift as he views more homes on the market.

Because such a wide range of variables enter into any housing search undertaken by a buyer with a real estate agent, and because agents are financially motivated to match qualified buyers with willing sellers as quickly as possible, one should expect to see a significant degree of differential treatment of the same buyer by different agents and by the same agent of different buyers. Therefore, the credibility of any general conclusion that identifies purposeful discrimination as the cause of observed differences in the options offered to minority and nonminority home seekers, whether testers or bona fide buyers or tenants, will depend on whether the study on which the conclusion is based adequately accounted for the highly variable nature of the home-buying and -selling process.

LACK OF EVIDENCE FOR SYSTEMATIC RACIAL STEERING

The authors of the Housing Discrimination Study (HDS) acknowledge that random factors frequently can explain why one tester receives different treatment than another.[1] Despite this acknowledgment, the HDS authors contend that "gross" measures of unfavorable treatment of the minority tester are a legitimate indicator of systematic discrimination, notwithstanding a large number of observations that showed the minority tester to have received favorable treatment.[2] Later in the report, the HDS authors assert that use of multinominal logit analysis permits the isolation of those instances of unfavorable treatment of minorities that can be explained by systematic as opposed to random factors. Yet the HDS authors admit that even the multinominal logit analysis leads "to either an under- or overstatement of discrimination."[3]

If one examines the raw data in tables A-1, A-2, and A-3 at the conclusion of the HDS report, the effect of randomness becomes quite striking. For example, table A-2 records differential treatment for "contributions to transaction," or whether the minority and nonminority testers experienced differences in the effort expended by the agent to consummate a sale or rental transaction involving that tester. The composite index for black/white rental audits shows that whites received favorable treatment 44.5 percent of the time, blacks were favored 24.9 percent of the time, and no difference was observed 30.6 percent of the time. Composite indexes for black/white sales audits and Hispanic/Anglo sales and rental audits do not differ markedly from the composite index for black/white rental audits.

To be sure, the "white-favored" category contains the largest number of observations. But overall, there are a greater number of observations in which the black or Hispanic auditor was favored or "no difference" was observed. If systematic racial discrimination were in fact being practiced as a general rule by real estate agents, one certainly would not expect to see black auditors favored, or no measurable difference, in 55.5 percent of the rental audits.

The HDS data in table A-3 relating specifically to racial steering are similarly revealing. Black/white sales audits showed that whites were "favored" 20.9 percent of the time, in terms of being shown neighborhoods with a higher white population and per capita income as well as a higher median housing value. On the other hand, blacks were favored 11.6 percent of the time, and 67.5 percent of the time no difference was observed in the treatment of the white and black testers. Comparable figures for Hispanic/Anglo sales audits show that

Anglos were favored 21.3 percent of the time, Hispanics were favored 16.7 percent of the time, and no differences were observed 62.1 percent of the time.

The HDS data do suggest that some degree of systematic racial steering is occurring because whites were "favored" 20.9 percent of time. But the data showing that the black tester received "favored" treatment 11.6 percent of the time, and that no difference was observed 67.5 percent of the time, cannot be dismissed as irrelevant to the issue of whether real estate agents are engaging in deliberate or systematic forms of racial steering and, if so, to what extent. Certainly, these figures undermine any conclusion that systematic racial steering occurs in one out of every five encounters between a real estate agent and a black home seeker, as the HDS authors contend.[4]

The HDS report also acknowledges that while steering favoring whites is measurable in 20.9 percent of the tests, the severity of the steering that occurred is quite small. In tests in which the white tester was favored, the neighborhoods offered to the black tester had only a 3 percent higher black population, and the median value of the homes shown to the black tester was only $1,700 less than that of homes shown to the white tester. Even smaller differences were found in the Hispanic/Anglo tests.

These data, however, are rendered virtually useless in measuring the true scope of any systematic racial steering by real estate agents because all HDS tests were "anchored" to advertisements found in newspapers of general circulation in the relevant market area. Testers were each told to begin their test by asking about a specific property that appeared in a newspaper advertisement. Because the properties appearing in local newspapers tended to be located in predominantly white neighborhoods, the housing options offered to both white and black testers were located, not surprisingly, in predominantly white neighborhoods.

LACK OF RELATIONSHIP BETWEEN REAL ESTATE MARKETING AND RESIDENTIAL SEGREGATION

In chapter 3 of this volume, Margery Austin Turner acknowledges the difficulty in drawing reliable conclusions based on the HDS steering data because the tests were anchored to advertisements of properties that were located in predominantly white neighborhoods. Turner then postulates that differences may exist between black and white home-seekers in the degree to which they rely on newspaper advertising to locate suitable housing. To test this hypothesis, Turner reports the results of an exploratory survey of recent home buyers in white, black, and integrated areas of Washington, D.C., and Prince George's County, Maryland. This survey showed that white and black home seekers used similar search methods to locate suitable properties, and both groups showed a similar reliance on newspaper advertising. Nevertheless, Turner's data also showed that houses in minority or integrated neighborhoods were statistically less likely to be advertised in a major metropolitan newspaper.

In her conclusions, Turner offers the hypothesis that there exist clear differences in the way houses in minority and nonminority neighborhoods are marketed and that these differences, especially the failure to advertise houses in minority neighborhoods in major metropolitan newspapers, contribute to residential racial segregation. Finally, Turner recommends that, given these findings, enforcement techniques should be developed to prohibit real estate agents from, among other things, (1) marketing listings in minority and integrated neighborhoods differently than listings in predominantly white neighborhoods, (2) establishing offices only in predominantly white neighborhoods, and (3) turning down listings in minority or integrated neighborhoods or referring these listings to smaller, localized firms with fewer marketing resources.

The basic flaw in the Turner proposals is that they fundamentally misperceive the function real estate agents play in the home-buying and -selling process. Blacks and whites continue to reside in segregated neighborhoods, not because of the manner in which houses in these neighborhoods are advertised or not advertised, but because whites, in the aggregate, choose not to live in neighborhoods that are integrated or predominantly minority. As long as whites (1) equate integrated or predominantly minority neighborhoods with a lower social status, (2) are free to move if motivated and capable of doing so, and (3) are able to locate an affordable supply of housing choices in predominantly white neighborhoods, residential segregation will continue.

It is also true that many blacks prefer to live in neighborhoods in which there are already a reasonable number of other blacks. Significantly, blacks generally require a higher percentage of minority residents to be present before they will define a neighborhood to be integrated than do whites. Unlike whites' perceptions of black neighborhoods, blacks do not generally equate predominantly white neighborhoods with a lower social status. Rather, blacks are simply expressing a natural desire to live in a neighborhood in which they share a similar ethnic and cultural background with at least some of the other residents.

Given this background, to ascribe racial segregation to the marketing practices of real estate brokers is truly to miss the forest for the trees. This becomes abundantly clear when one revisits the role real estate brokers play in the home-buying and -selling process. Brokers are retained to bring about a result, namely a sale to a qualified buyer on terms the seller is willing to accept. Because brokers and their agents are paid if and only if a successful transaction occurs, their level of income is a direct function of the number of transactions they can arrange in a given period of time. Also, the contingent nature of the broker's commission results in the broker's earning the same fee whether a buyer is found only after weeks of intense marketing at substantial cost to the broker or a buyer is found the day after the listing is taken with literally no resources spent on marketing. As a result, brokers maximize their income in two fundamental ways: (1) by selling as many houses as they can in a given period of time and (2) by selling them as early as possible during the listing period so that marketing expenses are minimized and profits maximized.

An economically rational real estate agent therefore will develop a marketing plan for a particular listing that is designed to produce a ready, willing, and able buyer in the shortest period of time. Whether this marketing plan will include classified advertising, open houses, brochures, or yard signs will depend on the broker's judgment concerning which technique, or combination thereof, will be most cost-effective in reaching the buyer most likely to buy the listed property. Simple logic dictates that homes in different neighborhoods, with different prices, and with different features and amenities will be promoted and marketed differently. Logic also dictates that an economically rational real estate broker will not sacrifice profits by wasting valuable resources on any marketing technique, such as newspaper advertising or open houses, that experience shows is not efficient in reaching the buyer most likely to buy a listed property.

Analysis of real estate marketing practices further shows that in most residential markets, a real estate agent's best source of potential buyers is personal referrals generated through the agent's network of community contacts. These contacts result from satisfied customers and clients, as well as the agent's membership in churches, clubs, business leagues, and other local organizations. Other sources of buyers include yard signs and the cooperative efforts of other agents in a multiple listing service. The most costly and least effective form of marketing a specific listing is newspaper classified advertising. But while the techniques employed to market a particular listing may vary, the goal of the marketing plan is always the same regardless of the location, price, or style of the house: the production of a ready, willing, and able buyer in the shortest period of time.

It thus misses the point to focus on differences in marketing techniques to determine whether real estate agents are discriminating on the basis of race in the manner in which they sell homes in different neighborhoods. A better measure of any discriminatory treatment in the marketing of properties in minority and white neighborhoods would be whether homes in predominantly white neighborhoods consistently sell faster and at a higher percentage of list price than homes in black or integrated neighborhoods. If a real estate broker's success is measured by the frequency and speed with which results are achieved, rather than by the resources spent to achieve the results, then comparing the quality of the results achieved in different neighborhoods is the best measure of whether real estate agents are according less favorable treatment to one neighborhood or another. The results of any study of this type would most likely show that, over time, houses in all neighborhoods in a single housing market experience similar average times on the market, and list-price-to-sales-price ratios, even though the marketing techniques may well vary from neighborhood to neighborhood.

When one reexamines the Turner enforcement initiatives in this light, one sees that they are, in fact, unrealistic proposals intended to alter the fundamental economics of the real estate and real estate brokerage markets. Compelling uniformity in the marketing of all homes is the equivalent of compelling real estate brokers to disregard the reality that different homes in the same neighborhood, or similar homes in different neighborhoods, appeal to different types of buyers, who respond to different marketing techniques. Turner apparently assumes that if all homes were marketed in the same manner, this somehow would bring about a uniformity of demand for all housing across all racial groups.

Central to Turner's proposals is the false assumption that if brokers who presently sell homes in white neighborhoods opened offices or took listings in minority neighborhoods, then these brokers would stimulate more white demand for homes in minority neighborhoods.

The truth is that the demand for homes in white and minority neighborhoods would remain unchanged because real estate brokers do not create demand, they simply develop marketing techniques that respond to it. The only change that would result from Turner's proposals is that brokers currently doing business in minority neighborhoods would face more competition as the brokers operating in white neighborhoods entered those markets. These new entrants would not increase the number of buyers willing to buy in minority neighborhoods. There would simply be more brokers competing to locate the buyers already willing to buy in these neighborhoods and match them with houses for sale.

The inescapable reality is that the persistent residential racial segregation that Turner wishes to change is not caused by the behavior of real estate agents. It is caused by the forces of supply and demand for housing, which are, in turn, greatly influenced by the unwillingness of most of the white majority to live in integrated neighborhoods, and to a lesser extent by the preference of the black minority to live in neighborhoods that are already integrated to some degree. Real estate agents are basically powerless to change these forces. All that can and should be demanded of real estate agents is that they eliminate race, or any other prohibited criteria, from their individual marketing efforts. As long as a real estate agent accords all persons an equal opportunity to buy or rent any housing for which they are financially qualified, the agent has met his burden under the fair-housing laws. To demand more is to hold real estate agents accountable for economic and demographic forces over which they have no control.

The HDS report and the Turner chapter on racial steering, when reviewed objectively, strongly suggest that the real estate industry is not, as a general rule, engaging in deliberate racial discrimination. The test results instead reflect the highly individualistic nature of real estate sales. Also unique are those who buy, sell, and rent real estate and the agents who are paid to arrange successful real estate transactions. These differences, together with random events, necessarily result in different buyers having different experiences with real estate agents in the same market, or even the same real estate firm. While the HDS data do suggest that a degree of systematic racial discrimination persists in today's housing markets, these data do not at all present a picture of a real estate industry deliberately attempting to deprive Americans of an equal opportunity to buy or rent homes wherever they choose to live.

Notes

1. Turner, M. A., R. Struyk, and J. Yinger. 1991. "Housing Discrimination Study: Synthesis." Washington, D.C.: U.S. Department of Housing and Urban Development, pp. 7–8.

2. *Id.* at 8.

3. *Id.* at 41.

4. *Id.* at 25.

Chapter Four

THE URBAN INSTITUTE AUDIT STUDIES:
THEIR RESEARCH AND POLICY CONTEXT

Ronald B. Mincy

INTRODUCTION

In recent years concern about the poor labor market performance of young males has dominated public, academic, and policy-making discussions of social distress among inner-city blacks and Hispanics. When compared with young white males of the same age, young black and Hispanic males have higher unemployment rates, lower labor force participation rates, and lower mean wages. The decreasing labor market participation among black males is a new phenomenon. Without a firm foothold in the labor market, young black and Hispanic males are unable to form and support families. Many observers believe that this has contributed to rising rates of female-headed and welfare-dependent families in black and Hispanic communities.

Sociologists and other social scientists have revisited a few arguments to explain these labor market outcomes. The most frequently cited explanations emphasize changes in the structure of urban labor demand that have produced skills or spatial mismatches to the detriment of young black and Hispanic workers. Competition from women and recent immigrants is another argument advanced to explain poor labor market outcomes. Only rarely do theorists raise the possibility that labor market discrimination explains the poor labor market performance of black and Hispanic males.

Because discrimination has been such a neglected subject, the Urban Institute (UI) audit studies of hiring are potentially very important. The results of these studies—if they hold up to scrutiny—will remind observers that labor market discrimination still limits the employment opportunities of young males in some metropolitan areas where poverty and social distress remain high. The purpose of this chapter is to review these findings in light of (1) the literature on the role of labor markets in high rates of social distress among blacks and

Hispanics, (2) theoretical and empirical research on labor market discrimination, (3) findings from hiring audits in the United States and Great Britain, and (4) developments in public policies toward labor market discrimination.

LABOR MARKETS AND THE URBAN UNDERCLASS

Explanations of the social distress of inner-city minorities usually ignore the role that employment discrimination can play in reducing the employment opportunities of blacks and Hispanics. Instead, most observers emphasize changes in urban economics or changes in attitudes as factors. Beginning with *The Declining Significance of Race*, Wilson (1980) has drawn attention away from racially and ethnically centered explanations for inner-city dislocations, instead emphasizing the adverse effects of changes in the structure of urban economies (Wilson 1987). The most important structural change has been the decline in manufacturing establishments in urban areas and the replacement of manufacturing jobs by jobs in the high-skilled or low-skilled service sectors.

Other observers have also de-emphasized issues of race and ethnicity. Kasarda (1988) argues that the decline in employment opportunities for young black males in Chicago and, by extension, in other major metropolitan areas is the result of spatial mismatch. According to Kasarda, during the 1970s and 1980s opportunities for low-skilled employment moved from central-city areas with large concentrations of black and Hispanic residents to the suburbs, where few blacks and Hispanics live. Low-skilled employment thus became inaccessible to inner-city residents. Ellwood (1986) argues that "race not space" explains the reduction in employment opportunities, although he does not discuss the implications of continued discrimination for public policy. More conservative writers, such as Meade (1986), have explicitly pronounced that discrimination is no longer a barrier to employment opportunities for blacks and Hispanics because of successful civil rights enforcement.

By turning attention away from issues of race and ethnicity these authors hope to encourage policymakers to shift their focus. Old policies tried to correct the human capital deficiencies of individual workers or the misdeeds of individual employers. New policies, according to these authors, should try to adjust for macro-structural changes in the economy or for changes in attitudes about the social obligations of citizens. Even if these larger forces could account for some growth in poverty and dislocations among inner-city blacks and Hispanics, the effect of the change in focus has been that discrimination has disappeared from view.

PREVIOUS STUDIES

Because of the predictions of economic theory, empirical work by economists has emphasized wage discrimination and neglected hiring discrimination. Economists have focused on wage discrimination because the earliest theories of discrimination rested on assumptions about employer preferences for minority and majority workers. In these theories, only wage discrimination could account for hiring discrimination (Cain 1986).

Hiring discrimination can result because employers, workers, or customers prefer majority workers. If some employers in a labor market practice hiring discrimination to indulge their own preferences for majority workers, wage and hiring discrimination results. Employers with such preferences hire only majority workers and, because they are in greater demand, pay them higher wages than nondiscriminating employers pay minority workers. If some employers practice hiring discrimination to indulge worker or customer preferences, however, there should be no wage discrimination. In other words, data on hiring discrimination are consistent with employer, worker, or customer discrimination, but data on wage discrimination reveal that employer preferences dominate.

Another branch of the economic theory of discrimination also focuses on wages. In these statistical theories, employers pay different wages to minority workers because race and ethnicity are inexpensive ways to predict the productivity of workers. If employers have reason to believe that majority workers are more productive than minority workers, then color or accent provides an inexpensive signal of a worker's productivity. To offset the expected lower productivity of minority workers, employers offer all minority job applicants lower wages, even if particular minority applicants may be as productive as the average majority applicant. In low-wage labor markets, such wage discrimination can result in hiring discrimination when the wage offer to minority workers falls below the legal minimum, so that employers cannot legally hire them.

Besides economists' studies of wage discrimination, a few new studies by other social scientists simply document the extent of hiring discrimination. The most important studies for comparision are previous audit studies that focus on discrimination in entry-level employment, relying for data on personal contacts between auditors and employers. (The studies of discrimination in higher-level positions get much of their data from employer responses to cover letters and resumes, while the hiring process for entry-level jobs rarely uses cover letters and resumes.)

McIntosh and Smith (1974) tested for discrimination against Greek, Indian, Pakistani, and West Indian immigrants applying for unskilled and semiskilled jobs in Britain. The authors found substantial discrimination against nonwhite immigrants and much less discrimination against white (Greek) immigrants. This finding suggested that British employers discriminated on the basis of both color and immigrant status. The UI studies examined both kinds of discrimination by U.S. employers.

Two features of the McIntosh and Smith study make it difficult to generalize from their results. First, they did not rely on a random sample of employers. Instead, they sent auditors to make "cold contacts" with any employer in two areas of British cities with high concentrations of low-skilled manufacturing employment. An unknown number of these employers lacked an opportunity to discriminate because they lacked vacancies. Further, the results could not be generalized beyond the two areas studied or beyond manufacturing employers.

A second troubling feature of the McIntosh and Smith audits was their reliance on professional actors who were not necessarily matched to form visually comparable teams. Instead, in one city the researchers matched one white actor with eight immigrant actors (two West Indians, two Pakistanis, two Indians, and two Greeks) to form eight audit teams. In another city, the authors matched two white actors with the same group of immigrants. The researchers gave both immigrant and nonimmigrant auditors biographies mentioning previous experience in unskilled jobs. Still, there were many idiosyncratic differences between the members of the audit teams that could have accounted for differential treatment.

Culp and Dunson (1986) conducted the only previous and closely related study of entry-level employment discrimination by U.S. employers. They relied on a nonrandom sample of 21 graduating, but non-college-bound, male high school seniors. Many blacks wanted to participate in the study, partly because they had not found full-time jobs by the summer after they graduated. By contrast, few whites wanted to participate, and some who began the study failed to complete the audit phase because they later found full-time employment.

At best, the Culp and Dunson study hints at what an actual audit might find. The researchers did not pair the students or give them falsified biographies to convince prospective employers that the students were comparable on productivity characteristics. And because of attrition in the sample, the researchers were unable to have the students apply for vacancies with the same employers. Instead, Culp and Dunson first examined the employment-relevant characteristics of their entire sample of seniors. Then they looked at how large employers in the same county treated the subsample of students who completed the study. But because these students made cold contacts rather than responding to known vacancies, once again, an unknown number of contacted employers lacked an opportunity to discriminate.

Culp and Dunson presumed that employers would find that their sample of black and white seniors had similar employment-relevant characteristics. Specifically, all the students had limited previous employment experience and few references. Four black students and one white student completed a survey questionnaire about their treatment by 45 contacted employers.

The four blacks reported less favorable treatment by employers, who were less likely to treat them courteously (i.e., to call them "Mr.," offer them a seat, shake their hand, engage them in a conversation, and so on). Besides these aspects of employer behavior—which are important because they can discourage applicants—there were at least two clear signs of discrimination: Employers were less likely to tell the black applicants about employment prospects, and they quoted black applicants lower wages. While there was evidence that differential treatment varied by industry, none of the results were statistically significant.

URBAN INSTITUTE AUDIT STUDIES

The UI audits (Cross et al. 1990; Turner et al. 1991) were executed with great care and were improvements over previous studies in three important respects. The earlier studies were hampered by incomplete matching of white and nonwhite auditors, nonrandom samples of employers, and uncertainties about the availability of vacancies.

While there had been a previous study of employment discrimination against blacks in the United States, until the UI audits there had been no study of employment discrimination against Hispanics.

The UI research teams chose, matched, and trained auditors carefully. All the auditors were college students who had applied for jobs as study participants. First, the research staff evaluated each applicant and eliminated applicants they felt were too zealous, had inadequate motivation, or were difficult to match. Second, the staff matched the successful black or Hispanic applicants with successful white or Anglo applicants of similar height, weight, and general appearance. Third, outside project consultants reevaluated audit teams, making a few necessary changes. Once the research staff had finalized the audit teams, who consisted of one Anglo and one Hispanic (or one white and one black) auditor, auditors worked with the same team member in the field.

These and other procedures contributed to high-quality audits. The auditors applied for jobs requiring no more than a high school education, so they were all overqualified. Auditors had falsified, but believable, biographies to support the illusion of comparability on productivity characteristics. Employers thus saw credible applicants, and, as far as possible, the only basis for choosing one team member over another was race and ethnicity.

Employer selection and auditor training emphasized standardization. The researchers selected employers from a random sample of advertisements for entry-level jobs in the Sunday editions of major metropolitan newspapers, which resulted in some variance in employer characteristics, such as size and industry. Auditor teams contacted employers within three days. By relying on advertised vacancies instead of cold contacts, the studies had fewer trials in which there was no opportunity to discriminate, though employers had sometimes filled vacancies before the initial auditor call.

Each audit followed a standard procedure, beginning with a phone call to find out if the advertised vacancy was still available. White (or Anglo) and black (or Hispanic) auditors alternated making the first call. If permitted, the auditor made a personal visit to the employer to obtain and complete an application and request a personal interview. If the employer granted the interview, the auditor presented his qualifications using the interview skills he learned during training sessions. After the interview, the auditor called the employer to learn of the employer's decision. If offered a job, the auditor declined within a few hours. At every stage of this process, the auditor completed standardized forms detailing the employer's response in various requests and some indications of the way the employer had treated the auditor. Finally, auditors received a flat salary, which removed any incentive for them to discover discrimination where there was none.

Brief Review of Findings

The UI audit studies examined the outcomes of young black, Hispanic ("foreign looking and foreign sounding"), and Anglo (or white) men seeking entry-level employment. Audits involving Hispanic and Anglo applicants took place in Chicago and San Diego. Audits involving black and white applicants took place in Chicago and Washington, D.C.

The two sets of audits used a common three-stage model of the effect of hiring discrimination on employment of young black and Hispanic men (figure 4.1). In this model, young men seek entry-level employment by reviewing advertisements in major metropolitan area newspapers. After identifying vacancies for which they qualify, potential applicants call to find out whether vacancies are still available and whether they can fill out an application.[1] Opportunities for unfavorable treatment begin at this point and proceed through two further stages. First, if the employer permits only one applicant to fill out an application, that applicant is counted as having received favorable treatment at the application stage. Second, if the employer permits both auditors to complete applications but grants an interview to only one applicant, that applicant is counted as having received favorable treatment at the interview stage. Third, the employer interviews both applicants but makes only one applicant an offer, that applicant is counted as having received favorable treatment at the offer stage.

The Hispanic/Anglo and black/white audits used somewhat different questions about job-seeking outcomes. The Hispanic/Anglo audits were aimed at finding out (1) whether Anglo applicants progressed further through the hiring process than did Hispanic applicants and (2) whether Anglo and Hispanic applicants had different numbers of completed applications, interviews, and job offers. Thus the study included the possibility of reverse discrimination.

Besides these two outcomes, the black/white audits also were aimed at finding out whether black and white auditors experienced differential treatment at various stages in the hiring process. For example, black applicants may have been required to wait longer for interviews, or may have met with clerical staff instead of with managers who would be making hiring decisions. Even if employers accepted appli-

Figure 4.1 DIFFERENTIAL OUTCOMES AND DIFFERENTIAL TREATMENT IN THE HIRING PROCESS

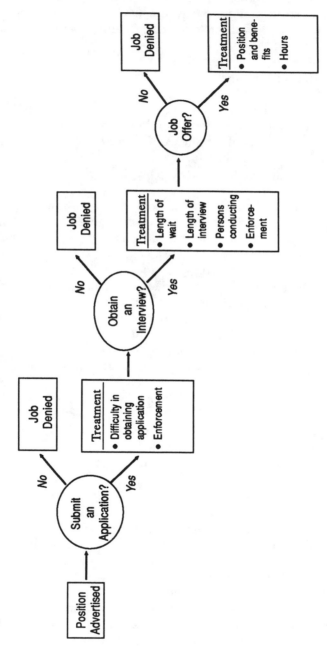

Source: Turner et al. 1991.

cations from black applicants and interviewed them, such differential treatment could have discouraged them from pursuing the job further.

The UI audits took place in three large metropolitan areas: Washington, D.C., San Diego, and Chicago. In 1990, the Washington, D.C., metropolitan area had almost 4 million people, San Diego had just under 2½ million, and Chicago had 7 million (see table 4.1).[2] Blacks and Hispanics represented 32 percent of the population in Washington, D.C., less than 1 percent of the population in San Diego, and 31 percent of the population in Chicago.

Findings of discrimination against blacks and Hispanics applying for entry-level employment could be significant in these cities because each city had high rates of poverty and social distress. In 1980, family poverty rates in these metropolitan areas ranged from a high of 16.8 percent in Chicago to a low of 9.2 percent in San Diego (U.S. Bureau of the Census 1988).

Overall, the audit results show that blacks and Hispanics experience roughly equal treatment at the application stage; but at subsequent stages black, and especially Hispanic, applicants are more likely to encounter unfavorable treatment.[3] In the Hispanic/Anglo audits, Anglo applicants received favorable treatment at the interview stage 22 percent of the time, while Hispanic applicants received favorable treatment 6 percent of the time (table 4.3). Anglo auditors received favorable treatment at the offer stage 22 percent of the time, while Hispanic auditors received favorable treatment 8 percent of the time. In the black–white audits, white applicants received favorable treatment at the interview stage 9 percent of the time, while black applicants received favorable treatment 3 percent of the time. White audi-

Table 4.1 RACIAL/ETHNIC DISTRIBUTION OF POPULATION AND POVERTY FOR FOUR METROPOLITAN AREAS (1980)

Measure	Washington, D.C., CMSA	San Diego SMSA	Chicago CMSA[a]	Denver CMSA
Total population (in thousands)	3,924	2,498	7,261	1,848
% of population black	26.6	0.1	19.6	0.1
% of population Hispanic[b]	5.7	0.2	11.5	0.1
% of families below poverty line, 1979	15.1	9.2	16.8	10.3

Sources: Early release 1990 census data; U.S. Bureau of the Census 1988.
[a]Includes the six counties that were part of the Chicago SMSA in 1980.
[b]Persons of Hispanic origin can be of any race.

Table 4.2 STAGE AT WHICH UNFAVORABLE TREATMENT OCCURRED

Stage	Black/white audit (%)	Hispanic/Anglo audit (%)
Application		
Anglo or white favored	2	6
Black favored	0	—
Hispanic favored	—	2
Interview		
Anglo or white favored	9	22
Black favored	3	—
Hispanic favored	—	6
Job offer		
Anglo or white favored	8	22
Black favored	4	—
Hispanic favored	—	8

Sources: Cross et al. 1990; Turner et al. 1991.

tors received favorable treatment at the offer stage 8 percent of the time, while black auditors received favorable treatment 4 percent of the time.

These results are revealing beyond what they tell us about discrimination. Consider what the results meant to the sample of young men who were seeking employment. For the UI researchers, the only valid audits were those in which employers allowed at least one auditor to complete an application. In some cases employers allowed neither auditor to complete one, but both kinds of audits convey information about the difficulty these young men experienced finding jobs.

Counting both kinds of audits, only about half of the employers who advertised vacancies allowed both auditors to complete an application. Thus even without any discrimination on the part of employers, jobs are scarce. Further, black and Hispanic applicants could expect to be offered a job at most 5 percent of the time they filled out applications. In the face of these results, the low and falling parts of labor force participation of black and Hispanic men should not surprise observers.

Unfavorable treatment experienced by blacks and Hispanics varied across metropolitan areas. Black auditors in Washington, D.C., experienced more unfavorable treatment than did black auditors in Chicago, and Hispanic auditors in Chicago experienced more unfavorable treatment than did Hispanic auditors in San Diego.

Within metropolitan areas, there also were variations by occupation and industry. For example, Hispanic auditors in Chicago experienced more unfavorable treatment in applying for jobs in management and service occupations and in the manufacturing and construction industries. Black auditors in Washington, D.C., experienced more unfavorable treatment in applying for jobs in service industries and in white-collar or sales occupations. These findings are consistent with hypotheses that discrimination is more likely to occur in higher-paying or higher-status jobs and in jobs with substantial amounts of customer contact. Finally, the black–white audits showed that unfavorable treatment of black applicants occurred in subtle ways. For example, employers steered black applicants to less favorable jobs (with lower wages, less desirable hours, or lower status), made negative comments to them about the job, made them wait longer for interviews, or interviewed them for shorter periods of time.[4]

DENVER AUDIT STUDY

James and DelCastillo (1991) recently completed an audit study of hiring discrimination in the Denver metropolitan area. Like the UI studies, this study focused on young black and Hispanic men who applied for entry-level employment, using high-quality audits. The researchers carefully selected, trained, and matched auditors and used a random sample of employers who had advertised vacancies in a major metropolitan newspaper. Unlike the UI studies, the Denver study found almost no evidence of discrimination. The only evidence of discrimination was that large employers (with 15 or more employees) never favored the black applicant. Several methodological and substantive issues could account for differences in the results of these studies.

First, auditor selection, training, matching, and compensation differed in ways that make comparisons of the two groups of audits difficult. The most important difference was the characteristics of the Hispanic auditors. The UI Hispanic/Anglo audits used "foreign-looking and foreign-sounding" Hispanics. The Denver audits had no such requirements.[5] Recent amendments to the Immigration Reform and Control Act provide for stiffer sanctions against employers who hire undocumented aliens. A possible and perverse side effect of these sanctions is discrimination against persons who appear to be illegal immigrants because of their Hispanic appearance or accent. The U.S. General Accounting Office commissioned the UI studies to determine the extent of such discrimination, but because effects of changes in immigration law were not under examination in the Denver audits, those audits used native-born Hispanics who did not necessarily have Hispanic accents or appear Hispanic.

Other methodological differences could also account for the different results. For example, the Denver study recruited Anglo and white auditors from college campuses but contacted local civil rights agencies to recruit black and Hispanic auditors, who may therefore have been more aggressive than the white and Anglo auditors in the job search process. In particular, black and Hispanic auditors made more post-interview follow-up calls than did white or Anglo auditors, though orientation and training should have eliminated any such differences.

Finally, the Denver and UI studies paid auditors differently. Denver auditors received a bonus when at least one member of the team completed an application. They received another bonus when at least one member completed an interview and a third bonus when at least one member got a job offer. James and DelCastillo provided these bonuses so that the auditors would have monetary incentives similar to the incentives real job searchers have. Whether these incentives differentially affected team members is unclear because black and Hispanic auditors made more follow-up calls. By contrast, UI auditors received a flat salary, which removed any incentive to find discrimination but also removed the monetary incentive real job seekers have.

These and other aspects of the Denver and UI studies create arguable biases that hamper comparisons between the Denver and UI results.[6] The more important point, however, is that the Denver and UI studies used higher-quality audits than did previous audit studies. Therefore, while comparisons across these studies are risky, each presents reliable evidence of discrimination in the respective labor markets.

Assuming the Denver results are reliable, what could account for the absence of any findings of discrimination in Denver? The authors emphasize two factors. First, blacks in Denver made up a smaller fraction of the metropolitan area population than did blacks in the UI audit cities (Chicago and Washington, D.C.). Perhaps low-skilled white and Anglo workers in Denver felt less threatened by blacks and, therefore, put less pressure on Denver employers to discriminate against them.

Second, blacks and Hispanics in Denver have higher levels of educational attainment on average than do minorities in Chicago and Washington, D.C. Denver employers would thus have historically observed less disparity in the educational attainment of entry-level minority and nonminority workers, which could have contributed to their lower levels of statistical discrimination against minority workers. Unfortunately, the authors provide no evidence for this theory, and data for 1980—on the proportions of blacks and Hispanics who completed high school and college in the respective cities—provide very weak support (table 4.3)

IMPLICATIONS FOR POLICY AND RESEARCH

The UI studies documented significant hiring discrimination against young black and Hispanic men in three metropolitan areas where indicators of poverty and social distress are high. A high-quality audit of employers in Denver revealed almost no discrimination. Since these audits represented improvements over the previous research, their results are the most reliable evidence available of the extent of discrimination. This evidence has important implications for future research and policy, especially antidiscrimination policy.

Labor Market Performance

The most obvious implication is as a reminder to the public, policymakers, and researchers that discrimination constrains the already limited employment opportunities of black and Hispanic males in some metropolitan areas. To improve the poor labor market performance of these men, policies must pay more attention to the demand for their labor. Policymakers can improve the labor market performance of young black and Hispanic men by using three strategies: (1) reducing discrimination against them, (2) increasing their human capital, and (3) increasing the demand for their labor, for example,

Table 4.3 PERCENTAGE OF BLACKS AND HISPANICS IN FOUR SMSAs COMPLETING HIGH SCHOOL AND COLLEGE (1980)

SMSA	Blacks		Hispanics	
	4 years of high school	4 years of college	4 years of high school	4 years of college
Chicago	29.6	8.4	20.1	6.2
Washington, D.C.	32.8	14.7	27.2	27.4
Denver	34.5	14.2	29.4	8.4
San Diego	35.3	11.1	25.6	7.8

Source: Census tracts, 1980 Census of Population and Housing, U.S. Bureau of the Census, PHC80-2 series.

through public service employment. The hiring audit data suggest that the third strategy should receive top priority.

Many observers blame supply-side factors for the low labor force participation rates of young Hispanic and, especially, black males. For example, Meade (1986) argues that these young males have high reservation wages and poor human capital. The employment audit results provide significant evidence against this interperetation because the supply-side characteristics of minority and nonminority workers are identical.

The demand side is responsible for the differential results. That is, the audits took place in labor markets with few opportunities, even for young men willing to work at prevailing wages. Only half the employers who advertised vacancies allowed both auditors to complete an application. Despite nearly 30 years of forceful antidiscrimination policies, since the Civil Rights Act of 1964, white and Anglo men were two to three times more likely to get a job offer in the UI audits than were equally overqualified black or Hispanic men. This meant that blacks and Hispanics could expect to get a job offer for at most 5 percent of the unfilled vacancies they found. Given these odds, observers should not be surprised that labor force participation rates of these men are low and falling.

Antidiscrimination Policies

State and federal budget crises may not permit new expenditures to increase the demand for young black and Hispanic men. Still, policymakers should guarantee that the opportunities created by the market are equally available to all workers. Policymakers now use widely or selectively targeted sanctions to achieve this goal. Widely targeted sanctions affect the decisions of all employers in a labor or product market simultaneously; selectively targeted sanctions affect the decisions of those employers who have direct contact with enforcement agencies.

Current Policies for Targeting Sanctions

The most important vehicle for widely targeted sanctions is Executive Order No. 11246, as amended by Executive Order No. 11375 and administered by the Office of Federal Contract Compliance Programs (OFCCP). These orders impose a basic obligation on federal contractors not to discriminate, require them to take affirmative action to employ minorities and women, and require them to get similar commitments from their subcontractors (Amaker 1988). Because the orders affect all employers who bid on federal construction contracts, the sanctions for violations are widely targeted. These sanctions include back-pay orders, retroactive seniority requirements, cancellation or suspension of existing contracts, and debarment from bids on future government contracts.

The major vehicle for selectively targeted sanctions is Title VII of the Civil Rights Act, which allows individuals to sue employers for employment discrimination. The act also gives the Equal Employment Opportunity Commission (EEOC) authority to impose sanctions for discrimination by private employers and federal agencies in administrative or judicial proceedings. Historically, the EEOC has used this authority to establish an arsenal of broad legal principles which private citizens have used to win multimillion-dollar judgments against discriminating employers (Leonard 1990). Title VII also gives the Justice Department responsibility to bring suits against state and local government units charged with employment discrimination.

Affirmative action involves weak and unstable sanctions. Its weakness derives from its being targeted only against government contractors; its instability derives from its reliance on enforcement by federal agencies whose commitment is subject to swings in political will.

The employment audit data suggest that affirmative action requirements imposed on government contractors have little potential to reduce employment discrimination against young black and Hispanic males. Indeed, 85 percent or more of the audited employers were in retail trades and service industries, which have few federal government contractors (Smith and Welch 1984). So there is no reason to expect that policymakers can increase their impact on the hiring practices of employers who fill entry-level positions by continuing to widely target government contractors. Further, in a series of studies reviewed by Leonard (1990), economists have shown that this type of antidiscrimination program has had only modest effects on black employment.

From 1964 until 1981, enforcement of antidiscrimination policies by the EEOC, the OFCCP, and the Justice Department established new legal precedents for the fight against discrimination. But subsequent actions by the same federal agencies have weakened antidiscrimination policies considerably. Many observers who bemoan this reversal fail to realize that it was inevitable. The most effective way to promote or change policy is through leadership and control of federal agency purse strings. Thus, in the 1980s, the heads of these federal agencies challenged the principles established by their predecessors, including (1) the use of timetables and numerical goals in the affirmative action plans of federal contractors and (2) race-conscious hiring plans in judgments and conciliation agreements involving state and local government bodies found guilty of past discrimination. Further, the EEOC and the Justice Department reduced the number of complaints of discrimination by private employers settled by administrative and judicial law.

Before 1989, selectively targeted sanctions, brought through private litigation under Title VII, were the most effective antidiscrimination strategy (Leonard 1990). But recent Supreme Court decisions, especially *Wards Cove Packing Co. v. Atonio*, 490 U.S. 642 (1989), weakened selective sanctions. Because of this decision, plantiffs must go beyond showing that employment practices result in numerical imbalances. They must identify the practices specifically and show that they are not a business necessity. Obviously, hiring audits can provide powerful documentation for such efforts.

USING HIRING AUDITS TO TARGET SANCTIONS

As discussed earlier, widely targeted sanctions have limitations, and selective sanctions impose high costs on plantiffs, who must pay for legal representation and wait months for a complaint to be adjudicated in the courts. While many have complained about selective targeting, it may be the most effective strategy for enforcement when there is no systematic pattern to the employment discrimination (Wallace 1973). When there are patterns, however, policymakers can target sanctions to affect a wide range of employers.

The earlier discussion of the economic theory of discrimination suggests that patterns of discrimination vary by industry. Responding to competitive market pressures, employers discriminate to indulge worker or customer preferences. If they don't discriminate against minorities, they must pay their workers higher wages or lose customers to other firms that employ only majority workers. Thus, markets in which worker and customer preferences dominate decisions about hiring are appropriate markets for widely targeted sanctions.

One such appropriate market is the construction industry, where employers sometimes discriminate against minorities to indulge their workers. Construction worker preferences for nonminority co-workers are a simple extension of nepotism, which has operated in unionized construction for decades. By requiring all construction contractors with federal contracts (and their subcontractors) not to discriminate, policymakers make it easier for employers to resist the discriminatory demands of their workers. This antidiscrimination policy also extends to unions, which have been subjected to scrutiny by the EEOC (Wallace 1973).

Construction is not the only product market where policymakers should try to reduce competitive pressures on employers to discriminate in hiring. Two other obvious candidates for widely targeted sanctions are the retail trade and service industries in highly segregated areas. These industries have many positions with high customer contact and employ large numbers of entry-level workers. If the economic theory is correct and customers in highly segregated areas are more likely to prefer service by majority workers, hiring discrimination in these industries will be widespread.

Widely targeted sanctions in these industries could work in two ways. Policymakers could audit every retail or service employer in a highly segregated area (or every employer with an advertised vacancy) and sanction discriminating employers. Alternatively, policymakers could audit a random sample of retail and service employers. If the audits uncovered employers who discriminate, policymakers could affect the hiring decisions of nonsampled employers through publicity—for example, by letting the public know, through journalists, that an "ongoing program" of random audits in the area was the source of the evidence used to bring suit against the discriminating employers. Such publicity would raise the expected cost of discrimination to all retail and service employers in the area.

The evidence from the audit studies also suggests that discrimination in entry-level employment varies from one metropolitan area to another. This kind of evidence could help policymakers allocate scarce enforcement resources more effectively. For example, the audits suggest that because blacks in Chicago and Washington, D.C., suffer more from discrimination than do blacks in Denver, the scope of any equal opportunity enforcement effort should be smaller in Denver.

Evidence gathered by hiring audits also could strengthen selective sanctions. Courts have already ruled that audit testers in the housing discrimination area have standing to bring suits against housing owners who discriminate. Similar standing could be granted in the hiring discrimination area. Thus, audits could be used to show whether specific hiring practices systematically favor majority applicants. These practices include, for example, (1) differential screening of minority and nonminority applicants by accepting fewer applications from minorities, denying them personal interviews, or conducting shorter interviews with them; and (2) supplying less favorable information to black or Hispanic applicants about wages or promotion opportunities.

Suggestions for Future Research

While the UI audits provide valuable information for researchers and policymakers, two features need adjustment in future work. First, the audits gathered and reported very little information on wages and other terms or conditions of employment. This information is valuable for research and for use as evidence in selective sanctions. Economists need information about wage offers (and other terms and conditions of employment) to help determine whether employer, worker, or customer preference drives hiring discrimination. This information also can help determine whether antidiscrimination policies should be targeted widely or selectively.

Litigants need such information to provide unambiguous evidence of discrimination. Subjective evaluation of candidates is an arguably valid reason for not accepting an application from a non-Anglo male, not granting an interview, or cutting an interview short. But there is no valid reason for quoting Anglo and non-Anglo applicants different wages, hours, or working conditions for the same job. Audits seeking to gather such information would require larger samples because many employers exclude black and Hispanic applicants before they have a chance to ask about wages and other conditions of employment.

Second, future research should try to reconcile the results of the hiring audits in Denver and in the UI cities. There were methodological differences between these studies, but there also was a major substantive difference. Blacks and Hispanics represent small fractions of the population in Denver, but they represent large fractions of the population in the UI cities. Theory predicts that there should be less discrimination in cities like Denver. A more reliable test of this hypothesis could be undertaken using another city where minorities represent a small fraction of the population, using the UI methodology. Unfortunately, a test of discrimination against "foreign-looking and foreign-sounding" Hispanics in a city with few Hispanics is not feasible because immigrants locate in areas where there is an established immigrant community.

Finally, the UI audits focused on male applicants—for good reasons—but many observers would like to see the results of employment audits involving women. The number of critical variations multiplies quickly. Some observers are most concerned about the economic status of women; they want to know whether employers favor men over women for entry-level jobs in traditionally male occupations. Other observers want to know whether employers pay men and women differently for comparable jobs. Answering that question would shift the focus away from hiring decisions and require more data on wages for comparable jobs.

Observers concerned about the economic status of blacks and Hispanics are also interested in questions that audits involving women could answer. For example, do employers favor women over men, especially minority men, for jobs in industries with high customer contact? The shift in urban employment from manufacturing to service and low-wage retail industries gives this question more importance. Still other observers want to know whether employers favor white or Anglo women over black or Hispanic women in certain occupations. The steadily increasing number of female-headed families in the black and Hispanic communities adds importance to this question. Setting priorities among these variations will be a difficult task.

THE ROLE OF AUDITS

Poverty and social distress among blacks and Hispanics have increased dramatically in the past two decades. Explanations for these changes emphasize the poor labor market performance of young men and rarely consider the role of employment discrimination. The Urban Institute hiring audits show that young black and Hispanic males experience substantial discrimination when they apply for entry-level employment. But discrimination does not exist everywhere. The recent audit of employers in the Denver metropolitan area found almost no evidence of discrimination.

These studies are important because they remind observers that employment opportunities are scarce for young male workers. Overqualified young men, willing to work for prevailing wages, found few vacancies in the four major metropolitan areas studied. Thus, increasing the demand for the skills of young male workers is the best way to improve the labor market performance of young black and Hispanic men. Besides poor demand for their labor, young black and Hispanic men face substantial discrimination in metropolitan areas where they are no longer racial and ethnic minorities. After 30 years of hotly debated antidiscrimination policy, this is an intolerable situation.

Antidiscrimination policies have been ineffective for these young men, either because they rely on costly, selective sanctions that few of them can afford or because they rely on sanctions widely targeted at employers who hire few young men.

The audit results suggest ways of making selectively and widely targeted sanctions more effective. Under rules forthcoming from recent Supreme Court decisions, hiring audits can provide the evidence plaintiffs need to show how specific hiring practices systematically favor majority applicants. But the direction of antidiscrimination policy may make it harder for policymakers to use this evidence. Since 1981, federal agencies charged with enforcing antidiscrimination laws have tried to restrict remedies for discrimination to actual victims. If their effort continues, only audits involving real job applicants will be able to be used to sanction discriminating employers. Nevertheless, policymakers can use publicized hiring audits and the threat of sanctions to increase the costs of discrimination for all employers serving customers in one product market, thus enabling these employers to resist customer demands for hiring discrimination.

Notes

This chapter is a product of the Underclass Research Project. I thank Susan Wiener for her research assistance.

1. The UI research teams treated the initial telephone calls differently. The Hispanic auditors had accents so that employers could determine ethnicity from the initial telephone contact. Therefore, the Hispanic–Anglo research team counted an audit valid if, on the basis of the initial telephone call, employers refused to allow the Hispanic auditor to obtain and complete an application but allowed the Anglo auditor to do so. The black–white research team did not assume that employers could identify a black accent over the telephone. Therefore, this research team invalidated audits in which the employer screened out one auditor on the basis of the initial telephone call. Instead, the first opportunity for discrimination (i.e., for a valid audit) occurred when employers allowed both auditors to obtain applications.

2. The data in table 4.1 reflect the six Chicago counties that were in the Chicago SMSA in 1980. The other consolidated metropolitan areas in the table had the same (or virtually the same) counties in 1980 SMSAs and 1990 consolidated CMSAs.

3. Discrimination is only one of the reasons that employers deny job offers to black and Hispanic job seekers. Therefore, at best, the UI studies document whether whites and Anglos were systematically favored over black and Hispanic applicants. For this reason, the studies report findings in terms of the number or percentage of audits in which employers treated particular types of auditors unfavorably. I follow this language. The findings suggest discrimination if differences in unfavorable treatment between two members of a team of auditors are statistically significant.

4. Additional findings from the employment audits is presented in the appendix.

5. The Hispanic auditors had dark hair and dark complexions, but did not necessarily have accents.

6. A lengthy correspondence between the authors of the UI and Denver studies is available for the interested reader.

References

Amaker, Norman C. 1988. *Civil Rights and the Reagan Administration*. Washington, D.C.: Urban Institute Press.

Cain, Glen G. 1986. "The Economic Analysis of Labor Market Discrimination: A Survey." In *The Handbook of Labor Economics, Volume I*, edited by O. Ashenfelter and R. Layards. Netherlands: Elsevier Science Publishers B.V.

Culp, Jerome, and Bruce H. Dunson. 1986. "Brothers of a Different Color: A Preliminary Look at Employer Treatment of White and Black Youth." In *The Black Youth Employment Crisis*, edited by R. Freeman and H. Holzer. Chicago: University of Chicago Press.

Cross, Harry, Genevieve Kenney, Jane Mell, and Wendy Zimmerman. 1990. *Employer Hiring Practices: Differential Treatment Of Hispanic and Anglo Job Seekers*. Washington, D.C.: Urban Institute Press.

Ellwood, David. 1986. "The Spatial Mismatch Hypothesis: Are There Teenage Jobs Missing in the Ghetto?" In *The Black Youth Employment Crisis*, edited by R. Freeman and H. Holzer. Chicago: University of Chicago Press.

James, Franklin J., and Steve W. DelCastillo. 1991. "Measuring Job Discrimination by Private Employers Against Young Black and Hispanic Males Seeking Entry Level Work in the Denver Metropolitan Area." Unpublished Report. Denver: University of Colorado.

Kasarda, John D. 1988. "Jobs, Migration, and Emerging Urban Mismatches." In *Urban Change and Poverty*, edited by Michael G. H. McGeary and Laurence E. Lynn, Jr. Washington, D.C.: National Academy Press.

Leonard, Jonathan S. 1990. "The Impact of Affirmative Action Regulation and Equal Employment Law on Black Employment." *Journal of Economic Perspectives*, 4 (fall): 47–63.

McIntosh, Neil, and David J. Smith. 1974. *The Extent of Racial Discrimination*, XL, Broadsheet No. 547. London: PEP, The Social Science Institute.

Meade, Lawrence M. 1986. *Beyond Entitlement: The Social Obligations of Citizenship*. New York: Free Press.

Ricketts, Erol, and Isabel Sawhill. 1988. "Defining and Measuring the Underclass." *Journal of Policy Analysis and Management*, 7 (2): 316–25.

Smith, James P., and Finish Welch. 1984. "Affirmative Action and Labor Markets." *Journal of Labor Economics*, 2 (2): 269–301.

Turner, Margery A., Michael Fix, and Raymond Struyk. 1991. *Opportunities Denied, Opportunities Diminished: Racial Discrimination in Hiring*. UI Report 81–9. Washington, D.C.: Urban Institute Press.

U.S. Bureau of the Census. 1988. *County and City Data Book, 1988*. Washington, D.C.: U.S. Government Printing Office.

Wallace, Phyllis A. 1973. "Employment Discrimination: Some Policy Considerations." In *Discrimination in Labor Markets*, edited by Orley

Ashenfelter and Albert Rees. Princeton, N.J.: Princeton University Press.

Wilson, William Julius. 1987. *The Truly Disadvantaged*. Chicago: University of Chicago Press.

————. 1980. *The Declining Significance of Race: Blacks and Changing American Institutions*. Chicago: University of Chicago Press.

Chapter Five

THE URBAN INSTITUTE AUDIT STUDIES: THEIR METHODS AND FINDINGS

James J. Heckman and Peter Siegelman

INTRODUCTION

Policy discussions often revolve around concepts that defy precise definition or measurement. The current controversy over the prevalence of discrimination by race, ethnicity, and gender and the remedies for such discrimination is fueled by the lack of hard evidence. Most people agree with the definition of labor market discrimination. It occurs if persons in one group with the same relevant productivity characteristics as persons in another group are treated unfavorably by the labor market solely as a consequence of their demographic status, which is assumed to be irrelevant to productivity.

A large and sometimes polemical literature has emerged about what characteristics of persons are relevant to their productivity and how they can be measured. Especially problematic is the possibility of statistical discrimination that may arise if the same levels of observed characteristics convey different information about true productivity for different demographic groups. In order to assess true productivity, we need to acquire much more information about individuals and jobs than is generated in standard data on labor market transactions. The available data on the operation of the labor market are meager and unsatisfactory; so is our understanding of the prevalence and sources of discrimination.

The current empirical literature in labor economics focuses most of its attention on widely available wage data. An enormous literature summarized in Cain (1986) documents the existence of demographic wage differentials even after controls are made for available measured "productivity" characteristics. Because of the absence of standardized, economywide data on hiring, promotion, and firing decisions, there is much less evidence on discrimination in these important dimensions of labor market activity. What we know about hiring and promotion mostly comes from court cases or selected studies of firms, with their attendant uncertain generality.

Audit studies are a potentially promising method for extending our understanding of hiring discrimination. Although such studies can overcome some of the limits inherent in traditional analyses of discrimination, they also pose a number of important and subtle challenges. Both the generation of the audit pair data and its interpretation need to be conducted with extreme care if the potential usefulness of hiring audits is to be realized.

Despite suggestive rhetoric to the contrary, audit pair studies are not experiments or matched pair studies. Race or ethnicity cannot be assigned by randomization or some other device as in experimental or matched pair analyses. Race is a personal characteristic and adjustments must instead be made on "relevant" *observed* characteristics to "align" audit pair members. Some characteristics can be controlled by the audit analyst: e.g., which firms to sample. Audit pair studies are, then, a variant of statistical matching in which some of the match characteristics can be manipulated. Because there is partial control on auditor characteristics, such studies may improve on matching methods. But audit pair studies suffer from the main defect of matching methods: they do not account for unobservables that affect outcomes. Indeed, as we document below, matching on observables may exacerbate the problem of non-alignment of audit pairs by accentuating differences in unobservables among audit pair members. Audit pair evidence of the sort reported in this volume is not necessarily clear or convincing.

This chapter critically examines the methods and findings of two recent Urban Institute studies and a study of the Denver labor market patterned after them.[1] For brevity, the Urban Institute black/white study will henceforth be denoted UIBW, the Urban Institute Anglo/Hispanic study will be denoted UIAH, and the Denver study will be called just that. In this chapter, we draw heavily on our recent research on audit pair methodology (Heckman and Siegelman 1993). In that work, we develop explicit models of employment and use them to define discrimination. Both large sample and exact small sample tests are developed to analyze audit pair data. We also use this apparatus to analyze the available data. Our framework can also be used to design "optimal" audit pair studies. A major methodological finding of our research is the potentially misleading character of large sample statistical methods that are widely used to design and interpret audit pair studies. Conventional large sample methods, if correctly adapted to small samples, produce less evidence of discrimination than is found when optimal exact small sample tests are used. If taken literally, conventional large sample methods produce misleading advice on optimal experimental design. Here we communicate the main ideas in our work.

The rest of this chapter is executed in seven sections. The second section presents a description of the audit pair methodology. The third section considers the potential of the UI studies for understanding discrimination in hiring. The fourth section presents the evidence set forth in the UI and Denver studies and an intuitive discussion of alternative measures of discrimination. We present large sample statistical tests for the absence of discrimination.

Using a variety of tests, and the measure of discrimination that seems most satisfactory, we find little evidence of discrimination against Denver blacks and Denver Hispanics. For Chicago blacks, the evidence in support of discrimination is at best marginal. For Washington, D.C. blacks and Chicago and San Diego Hispanics, our tests reveal evidence of what might be termed discrimination.

In the fifth section we subject this evidence to further scrutiny. We question the representativeness of the UI sampling frame. We raise concern about "experimenter effects," that is, inadvertent contamination of the audit studies by motivational devices. We also point out an important ambiguity that plagues the UI Anglo/Hispanic study: that all Hispanics had accents and facial hair while none of the Anglos possessed these characteristics.

In the sixth section we show that the UI studies do not shed much light on the magnitude of the wage gap or on the source of the 25-year decline in the labor force participation rate for black males relative to white males. We go on to note that the evidence in the Denver and UI studies does not support the claim that affirmative action has led to reverse discrimination, at least in low-wage labor markets.

We further note that the Denver and UI studies appear to differ in the extent of homogeneity across audit pairs. The Denver pairs are not comparable with each other. Since both Denver and UI claim to match testers within and across pairs at comparable levels, this conflict in the evidence demonstrates the difficulty in objectively verifying the quality of the matches, on which the employment audit method depends.

In the seventh section, we summarize a formal model of firms' employment decisions developed in appendix 5.D that enables us to assess the intuitive definitions of labor market discrimination. We establish the conditions required to justify them. Appendix 5.D is a condensed version of our companion paper. We make two important observations about the limitations of audit pair methodology: (1) Standardization on *observed* productivity characteristics may either accentuate or attenuate measured racial differences in hiring rates compared with what occurs in actual labor markets; (2) The choice of a particular observed productivity level at which to standardize may produce much more (or less) evidence of discrimination than standardization at another level. More thought should go into the choice of a standardization level. A variety of levels across audit pairs should be used to present a more accurate picture of actual labor market hiring practices. The chapter concludes with suggestions for future research.

HOW AUDITS WORK

Audits have been adopted by social scientists from techniques employed by legal activists, who pioneered their use in the enforcement of fair-housing laws during the late 1960s. The audit procedure can be conveniently divided into two parts.[2] First is the selection and training of auditors. Groups of two individuals, one white or Anglo and one black or Hispanic, are selected from a group of applicants to resemble each other as closely as possible except for race. Testers are typically matched on such attributes as age, education, physical appearance (subjective level of attractiveness), physical strength, and level of verbal skills, as deemed relevant.[3] The goal is to produce pairs of testers who are identical in all *relevant* characteristics so that any systematic difference in treatment within each pair can be attributed only to the effects of race.[4] In addition to their outward similarities, testers are given training about how they are supposed to behave during the course of the audits. Such training typically includes developing synthetic biographies (current and past employment, references, education, and so on), behavioral alignment (e.g., level of aggressiveness and overall "presentation of self"), and experience in role-playing, simulating the kind of transaction being audited.

An important element of subjective judgement enters at this stage. Audit pair analysts assume that they know which characteristics are relevant to employers, and when such characteristics are "sufficiently" close to make majority and minority audit pair members "indistinguishable." Audit pair members must be matched on each of the relevant characteristics. Alternatively, audit analysts assume that they know how employers trade off characteristics. For the housing market, where the original audit studies were conducted, fewer characteristics (wealth, income, credit status, etc.) are essential attributes of purchasers. For the case of the labor market, many more characteristics are likely to be relevant and different employers are likely to place different weight on those characteristics. Thus audit methods seem less well-suited to the labor market than to the housing market.

Given the current low level of factual knowledge about which characteristics employers value and how attributes trade off in productive content, and given the likely heterogeneity among employers in making these assessments, it is not obvious that audit analysts would possess the relevant information required to make perfect matches. There is a presumption of knowledge about "what is really important" that is difficult to demonstrate objectively. This inability to defend, or even fully enunciate, the criteria used to match audit pair members constitutes the Achilles heel of the audit pair methodology. In the UIBW study five audit pairs were chosen in Chicago and Washington from a group of male college students between the ages of 19 and 24 at the major universities in those environments (excluding junior colleges and community colleges) who applied to perform the audits. Job announcements were mailed to university employment and placement offices, social science departments, minority affairs offices, and selected professors. There were 23 applicants in Washington and 31 in Chicago, who were winnowed to five audit pairs in each site. The choice among potential audit pair partners was thus rather limited. One of two implicit assumptions must be made at this stage. Either there are (many) fewer than thirty relevant characteristics of workers valued by employers, so that exact matches can be formed among potential auditors, or else UI analysts know the isoproductivity trade-off curves of firms which are assumed to be identical at all places of employment.

The small size of the list of potential match partners, coupled with the likely large number of relevant productivity attributes, makes the probability of five successful matches rather low. To take an example, suppose that as in Washington there are 10 potential white match partners for 10 potential black partners. Suppose that there are five productivity attributes that describe each worker, each independently distributed as binomial with probability of one-half for each value of each attribute. (The case of discrete attributes is most favorable to matching.) Black and white distributions are identical. Then the number of expected successful matches is less than 2.7, whereas UI reports 5 such matches in Washington. If the number of attributes is increased to 10, the expected number of successful matches is less than 0.1. It seems unlikely that five exact matches were found in Washington given that there are likely to be more than 10 characteristics valued by employers, that some characteristics are continuously distributed, and that black and white productivity distributions are likely to be different.

Payment was made to applicants for a fixed sum of $3,000 for six weeks of work. It was not made contingent on performance in the audit study. Each audit pair partner applied without knowledge of the employment outcomes of the other partner.

The second phase of an audit study is the generation of the data. Job openings to be audited are selected at random for certain types of entry level jobs sampled from help-wanted advertisements in local newspapers. Members of an audit pair are then sent in random order to apply for the job, typically within a few hours of each other. (If the first member of a pair is offered a job, he is instructed to turn down the offer so as to leave the vacancy available for his teammate.) Each pair typically conducts many tests, so repeated observations are available for each person in each pair. However, in these studies, the same firms are not visited by more than one audit pair.

The data generated by these tests document the way each member of an audit pair was treated in the process of applying for a job. In the employment context, the possible outcomes might look like those described in figure 5.1.

Outcomes are typically limited to only a few, discrete possibilities and there is usually only a small sample of observations for each audit pair. Statistical analyses must cope with the small numbers in these samples.

Figure 5.1 A SCHEMATIC REPRESENTATION OF OUTCOMES IN AN
EMPLOYMENT AUDIT

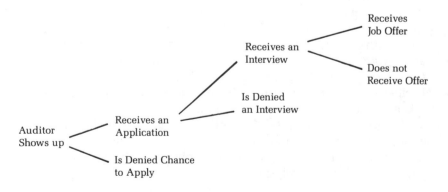

Auditors often collect data on aspects of employer treatment apart from employment offers. Such supplemental data might include the amount of time the auditor had to wait for an interview, the kinds of remarks interviewers made, or other subjective features of interviewee treatment. While such data can be enlightening, and are especially useful in illuminating potential *causes* of discriminatory treatment (Yinger 1986), we concentrate on the analysis of the bottom line employment variable.

HOW THE AUDIT METHOD MIGHT IMPROVE OUR KNOWLEDGE OF LABOR MARKET DISCRIMINATION

Virtually all subsequent analyses of discrimination follow Gary Becker's *The Economics of Discrimination* ([1957] 1975), and examine employment segregation and wage differentials. They do not explicitly consider the hiring process that is the focus of the studies under review here.[5] One crucial benefit of audit studies is that they offer a chance to examine an important aspect of labor market behavior—discrimination in hiring—that has been largely inaccessible to social scientists until now.

The other major advantage of the audit technique is that it allows more control over the characteristics that are thought to be relevant to the employment decision than is possible in conventional ex-post regression analyses. For example, regression studies typically use years of education as a control variable in explaining wage discrimination. But this is an extremely crude control, ignoring as it does differences in educational quality and performance between workers with the same number of years of education. In an audit, by contrast, the two testers can be matched exactly on certain characteristics (by giving them identical educational histories, including schools attended, GPA, and so forth), providing a much cleaner measure of the demand-side response to race and ethnicity than techniques based on passive observation. In addition, by sending pairs of auditors to the same firms, one gains partial control over idiosyncratic differences in firm valuations of common bundles of characteristics that plague ordinary observational studies. In Heckman and Siegelman (1993), we demonstrate the gains in statistical power that accrue from sending pairs to the same firm rather than sending team members to separate firms. Eliminating common unobserved components makes it possible to construct better tests of the hypothesis of no discrimination.

Evidence for Discrimination in Hiring

Several measures of discrimination were developed in the UI studies, and several measures were not used that might have been. This section presents the main empirical findings. We then discuss ways of measuring discrimination, comment briefly on their theoretical justification, and show how they operate when applied to the audit data under consideration. A more extensive theoretical analysis of these methods and definitions is reserved for later sections of this paper.

Discrimination in What?

Table 5.1 presents summaries of outcomes for each black/white audit pair in Washington, D.C., and Chicago. Table 5.2 presents comparable summaries from the UIAH study, in which similar definitions are used. Table 5.3 presents the aggregate data from Denver.[6] See table 5.10 for the disaggregated data.

The first question one needs to ask in analyzing these data is, "What constitutes an 'outcome' that exhibits discrimination?" In one context, the question becomes whether one is interested only in differences within pairs in the rate of job offers, or whether one also cares about disparities in getting interviews or opportunities to apply— what we call "favorable audits."[7] Additionally, incidental treatment (what the UIBW study refers to as "opportunities-diminished" variables)—such as length of waiting time for an application, length of interview, number of interviewers, or positive and negative comments made during an interview—can be used to measure discrimination. Based on these variables, UIBW constructed a composite index for each auditor in each audit, with differences in this index between auditors indicative of discrimination. Given the ambiguity in interpreting an index, and the clear bottom-line nature of a job offer, we focus on the "get-a-job" measures of discrimination in this chapter.[8]

Unequal Treatment of "Identical" Pairs as a Measure of Discrimination

One intuitively plausible measure of the existence of discrimination is the proportion of times that two members of an audit pair who are identical (except for ethnicity or race) are treated differently by potential employers. This measure cannot be formalized into a statistical test until we have a precise measure or range of measures specifying whether any given sample proportion is large or small. Nevertheless,

Table 5.1 OUTCOMES IN THE URBAN INSTITUTE BLACK/WHITE STUDY IN CHICAGO AND WASHINGTON, D.C. (Get Job or Not)

Number of Audits	Pair	(a) Both get job	(b) Neither gets job	a + b	White yes, black no	White no, black yes
Chicago						
35	1	(5) 14.3%	(23) 65.7%	80%	(5) 14.3%	(2) 5.7%
40	2	(5) 12.5%	(25) 62.5%	75%	(4) 10.0%	(6) 15%
44	3	(3) 6.8%	(37) 84.1%	90.9%	(3) 6.8%	(1) 2.3%
36	4	(6) 16.7%	(24) 66.7%	83.4%	(6) 16.7%	(0) 0%
42	5	(3) 7.1%	(38) 90.5%	97.6%	(1) 2.4%	(0) 0%
197	Total	(22) 11.2%	(147) 74.6%	85.8%	(19) 9.6%	(9) 4.5%
Washington						
46	1	(5) 10.9%	(26) 56.5%	67.4%	(12) 26.1%	(3) 6.5%
54	2	(11) 20.4%	(31) 57.4%	77.8%	(9) 16.7%	(3) 5.6%
62	3	(11) 17.7%	(36) 58.1%	75.8%	(11) 17.7%	(4) 6.5%
37	4	(6) 16.2%	(22) 59.5%	75.7%	(7) 18.9%	(2) 5.4%
42	5	(7) 16.7%	(26) 61.9%	77.6%	(7) 16.7%	(2) 4.8%
241	Total	(40) 16.6%	(141) 58.5%	75.1%	(46) 19.1%	(14) 5.8%

Note: Results are percentages; figures in parentheses are the relevant number of audits.

Table 5.2 OUTCOMES IN THE URBAN INSTITUTE ANGLO/HISPANIC STUDY IN CHICAGO AND SAN DIEGO (Get Job or Not)

Number of Audits	Pair	(a) Both get job	(b) Neither gets job	a + b	Anglo yes, Hispanic no	Anglo no, Hispanic yes
Chicago						
33	1	(9) 27.3%	(16) 48.5%	75.8%	(7) 21.2%	(1) 3%
32	2	(4) 12.5%	(18) 56.3%	68.8%	(9) 28.1%	(1) 3.1%
39	3	(9) 23.1%	(20) 51.3%	74.2%	(7) 17.9%	(3) 7.7%
38	4	(4) 10.5%	(19) 50.0%	60.5%	(10) 26.3%	(5) 13.2%
142	Total	(26) 18.3%	(73) 51.4%	69.7%	(33) 23.2%	(10) 7.0%
San Diego						
39	1	(5) 12.8%	(24) 61.5%	74.3%	(6) 15.4%	(4) 10.3%
37	2	(8) 21.6%	(18) 48.7%	70.3%	(9) 24.3%	(2) 5.4%
44	3	(14) 31.8%	(17) 38.6%	69.4%	(11) 25%	(2) 4.6%
40	4	(9) 22.5%	(18) 45.0%	67.5%	(8) 20%	(5) 12.5%
160	Total	(36) 22.5%	(77) 48.1%	70.6%	(34) 21.2%	(13) 8.1%

Note: Results are percentages; figures in parentheses are the relevant number of audits.

Table 5.3 OUTCOMES IN THE DENVER STUDY (Aggregate Data)

Total	Pair	Majority favored	Minority favored	Neither favored
140	Hispanic/Anglo	(26) 18.6%	(36) 25.7%	(78) 55.7%
145	Black/White	(17) 11.7%	(15) 10.3%	(113) 77.9%

Notes: Results are percentages; figures in parentheses are the relevant number of audits. The study is reported in James and DelCastillo (1991).

one of the most striking features of all three tables is the relatively high proportion of trials in which there was no difference in treatment by race/ethnicity—roughly 80 percent by the get-a-job measure. The Denver Hispanic/Anglo study showed the smallest proportion of equal treatment, but in that study Hispanics were actually favored over Anglos. Compared with the housing audit studies of Yinger (1986) or the car negotiations tested by Ayres and Siegelman (1993), the proportion of tests in which applicants received equal treatment is very high. By focusing on the disparities between the treatment of majority and minority group members, the Urban Institute studies deemphasize the high proportion of audits in which equal treatment of both partners was found. An appropriate question, therefore, is "whether the glass is one-quarter empty or three-quarters full?" In all of the audit pair studies it seems quite full to us.

Symmetrical Treatment vs. Zero Differences

Any measure of discrimination can be justified only in terms of an implicit or explicit model of how discrimination arises. In a later section we present a model that seems rich enough to enable us to evaluate various measures. The UIBW study (though not the UIAH study) defines discrimination by the proportion of trials in which members of a pair of matched testers were treated differently.[9] While this definition has some appeal, it has some peculiar implications and is based on a somewhat implausible model of an error-free hiring process.

For example, consider the following hypothetical audit pair outcome:

	Tester's Race	
Firm	White	Black
1	Offer	No offer
2	No offer	Offer

Under the UIBW definition, if the white tester gets a job offer from firm 1, while the black tester doesn't, we conclude that there is discrimination in favor of the white tester at firm 1. If the black tester gets a job offer from firm 2, and the white tester does not, we conclude that there is discrimination at firm 2 as well (although, of course, in the opposite direction). The UIBW definition therefore implies that we are observing discrimination at both firms. Suppose that, consistent with these results, firm 1 openly advertises that it will hire only white applicants, while firm 2 makes it clear that it will hire only black applicants.[10] These behaviors would both be a clear violation of race-neutral hiring, so the definition seems appropriate in this setting—we would want to sum the differences in treatment across firms to determine how much discrimination there was. Applying this definition to the numbers in the second panel of table 5.1 suggests that 14.1 percent of the audit observations in Chicago were consistent with discriminatory behavior on the part of firms.

But another possibility is also worth considering. Suppose that testers A and B are identical in all respects (except for race), that both firms saw the two candidates as very close, but that "random factors" led firm 1 to prefer the white tester and firm 2 to prefer the black. As long as there is some uncertainty about future productivity, or there are characteristics valued by a firm that cannot be perfectly aligned in an audit pair and there is scope for intrafirm variability in the ranking of the two candidates unrelated to their race or ethnicity, there is no reason to imagine that every instance of differential treatment constitutes discrimination. It could rather be the case that both testers face the same chance of getting a job at either of these two firms (and at every other firm in this hypothetical economy).

This possibility suggests a different definition of what constitutes discrimination. Discrimination exists whenever two testers in a matched pair are treated differently in the aggregate or on average. Thus, rather than suggesting discrimination at both firms, the hypothetical outcomes presented above could also support an inference of no discrimination in the aggregate.[11] Rather than summing the differences in treatment, we would subtract them to arrive at a net amount that reflects average treatment across all firms.[12]

The net, or symmetric treatment, definition is consistent with the view that whites experience no discrimination and that the proportion of trials in which blacks are hired and whites are not constitutes a benchmark measure for "randomness" in employment decisions. (It is also consistent with the view that one cannot measure an absolute level of discrimination in the labor market but that asymmetry of treatment of "identical" persons constitutes evidence of discrimination.) By this measure, there is evidence of discrimination in only 7.1

percent of the Chicago audits summarized in the first panel of table 5.1. This second definition asks whether in the aggregate the two testers in a pair are "exchangeable"—whether there is *symmetric* treatment of the two testers—while the first definition sees each instance of disparate treatment as evidence of discrimination. The second definition is only an aggregate measure and is consistent with an economy in which half the firms employ only blacks and half employ only whites and both black and white workers sample from the same universe.

The UIBW study essentially adds a measure of asymmetric treatment favoring whites (the proportion of times a white is hired and a black is not) and asymmetric treatment favoring blacks (the proportion of times a black is hired and a white is not) to arrive at a total amount of discrimination. But this makes sense only if one believes that asymmetric treatment of both blacks and whites is race based. If asymmetric treatment against blacks is race based but asymmetric treatment against whites simply reflects employer "errors" in the hiring process, it is meaningless to add the two measures to form an index of overall discrimination.[13]

The choice between the two definitions of discrimination is not entirely straightforward. We would not want to preclude the possibility of detecting reverse discrimination, should it be occurring. The UIBW study properly raises this possibility, although only implicitly.

However, the exchangeability or symmetry definition of no discrimination, which allows for random errors in hiring, is the natural point of departure for any statistical testing procedure. The first definition is a special case of the second in which blacks and whites are treated symmetrically both on average (as in the second definition) and in each instance. (The first definition of no discrimination requires symmetry in the sense that the probability that a black is hired and a white is not should equal the probability that a white is hired and a black is not, and *both should equal zero*.) In terms of testing hypotheses, it is desirable to start with the weaker version. If blacks and whites are treated asymmetrically by the second definition, they cannot be treated symmetrically by the first definition.

The choice of a measure of discrimination vitally affects the interpretation of the evidence in tables 5.1 through 5.3 and the choice of an appropriate test statistic. To see this it is useful to be more precise. Let P_i be the population probability of outcome i. There are four mutually exclusive and exhaustive outcomes in the second panel of table 5.1: (a) Both auditors get a job ($i = 1$); (b) neither gets a job ($i = 2$); (c) white gets a job but black does not $5(i = 3)$; (d) black gets a job but white does not ($i = 4$). The underlying probability model is thus multinomial.

By definition,

$$\sum_{i=1}^{4} P_i = 1.$$

Under the UIBW definition of discrimination, the null hypothesis being tested is H_0: $P_3 + P_4 = 0$. That is, $P_3 = P_4 = 0$, since both P_3 and P_4 are nonnegative. Using large-sample test statistics, UIBW presents evidence that rejects this hypothesis. The study therefore concludes that there is significant discrimination in hiring.

Under the alternative definition, the appropriate hypothesis is one of exchangeability or symmetry of outcomes: H_0': $P_3 = P_4$. This definition is intuitively more plausible because it allows for the possibility of race neutral chance or randomness in the hiring and screening process in a way that H_0 does not. Obviously H_0 implies H_0'. Rejection of H_0' implies rejection of H_0.

Hypothesis H_0 raises a technical problem that is finessed in the UIBW study by its use of normal approximations to multinomial cell means. The problem is that of testing for a zero probability. UIBW uses standard t-tests to compare sample proportions with zero. The study ignores the fact that the exact variance of the test statistic is zero under the null hypothesis, which implies that standard classical test statistics are invalid.[14] Thus, on purely technical grounds, H_0 is not an attractive null hypothesis. There is no nonrandomized test of the hypothesis with size α (> 0), although if the estimated cell probabilities are nonzero one can safely reject the null with size $= 0$ (i.e., the probability of a type I error equals zero). This problem is alleviated by testing the weaker null hypothesis H_0', the net definition.

Even in situations in which the maintained hypothesis bounds the P_i away from one or zero, some caution is required in using large-sample theory to test hypotheses given the small samples that are an intrinsic feature of audit pair studies. In both the design of the study (i.e., sample size and power calculations) and the interpretation of the evidence, it would be more appropriate to use exact small-sample theory for multinomial models. In Heckman and Siegelman (1993), we consider matters of optimal sample design and the issue of the suitability of large sample theory for small-sample audit studies. For the main tests of interest, large-sample theory is often very inappropriate. It is unfortunate that it has become enshrined in sampling textbooks, and was used by UI to design its samples and interpret its evidence.

Tests for Homogeneity across Pairs (Pooling)

Before presenting tests of hypothesis H'_0, it is necessary to address an important problem not considered in the UI studies: whether it is possible to pool the data across audit pairs. The UIBW and Denver studies assumed that simple pooling (i.e., adding up estimates across audit pairs using unweighted observations) produces valid statistical inferences. Both the UI and the Denver studies pooled observations across individual audit pairs within sites. Such pooling is valid if there is homogeneity in the selection of firms across pairs and if audit pairs are comparably matched (which means only that any discrepancies between minority and majority members are uniform across pairs, not that the two members of each pair are identically matched). Homogeneity across audit pairs is a testable hypothesis, which we now examine. Below we demonstrate that homogeneity in the skill level across pairs in any given site is not necessarily a desirable feature of an audit study. Homogeneous data characterizes only a single skill level and may not represent the dispersion across types in a given demographic group that typifies actual labor markets.[15] A study that forces homogeneity across pairs may not present a valid description of the market for all workers in the sites being studied. Evidence of homogeneity is, however, consistent with the claimed uniformity across audit pairs in the UI and Denver reports, and a test of homogeneity is a test of the efficacy of the auditor matching and selection procedures. Tests for inhomogeneity may indicate whether a single (possibly misaligned) audit pair drives the results of tests for discrimination at any site, although inhomogeneity may also arise if auditors are perfectly aligned within pairs but different levels are selected across pairs.

To examine this issue, we use a standard test for equality of cell proportions across rows for each of the panels in tables 5.1 and 5.2. More formally, we test for homogeneity of rows in contingency tables assuming product multinomial sampling for pairs—the scheme actually used in the UI studies. (See Bishop et al. 1975, 63, for a definition of this sampling scheme.) A detailed description of the test is given in appendix 5.A. Table 5.4 presents the results of these tests for the get-a-job tables. The evidence suggests homogeneity across audit pair teams except for Chicago blacks. (These results are confirmed

Table 5.4 COMPARISON OF χ^2, "AUGMENTED CELL" χ^2, AND CRESSIE-READ
TESTS FOR POOLING OF OUTCOMES ACROSS PAIRS

Blacks vs. Whites	
Washington, D.C.	
$\chi^2_{(12)}$	3.27
Augmented[a]	3.02
Cressie-Read[b]	3.26
Chicago	
$\chi^2_{(12)}$	25.09*
Augmented	21.46*
Cressie-Read	24.49*
Both Cities	
$\chi^2_{(27)}$	38.68
Augmented	34.68
Cressie-Read	39.03

Hispanics vs. Anglos	
Chicago	
$\chi^2_{(9)}$	8.50
Augmented	7.49
Cressie-Read	8.48
San Diego	
$\chi^2_{(9)}$	9.01
Augmented	8.41
Cressie-Read	9.02
Both Cities	
$\chi^2_{(21)}$	18.29
Augmented	16.65
Cressie-Read	18.37

*Significantly different from zero at the 5 percent level for a χ^2 test with the appropriate
degrees of freedom.
[a]Calculated by adding 0.5 to the value in each cell and computing a χ^2 statistic.
[b]Cressie-Read evaluated at $\lambda = 0.666$.

when Fisher's exact test for pooling is performed.) In the analysis of the Denver data, below, we test for, and reject, homogeneity across audit pairs.

For Chicago blacks, audit pairs 2 and 5 are the sources of the in-homogeneity. Interestingly, these appear to be the pairs that evidence little asymmetry of treatment between minority and majority auditors. Table 5.5 presents the cell-by-cell difference between the proportion predicted under homogeneity and the actual cell. These residuals are asymptotically normal and confirm the claim that the main source of inhomogeneity in the Chicago data is in audit pairs 2 and 5.

Appendix 5.B presents evidence that large sample theory is producing correct inferences in the homogeneity tests. The "Cressie-Read" statistics are a family of asymptotically equivalent test statistics that can produce different inferences in small samples. When they do not, we have greater confidence in applying large sample methods. Evidence from Fisher's exact test reported in Heckman and Siegelman (1993) confirms the validity of the asymptotic test statistics for testing homogeneity.

Tests for Symmetry of Treatment

Visual inspection of tables 5.1 through 5.3 reveals that one can decisively reject the strong hypothesis H_0—the "gross" definition of no discrimination in treatment ($P_3 = P_4 = 0$). This test has a zero type I error, but the hypothesis is implausibly strong. The evidence against the weaker symmetry in aggregate treatment hypothesis H_0' ($P_3 = P_4$) is less clear-cut.

Table 5.6 presents large-sample tests of symmetry for each audit pair and for sites as a whole. On a pair-by-pair basis, one can reject symmetry for only one Washington black audit pair and only one Chicago black audit pair using 5 percent significance levels. For the Washington pairs taken together, however, one rejects symmetry for the entire set of audit pairs. For Chicago pairs as a whole, one also rejects symmetry (although pooling the Chicago data is not legitimate, as indicated above). The source of the rejection is audit pair 4. For the Hispanic/Anglo comparisons in table 5.6, two of the four pairs in each site allow one to reject symmetry, so the hypothesis is rejected overall in both sites.

Elsewhere (Heckman and Siegelman, 1993) we investigate exact versions of the large-sample tests for symmetry on these data tests and demonstrate the fragility of the asymptotic statistics for all audit pairs, especially for Chicago blacks. This is already apparent from the Cres-

Table 5.5 RESIDUAL ANALYSIS OF AUDIT PAIR HOMOGENEITY

Pair	Both Got	Neither	W+, B−	W−, B+	Total	Residual*			
Blacks, Washington									
1	5	26	12	3	46	−1.16	−0.30	1.34	0.23
2	11	31	9	3	54	0.85	−0.19	−0.51	−0.09
3	11	36	11	4	62	0.28	−0.08	−0.31	0.25
4	6	22	7	2	37	−0.07	0.13	−0.03	−0.11
5	7	26	7	2	42	0.01	0.49	−0.44	−0.32
Total	40	141	46	14	241				
Blacks, Chicago									
1	5	23	5	2	35	0.65	−1.33	1.03	0.36
2	5	25	4	6	40	0.30	−1.97	0.09	3.54
3	3	37	3	1	44	−1.04	1.64	−0.72	−0.83
4	6	24	6	0	36	1.16	−1.21	1.58	−1.45
5	3	38	1	0	42	−0.93	2.66	−1.80	−1.60
Total	22	147	19	9	197				

Pair	Both Got	Neither	A+, H−	A−, H+	Total	Residual			
Hispanics, San Diego									
1	5	24	6	4	39	−1.66	1.93	−1.03	0.56
2	8	18	9	2	37	−0.15	0.07	0.52	−0.69
3	14	17	11	2	44	−1.74	−1.48	0.71	−1.02
4	9	18	8	5	40	0.00	−0.46	−0.22	1.17
Total	36	77	34	13	160				
Hispanics, Chicago									
1	9	16	7	1	33	1.52	−0.38	−0.31	−1.03
2	4	18	9	1	32	−0.97	0.62	0.74	−0.98
3	9	20	7	3	39	0.90	−0.02	−0.92	0.19
4	4	19	10	5	38	−1.45	−0.20	0.52	1.72
Total	26	73	33	10	142				

*Residual calculated as $R_{ij} = \dfrac{N_{ij} - N_i N_j / N}{[(N_i N_j / N)(1 - N_i / N)(1 - N_j / N)]^{1/2}}$ where N_i is number in row i, N_{ij} is number in cell ij, etc.

sie-Read diagnostic statistics reported in appendix 5.B. Asymptotically equivalent test statistics produce very different inferences for the symmetry hypothesis. Using an exact small sample version of a conventional likelihood ratio test and standard 5 percent significance levels we cannot reject symmetry for all UI sites. From this test, we would conclude that the evidence of discrimination is less clear and convincing than the title of this volume seems to suggest. We also fail to reject symmetry for the Denver audit studies using the same test.

But another, and better, way to look at the data is to notice their sign pattern. In UIAH, the pattern of outcomes is always in the same direction. That is, the minority-favored proportion $(\hat{P}_4)$ is always smaller than the majority favored proportion $(\hat{P}_3)$. Conditioning on observations that are in a 3 cell or a 4 cell, under the null hypothesis of symmetry, the probability of a "3" or a "4" is one-half. Sizable departures of

$$\hat{\theta} = \frac{\hat{P}_3}{\hat{P}_3 + \hat{P}_4}$$

from 1/2 in one direction indicate asymmetry in that direction. The UIAH patterns in both sites could happen only with probability $(\frac{1}{2})^8 = 1/256 = 0.3\%$. For each site (Chicago/San Diego separately), the probability is $(\frac{1}{2})^4 = 1/16 = 6.25\%$. These are relatively rare events under the null of symmetry. In UIBW, there is one reversal in ten audits. This happens with probability $\binom{10}{9}(\frac{1}{2})^{10} = 0.97\%$. There are no reversals in Washington $(p = 3.1\%)$ and one reversal in Chicago $(p = 15.62\%)$. With the exception of the test for Chicago blacks, the conditional sign test appears to support the UI conclusions much more than do conventional tests, an intuition that we make rigorous in our companion paper.

Tests based on $\hat{\theta}$ are conditional tests. They are so named because they are conducted on samples defined by certain conditioning events. In our case, the conditioning event is that only one member of an audit pair receives a job offer. There are two main advantages of such tests: (a) their size (probability of a type I error) does not depend on specific values of P_1, P_2, P_3 and P_4 which are generally unknown, and (b) they are uniformly most powerful compared to other test statistics for either one-sided or two-sided versions of the hypothesis of no discrimination,

$$H_0: \theta = \frac{P_3}{P_3 + P_4} = 1/2.$$

Table 5.6 LIKELIHOOD RATIO TESTS FOR SYMMETRICAL TREATMENT OF TESTERS WITHIN PAIRS, AND ACROSS PAIRS AND CITIES

Pair	Both got job	Neither got job	W yes B no	W no B yes	Total	$\chi^2(1)$
Part I: Blacks vs. Whites						
Washington						
1	5	26	12	3	46	5.78*
2	11	31	9	3	54	3.14
3	11	36	11	4	62	3.40
4	6	22	7	2	37	2.94
5	7	26	7	2	42	2.94
Aggregated	40	141	46	14	241	17.98*
Total $\chi^2(5)$						18.20*
Chicago						
1	5	23	5	2	35	1.33
2	5	25	4	6	40	0.40
3	3	37	3	1	44	1.05
4	6	24	6	0	36	8.32*
5	3	38	1	0	42	1.39
Aggregated	22	147	19	9	197	3.65
Total $\chi^2(5)$						12.48*
Grand Total	62	288	65	23	438	20.89*
$\chi^2(10)$						30.68*

Part II: Hispanics vs. Anglos

San Diego					
1	5	24	6	4	39	0.40
2	8	18	9	2	37	4.82*
3	14	17	11	2	44	6.86*
4	9	18	8	5	40	0.70
Aggregated	36	77	34	13	160	9.72*
Total $\chi^2(4)$						12.78*
Chicago						
1	9	16	7	1	33	5.06*
2	4	18	9	1	32	7.36*
3	9	20	7	3	39	1.65
4	4	19	10	5	38	1.70
Aggregated	26	73	33	10	142	12.97*
Total $\chi^2(4)$						15.77*
Grand Total	62	150	67	23	302	22.46*
$\chi^2(8)$						28.55*

Notes: Likelihood ratio tests calculated as $2[\ln(L_u) - \ln(L_c)]$, where

L_u = unconstrained likelihood = $(N!/(N_1! \cdot N_2! \cdot N_3! \cdot N_4!)) \cdot (N_1/N)^{N1}(N_2/N)^{N2}(N_3/N)^{N3}(N_4/N)^{N4}$

L_c = constrained likelihood = $(N!/(N_1! \cdot N_2! \cdot N_3! \cdot N_4!)) \cdot (N_1/N)^{N1}(N_2/N)^{N2}([N_3 + N_4]/2N)^{N3+N4}$

* = Significant at the 5% level (critical value for $\chi^2(1) = 3.84$)

Aggregated is computed summing the first four audit pairs and treating them as one pair.

Total and Grand Total refer to the sums of the likelihood ratio statistics for the audit pairs in each table, and overall, respectively.

(See, e.g., Lehmann 1986, or Pratt and Gibbons 1981.)[16]

Neither property is shared by the classical and widely used likelihood ratio test statistic or the small sample t-test approximation to it. Because the small sample distribution of the likelihood ratio test statistic depends on particular values of P_3 and P_4, while the distribution of our conditional test statistic does not, the large sample properties of the likelihood ratio test statistic are a poor guide for small sample inferences. Within the classical (large sample) statistical model, this dependence on P_3 and P_4 is handled by picking as a testing point the *worst case* null (among all possible combinations of P_3 and P_4 that set $\theta = \frac{1}{2}$) so that the probability of a type I error is *no greater than* α (where α is usually .05 or .10). Such procedures are inherently conservative—there are many values of P_3 and P_4 for which the true type I error rate is much less than α. (In our companion paper we show that there are values of P_3 and P_4 near zero that make the type I error rate arbitrarily small.)

A more efficient use of the inherently small sample information available from audit pair studies is based on conditional inference. When it is used, the evidence, on a pair by pair basis, *rejects* H_0: $\theta = \frac{1}{2}$ more frequently (i.e., finds more evidence of disparity in treatment) than when widely used likelihood ratio tests are correctly employed. In our companion paper we develop in detail the argument that conditional inference is the more appropriate framework for analyzing small sample audit pair data. Details of the construction of the conditional test are given in appendix 5.C.

All of this discussion is conducted for a single pair. What is the appropriate procedure for combining evidence across pairs within a given study? If the pairs are homogeneous (identical under the null and identical under the alternative $\theta \neq \frac{1}{2}$), the appropriate way to pool the data across pairs is to combine the results from all pairs to make a single "synthetic" pair and then use the conditional procedures just described to test H_0: $\theta = \frac{1}{2}$. When the alternatives are not the same for all pairs, the matter is more delicate. A full analysis is presented in our companion paper.

One way to combine information in this more general setting is to use the tools of meta-analysis (see, e.g., Hedges and Olkin, 1985). An easy way to deal with heterogeneous alternatives is to use Fisher's pooling method for p values, adjusting for continuity using the method of Pearson (1950).[17]

Table 5.7 presents evidence on these issues. For each pair, for the synthetic pair created by aggregating over all pairs, and for two pooling procedures, we examine the conflict in inference that arises from using alternative testing procedures. The first column records the study. The second records the pair number. The third reports the conventional likelihood ratio test for each pair, for the synthetic pair formed by adding the results for each of the pairs ("Aggregate"), and for the sum of the likelihood ratios for each pair ("$\Sigma 2$lik ratio").

The fourth column reports the inference from a 5 percent exact one-sided test: H_0: $\theta = \frac{1}{2}$ vs. H_0: $\theta > \frac{1}{2}$. "R" means reject. "R(b)" means reject $b \times 100\%$ of the time using a randomized testing procedure. (Randomization is required to produce exact α percent values.) The higher is "b", the more confident we would be in rejecting the hypothesis (i.e., the more likely it is that the outcome in hand would produce a rejection on a randomized test). The fifth column reports the inference from an exact two-sided test (H_0: $\theta = \frac{1}{2}$ vs. H_A: $\theta \neq \frac{1}{2}$). The last column reports the Fisher pooled p value test using one-sided tests (and adjusting for discontinuity in the p values). This test recognizes that the pairs may be heterogeneous, as is certainly the case for Chicago blacks, and Denver blacks and Hispanics. We do not report the conservative small sample adjustment to the likelihood ratio statistics. These adjustments mark up the size of the "true" (least favorable) type I error associated with the conventional likelihood ratio test statistic. The individual Denver data are presented in table 5.10 (p. 221).

The general pattern is that the exact tests tend to reject the null H_0: $P_3 = P_4$ at the 5 percent level more often than the conventional likelihood ratio tests on a pair-by-pair basis. This is even true for the synthetic pairs. The summed likelihood ratio tests are larger than the synthetic pair likelihood ratio tests, but this difference is misleading because the latter are $\chi^2(1)$ whereas the former are $\chi^2(4)$ or $\chi^2(5)$. Pooled p values aggregated in the manner of Fisher, produce much less sharp rejections of the null. The "optimal" pooling procedure across pairs is discussed in our companion paper. Pooling data by forming synthetic pairs overstates the strength with which we can reject the null hypothesis of symmetry.

Appendix 5.C presents evidence from another statistical model that allows for heterogeneity among the audit pairs in each UI site. This heterogeneity can arise as a consequence of sampling variability in the set of firms selected for a particular audit pair member. If we assume that the P_i from each site are observations from a Dirichelet distribution, it is possible to estimate the distribution of the P_i and test the hypothesis of symmetry. The test in this case is of the hypothesis that the marginal distributions of P_3 and P_4 are equal. The hypothesis is rejected in all studies except for Chicago blacks.

Table 5.7 INFERENCE ON H_0: $P_3 = P_4$ FROM LARGE SAMPLE, EXACT TESTS, AND POOLED P VALUES

Study	Pair	Likelihood Ratio Statistic	Exact One Sided[c] 5% Test	Exact Two Sided 5% Test	Fisher Pooled Test with Pearson Continuity Correction (One Sided Test)[g]
Black vs. Whites Washington	1	5.78	R[d]	R[d]	
	2	3.14	R(.57)[e]	R(.11)[e]	
	3	3.40	R(.77)	R(.18)	
	4	2.94	R(.77)	R(.77)	
	5	2.94	R(.77)	R(.77)	
	Aggregate[a]	17.98 ($\chi^2(1)$)	R	R	28.61 ($\chi^2(10)$)
	Σ2lik ratio[b]	18.20 ($\chi^2(4)$)			
Blacks vs. Whites Chicago	1	1.33	NR	NR	
	2	.40	NR	NR	
	3	1.05	NR	NR	
	4	8.32	R	R	
	5	1.39	R(.10)	R(.05)	
	Aggregate[a]	3.65 ($\chi^2(1)$)	R	R(.28)	15.40 ($\chi^2(10)$)
	Σ2lik ratio[b]	12.48 ($\chi^2(5)$)			
Hispanics vs. Anglos San Diego	1	.40	NR	NR	
	2	4.82	R	R(.71)	
	3	6.86	R	R	
	4	.70	NR	NR	
	Aggregate[a]	9.72 ($\chi^2(1)$)	R	R	20.24 ($\chi^2(8)$)
	Σ2lik ratio[b]	12.78 ($\chi^2(4)$)			
Blacks vs. Whites Washington	1	5.06	R	R(.68)	
	2	7.36	R	R	
	3	1.65	NR	NR	
	4	1.70	NR	NR	

Aggregate[a]	12.97 (χ²(1))	R	R	23.07 (χ²(8))
Σ2lik ratio[b]	15.77 (χ²(4))			
Black vs. Whites				
Denver				
1	6.93	NR	R(.8)	
2	13.86	R	R	
3	1.39	R(1)	R(.05)	
4	0.34	NR	NR	
9	0	—[f]	—	
Aggregate	1.33 (χ²(11))	NR	NR	15.25 (χ²(10))
Σ2lik ratio[b]	22.52 (χ²(4))			
Hispanics vs. Anglos				
Denver				
5	1.39	R(.1)	R(.05)	
6	7.72	NR	R	
7	0	—[f]	—	
8	1.02	NR	NR	
Aggregate[a]	3.06 (χ²(4))	R(.64)	NR	2.75 (χ²(10))
Σ2lik ratio[b]	13.19 (χ²(4))			

Notes: [a] Aggregate treats data from all pairs as a single pair. This is the correct procedure if P_1, P_2, P_3, P_4, values are the same across pairs under the null and the alternative.

[b] Sum of 2ln likelihood across audit pairs: $\chi^2(4) = 9.49$ at 5%; $\chi^2(5) = 11.07$ at 5%.

[c] The one-sided alternative considered is $P_3 > P_4$.

[d] R means reject at 5% significance level using Uniformly Most Powerful Unbiased Test (UMPU). NR means we do not reject equality.

[e] R(.57) means that 57% of the time one would reject the hypothesis at a 5% significance level using a randomized test.

[f] Cannot be evaluated.

[g] This is the Fisher Aggregation Test for Pooling p-values for one-sided test $\frac{P_3}{P_3 + P_4} = 1/2$ vs. $\frac{P_3}{P_3 + P_4} > 1/2$ using Pearson's (1950) continuity correction as obtained from the median of 1,000 trials to correct P values for discontinuity in the data. It is distributed $\chi^2(2K)$ where K = number of pairs. $\chi^2(10) = 18.31$ at 5% level; $\chi^2(8) = 15.51$ at 5% level; $\chi^2(1) = 3.84$ at 5% level. The test statistic is $-2 \sum_{k=1}^{K} \ln p_k \sim \chi^2(2K)$ where p_k is the one-sided p value (for $\theta > 1/2$) and K is the number of audit pairs. See Hedges and Olkin (1986).

One should be cautious about this particular piece of evidence, however, because the justification for it is based on large sample statistics. This test is discussed further in Heckman and Siegelman (1993). In that paper we also present exact small-sample tests based on the multinomial distribution. Accounting for the composite nature of the null hypothesis $P_3 = P_4$ (see Lehmann 1989) and the composite nature of the alternative ($P_3 \neq P_4$), these tests do not support the inferences based on the standard asymptotic distributions. The classical large sample tests conventionally applied understate the size of tests, sometimes badly so. The bias in using conventional testing methods is toward rejecting equality of treatment, i.e., toward finding discrimination.

Our reanalysis of the data produces the following conclusions. For Chicago blacks, Denver blacks and Denver Hispanics, conventional likelihood ratio test statistics do *not* reject the hypothesis of symmetry of treatment. When adjusted for their small sample dependence on P_3 and P_4, the evidence produced from these statistics is much less strong (see our companion paper). However, use of exact small-sample conditional statistics produces sharper evidence against the null of symmetric treatment.

In this paper, we have not presented a thorough analysis of aggregation across pairs when there is interpair heterogeneity. Tests based on synthetic pairs reject the null of symmetry much more strongly than tests that allow for heterogeneity. Our companion paper pursues this point at length.

In sum, our analysis to date demonstrates (a) the value of making pairs homogeneous and (b) the value of using exact conditional testing procedures to test the hypothesis of symmetry. Large sample tests are misleading in light of their true small sample performance. Tests that rely on large sample methods to design and evaluate an intrinsically small sample problem fail to exploit the full promise of the audit method.

We next turn to the question of what the evidence from the large sample tests would mean about the prevalence of discrimination in the tested labor markets if it were taken at face value.

QUALIFYING THE URBAN INSTITUTE CONCLUSIONS: SOME LIMITATIONS OF THE EVIDENCE

This section addresses four aspects of the audit methods used in the employment discrimination studies. The first is the question of the proper sampling frame for selecting the firms and jobs to be audited. The second is the possibility of "experimenter effects." The third is the possible bias induced by using false credentials to align audit pair members within a pair and to the skill level of the market being studied. The fourth is the possible problem posed by the presence of facial hair and accents among the Hispanic testers.

Sampling Frame

The Urban Institute studies presented persuasive reasons for sampling jobs from newspaper advertisements. Employers seeking applicants through this route clearly signal the availability of jobs. For audit studies with limited budgets and operating over limited time frames, it is clearly much more cost-efficient to sample firms with jobs than it is to sample the universe of all firms to determine subsamples of firms that are hiring.

An important drawback to the use of newspaper advertisements in constructing the sampling frame, however, is that relatively few actual jobs are obtained through this route, even for youth participating in the unskilled labor markets analyzed in the Urban Institute and Denver studies. Recent evidence by Holzer (1988), presented in tables 5.8 and 5.9, indicates that friends and relatives and direct contact of firms by applicants are much more common sources of jobs in searches by both employed and unemployed youth. For employed youth, only 26 percent of search time is spent on contacts generated by newspaper advertising. For unemployed youth, the corresponding figure is only 18 percent (see table 5.8.). Table 5.9 documents that job acceptances from newspaper-generated searches are much less common than acceptances from other sources. In sum, youths' job searches are characterized by primary use of informal networks.[18] Sampling from these networks poses a major challenge to the audit pair methodology.

Holzer's evidence suggests that the sampling frame adopted in the UI studies is not representative of the job search process followed by most workers. The UI studies claim that this lack of representativeness leads to an understatement of the extent of labor market discrimination as measured by their studies. Their argument is that discriminatory firms are more likely to use informal employment sources, rather than publicly advertising for applicants, in an effort to conceal their discriminatory practices and avoid prosecution under employment discrimination laws.

The claim that firms that hire through networks are inherently more discriminatory than firms that hire from newspaper advertisements

Table 5.8 SEARCH METHODS OF EMPLOYED AND UNEMPLOYED JOB SEEKERS:
MEANS AND STANDARD DEVIATIONS

Search Method	Employed		Unemployed	
Number of methods used	2.723		3.285	
	(1.283)		(1.261)	
Percentage using:				
Friends/relatives	.873		.852	
Direct contact	.693		.796	
State agency	.303		.538	
Newspaper	.449		.578	
Other methods[a]	.409		.524	
Time[b] spent by those using:				
Friends/relatives	167.81		295.97	
	(309.71)		(516.37)	
Direct contact	271.71		363.28	
	(238.69)		(536.28)	
State agency	147.07		212.23	
	(148.37)		(298.09)	
Newspapers	251.04	26%	237.74	18%
	(454.99)		(309.11)	
Other methods[a]	121.55		218.65	
	(113.46)		(251.11)	
Total minutes	959.2		1328.00	

Sources: National Longitudinal Survey New Youth Cohort, 1981 panel. Holzer, July 1987, table 1.
Notes: All means are weighted. Sample sizes are 438 for employed seekers and 609 for unemployed seekers.
[a]Other methods include private agencies, school placement offices, labor unions, and community organizations.
[b]Minutes spent on the search method.

must be treated with caution, however. The use of informal networks may simply be an efficient means of screening prospective workers, in that firms may prefer to rely on the information and reputation of existing workers when considering new applicants. In light of the great gains made by minority workers in unskilled markets in the past 25 years, it is not obvious that informal networks now act to exclude minorities. Indeed, in unskilled markets like those studied by the Urban Institute, it seems likely that there are both majority and minority networks that certify applicants by word of mouth.

Nevertheless, Holzer (1987) reports that the fraction of blacks using each search method is virtually identical to that of whites but that job offers from friends and relatives and direct contacts are greater for whites than for blacks. Whites spend more time searching by direct

Table 5.9 OUTCOMES OF SEARCH METHODS USED BY UNEMPLOYED YOUTH

Outcome	Percentage
Percent of job seekers who reported:	
One offer	.220
Two or more offers	.120
Percent of job seekers who reported:	
Friends/relatives	.177
Direct contact	.186
State agency	.089
Newspaper	.099
Other methods	.078
Percent of job seekers who reported:	
One job acceptance	.243
Two or more job acceptances	.043
Percent of job seekers who reported acceptances from use of:	
Friends/relatives	.143
Direct contact	.121
State agency	.048
Newspaper	.040
Other methods	.050

Source: Holzer (1987).
Notes: Samples for those reporting offers and acceptances for each method include only those who used each one. All means are weighted.

application and through leads generated by friends and relatives than do blacks (397 minutes vs. 252 minutes, respectively, for searches via friends and relatives). Blacks spend more time on searches at state agencies (292 minutes vs. 187 minutes), newspaper searches (292 minutes vs. 223 minutes) and other methods (266 minutes vs. 205 minutes). Assuming rational search behavior by both blacks and whites, this pattern provides indirect support for the UI claim that firms advertising in newspapers are less discriminatory.

Future research should make an effort to audit jobs obtained through informal networks, such as those obtained by word of mouth. Such jobs are clearly much more difficult to identify, and the paired-tester approach is unlikely to be a feasible way to sample most of the hiring action in the labor market. Accordingly, evidence from labor market audit studies has uncertain generality.[19]

Experimenter Effects

By experimenter effects, we mean that "the experimenter is not simply a passive runner of subjects, but can actually influence the results" of an experiment (Lindzey and Aronson 1975, 66). When it exists, such influence is not exerted by any deliberate or conscious actions on the part of the experimenter but, rather, occurs because of unconscious motivations or because subjects may have a desire to conform to (what they perceive as) the experimenter's wishes.

Social psychologists, who have a much longer and more sophisticated tradition of behavioral experiments than do economists, take experimenter effects extremely seriously. In one experiment involving learning in rats, for example, "each experimenter was randomly assigned a rat after being told that the animal had been specially bred for brightness or dullness. Lo and behold, when the results were tabulated, the so-called bright rats learned more quickly than the so-called dull rats" (Lindzey and Aronson 1975, 67).[20]

Anyone who doubts the importance of experimenter effects need only consider the importance of controls in the testing of new drugs. According to one expert, "it is not at all unusual to find placebo effects that are more powerful than the actual chemical effects of drugs whose pharmacological action is fairly well understood" (Rosenthal 1976, 134). Studies evaluating the effects of drugs are always double blind (neither the patient nor the experimenter knows whether the drug being administered is a placebo or the real drug) precisely to minimize such effects.

Both of the Urban Institute studies, as well as the Denver audits, are potentially subject to experimenter effects. All three studies made a point of stressing the nature of the experiment and its expected findings to the testers in several days of training. This was done in part to minimize the psychological impact of discriminatory treatment on minority auditors, but it may have had perverse unintended effects. (However, the performance of the other testers in the project was not revealed to any tester, so at least there was no contamination from direct feedbacks.) An explicit part of the training of auditors was a general discussion of the pervasive problem of discrimination in the United States.

In the UIBW study, part of the first day of the five-day auditor training session included an introduction to employment discrimination and equal employment opportunity and a review of project design and methodology. Similar protocols were used in UIAH. In both studies, participants were warned about the employer bias they might encounter and how they should react to it. We would prefer an experimental design in which the testers themselves were kept ignorant of the hypothesis being tested (discriminatory hiring) and the fact that they were operating in pairs.

Posing and the Use of False Credentials

All of the studies supplied applicants with partially false credentials in order to make audit pair members resemble each other more closely. All of them used college students who masqueraded as blue collar workers seeking entry level jobs. Apart from the ethical issues involved, this raises the potentially important problem that the tester/actors may not have experienced what actually occurs in these labor markets among real participants. For one thing, the auditors may have been overqualified, or have been perceived as overqualified by employers. These suspicions may have been reinforced by the time of year at which the applicants appeared at the door. The audits were conducted in the summer, in order to accommodate the summer schedule of the auditors. At such times, it would be natural for employers seeking long-term workers to be suspicious that the auditors were actually college students who would not stick around in the fall. Credentials may be more closely checked in summer months for this reason, especially for persons who appear to be overqualified. If race or ethnicity is a factor in arousing employer suspicion, differential checking rates by race/ethnicity of applicant, and subsequent discovery of falsified data, might account for the UI findings of no discrimination. Since whites are more likely to attend college than blacks (Cameron and Heckman 1992), white credentials may be more likely to be checked. If the discovery of forged credentials leads to lower white hiring rates, black/white differentials in job offer rates would be understated. On the other hand, discrimination on the part of employers may take the form of greater suspicion of blacks and their credentials than of whites and their credentials. More checking of black credentials, and greater subsequent discovery of false credentials, could lead to an overstatement of true black-white racial disparity in hiring.

If credentials are not, in fact, checked by firms, as UI staff have claimed is the case, this would allay our concerns. It would be helpful to document that the concerns raised in this subsection are irrelevant, if in fact they are.

Facial Hair and Accents

In the Urban Institute study, all the Hispanic testers in San Diego had facial hair and strong Hispanic accents.[21] The presence of accents, facial hair, or any other characteristic across *all* testers of one type is unfortunate because it means that the hypotheses of discrimination against "accents" or "hair" are observationally equivalent to (indistinguishable from) the hypothesis of discrimination against Hispanics per se. There is some evidence that employers are sensitive to the general appearance or "attractiveness" of applicants.[22] Thus, it is interesting and important to know whether Hispanic men without beards and/or accents do better relative to whites than do those with these characteristics.[23] The fact that in Denver, Hispanic men were more like Anglo men in these characteristics, and did not experience discrimination, indicates that this problem is potentially serious.

Using the presence of facial hair or an accent—rather than race/ethnicity itself—to make hiring decisions could constitute discrimination that would subject an employer to "disparate impact" liability under Title VII of the 1964 Civil Rights Act.[24] Since effect, not intent, is what is at issue in such cases, if Hispanics were disproportionately hurt by a "no beards" or "no accents" rule, one might be able to mount a legal challenge to such a rule. Still, it makes an important difference to policy whether employers are using ethnicity directly in making hiring decisions, or are instead relying on apparently neutral rules that disproportionately hurt minorities. Moreover, in the context of the audit pair methodology, in which Anglo and Hispanic testers were virtually identical in all other observable productivity-related characteristics, slight differences in accents (or facial hair) could have ended up being more important in employers' decisions than they ordinarily are. In other words, employers might have used accents or facial hair only to "break a tie" between candidates who were otherwise identical. This kind of behavior might well constitute discrimination, but it is probably an unusual kind of discrimination compared to what typically occurs in the market, with very different policy implications.[25]

ADDITIONAL COMMENTS ON THE AUDIT STUDIES

Evidence on Reverse Discrimination

Those who see reverse discrimination as a more serious problem than discrimination against racial/ethnic minorities will find no support in any of these findings. In virtually no dimension did white and Anglo auditors consistently do worse than their black and Hispanic partners.

Evidence on the Role of Hiring Discrimination in Explaining the Wage Gap

Using large sample test statistics, a clear pattern of discrimination against blacks is found in the UIBW Washington study. Since government jobs were excluded from the universe from which employers were sampled, it is not clear how seriously these findings are to be taken as a general description of that market.

Taken at face value, the disparity between black and white job offer rates is substantial. Whites were offered jobs in 35.7 percent of the interviews, while blacks were offered jobs in only 22.4 percent of the interviews. These figures imply that blacks would have to sample about 50 percent more jobs than whites to get an offer.

In a simple model of job search with identical fixed-costs components for blacks and whites, as well as common wage offer distributions and discount rates, these results indicate that blacks would have lower reservation wages and lower accepted wages than whites. Wages observed for working blacks would be lower than wages observed for working whites even if employers made identical wage offers to accepted blacks and whites.

However, it does not follow that blacks would necessarily have higher unemployment rates than whites, although it does follow that with identical nonmarket opportunities, blacks would have lower labor force participation rates. For hiring discrimination to produce higher black unemployment rates requires special conditions on the shape of the wage offer distribution (see Flinn and Heckman 1983 or Van den Berg 1991). Lower reservation wages may offset the effect of lower job offer rates. For the Urban Institute to translate its evidence into convincing stories about unemployment, and about the contribution of hiring discrimination to the wage gap, it will be necessary to collect information on offered wages. In order to gain a more complete understanding of labor market disparities between blacks and whites, it is necessary to know the rate of arrival of potential job offers to race groups. The audit studies produce no information on this question because majority and minority partners are necessarily sent to the same firms at the same rate. It would be necessary to supplement the audit data with conventional labor market surveys in order to parse out the roles of individual search and firm behavior in accounting for majority/minority differences in unemployment and labor force attachment.

No evidence is offered in any of the studies under consideration that discrimination in hiring has increased over time or that the post-

1966 decline in relative labor force participation rates for black males compared with white males is a consequence of increased discrimination in hiring.

Comparing the Denver and Urban Institute Studies

An interesting problem posed by the collection of audit studies considered here is the apparent disparity in the results between the two Urban Institute studies on one hand and the Denver studies on the other.[26] While the Urban Institute studies based on large sample testing methods apparently find evidence of discrimination against Hispanics in San Diego and Chicago, and in Washington, D.C. against blacks, the Denver study suggests virtually no discrimination against either of these groups.

Two explanations for these divergent results should be considered. One possibility is that the differences are simply artifacts of methodological differences between the two groups of studies. Although the methodology used in Denver was patterned after that of the Urban Institute studies, there were some differences that may have had an effect on the results. The second possibility is that there is actually less discrimination (against both blacks and Hispanics) in Denver than in Chicago, San Diego, or Washington, D.C.

Of course, these are not mutually exclusive explanations—both could be operating at the same time. In fact, our view is that the differences between Denver and the other cities seem small enough to be explained by either of the two sources, or both together.

The disaggregated data from the Denver experiments are presented in table 5.10. While we do not resolve this issue definitively in this paper (but see Heckman and Siegelman 1993), the data strongly suggest that the pairs of Denver auditors were much more heterogeneous (diverse) than are the pairs in either UIBW or UIAH. Thus, while the aggregate experience for *all* Denver audit pairs reveals little evidence of discriminatory treatment, this aggregation conceals large differences in the way certain pairs were treated. A Fisher exact test rejects the hypothesis of across-pair homogeneity, as does a large sample test.

Table 5.10 reveals that overall, black auditors got a job when their white partner did not in 7 out of 145 audits (4.8 percent); white auditors were favored in 12 audits (8.3 percent). According to the analysis presented in Table 5.7, this relatively small difference does not provide statistically significant evidence of the existence of discrimination at the aggregate level or at the individual level.

Table 5.10 DISAGGREGATED DENVER DATA: "GET A JOB" MEASURE

Pair	Both get job	Neither gets job	Black/White White yes, Black no	White no, Black yes	Total
1	(2) 11.1	(11) 61.1	(0) 0.0	(5) 27.8	(18)
2	(2) 3.8	(41) 77.4	(10) 18.9	(0) 0.0	(53)
3	(7) 21.2	(25) 75.8	(0) 0.0	(1) 3.0	(33)
4	(9) 60.0	(3) 20.0	(2) 13.3	(1) 6.7	(15)
9	(3) 11.5	(23) 88.5	(0) 0.0	(0) 0.0	(26)
Total	(23) 15.8	(103) 71.1	(7) 4.8	(12) 8.3	(145)

Pair	Both get job	Neither gets job	Hispanic/Anglo Anglo yes, Hispanic no	Anglo no, Hispanic yes	Total
5	(0) 0.0	(11) 91.7	(0) 0.0	(1) 8.3	(12)
6	(4) 7.8	(30) 58.8	(3) 5.9	(14) 27.5	(51)
7	(1) 2.8	(35) 97.2	(0) 0.0	(0) 0.0	(36)
8	(2) 4.9	(30) 73.2	(6) 14.6	(3) 7.3	(41)
Total	(7) 5.0	(106) 75.7	(18) 12.8	(9) 6.5	(140)

Note: Results are percentages; figures in parentheses are the relevant number of audits.
Source: Denver study.

The aggregate results conceal a widely disparate set of outcomes among the different pairs of testers, however. For example, consider pairs 1 and 2. In pair 1, the black tester was favored over his white partner in 5 out of the 18 tests, while the white tester was never favored. For pair 2, the results are dramatically opposite: the white tester was favored in 10 of the 53 tests, while the black tester was never favored. Roughly similar patterns can be observed for Hispanic/ Anglo pairs 6 and 8. In the notation developed earlier, the quantity $(P_3 - P_4)$ ranges from 28 percent to -19 percent for the black audit pairs, and from 21.6 percent to -7.3 percent for the Hispanic pairs. There are large differences among the different audit pairs that are masked when the experiences of all the pairs are aggregated.

The heterogeneity found in the Denver data raises three important issues. First, it demonstrates the importance of providing data at the disaggregated (pair-by-pair) level. Aggregation of audit pair results by city can obscure some important differences in the way individual pairs were treated, which can in turn influence the interpretation of the aggregate results. We note that the authors of all three studies were willing to furnish us with the disaggregated data. But these data were not part of the main bodies of the reports prepared by any of the audit teams. (The data were included in an appendix to UIAH.) We strongly urge that pair-by-pair data be included, as a matter of course, in future studies of this kind.

Second, both the Denver and UI studies show how difficult it is to draw inferences about the homogeneity of pairs from verbal descriptions of the selection and matching procedures by themselves. Looking only at the *descriptions* of the rigorous and careful procedures used in the Denver (or UI) studies, one would naturally be inclined to assume that the pairs were all quite homogeneous. In fact, however, we reject homogeneity in three of the six race/city sites (Denver blacks, Denver Hispanics, and Chicago blacks). In spite of the extremely careful efforts made by all of the researchers to ensure that all the pairs of testers resembled each other, the pairs appear to have been treated quite differently in their respective labor markets.

This raises a final problem. Why should the audit pair analysts have found it relatively difficult to control for heterogeneity across pairs? The answer must rest on the difficulty of comparing and matching large numbers of auditor characteristics, many of which are intangible or difficult to describe. If mismatching in characteristics occurs in half of the city/race sites despite the best efforts of the testers to prevent it, it would seem that our knowledge of the hiring process being audited is rife with uncertainty. One should be wary of assuming that much is known about how hiring decisions are actually made. The burden of proof that audit pairs are properly aligned must be assumed by audit pair analysts. More objective demonstrations of the matching methods actually used would increase the value of audit pair evidence.

THE VALUE OF HAVING MORE THAN TWO TESTERS

There is potentially great value in having two or more testers from each race/ethnic group. (See McIntyre et al., 1980, who use this method in a resume audit study.) Access to evidence from such audit pair studies would permit calibration of background noise and would provide valuable corroborating evidence on the capacity of UI to match on "relevant" productivity characteristics. It would also help to settle the choice of an operational definition of discrimination.

Thus for two majority group members it would be possible to estimate P_3 and P_4 (proportions that one is hired and the other is not) and determine whether a $P_3 + P_4 = 0$ definition of no discrimination is reasonable. A similar check would be of value for minority group members. Evidence that $P_3 \neq P_4$ would indicate problems in making identical matches. If, in fact, "identical" matched pairs show $P_3 \neq P_4$, even after accounting for sampling variation, tests of symmetry ($P_3 = P_4$) should be modified. It would be more appropriate to test whether $P_3 - P_4$ lies in an *interval* determined from the "noise band" estimated from the analyses of audit pair members of the same demographic group. Such a band would make audit evidence both intuitively and formally more convincing.

A BEHAVIORAL MODEL OF FIRM'S JOB OFFERS TO HETEROGENEOUS WORKERS

We have discussed the UI and Denver studies on their own terms: as intuitive models of the job offer process. Intuitive models are informative guides to data but can take one only so far. When the researchers in UIBW use the models developed by McFadden (1973) to analyze their data, they implicitly appeal to a particular decision process for firm job offers. In appendix 5.D, we present a rigorous model of firm hiring decisions; we evaluate the methods used by the Urban Institute; and we consider what specifications of these models justify the definitions of discrimination used in the UI studies. A more complete analysis is presented in Heckman and Siegelman (1993).

Three important conclusions emerge from this analysis. First, our model reveals some of the underlying assumptions needed to support each of the various definitions of (and tests for) discrimination. In particular, we demonstrate that the distributions of unobserved (by the UI) worker characteristics within an audit pair must be identical to justify the "symmetrical treatment" definition of discrimination adopted in the UIAH study; an even stronger assumption is necessary to support the "zero difference" definition of discrimination in UIBW—namely that there are no relevant unobservables omitted by the UI analysts.

Second, we point out that standardizing on *observed* productivity characteristics for members of an audit pair may, paradoxically, accentuate the discrepancy in job offer rates between the two audit pair members as compared with what would be measured from observing two randomly selected job searchers. Under certain circumstances, data from randomly selected pairs would provide closer approximations to job offer patterns in an actual labor market.

Third, our model demonstrates that the choice of an observed productivity level for an audit pair may drive the resulting estimates of job offer discrimination produced by the audits. In other words, standardizing the observed productivity level of two auditors at one level can produce much more (or less) evidence of discrimination than standardizing at another level.

By a suitable choice of an observed productivity level, it is always possible to produce evidence of no discrimination, of favoritism toward minorities, or of discrimination against minorities, provided only that minority and majority distributions of unobservables are not identical. A corollary of our analysis is that any evidence of firm-based discrimination can also be interpreted as evidence of differences in the variance of unobservables between majority and minority group members.

These considerations suggest that much more thought should be given to the choice of an appropriate level of auditor productivity characteristics in designing audit pair studies and that a variety of levels across audit pairs should be used to present a more complete picture of labor market hiring practices. The relatively weak evidence of discrimination found in Chicago might simply be a consequence of an unfortunate choice of observed productivity level. It also suggests that audit studies are crucially dependent on an unstated hypothesis: that the distributions of unobserved (by the testers) productivity characteristics of majority and minority workers are identical. The UIBW study is based on the even stronger assumptions that there are no relevant unobservables and that observables can be perfectly matched within audit pairs.

IMPLICATIONS FOR POLICY AND FUTURE RESEARCH

The key item on the agenda for future research is to design audit studies that provide more effective answers to the question of *why* discrimination occurs. Without such answers, policy recommendations are unlikely to be very helpful, because the kind of policies one would favor depend on the kind of discrimination one observes.

We strongly encourage the use of more than two testers at each firm.[25] This would allow analysts to distinguish between random and race-based explanations for differences in treatment. If both white males consistently got job offers while the black males, for example, did not, one would have a stronger case for the race-based explanation.

If only one of the white males consistently got the job, however, the random explanation would seem more plausible. Use of additional applicants would further facilitate measurement of randomness or "background noise" at firms. Use of extra testers would also enable analysts to determine how well relevant characteristics have been aligned. Using extra testers, it is possible to adjust the gross index of discrimination used by UIBW by subtracting the summed gross index for the two demographically comparable patterns from the gross index for two demographically disparate partners.

More attention should be paid to firm-specific variables. The multinomial logit analyses reported in the appendixes to both Urban Institute reports head in the right direction (although they inappropriately pool across audit pairs in Chicago), but we need to go further. What, if anything, distinguishes firms that discriminate against blacks or Hispanics from those that discriminate against whites or do not discriminate at all? Are some firms operating under a quota constraint while others are free to practice discrimination against blacks? Obtaining answers to questions such as these is vital before strong policy recommendations can be made.

We also urge further consideration of the attributes of the testers. It is essential to present more objective evidence on the comparability of the white and minority testers in a pair. The difference between each tester's characteristics and the employer's stereotype or belief about the characteristics of the average applicant of that race may also matter. Thus, it would be useful to know if it makes a difference whether the testers both resemble the typical white applicant or both resemble the typical black applicant in the relevent productivity attributes. In light of the analysis summarized in the previous section, and developed in appendix 5.D and in our companion paper, it is essential to consider a range of observed skill levels across the audit pairs in order to sample market outcomes. Otherwise, there is great danger in picking an anomalous value of skill levels that may understate or overstate actual differences in firm's hiring rates.

As a relatively new research technique, audit studies may benefit from some nontraditional strategies for documenting their results. For example, ABC Television's recent PRIMETIME LIVE feature "True Colors," (9/26/91) used only a single audit pair, filming the two testers as they went about many of the activities of everyday life. This was an exercise in investigative journalism, rather than social science, and we should not judge academic research by the standards it set (or vice versa). Nevertheless, one of the reasons the results were so powerful is that the audience could clearly see how similar the two testers actually were. Perhaps employment audits could also make use of some of these techniques and provide both visual and oral evidence of alignment by making videotapes of audit pairs available.

The UI studies provide suggestive evidence on the prevalence of discrimination in job hiring. Much more information must be collected on the job offer process, especially on offered wages, before the UI studies can be said to document discrimination on the basis of race or ethnicity.

Richer sampling plans for firms must be undertaken in order to get a more representative picture of the labor market. Mechanisms for sampling of job search methods other than newspaper advertising must be devised if we are to achieve a truly representative view of the labor market. Concerns about the use of falsified credentials should be met. Audits should be conducted using real rather than simulated low-skilled market participants. To understand the conflict between the findings of the UIAH study and the Denver Hispanic study, it is essential to unbundle accents, facial hair, and Hispanic status.

We also urge that the Denver study be replicated following the Urban Institute protocol as closely as possible. Ultimately, this will be the only way of deciding whether the apparent difference in results stems from lower levels of discrimination in Denver or is attributable to the differences in research design. Such replication would be extremely useful to others planning future work in this field; given our limited experience with audits, we are almost completely ignorant about how sensitive the findings are to small changes in methodology. A replication of the Denver audits using the strict UI methods would give us some important information about the robustness of the audit technique.

Finally, we urge further work on the statistical aspects of the design of audit studies and the testing of hypotheses using audit data. Because audit studies are expensive to conduct, sample sizes in such studies are likely to be relatively small, especially for studies conducted by civil rights organizations. Moreover, most of the outcomes being studied, at least in the employment context, are discrete (either the tester is offered a job or he is not) rather than continuous. The combination of small sample size and discrete outcomes means that researchers should make more use of small sample, multinomial statistical techniques in sample design and hypothesis testing, rather than relying on large sample normal approximations. We have explored some of these questions in appendix 5.D, and do so in greater depth in our companion paper (Heckman and Siegelman 1993). We establish that conventional large sample methods do not efficiently exploit audit pair data.

None of these comments detracts from our admiration for these pioneering studies. The audit pair methodology, properly augmented, promises to shed much valuable new light on the nature of racial and ethnic disparities in labor market outcomes.

Notes

We would like to thank Jerry Marschke and Allison Sylvester for competent research assistance. Moshe Buchinsky, Hector Cordero-Guzmann, Robert LaLonde, Allan Lind, Richard Robb, John Yinger, and Mahmoud Zaidi made valuable comments on this work. We are especially grateful to Gary Becker for insightful comments.

1. The work we focus on is a study of black-white pairs in Washington and Chicago reported in Turner, Fix, and Struyk, *Opportunities Denied, Opportunities Diminished: Racial Discrimination in Hiring* (Urban Institute, September, 1991); a study of Hispanics and Anglos in San Diego and Chicago by Cross, *Employer Hiring Practices: Differential Treatment of Hispanic and Anglo Job Seekers* (Urban Institute, 1990) and the study of blacks, whites and Hispanics in the Denver labor market by James and Del Castillo (March, 1991).

2. We concentrate on employment audits. For more detailed description of the audit techniques used in this context, see the methodological appendixes to Turner et al. (1991) and Cross et al. (1991). Newman (1978) and McIntyre et al. (1980) used resumes, rather than live auditors, to test for differences in the treatment of applicants. For the use of the audit technique in other contexts, see Ayres (1991) (cars), Ayres and Siegelman (1993) (cars), and Yinger (1986) (housing).

3. Fair-housing testers have typically been matched on relatively few characteristics, while employment testers have been matched on many more, reflecting the greater variety of characteristics likely to be relevant in hiring decisions.

4. The similarity of testers *across* pairs is also relevant if, as is almost always the case, data from the pairs are to be aggregated for statistical analysis. We discuss this issue at greater length below.

5. The empirical and theoretical literature on labor market (mostly wage) discrimination is surveyed by Cain (1986). His pessimistic conclusion is that " . . . the results are so varied that they reveal as much about our ignorance as about our knowledge of labor market discrimination" (p. 743). Our ignorance of hiring discrimination is at least an order of magnitude greater than it is with regard to discrimination in wages.

6. See table 5.10 below for the Denver microdata and Heckman and Siegelman (1993) for their extensive analysis.

7. That is, if tester A is denied an interview, while tester B is interviewed but is nevertheless rejected for the job, should one consider this outcome as evidence of discrimination?

8. For one thing, the raw, pair-by-pair data for this index were not available to us for analysis. Moreover, while looking at "nonoutcome" aspects of the hiring process can produce some potentially useful evidence, the relationship between the categories and discrimination is somewhat tenuous. Is being interviewed for a shorter period of time necessarily evidence of discrimination? Is the number of positive comments (as opposed to their strength) necessarily a measure of favoritism? Under the circumstances, these crude measures are probably the best we can hope for, but they should be interpreted with caution. It seems unwise to build much of the case for the existence of discrimination on such subjective measures.

9. Turner et al. (1991).

10. We should note that reverse discrimination could come from black-owned firms, or firms with largely black customers or work forces, that dislike white employees. Or, as seems more likely, this kind of discrimination could be the result of legal pressures to increase hiring of blacks. See, for example, Leonard (1984) for further analysis.

Interestingly, Title VII and other antidiscrimination legislation could also have a negative impact on black hiring. The reason, as suggested by Donohue and Siegelman (1991), is that most litigation under Title VII now contests discriminatory discharge rather than discriminatory failure to hire. Thus, employers may see little costs for failing to hire a minority applicant but potentially high costs to hiring and possibly firing at some later date.

11. This point is developed more formally in the model of job hiring presented in appendix 5.D.

12. One could also take the ratios of the number of tests in which there was disparate treatment. In a companion to this paper, we show that the choice of which test statistic to use may not be innocuous.

13. For an interesting analysis of errors in the hiring process, see McIntyre et al. (1980), who conclude, using employment audits based on resumes rather than live testers, that identical whites are treated differently approximately 12 percent of the time.

14. Let $X_N = (X_{N1}, \ldots, X_{NT})$ have the multinomial distribution $M(N, \underline{P})$ where $\underline{P} = (P_1, \ldots, P_T)$. Then

$$E(X_N) = N(\underline{P})$$

$$Cov(X_N) = N(D_P - \underline{P}'\underline{P})$$

where $D_P = \text{Diag } \underline{P}$.

$$\hat{P} = \left(\frac{1}{N}\right) X_N.$$

$\sqrt{N}(\hat{\underline{P}} - \underline{P})$ converges under random sampling to

$$\sqrt{N} (\hat{\underline{P}} - \underline{P}) \doteq N(0, D_P - \underline{P}'\underline{P}).$$

Thus, asymptotically, under H_0

$$\sqrt{N} (\hat{P}_3 - P_3) \doteq N(0, 0)$$

$$\sqrt{N} (\hat{P}_4 - P_4) \doteq N(0, 0),$$

degenerate normal random variables.

15. Homogeneity is desirable from a statistical point of view in the sense that it justifies a simple pooling of observations. If pooling is not possible and each audit pair must be treated separately, the power of audit methods to detect discrimination is reduced. See Heckman and Siegelman (1993) for further discussion of this point.

16. The test statistic in one-sided form is to check if $\hat{\theta} \geq c$, where c is determined so that the probability of a type I error is α percent. In two-sided form, the test is to determine c_1, c_2 such that $\hat{\theta} \geq c_1$ or $\theta \leq c_2$ for c_1 and c_2 determined so that the overall error rate is α percent. For more details, see descriptions in the Lehmann (1986) or Pratt and Gibbons (1981) or the example in Appendix 5.C.

17. More specifically, in the results we report below, we perform a Monte Carlo analysis on the Pearson adjustment to the Fisher method and use the median of 1000 draws using the method. For more details, see our companion paper. The Fisher method is based on the observation that the p value for a one-sided test is distributed uniformly. Minus twice the log of the p value for a one-sided test is distributed uniformly. Minus twice the log of the p value is distributed $\chi^2(2)$. Twice the sum of logs of the p values is distributed $\chi^2(2K)$ where K is the number of audit pairs, i.e.,

$$-2 \sum_{k=1}^{K} \ln p_k \sim \chi^2(2K).$$

18. Mahmoud Zaidi has pointed out to us that the use of major newspapers as the sampling frame may be problematic. His research suggests that black and Hispanic youth often use community or local newspapers in their job searches, rather than the major newspapers from which the Urban Institute studies sampled.

19. Studies that use resumes, rather than (or in addition to) live auditors, could be potentially useful in this regard. See Newman (1978) and McIntyre et al. (1980).

20. For a massive collection of additional evidence on experimenter effects, see Rosenthal (1976).

21. The accents were deemed appropriate because the study was designed to uncover whether reform of the immigration laws caused employers to discriminate against "foreign-sounding" Hispanics. The UIAH study is careful to note that its results may not generalize to the larger population of Hispanics in the United States. Others, however, have interpreted the results more broadly than the authors presumably intended they would.

22. Dipboye et al. (1975).

23. Note that the Denver study found virtually no evidence of discrimination against Hispanics; it appears that Denver testers had less strong accents than those in the Urban Institute study, although this is not clear. No mention was made of facial hair in the Denver study. There were other differences between the studies as well, as we discuss later.

24. See *Bradley v. Pizzaco of Nebraska* 926 F.2d 714 (8th Cir. 1991) (a no-beards rule meets plaintiff's prima facie burden for asserting a disparate impact challenge).

25. This point is illustrated by the model of the hiring decisions developed below.

26. One should also mention two other studies that use a modification of the audit technique. McIntyre et al. and Newman used resumes, rather than live job applicants, to test for discrimination. Both found statistically significant discrimination in *favor* of black and women applicants. The studies were done more than a decade ago, however, and did not allow applicants to apply for jobs (and hence to receive job offers). The sampling frames were also different (consisting of employers who advertised in *College Placement Annual* that they were accepting written job applications). It is conceivable that employers discriminate in favor of women and minorities at the early stages of the hiring process, but nevertheless discriminate against them when it comes to the actual hiring decision itself.

APPENDIX 5.A

MATHEMATICAL APPENDIX

Our test for homogeneity in the contingency table of audit pairs is standard. Assume product multinomial sampling. For row i and column j, we construct the estimated number in cell ij (assuming no auditor effects) as

$$N_{ij} = \frac{N_i}{N} \frac{N_j}{N} N \qquad \text{all } i, j$$

where N_i is the row i total (summing across i) and N_j is the column j total (summing across j). This can be tested using standard $\chi^2[(R-1)(C-1)]$ statistics. (R is the number of rows; C is the number of columns.) Also, one can form cell-by-cell asymptotically normal deviates to examine which cells produce the departure from normality if there is one.

The likelihood ratio statistic is a special case of a whole class of "Cressie-Read directed divergence" statistics that nest classical Pearson, modified Pearson, and likelihood ratio statistics as special cases. It produces a class of test statistics that should produce equivalent inferences if the asymptotic theory used to conduct conventional tests is any good. Computation of different versions of the statistic therefore provides evidence on the validity of the asymptotics. Let $\hat{P}_{ij}$ be the sample proportion in cell ij. Let $\hat{P}_{ij}^{(r)}$ be the restricted sample proportion in cell i, j under a particular hypothesis. Then the directed divergence test statistic is, for sample size N,

$$I(\hat{P}_{ij}; \hat{P}_{ij}^{(r)}, \lambda) = \frac{\sum\limits_{i,j}^{R, C} N \hat{P}_{ij}}{\lambda(\lambda + 1)} \left(\left[\frac{\hat{P}_{ij}}{\hat{P}_{ij}^{(r)}} \right]^{\lambda} - 1 \right),$$

$$-\infty < \lambda < \infty \qquad \lambda \neq -1. \quad (1)$$

$2I$ is χ^2 with the number of degrees of freedom specified by the null. In the case of independence, the number of degrees of freedom is $(R-1)(C-1)$. When $\lambda = 0$, the classical likelihood ratio is produced. When $\lambda = 1$, the classical Pearson χ^2 is produced. High values of λ downweight high ratios of $(\hat{P}_{ij}/P_{ij}^{(r)})$ that may be due to sampling variation.

For testing symmetry within audit pairs, the same type of statistic can be used. Let there be K outcomes for each audit pair. Let the hypothesis in question be $P_{K-1} = P_K$ (i.e., equality in audit pair outcomes for outcomes K and $K-1$). In our case, these outcomes are those in which one demographic group is treated differently from another.

The test of symmetry for any audit pair is based on

$$2I(\hat{P}_i; \hat{P}_i^{(r)}, \lambda) = \frac{2}{\lambda(\lambda + 1)} \sum_{i=1}^{K} N \hat{P}_i \left(\left[\frac{\hat{P}_i}{\hat{P}_i^{(r)}} \right]^{\lambda} - 1 \right). \tag{2}$$

This statistic is chi-square one. In the case of the symmetrical treatment hypothesis, there is one degree of freedom for each audit pair and

$$\hat{P}_i^{(r)} = N \left[\frac{N_i}{\sum_{i=1}^{K-2} N_i + 2 \left(\frac{N_{K-1}^{\frac{1}{\lambda+1}} + N_K^{\frac{1}{\lambda+1}}}{2} \right)^{\lambda+1}} \right]$$

for $i \neq K, K-1$.

$$\hat{P}_{K-1}^r = \hat{P}_K^r = \frac{1}{2} \left(1 - \sum_{i=1}^{K-2} \hat{P}_i^{(r)} \right).$$

APPENDIX 5.B

PLOTS OF CRESSIE-READ STATISTICS FOR TESTS OF HOMOGENEITY AND TESTS OF SYMMETRY

We present plots of the Cressie-Read statistics for the values of λ indicated. The labels identify the sites and demographic groups. The figures with one line are for the tests of homogeneity, and the figures with multiple lines are for the tests of symmetry. Each line corresponds to a particular audit pair. A flat line indicates that the same asymptotic inference is being produced by the range of asymptotically equivalent Cressie-Read statistics. Flatness generates confidence in the asymptotic inference. Curvature (as in the audits of Chicago blacks for a single audit pair) casts doubt on the validity of the asymptotic inference.

For $\lambda = 1$, the Cressie-Read statistic is a classical χ^2 statistic, with degrees of freedom indicated in each figure.

Figure 5.B.1 CRESSIE-READ STATISTICS TESTING THE HYPOTHESIS OF
HOMOGENEITY ACROSS PAIRS OF TESTERS FOR BLACK/WHITE
PAIRS, WASHINGTON, D.C.

$$F(\lambda) = \chi^2_{(12)}$$

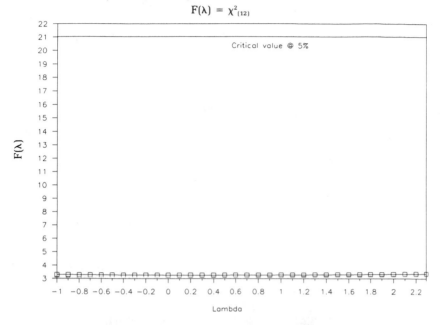

Figure 5.B.2 CRESSIE-READ STATISTICS TESTING THE HYPOTHESIS OF
HOMOGENEITY ACROSS PAIRS OF TESTERS FOR BLACK/WHITE
PAIRS, CHICAGO

$$F(\lambda) = \chi^2_{(12)}$$

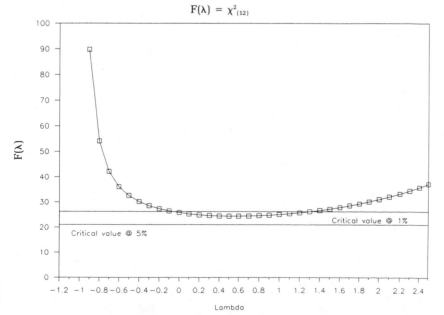

Figure 5.B.3 CRESSIE-READ STATISTICS TESTING THE HYPOTHESIS OF
HOMOGENEITY ACROSS PAIRS OF TESTERS FOR ANGLO/HISPANIC
PAIRS, SAN DIEGO

$$F(\lambda) = \chi^2_{(9)}$$

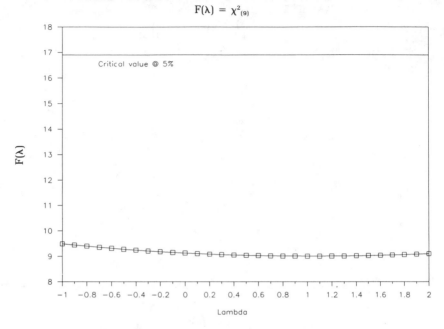

Figure 5.B.4 CRESSIE-READ STATISTICS TESTING THE HYPOTHESIS OF
HOMOGENEITY ACROSS PAIRS OF TESTERS FOR ANGLO/HISPANIC
PAIRS, CHICAGO

$$F(\lambda) = \chi^2_{(9)}$$

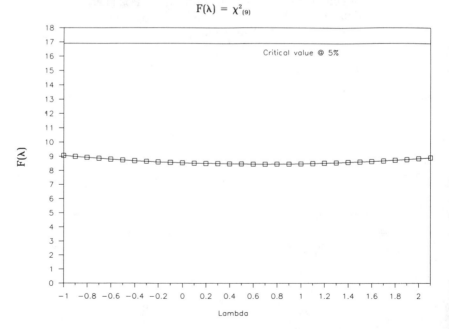

Figure 5.B.5 CRESSIE-READ STATISTICS TESTING THE HYPOTHESIS OF
HOMOGENEITY ACROSS CITIES FOR BLACK/WHITE PAIRS

$$F(\lambda) = \chi^2_{(27)}$$

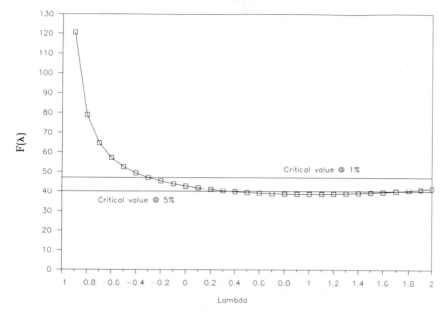

Figure 5.B.6 CRESSIE-READ STATISTICS TESTING THE HYPOTHESIS OF
HOMOGENEITY ACROSS CITIES FOR ANGLO/HISPANIC PAIRS

$$F(\lambda) = \chi^2_{(21)}$$

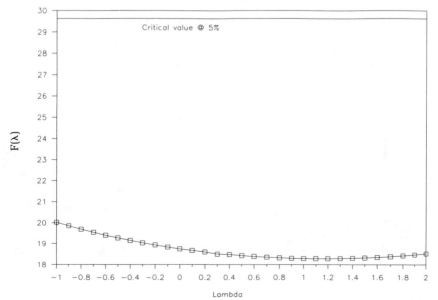

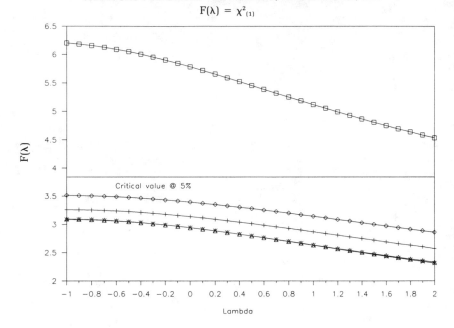

Figure 5.B.7 CRESSIE-READ STATISTICS TESTING THE HYPOTHESIS OF SYMMETRICAL TREATMENT OF MAJORITY AND MINORITY AUDITORS FOR BLACK/WHITE PAIRS, WASHINGTON, D.C.

$$F(\lambda) = \chi^2_{(1)}$$

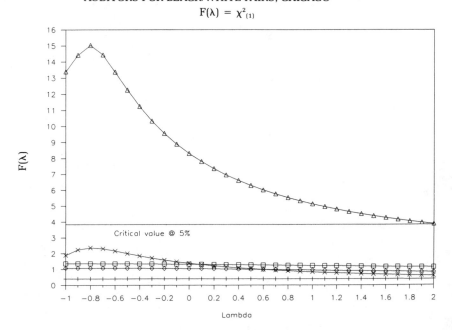

Figure 5.B.8 CRESSIE-READ STATISTICS TESTING THE HYPOTHESIS OF SYMMETRICAL TREATMENT OF MAJORITY AND MINORITY AUDITORS FOR BLACK/WHITE PAIRS, CHICAGO

$$F(\lambda) = \chi^2_{(1)}$$

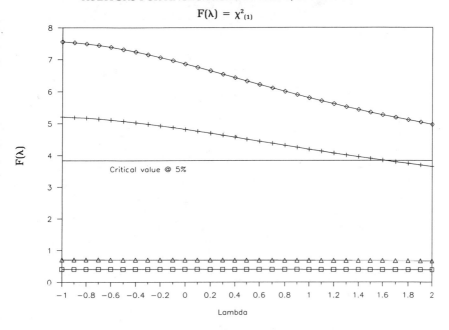

Figure 5.B.9 CRESSIE-READ STATISTICS TESTING THE HYPOTHESIS OF SYMMETRICAL TREATMENT OF MAJORITY AND MINORITY AUDITORS FOR ANGLO/HISPANIC PAIRS, SAN DIEGO

$$F(\lambda) = \chi^2_{(1)}$$

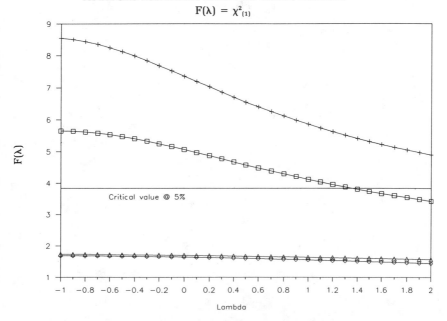

Figure 5.B.10 CRESSIE-READ STATISTICS TESTING THE HYPOTHESIS OF SYMMETRICAL TREATMENT OF MAJORITY AND MINORITY AUDITORS FOR HISPANIC/ANGLO PAIRS, CHICAGO

$$F(\lambda) = \chi^2_{(1)}$$

Figure 5.B.11 CRESSIE-READ STATISTICS TESTING THE HYPOTHESIS OF SYMMETRICAL TREATMENT OF MAJORITY AND MINORITY AUDITORS FOR BLACK/WHITE PAIRS AGGREGATED BY CITY

$$F(\lambda) = \chi^2_{(1)}$$

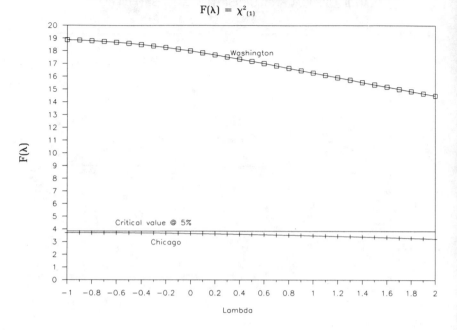

Figure 5.B.12 CRESSIE-READ STATISTICS TESTING THE HYPOTHESIS OF SYMMETRICAL TREATMENT OF MAJORITY AND MINORITY AUDITORS FOR ANGLO/HISPANIC PAIRS AGGREGATED BY CITY

$$F(\lambda) = \chi^2_{(1)}$$

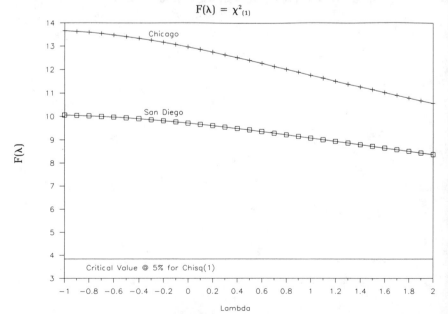

APPENDIX 5.C

EMPIRICAL BAYES METHODS AND THE SIGN TEST

Empirical Bayes procedures postulate a distribution of outcome probabilities $F(\underline{P})$. These can arise from heterogeneity across pairs in the match of auditors or in the firms they sample. For multinomial data, the Dirichelet prior is a conjugate prior widely used in the literature (see, e.g. Good 1965 or DeGroot 1970).

The density of $\underline{P}$ is

$$f(\underline{P}) = \frac{\prod\limits_{i=1}^{K} \Gamma(\alpha_i)}{\Gamma(\Sigma\alpha_i)} \prod\limits_{i=1}^{K} P_i^{\alpha_i - 1} \qquad \sum\limits_{i=1}^{K} P_i = 1, \, \alpha_i \geq 0 \, \forall .$$

Γ is the gamma function. The density for the multinomial likelihood assuming random sampling with samples of size N and with N_i observations in cell i is

$$f = \binom{N}{N_1, N_2, \ldots N_K} \prod\limits_{i=1}^{K} P_i^{N_i}.$$

Ignoring inessential constants, the expected probability given observation vector $(N_1, \ldots, N_K)$ is

$$E(P_1^{N_1} P_2^{N_2} \ldots P_K^{N_K}) = \frac{\Gamma\left(\sum\limits_{i=1}^{K} \alpha_i\right) \prod\limits_{i=1}^{K} \Gamma(\alpha_i + N_i)}{\prod\limits_{i=1}^{K} \Gamma(\alpha_i) \, \Gamma\left(\sum\limits_{i=1}^{K} (\alpha_i + N_i)\right)}.$$

This expression is the basis for the empirical Bayes material we report below. The test of the hypothesis of equality in mean probabilities for outcome i and outcome j is a test of $\alpha_i = \alpha_j$, $i \neq j$.

$$E(P_i) = \alpha_i^* \bigg/ \sum_{j=1}^{K} \alpha_j^*$$

$$\text{Var}(P_i) = (\alpha_i^*)\left(\sum_{j=1}^{K} \alpha_j^* - \alpha_i^*\right)\bigg/\left(\sum \alpha_j^*\right)^2 \left(\sum \alpha_j^* + 1\right).$$

where

$$\alpha_i^* = \alpha_i + N_i.$$

The Sign Test

Details of this test are given in Pratt and Gibbons (1981) or Lehmann (1986). Here we illustrate its computation by way of an example. Consider Chicago black audit pair 3. Of 44 interviews, only four firms treated pairs differently. $N_3 = 3$ (W yes; B no) and $N_4 = 1$ (W no; B yes). The conditional sign test proceeds *conditional* on $N_3 + N_4 = 4$.

Under the null that $P_3 = P_4$ ($\theta = \frac{1}{2}$), the probability of j outcomes where whites are hired and blacks are not is

$$\Pr(j \text{ whites hired} \mid N_3 + N_4 = 4) = \binom{4}{j} (1/2)^4.$$

Suppose that we seek values c_1 and c_2, $c_1 \leq c_2$, such that if $\theta = \frac{1}{2}$,

$$\Pr(j \leq c_1 \text{ or } j \geq c_2 \mid \theta = 1/2, N_3 + N_4 = 4) = .10$$

which is the probability of a type I error. Thus c_1 and c_2 are critical values.

Because of the binomial nature of j, in general it is not possible to find values of c_1 and c_2 that exactly set the type I error to 10%. If we set $c_1 = 0$ and $c_2 = 4$, the error rate is 12.5%. To attain exact error rates of 10%, we must randomize. Thus, if 80% of the time we reject if $j = 0$ or $j = 4$, we produce a randomized version of the test with the desired size (type I error rate). It can be shown that this test is uniformly most powerful and unbiased. The higher the randomized rate, the more likely are we to reject the null that $\theta = \frac{1}{2}$ if $j = 0$ or $j = 4$. In this sense, the test produces results closer to those obtained from conventional non-randomized tests. Observe that there is *no* 10% nonrandomized test in this example.

Table 5.C.1 LIKELIHOOD RATIO TESTS OF SYMMETRY

Study	Site	Outcome	Test Statistic $\chi^2_{(1)}$*
UIBW	Washington, D.C.	Get - job	17.90
UIBW	Chicago	Get - job	3.1
UIAH	Chicago	Get - job	11.04
UIAH	San Diego	Get - job	8.32

*Significant at the 5 percent level (critical value for $\chi^2_{(1)} = 3.84$).

Notes: UIBW = Urban Institute black/white audit; UIAH = Urban Institute Anglo/Hispanic audit. An interesting feature of the likelihood maximizing values of the α_i for each site is that the implied variances of α_i are very small, indicating that homogeneity among audit pairs is a valid description of the data.

APPENDIX 5.D

A MODEL OF THE HIRING DECISION

In our companion paper (Heckman and Siegelman 1993) we develop the following model of firm hiring decisions more completely.

The Model

Let C^{MIN} be the skill vector of a minority member and C^{MAJ} be the skill vector of a majority group member. Let γ^{MIN} be a firm's evaluation vector of the productivity of attributes of minorities and γ^{MAJ} be the firm's evaluation of the productivity of attributes of majority workers.[1] A constant is included among the elements of the C. The γ coefficient associated with the constant is a measure of the perceived productivity of the demographic group. Differences among groups could be due to animus-based discrimination. Thus, $\gamma^{MIN} C^{MIN}$ (a number) is the perceived increment to firm output from hiring a minority applicant and $\gamma^{MAJ} C^{MAJ}$ is the perceived contribution to firm productivity of a majority applicant. Assume that both applicants must be offered the same wage and impose the same hiring costs, K.

For a firm processing workers sequentially without recall of previous applicants, no explicit comparison of pairs of workers is made. In this case, a majority applicant is hired if $K \leq \gamma^{MIN} C^{MIN}$ and the majority group member shows up before any minority applicant.[2] Similarly, $K \leq \gamma^{MAJ} C^{MAJ}$ characterizes the case when a minority group member is hired. In the UI studies, inequalities may hold at a particular firm for each member of an audit pair if the first person offered the job declines it, so both persons may be offered a job.[3]

Differences between components of γ^{MAJ} and γ^{MIN} may arise because of discrimination in evaluating specific attributes or against a group as a whole (recall that C includes a constant). Alternatively, discrimination might reflect statistical information processing in the event of incomplete information about C, if the same observed characteristics convey different productivity information about majority and minority group members. A crucial unstated assumption in the UI analysis is that the absence of discrimination implies that $\gamma^{MAJ} = \gamma^{MIN}$ for each firm.[4] Audit pair studies as currently conducted cannot distinguish between animus-based discrimination and statistical discrimination, although it is of scientific and policy interest to do so.

Even if on average all firms treat majority and minority group members identically, firms may still differ in their evaluations of bundles of characteristics. Thus it is plausible that γ is a realization or a draw from a population distribution

$$P(\Gamma \leq \gamma) = F(\gamma).$$

The characteristics of applicant pairs are drawings from the distributions $G(c^{MIN})$ and $H(c^{MAJ})$ and C^{MIN} and C^{MAJ} are assumed to be statistically independent in the population. For simplicity, we assume that all firms offer the same wage, say as a consequence of sample design (i.e., by the restriction of samples to low wage markets). If some firms place a large, negative weight on the constant for minority group members, they are unlikely to hire minorities. As the weight becomes large in absolute value, the probability of hiring a minority group member becomes arbitrarily small. Such firms would not hire a minority at any finite price.

In the labor market at large, if job seekers randomly sample firms, and there are many firms and many workers of both types, the probability that a firm will offer a job to a randomly sampled minority group member in small time interval Δt is

$$\text{Prob}(\gamma^{MIN} C^{MIN} > K)\lambda_{MIN} (\Delta t),$$

where λ_{MIN} is the rate of arrival of minorities to the firm. Similarly, the probability that the firm will offer a job to a majority group member is

$$\text{Prob}(\gamma^{MAJ} C^{MAJ} > K) \lambda_{MAJ} (\Delta t).$$

Under standard conditions, the probability that both a majority and minority member arrive at the firm in a small time interval Δt is $\lambda_{MIN} \lambda_{MAJ}(\Delta t)^2$, which is negligibly small. Assuming that Γ and C are statistically independent, the job offer rate to minority group members is higher compared to that of majority group members (a) the higher their rate of arrival at firms relative to majority members, (b) the greater their skill endowments, and (c) the higher is γ^{MIN} compared to γ^{MAJ}.

Observe that minority job offer rates depend on the distribution of minority skills, the distribution of firm skill evaluation functions and the rate of arrival of minorities to vacancies. In the actual labor market, discrepancies in hiring rates between majority and minority group members can arise from any of these sources, only some of which plausibly constitute labor market discrimination. For example, minorities may do worse because they have lower skills (C), or lower firm encounter rates, which may not reflect employment or hiring discrimination.[5] Alternatively, minorities may fare worse because of differences in the way firms evaluate minority and majority members of equal skill.

The Urban Institute studies standardize the search component of job arrival rates by sending one minority member and one majority group applicant to the same firm in a short time period. Thus no information is gained about sources of racial differences in λ, since all attention is focused on the job offer rate to a given applicant pool of at least two workers.

In terms of this notation, the goal of the audit pair studies is to separate the effects of γ and C (firm evaluations and worker skills) on hiring. To test if $\gamma^{MIN} \neq \gamma^{MAJ}$, the UI studies attempt to align C^{MIN} and C^{MAJ} to a common value c^*. That is, the studies begin by matching the characteristics of the testers in an audit pair (including height, verbal facility, previous job history, and so on). If all characteristics could be aligned and wages and hiring costs were standardized across firms, and $\gamma^{MAJ} = \gamma^{MIN}$ for each audit trial at each firm, then

$$\text{Prob}(\gamma^{MAJ} c^* > K) = 0 \text{ or } 1$$

and

$$\text{Prob}(\gamma^{MIN} c^* > K) = 0 \text{ or } 1.$$

When all the characteristics of two applicants in an audit pair are perfectly matched, it is trivially true that the only way the members of the pair could be treated differently would be if $\gamma^{MAJ} \neq \gamma^{MIN}$. This model justifies the test of discrimination used in the UIBW study: $P_3 = P_4 = 0$.[6]

It seems more plausible, however, that only a subset of worker characteristics can be aligned by any pair matching procedure. In this case, it is fruitful to decompose the vector of characteristics relevant for hiring into observed and unobserved components, so that $C = (C_o, C_u)$. The audit pair researchers can control C_o, the characteristics they observe, but they cannot control C_u. Thus, for any two "paired" applicants, only a *part* of their productivity—the $\underline{C}_o$ part of $\gamma_o \underline{C}_o$—can be observed and aligned. The unobserved and uncontrolled productivity is $\gamma_u \underline{C}_u$. $\underline{C}_u$ is assumed to be known to the firm but not to those designing an audit pair study.

This interpretation assumes that firms consider a much wider variety of characteristics than the audit designers can observe or control. This assumption seems valid in light of our current factual ignorance about the way matching works in the labor market, the great heterogeneity across tasks at firms and in firm skill requirements, and the enormous heterogeneity in skills among persons. At the end of this appendix, we briefly discuss the implications of an alternative assumption about the information possessed by the firm implicitly used in UIBW.

In the absence of discrimination on the part of firms, the probability that a minority is offered a job at a particular firm given $\underline{C}_o^{\text{MIN}} = \underline{C}_o^{\text{MAJ}} = c_o$ and firm productivity and cost vectors $(\underline{\gamma}, K)$ is

$$\text{Prob}(\gamma_u \, \underline{C}_u^{\text{MIN}} > K - \underline{\gamma}_o \, \underline{c}_o \mid \gamma_u, \gamma_o, K, \underline{c}_o),$$

while the probability that the majority member is offered a job is

$$\text{Prob}(\gamma_u \, \underline{C}_u^{\text{MAJ}} > K - \underline{\gamma}_o \, \underline{c}_o \mid \gamma_u, \gamma_o, K, \underline{c}_o).$$

These rates will be equal for all values of K and c_o if and only if

$$\gamma_u \, \underline{C}_u^{\text{MAJ}} \text{ and } \gamma_u \, \underline{C}_u^{\text{MIN}}$$

have the same conditional distribution.[7] Ironically, the two conditional job offer probabilities may be *more* unequal than the job offer probabilities that arise from *not* standardizing on the observable characteristics, c_o. For minority applicants at a firm with skill evaluation vector $\underline{\gamma}$, this probability is

$$\text{Pr}(\underline{\gamma} \, \underline{C}^{\text{MIN}} > K \mid \underline{\gamma}, K)$$

and for majority applicants

$$\text{Pr}(\underline{\gamma} \, \underline{C}^{\text{MAJ}} > K \mid \underline{\gamma}, K).$$

The same can be said for the counterparts to these probabilities for the entire population of firms. That is, allowing for the distribution of γ across firms, the population hiring rate for minority group members is

$$\text{Pr}(\underline{\gamma} \, \underline{C}^{\text{MIN}} > K \mid K)$$

and for majority group members it is

$$\Pr(\underline{\gamma}\ \underline{C}^{\text{MAJ}} > K \mid K)$$

which are obtained by integrating the previous expressions that condition on γ with respect to the population distribution of γ. The population counterparts to the conditional distributions (with respect to c_o) are

$$\Pr(\underline{\gamma}_u\ \underline{C}^{\text{MIN}} > K - \underline{\gamma}_o\ \underline{c}_o \mid K, \underline{c}_o)$$

and

$$\Pr(\underline{\gamma}_u\ \underline{C}^{\text{MAJ}} > K - \underline{\gamma}_o\ \underline{c}_o \mid K, \underline{c}_o)$$

obtained by integrating the previously given conditional probabilities with respect to the population distribution of γ, invoking independence between $\underline{C}$ and $\underline{\gamma}$.

There is no guarantee that standardizing on (conditioning on) a subset $(\underline{C}_o)$ of the components of $\underline{C}$ makes the difference (or ratio) between majority and minority hiring rates smaller or larger than the difference (or ratio) between the population rates that do not condition on $\underline{c}_o$. By standardizing on observed characteristics, it is possible to greatly exaggerate the role of differences in productivity characteristics that play only a minor role in actual labor markets, a phenomenon we illustrate below. Evidence of exchangeable treatment $P_3 = P_4$ (as defined in the text) is consistent with $\gamma^{\text{MAJ}} = \gamma^{\text{MIN}}$ at each firm, or at least in equality in the population distributions of γ^{MAJ} and γ^{MIN}, and equality in the distributions of C_u^{MAJ} and C_u^{MIN}. However, a test of $P_3 = P_4$ has no power against an alternative in which $\gamma_o^{\text{MAJ}} = \gamma_o^{\text{MIN}}$ but $\gamma_u^{\text{MAJ}} \neq \gamma_u^{\text{MIN}}$, and the distribution of C_u^{MAJ} does not equal the distribution of C_u^{MIN}, but the distributions of $\gamma_u^{\text{MAJ}} C_u^{\text{MAJ}}$ and $\gamma_u^{\text{MIN}} C_u^{\text{MIN}}$ are identical (i.e., the γ_u and C_u distributions "offset" each other). Thus, even in the presence of discrimination, P_3 can equal P_4.

A Normal Characteristics Model

To illustrate the problems that partial standardization of tester characteristics can create, we present a simple example of the hiring model. We use this example to illustrate two points. First, standardizing on only a *subset* of relevant productivity characteristics may greatly exaggerate the measured level of disparity in racial hiring rates compared with what occurs in actual market settings. Second, the skill *level* at which standardization occurs greatly affects the results.

Depending on the level of skill at which one standardizes, it is possible to produce a wide array of disparities in majority vs. minority hiring rates.

Suppose that there are only two productivity characteristics that are relevant to the hiring decision (C_o, C_u), and both are normally distributed in the population. For simplicity, and without loss of any fundamental generality, the components are assumed to be statistically independent of each other. Both components are observed by the employer, but the testing organization observes only C_o and aligns tester pairs only on this characteristic. For example, suppose that the two relevant characteristics are height and "motivational level." We assume that researchers observe (and standardize) the height of both members in an audit pair, but do not observe the auditors' motivation levels.[8] We further assume that firms observe both auditors' heights and their motivation levels, and that the latter, because they are not standardized, may differ between the two auditors.

In our model, firms turn worker characteristics into expected output by means of an evaluation vector, γ (which has two components, γ_o and γ_u). The components of the vector can be thought of as the expected marginal product of the worker characteristics in the C vector. Thus, in the above example, γ_o is the expected marginal product of height—the extra output that is produced by one extra inch of height. The expected marginal product of an applicant with the vector of characteristics $C (= (c_o, c_u))$ is γC, a scalar.

To keep this example simple, suppose that no firms discriminate and that all firms place the same value on C_o and C_u in assessing productivity. Let us assign that value at $\gamma_o = \gamma_u = 1$ for both majority and minority attributes so there is no discrimination across firms. Later we introduce discriminatory behavior.

In the population at large,

$$C_o^{MIN} \sim N(\mu_o^{MIN}, \sigma_o^{2MIN}),$$

$$C_o^{MAJ} \sim N(\mu_o^{MAJ}, \sigma_o^{2MAJ}),$$

$$C_u^{MIN} \sim N(\mu_u^{MIN}, \sigma_u^{2MIN}), \text{ and}$$

$$C_u^{MAJ} \sim N(\mu_u^{MAJ}, \sigma_u^{2MAJ}),$$

where "$\sim$" denotes "is distributed as" and $N(a, b)$ denotes a normal random variable with mean a and variance b. σ_o^{2MIN} is the *variance* in observables for minorities. Let Z denote a standard normal random variable: $Z \sim N(0, 1)$. Thus the productivity of minority members is

$$P^{MIN} = C_o^{MIN} + C_u^{MIN}, \text{ where} \tag{1}$$

$$P^{MIN} \sim N(\mu_o^{MIN} + \mu_u^{MIN}, \sigma_o^{2MIN} + \sigma_u^{2MIN})$$

while

$$P^{MAJ} = C_o^{MAJ} + C_u^{MAJ}, \text{ with} \tag{2}$$

$$P^{MAJ} \sim N(\mu_o^{MAJ} + \mu_u^{MAJ}, \sigma_o^{2MAJ} + \sigma_u^{2MAJ}).$$

Suppose that firms face a fixed cost of hiring, which includes the wage paid plus any costs associated with the hiring transaction itself. Then it follows that in the population at large, the probability that a randomly selected minority will be hired is

$$\text{Prob}(P^{MIN} > K). \tag{3(a)}$$

Because both components are normally distributed, their sum is as well, so we can write

$$\text{Prob}(P^{MIN} > K) = \text{Prob}(C_o^{MIN} + C_u^{MIN} > K)$$

$$= \text{Prob}\left(Z > \frac{K - \mu_o^{MIN} - \mu_u^{MIN}}{(\sigma_o^{2MIN} + \sigma_u^{2MIN})^{1/2}}\right)$$

$$= \Phi\left(\frac{(\mu_o^{MIN} + \mu_u^{MIN}) - K}{(\sigma_o^{2MIN} + \sigma_u^{2MIN})^{1/2}}\right),$$

where Φ is the cumulative distribution function for Z. For the majority population, the comparable hiring rate is

$$\text{Prob}(P^{MAJ} > K) = \Phi\left(\frac{(\mu_o^{MAJ} + \mu_u^{MAJ}) - K}{(\sigma_o^{2MAJ} + \sigma_u^{2MAJ})^{1/2}}\right). \tag{3(b)}$$

Thus, *ceteris paribus*, the higher the mean productivity, the higher the probability of hiring a minority or majority applicant. Higher variability in skill ($\sigma_o^2 + \sigma_u^2$) lowers the hiring probability if $\mu_o + \mu_u > K$, while greater variability increases the hiring probability if $\mu_o + \mu_u < K$.[9] The audit pair methodology aligns values of $C_o = c_o$ for both groups. Then the *conditional* (on $C_o = c_o$) hiring rates for majority and minority group members are, respectively,

$$\text{Prob}(P^{MIN} > K \mid C_o^{MIN} = c_o) = \text{Prob}(C_u^{MIN} > K - c_o \mid C_o^{MIN} = c_o)$$

$$= \Phi\left(\frac{\mu_u^{MIN} + c_o - K}{\sigma_u^{MIN}}\right) \tag{4(a)}$$

and

$$\text{Prob}(P^{\text{MAJ}} > K \mid C_o^{\text{MAJ}} = c_o) = \Phi\left(\frac{\mu_u^{\text{MAJ}} + c_o - K}{\sigma_u^{\text{MAJ}}}\right). \qquad 4(b)$$

At issue is the comparison of the ratio of 4(a) to 4(b) (the standardized hiring rate) to the population hiring ratio (3(a) divided by 3(b)).

In the population the ratio of the minority to the majority hiring rate is thus

$$h = \frac{\Phi\left(\dfrac{\mu_o^{\text{MIN}} + \mu_u^{\text{MIN}} - K}{(\sigma_o^{2\text{MIN}} + \sigma_u^{2\text{MIN}})^{1/2}}\right)}{\Phi\left(\dfrac{\mu_o^{\text{MAJ}} + \mu_u^{\text{MAJ}} - K}{(\sigma_o^{2\text{MAJ}} + \sigma_u^{2\text{MAJ}})^{1/2}}\right)}. \qquad 5(a)$$

The ratio of hiring rates when the auditors have been matched on the observable characteristic (but not on the unobservable characteristic) is

$$h(c_o) = \frac{\Phi\left(\dfrac{\mu_u^{\text{MIN}} + c_o - K}{\sigma_u^{\text{MIN}}}\right)}{\Phi\left(\dfrac{\mu_u^{\text{MAJ}} + c_o - K}{\sigma_u^{\text{MAJ}}}\right)}. \qquad 5(b)$$

Using 5(a) and 5(b), the intuitive remarks made above can be justified. Suppose that the observable characteristic, height, is the major source of productivity variability. By this we mean that the variance of height is greater than the variance of motivation ($\sigma_o^2 > \sigma_u^2$) for both majority and minority group members. Letting $\sigma_o^{2\text{MIN}}$ and $\sigma_o^{2\text{MAJ}}$ become arbitrarily large, holding the other parameters fixed, both the numerator and the denominator of 5(a) approach one-half, so h approaches one. In this case C_o "swamps" C_u. Conditioning on $C_o = c_o$ eliminates this effect. Suppose that $\mu_u^{\text{MIN}} = \mu_u^{\text{MAJ}} = 0$. If $c_o > K$, and σ_u^{MIN} and σ_u^{MAJ} becomes arbitrarily small, but in such a way that the minority variance is relatively bigger than the majority variance, i.e.,

$$\lim_{\substack{\sigma_u^{\text{MIN}} \to 0 \\ \sigma_u^{\text{MAJ}} \to 0}} \frac{\sigma_u^{\text{MIN}}}{\sigma_u^{\text{MAJ}}} > 1,$$

a standard argument verifies that $h(c_o)$ approaches infinity. That is, minority hiring rates become infinitely large relative to majority hiring rates. To take a less extreme case, set $c_o = \mu_o^{MAJ} = \mu_o^{MIN}$ so the numerator within each probability in 5(b) is the same as in 5(a) but the denominators are different. Even small differences in the numerators, which are "swamped" in 5(a), become large in 5(b) if $\sigma_u^{MIN} = \sigma_u^{MAJ}$.

To gain further insight into the model, set $\mu_u = 0$ for both groups. For the special case $\mu_o^{MIN} = \mu_o^{MAJ} = K$, 3(a) and 3(b) reveal that in the population the hiring rate is the same for both majority and minority group members and equals $\frac{1}{2}$. Thus h, the relative hiring rate, equals 1. Suppose that the component of variance for the unobservable differs between the two populations, with the minority trait more dispersed $(\sigma_u^{2MIN} > \sigma_u^{2MAJ})$. Then, depending on the value of c_o, $h(c_o)$ may be bigger or smaller than one. See figure 5.D.1, which plots $h(c_o)$ for the special case $\sigma_o^2 = 1$, $\sigma_u^{2MIN} = 1.5$, and $\sigma_u^{2MAJ} = 1$. For values of c_o less than zero, $h(c_o) > 1$. As c_o gets smaller, $h(c_o)$ becomes much bigger than one. As c_o becomes large, $h(c_o)$ approaches one. The smallest value of $h(c_o)$ is .89. For values of c_o above zero, $h(c_o) < 1$.[10] The choice of the level of c_o determines both the magnitude and the direction of the bias in the relative hiring rate as detected by audit pair methods. In this example, any relative hiring rate between .89 and infinity can be produced. Standardizing on only a subset of the relevant productivity characteristics may produce a severely distorted impression of actual labor market discrimination, which in this example does not exist in the labor market. It should be obvious that the same phenomenon of dramatic misrepresentation of population hiring rates by audit-measured hiring rates will appear if we reverse the assumption about the ordering of the variances of the unobservables $(\sigma_u^{2MAJ} < \sigma_u^{2MIN})$ or if the variances of the unobserved components are smaller than the variances of the observed components, $Max(\sigma_0^{2MIN}, \sigma_0^{2MAJ})$.

A somewhat less trivial example is produced when $K = 1$, $\mu_o^{MIN} = \mu_o^{MAJ} = 0.9$. For this case $h = .75$, so that there is a sizable disparity between minority and majority hiring rates in the population. Again, depending on the level at which the observable skill is standardized (c_o), the standardized hiring ratio can be set as large as we like and as small as .662 and can attain any value in between, as figure 5.D.2 shows.

The gist of the argument presented so far can be seen in the following example. Suppose that there are two audit pairs. In one, both the auditors are 5 feet tall. In the other both are 6'6" tall. The model shows

Figure 5.D.1 STANDARDIZED RELATIVE HIRING RATE (MINORITY VS. MAJORITY) $h(c_o)$, AS A FUNCTION OF c_o, FOR:

$$K = \mu_u^{MIN} = \mu_u^{MAJ} = \mu_o^{MIN} = \mu_o^{MAJ} = 0;$$

$$\sigma_o^{2MIN} = \sigma_o^{2MAJ} = 1; \sigma_u^{2MIN} = 1.5, \sigma_u^{2MAJ} = 1$$

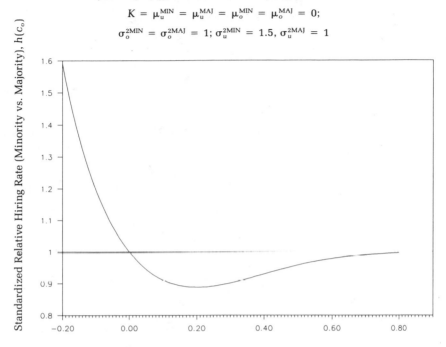

Standardized Relative Hiring Rate (Minority vs. Majority), $h(c_o)$

Level at which the observable characteristic is standardized (c_o)

$$\text{Min}(h(c_o)) = 0.89 \text{ at } c_o = 0.2$$

that under certain plausible conditions, the amount of "discrimination" (as measured by the difference in hiring rates within each of the two pairs) will be different for the two pairs.

Why should standardizing the level of the observable characteristic (say, height) at some value (c_o^*) below its mean favor black applicants, while standardization at a level above the mean favor whites? Recall that total productivity is derived from two components, height and motivation, only the first of which is observable by the researcher. Both height and motivation are observable by the firm that is evaluating job applicants, however, so when we use "unobservable," we refer only to what the researchers can observe. We further assume that minorities have a higher variance in the unobservable component than do whites, although the average motivation level is the same for both races.

Figure 5.D.2 STANDARDIZED RELATIVE HIRING RATE (MINORITY VS. MAJORITY) $h(c_o)$, AS A FUNCTION OF c_o, FOR:

$$K = 1; \mu_o^{MIN} = \mu_o^{MAJ} = 0.9; \mu_u^{MIN} = \mu_u^{MAJ} = 0;$$

$$\sigma_o^{2MIN} = \sigma_o^{2MAJ} = 10; \sigma_u^{2MIN} = 5, \sigma_u^{2MAJ} = 1$$

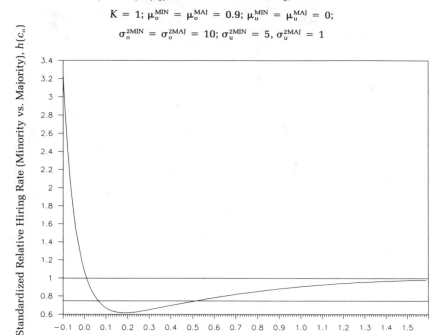

Level at which the observable characteristic is standardized (c_o)

$$Min(h(c_o)) = 0.662 \text{ at } c_o = 0.2$$

The model of hiring developed earlier suggested that there is some threshold value of productivity, K, such that any applicant whose productivity is above the threshold will be hired. Imagine that the experimenters pick some value for the observable component of total productivity. All auditors will have the identical value for the observable characteristic, height, which we will imagine is set at some value c_o^*, say 6 feet. In order for any 6-foot applicant to be hired, the sum of the two components must be greater than K, which implies that his motivation level must be greater than $(K - c_o^* = K - 6)$. In other words, conditional on a given height, the threshold for motivation (the component unobservable by the researchers) by itself is simply $K_u^* = K - c_o^*$.

Suppose we rescale so that the mean of the observable characteristic is now set to zero. If c_o^* is set below its mean of zero, then the threshold value for the unobservable variable, K_u^*, will be large and positive. All this says is that an applicant who is very weak in one of the two dimensions must be correspondingly strong in the other in order to overcome his handicap and meet the hiring threshold. Even though minorities and whites both have the same average level of motivation, our earlier variance assumptions imply that there are relatively fewer whites with either extremely high or extremely low values of this variable. Thus, for $c_o^* < 0$, a higher fraction of minority applicants will have motivation greater than the threshold (K_u^*) than will white applicants. Fixing c_o less than zero will therefore tend to favor the group with the larger variance in unobservables—in this case, minority applicants. The reverse is true for a positive value of c_o. An employer considering a very tall applicant need only worry whether the worker has an extremely low motivation level. Those with unusually low (or unusually high) motivation are more common among applicants from the high-variance applicant pool (in this case, minorities) than for those from the low variance pool.

These points are illustrated graphically in figure 5.D.3, which depicts the distribution of "motivation" for majority and minority applicants. The threshold value for the unobserved characteristic (K_u^*)

Figure 5.D.3 EFFECTS OF STANDARDIZING THE OBSERVED CHARACTERISTIC AT DIFFERENT LEVELS ON RELATIVE HIRING RATES FOR MINORITY AND MAJORITY TESTERS

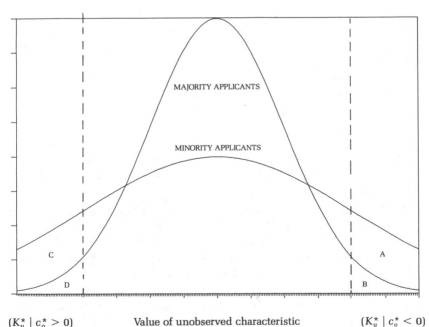

MAJORITY APPLICANTS

MINORITY APPLICANTS

C

D

A

B

$(K_u^* \mid c_o^* > 0)$ Value of unobserved characteristic $(K_u^* \mid c_o^* < 0)$

is the minimum value the applicant must have in order to be hired, conditional on some given value of height which has already been chosen by the auditors. The probability of hiring a randomly selected applicant from either of the two populations is simply the area under the relevant curve to the right of K_u^*. Suppose we set the standard height for the audit pairs very low, implying that K_u^* will be positive (so that applicants will need to be very highly motivated to be hired). Then the probability of hiring is greater for the minority applicant than for the majority applicant, as can be seen by comparing area $A + B$, the probability of hiring a minority applicant, to area B, the probability of hiring a white applicant. Conversely, if the audit pair members are both very tall, then K_u^* will be less than zero. Thus, the probability of being hired will be greater for the white applicant than for the minority applicant (compare $1 - (C + D)$ to $1 - D$)).

The following points are general features of the normal model. From 5(b), as long as $\sigma_u^{MIN} \neq \sigma_u^{MAJ}$, there always exists a c_o, c_o^* that sets $h(c_o^*) = 1$. That value is given by

$$c_o^* = \frac{\sigma_u^{MAJ} (\mu_u^{MIN} - K) - \sigma_u^{MIN} (\mu_u^{MAJ} - K)}{\sigma_u^{MIN} - \sigma_u^{MAJ}}.$$

Thus

$$h(c) > 1 \text{ for } c < c_o^* \text{ if } (\sigma_u^{MIN} > \sigma_u^{MAJ})$$

$$\text{or for } c > c_o^* \text{ if } (\sigma_u^{MIN} < \sigma_u^{MAJ}).$$

If unobserved characteristics are more heterogeneous in the minority population $((\sigma_u^{MIN} - \sigma_u^{MAJ}) > 0)$, it is always possible to find $h(c_o) > 1$ by picking a low enough level of c_o. That is, it is possible for audits to establish that there is no discrimination against minority members, even if such discrimination exists. This is evident from figures 5.D.1 and 5.D.2.

Comparing 5(a) and 5(b), it is clear that if $\sigma_u^{MIN} > \sigma_u^{MAJ}$, there exists a value of c_o such that $h(c_o) > h$. The proof entails use of L'Hospital's rule. It notes that for this case, $\lim_{c_o \to -\infty} h(c_o) \to \infty$, and by the continuity of $h(c_o)$, $h(c_o)$ assumes all values in the interval $(1, \infty)$. For the special case $\mu_u^{MIN} = 0$ and $\mu_u^{MAJ} = 0$, $h(c_o)$ reaches a global minimum at some $c_o > 0$. For the case $\mu_u^{MIN} = \mu_u^{MAJ}$ and $\mu_o^{MIN} = \mu_o^{MAJ}$ and $\sigma_o^{2MIN} + \sigma_u^{2MIN} > \sigma_o^{2MAJ} + \sigma_u^{2MAJ}$, it is always possible to find a value of c_o such that $h(c_o) > h$, since $h > 1$. For the case of $\sigma_u^{MIN} < \sigma_u^{MAJ}$ an obvious reversal of the previously stated results will hold.

Suppose that $h < 1$, so that the population hiring ratio exhibits discrimination against minorities. Regardless of the parameter values that produce this result, there always exists a value of c_o such that $h(c_o) > h$. That is, it will always be possible to choose a skill-level for the observable variable such that the audits produce less evidence of discrimination than actually exists. This follows from the observation that $\lim_{c_o \to \infty} h(c_o) = 1$ for all values of the parameters (assuming $\sigma_u^{MAJ} > 0$ and $\sigma_u^{MIN} > 0$). The absence of discrimination found in some of the UI and Denver audits may be a consequence of the implicit choice of c_o.

Note, finally, an alternative interpretation of any pair study. Suppose that C_o and C_u have unit variances for both minority and majority members. Then the previous examples also apply to the following model of discrimination in hiring. Let σ_u^{MIN} be the *firm* valuation placed on C_u^{MIN} while σ_o^{MIN} is the firm evaluation placed on C_o^{MIN}. Similarly, σ_u^{MAJ} and σ_o^{MAJ} are the firm's evaluations of C_u^{MAJ} and C_o^{MAJ} respectively. All firms place the same valuation on the characteristics. The case $\sigma_u^{MIN} > \sigma_u^{MAJ}$ is thus equivalent to the case in which minority unobservables are valued more than majority unobservables. This alternative interpretation highlights a fundamental ambiguity in audit pair methodology for the normal example considered here. Greater variability in minority unobserved skills and greater market valuation of minority skills are indistinguishable. Every result stated in terms of differential variability in skills has a dual ordering in terms of differences in the market valuation for minority and majority skills. From the audit studies, one cannot distinguish variability in unobservables from discrimination.

THE CASE MOST FAVORABLE TO THE URBAN INSTITUTE INTERPRETATION OF THE AUDIT PAIR STUDIES

The case most favorable to audit pair methodology arises when the audit analysts have access to a larger set of productivity characteristics than firms use in making hiring decisions *and* they have access to large pools of audit partners so that near perfect matches can be made. In this case, audit pair members are perfectly aligned. Firm by firm, audit pair members should be treated identically in hiring decisions. That is the benchmark that was used in UIBW. But this assumption seems implausibly strong in light of our current ignorance about the nature of firms' hiring decisions and the small samples of potential auditors available in the UI studies.

Notes, appendix 5.D

1. The individual components of the evaluation vector, γ, can be thought of as the marginal product of the associated component in the individual's skill vector, C. That is, the gamma vector maps an individual's skills (strength, reliability, etc.) into output.

2. We assume that because of its past history with job applicants, the firm has set K so as to equate the marginal benefits of making an offer to the current applicant (the immediate increase in output) with the expected marginal benefits of waiting for another applicant who may have higher productivity than the current candidate. For simplicity we assume a stationary evironment.

3. Note that this model explains the finding in the UI data that the first member of an audit pair who approaches a firm has a greater probability of receiving a job offer. The reason is that other applicants, some of whom are successful, may approach firms between the time that the first audit member leaves and the second applies.

4. Actually, all that is required under the definition of the absence of discrimination in the Anglo/Hispanic study, which defines equality of treatment by symmetry of treatment of majority and minority group members over a series of trials, is that the distributions of γ^{MAJ} and γ^{MIN} are equal. Thus, firms could draw a fresh γ each time a new applicant comes in. Although two applicants with identical bundles of characteristics (C) may be treated differently in any individual instance, as long as the draws are from the same distribution for all workers, so that the two members of a pair are treated the same on average, there is no discrimination. We forego this generality here and assume that firms have stable preferences over attributes. As we point out below, the definition of discrimination in the black/white study requires a much stronger assumption, namely that $\gamma^{MIN} = \gamma^{MAJ}$. In Heckman and Siegelman (1993) we test for, and reject, this random-draw model of employment.

5. The extent to which skill differences or differences in search behavior are attributable to the labor market or to forces outside of the labor market is difficult to sort out with either audit pair or standard observational data. Lower skills for minorities may be a consequence of their lower market rate of return to skill or due to nonmarket factors. Lower search intensity by minorities can be rationalized in the same conflicting ways.

6. Operationally, this definition requires that $\text{Prob}(\bar{\gamma}^{MAJ} c^* > K \wedge \bar{\gamma}^{MIN} c^* \leq K) = 0$ so that majority and minority group members are treated alike. In the absence of statistical or animus-based discrimination, members of a matched pair must be treated the same at all firms and will both be hired or rejected depending only on the values of K and γ for the firm.

7. The conditioning is on c_o, K, γ_u and γ_o.

8. In fact, all three of the studies did make efforts to control for demeanor, appearance, assertiveness, and other factors that might reflect motivation levels. We use this purely as an example of the kinds of characteristics that are difficult to control for.

9. This is trivially true algebraically: when the numerator of the term in brackets is positive ($\mu_o + \mu_u > K$), a large variance (in the denominator) makes the whole expression smaller. When the numerator is negative, an increase in the variance makes the entire expression larger. We offer a more intuitive explanation below.

10. Choices of c_o below zero are not implausible. If productivity is multiplicative in its components, c_o is log skill and can be negative, even if skill is positive.

References

Ayres, I. 1991. "Fair Driving: Gender and Race Discrimination in Retail Car Negotiations." *Harvard Law Review* 104 (4): 817–872.

Ayres, I., and P. Siegelman. 1993. "Race and Gender Discrimination in Negotiating for the Purchase of a New Car." Chicago: American Bar Foundation Working Paper, 1993.

Becker, G. 1975. *The Economics of Discrimination.* Chicago: University of Chicago Press.

Bishop, Y., S. Feinberg, and P. Holland. 1975. *Discrete Multivariate Analysis: Theory and Practice.*

Cain, G. 1986. "The Economic Analysis of Labor Market Discrimination: A Survey." In *Handbook of Labor Economics,* edited by O. Ashenfelter and R. Layard, vol. 1. Amsterdam: North Holland.

Cox, P. 1987. *Employment Discrimination.* New York: Garland Law Publishing.

Cressie, N., and N. Read. 1988. *Goodness of Fit Statistics for Discrete, Multivariate Data.* Berlin: Springer.

Cross, H., G. Kenny, J. Mell, and W. Zimmerman. 1990. *Employer Hiring Practices: Differential Treatment of Hispanic and Anglo Job Seekers.* Washington, D.C.: Urban Institute Press.

DeGroot, M. 1970. *Optimal Statistical Decisions.* New York: McGraw Hill.

Dipboye, R. 1975. "Relative Importance of Applicant Sex, Attractiveness, and Scholastic Standing in Evaluation of Job Applicant Resumes." *Journal of Applied Psychology* 60: 39–43.

Domencich, T., and D. McFadden. 1975. *Urban Travel Demand.* Amsterdam: North Holland.

Donohue, J., and P. Siegelman. 1991. "The Changing Nature of Employment Discrimination Litigation." *Stanford Law Review* 43(3): 983–1033.

Flinn, C., and J. Heckman. 1983. "Are Unemployment and Out of the Labor Force Behaviorally Distinct States." *Journal of Labor Economics* 1: 65–93.

Good, I.J. 1965. *The Estimation of Probabilities: An Essay on Modern Bayesian Methods.* Cambridge: MIT Press.

Heckman, J., and P. Siegelman. 1993. "The Audit Pair Methodology for Assessing Labor Market Discrimination: A Critical Assessment." Unpublished manuscript, University of Chicago.

Hedges, L., and I. Olkin, *Statistical Methods for Meta-Analysis,* 1985, San Diego: Academic Press.

Holzer, H. 1987. "Informal Job Search and Black Youth Unemployment." *American Economic Review* 77(3): 446–452.

_____. 1988. "Search Methods Used By Unemployed Youth." *Journal of Labor Economics* 6(1): 1–20.

James, F., and S.W. DelCastillo. 1991. "Measuring Job Discrimination by Private Employers Against Young Black and Hispanic Males Seeking

Entry Level Work in the Denver Metropolitan Area." Unpublished report. Denver: University of Colorado, Denver, March.

Lehmann, E. 1986. *Testing Statistical Hypotheses.* 2nd ed., New York: Wiley.

Leonard, J. 1984. "Anti-Discrimination or Reverse Discrimination: The Impact of Title VII, Affirmative Action, and Changing Demographics on Productivity." *Journal of Human Resources* 19: 145–169.

Lindzey, G., and E. Aronson. 1975. *The Handbook of Social Psychology.* 2nd ed., vol. 2. Reading, Mass.: Addison-Wesley.

Madden, J. 1987. "Gender and Race Differences in the Cost of Displacement: An Empirical Test of Discrimination in the Labor Market." *American Economic Review* 77: 246–251.

McFadden, D. 1973. "Conditional Logit Analysis of Qualitative Choice Behaviour." In *Frontiers of Econometrics,* edited by P. Zarembka. New York: Academic Press.

McIntyre, S., et al. 1980. "Preferential Treatment in Preselection Decisions According to Race and Sex." *Academy of Management Journal* 23.

Newman, J. 1978. "Discrimination in Recruitment: An Empirical Analysis." *Industrial and Labor Relations Review* 32: 15–23.

Pearson, E.S. 1950. "On Questions Raised by The Combination of Tests Based on Discontinuous Distributions." *Biometrika,* 37: 89–99.

Pratt, J., and J. Gibbons. 1981. *Concepts of Nonparametric Theory.* Berlin: Academic Press.

Rosenthal, R. 1976. *Experimenter Effects in Behavioral Research.* 2nd ed. New York: Irvington Publishers.

Thurstone, L. 1927. "A Law of Comparative Judgement." *Psychological Review* 34: 273–286.

Turner, Margery A., M. Fix, and R. Struyk. 1991. *Opportunities Denied, Opportunities Diminished: Racial Discrimination in Hiring.* Washington, D.C.: Urban Institute Press.

Van den Berg, G. 1991. "Results on the Rate of Arrival of Job Offers in a Search Model." *Review of Economic Studies* 62: 263–271.

Yinger, John. 1986. "Measuring Racial Discrimination With Fair Housing Audits." *American Economic Review* 76 (5): 881–893.

AUDIT METHODOLOGY: COMMENTS

John Yinger

Audits are a deceptively simple technique. By sending out equally qualified Anglos and minorities to apply for a job (or to look for housing) we can make inferences about discrimination, it would seem, by observing differences in the treatment of the Anglo and minority auditors. As many researchers have discovered, however, these inferences are not always so easy to make. Audits raise complex issues of study design and statistical method. Our understanding of these issues is still limited, so this chapter by Heckman and Siegelman, with its detailed look at audit methodology, is a welcome addi tion to the literature.

The chapter addresses many different topics. This comment focuses on the chapter's contribution to audit methodology. Thus I do not address topics such as the problems in nonaudit studies of labor market discrimination and the ability to make inferences about wage differentials from audit results.

The chapter's discussion of audit methodology falls into three broad topics: aspects of study design, simple statistical procedures, and behavioral models. This comment is organized about these three topics. These topics are not new; they have been extensively discussed in the literature on fair housing audits and, to some degree, in the employment audit studies that Heckman and Siegelman (henceforth H/S) review. The discussion of these topics in this comment draws heavily on the analysis of these topics for the Housing Discrimination Study (HDS), which is discussed elsewhere in this volume.

STUDY DESIGN

Heckman and Siegelman's discussions of study design are concentrated in the section "Qualifying the Urban Institute Conclusions," although comments on the topic are scattered throughout the chapter.

In general, their comments help the reader understand some of the issues that researchers confront in setting up an audit study, but they do not always provide practical solutions to the problems they identify. They provide some good evidence, for example, that many jobs are obtained through informal networks, not just through newspaper advertisements, but they do not show how to identify these jobs and thereby include them in an audit sampling frame.

I will not attempt a comprehensive review of the H/S comments on study design, but will instead focus on one issue that has not been widely discussed in previous studies, namely experimenter effects. This is a good issue to raise and H/S make some important points that audit researchers need to consider. But I believe their discussion underestimates the difficulties of running an audit study in which the purpose, namely measuring discrimination, is hidden from the auditors.

H/S report that auditors "were warned about the employer bias they might encounter and how they should react to it." What they do not report, however, is that people who encounter bias without being prepared for it often become upset or react in some other way that invalidates the audit—at least this was found to be the case in early housing audit studies. Without preparing auditors for bias, therefore, audits of the most flagrant discriminators would sometimes be invalid. In addition, it is crucial that the two members of an audit team go through exactly the same training. A group that is obviously half black and half white (or half Anglo and half Hispanic) will start trainees thinking and perhaps making up their own mind about what the study is or how they should behave. It makes more sense to me to keep participants from guessing by telling them the purpose of the study and to emphasize how important it is that they record exactly how they are treated by the employer.

H/S write that "All three studies made a point of stressing the nature of the experiment and its expected findings to the testers in several days of training." I would summarize the training sessions in a somewhat different way. Tester training sessions gave some historical background on discrimination, told the testers about possible outcomes, and emphasized the need for accurate reporting, but did not literally indicate the expected findings from the study.

Nevertheless, I think there is room for alternative audit designs that can explore the importance of experimenter effects. A design in which auditors were "blind" as to the purpose of the study and the existence of their teammate, for example, could be a useful experiment.

SIMPLE STATISTICAL PROCEDURES

A great deal of effort in the employment and housing audit studies has been devoted to coming up with simple summary measures of the incidence of "discrimination." This effort is inevitable with a topic that has such obvious significance for public policy; a study's results are more likely to be considered in the policy debate if they can be summarized in a few easily understood numbers and hypothesis tests.

The key problem confronting any audit study is that a simple easy-to-interpret measure of the incidence of discrimination is not available. Researchers all agree, including H/S I believe, that discrimination is appropriately defined as systematic unfavorable treatment of minority applicants; however, this phrasing leaves two key issues unresolved.

The first issue is whether to focus on the *absolute* incidence of unfavorable treatment of minority auditors or on the incidence of unfavorable treatment of minority auditors *relative to* that of majority auditors. The former approach, which is called the *gross* approach, is more closely tied to a legal notion of discrimination, in which unfavorable treatment of a black applicant by one employer cannot be offset by unfavorable treatment of a white applicant by another employer. In contrast, the latter approach, which is called the *net* approach, is more closely tied to a standard economic notion of discrimination, in which differences in treatment in a large sample, controlling for relevant factors, are of primary interest. Differences of opinion on this issue are fundamentally philosophical and cannot be resolved with statistical procedures.

The second issue is to define what is meant by "systematic," that is, to distinguish between systematic and random employer behavior. Economists are, of course, used to distinguishing between systematic and random factors. The problem is particularly difficult here because some systematic factors, such as employer prejudice, are not observed and because the multivariate methods on which economists rely often add complexity to the interpretation and explanation of measures of discrimination and associated hypothesis tests.

In this context, two simple approaches to measuring the incidence of discrimination (and testing hypotheses about it) have been used. The simple gross approach, which is emphasized by UIBW and HDS, defines the incidence of discrimination as the share of audits in which the minority auditor encountered unfavorable treatment. This approach can be used to measure the legal notion of discrimination, given the assumption that acts of unfavorable treatment always (or virtually always) are associated with observed or unobserved systematic factors, not with true random behavior. In the terms used by H/S, this approach estimates the value of $P3$ and tests the hypothesis that $P3 = 0$.

The simple net approach, which is emphasized by UIHA, the Denver study, and pre-HDS housing audit studies, defines the incidence of discrimination as the simple gross measure minus the share of audits in which the majority auditor encountered unfavorable treatment. This approach can be used to measure either the economic or the legal notion of discrimination, given certain assumptions. It is appropriate for measuring the legal notion of discrimination under the assumptions that (1) minority applicants are only favored for random reasons and (2) random factors have a symmetrical impact on the probability that minority and majority applicants are favored. Under these assumptions, subtracting the share of audits in which the minority auditor is favored from the share of audits in which the majority auditor is favored yields the share of audits in which the majority auditor is favored for systematic reasons alone, which is the definition of discrimination. Again in the terms used by H/S, this approach estimates the value of $(P3—P4)$ and tests the hypothesis that $P3 = P4$.

If the first of these assumptions is dropped (but not the second), the simple net measure yields the economic notion of discrimination. In other words, the simple net measure indicates the difference in the probability that majority and minority auditors will be favored.

This discussion is consistent, I believe, with the discussion in the H/S chapter. In fact, their discussion of these issues concludes that "The net, or symmetric treatment, definition is consistent with the view that whites experience no discrimination and that the proportion of trials in which blacks are hired and whites are not constitutes a benchmark for 'randomness' in employment decisions." They add, in parentheses, that "It is also consistent with the view that one cannot measure an absolute level of discrimination in the labor market but that the asymmetry of treatment of 'identical' persons constitutes evidence of discrimination."

H/S make the reasonable argument that the "symmetry definition of no discrimination which allows for random errors in hiring is the natural point of departure for any statistical testing procedure." They also point out that a rejection of the hypothesis of no discrimination using the net approach implies a rejection of no discrimination using the gross approach. "In terms of testing hypotheses," they conclude, "it is desirable to start with the weaker version."

Although I agree that the net approach is a good starting point, I do not think it is the whole story. A gross measure may be more appropriate for some purposes, such as determining the extent to which minorities encounter acts that violate the notion of equal treatment. Thus researchers may want to provide gross measures (along with the associated hypothesis tests, even though, as H/S explain, those tests are somewhat awkward) as well as net measures.

H/S provide a valuable discussion of alternative methods for testing the hypothesis that discrimination exists using the net or symmetry approach. They argue that a conditional sign test is the best method for audit data. When all audits at a site are pooled (an issue to which I return below), this method confirms the UIAH and UIBW conclusion that discrimination in hiring exists in all sites they studied, and the conclusion by the Denver study that the hypothesis of no discrimination cannot be definitively rejected.

In some sense, the simple net and gross measures of discrimination, as well as the associated hypothesis tests, are bound to be unsatisfactory because they are based on untested assumptions about the underlying behavior and do not draw on the available control variables in an audit study. Although H/S do not address this topic explicitly, they do raise three issues that are potentially very helpful in developing more satisfactory measures.

First, following an article by McIntyre et al., they propose the use of three-person audit teams consisting of two Anglo auditors and one minority auditor. This approach makes it possible to estimate the importance of random factors in the treatment of Anglo auditors and thereby to shed light on the first assumption, listed above, that supports the use of the simple net measure. They also show how three-person teams could be used to refine their hypothesis tests. A possible extension of this approach would be to use four-person teams, consisting of two Anglo and two minority auditors. This extension would make it possible to test the other assumption on which the net measure is based, namely that random factors have a symmetrical impact on the treatment of minority and majority auditors.

Second, H/S raise the important issue of homogeneity across audit pairs. This issue arises because an audit study uses several audit teams, each of which completes many audits. In the employment audit studies, the number of audits conducted by each team was between 30 and 60. The test for homogeneity provided by H/S determines whether differences between Anglo and minority auditors are concentrated in one or a few audit teams. If so (that is, if there is not homogeneity), then one cannot reject the hypothesis that there is something about this (or these) teams, such as imperfect matching, that causes unequal treatment. Rejecting homogeneity, in other words, would limit one's ability to make inferences about discrimination. This test for homogeneity is a valuable contribution to the audit literature, particularly in the employment case, in which each team conducts so many audits. Although H/S do not say so, this issue was considered by one of the UI studies. To be specific, the intracluster correlation coefficient calculated by UIAH is an alternative measure of homogeneity.

As it turns out, H/S cannot reject the hypothesis of homogeneity for the UI studies, except in one case (the Chicago audits in UIBW); for the most part, a lack of homogeneity does not limit one's ability to make inferences about discrimination from these studies. The calculations made by UIAH yield the same result. H/S can reject homogeneity for the Denver audits, however.

Drawing on their work in an unpublished companion paper, H/S also argue that a conditional sign test can be adjusted to account for heterogeneity across audit pairs. The results they present confirm the results from simpler tests, namely that the hypothesis of no discrimination can be rejected for the UI audits but not for the Denver audits, in every case except one, namely the UI black/white audits in Chicago. In that case, the H/S test statistic falls just short of statistical significance at the 5 percent level.

Third, H/S provide a formal behavioral model of hiring discrimination. This helpful model, which is discussed in more detail below, is summarized near the end of the chapter and presented in appendix 5.D. Because it explicitly addresses many of the issues that confound interpretation of simple summary measures, this model could form the basis for alternative summary measures of discrimination and for alternative tests of the hypothesis that discrimination exists.

An excellent chapter like this one emboldens the reader to ask for more. What I would like to see is the use of the formal, multivariate model of discrimination to derive alternative summary measures of discrimination and associated hypothesis tests that avoid the problems inherent in simple summary measures. As discussed below, H/S use their model to make some comments about hypothesis tests concerning discrimination, but they do not link the two main parts of the paper, the hypothesis tests and the formal behavioral model. This lack of linkage is particularly apparent when, on the basis of their homogeneity tests, they criticize the UIBW study for conducting multinomial, multivariate logit analysis with pooled data for the Chicago black/white audits. An alternative way to connect the homogeneity issue with a multivariate procedure would be to use the H/S model or some other one to determine the extent to which using auditor and employer control variables provides a partial control for heterogeneity, or to introduce a fixed effect for each audit pair (or even each audit) to deal directly with the heterogeneity problem. Although H/S do not put it this way, this chapter provides a great deal of good analysis for making this type of connection.

BEHAVIORAL MODELS

The third major topic in the H/S chapter, which is summarized at the end of the chapter and presented in detail in appendix 5.D, is a behavioral model of discrimination in hiring. This model is a valuable addition to the literature; as H/S point out, we cannot design sensible public policy to combat discrimination unless we first model and test theories about its causes.

Let me begin my discussion of this topic with a brief review of the H/S approach. Their behavioral model is one in which firms evaluate the expected productivity of an applicant based on his or her characteristics. An applicant is offered a job if the firm believes, on the basis of his characteristics, that he will be productive enough to offset the costs of hiring him. In the H/S terminology, characteristics are a vector labeled C and the weights or expected marginal productivities associated with each characteristic form vectors labeled γ^{MAJ} and γ^{MIN}. (For simplicity, I have left off vector indicators, namely the lines under these terms.) Since audit teammates are matched to have the same characteristics (except for unobserved characteristics, which are considered below), discrimination exists when the weights or expected marginal productivities assigned by firms to various characteristics are less favorable for blacks than for whites.

The key challenge for this type of model is to specify the possible causes of discrimination. According to H/S, "Differences between components of γ^{MAJ} and γ^{MIN} may arise because of discrimination in evaluating specific attributes or against a race group as a whole (recall that C includes a constant). Alternatively, discrimination might reflect statistical information processing in the event of incomplete information about C, if the same observed characteristics convey different productivity information about majority and minority group members."

As I understand this discussion, H/S are saying that there are two types of discrimination, animus-based and statistical. Animus-based discrimination exists if, because of their own prejudice, employers refuse to hire minorities who have the same expected productivities as whites they hire. This type of discrimination can be seen in lower values for the elements of γ^{MIN} than for those of γ^{MAJ}. If the employers' prejudice affects all minority candidates the same way, regardless of their characteristics, then the effect will appear in the element of γ^{MIN} associated with the constant term, but prejudice might also lead employers to assign lower values to some other element of γ^{MIN} with no productivity justification.

Statistical discrimination exists if employers assign lower values to some elements of γ^{MIN} than to γ^{MAJ} because minority applicants with a given value of the associated characteristics have lower productivity, on average, than majority applicants and because the employers have incomplete information about individual applicants' productivity.

In my view, the H/S discussion starts in exactly the right place, namely specifying alternative potential causes of discrimination. Building on their foundation, I would like to add three points.

First, even though statistical discrimination is based on expected productivity differences between minority and majority applicants with the same characteristics, it is just as illegal as animus-based discrimination. An employer who refuses to hire minority applicants because "the same observed characteristics convey different productivity information about majority and minority group members" is still discriminating. In other words, it is not legal to refuse to hire a minority candidate on the basis of information that is valid for minorities on average but that may not be valid for that individual.

Second, H/S point out that "Audit pair studies as currently conducted cannot distinguish between animus-based and statistical discrimination, although it is of scientific and policy interest to do so." I agree with this statement but would add that the H/S model itself does not provide a way to determine whether differences in the estimated γ^{MAJ} and γ^{MIN} vectors are due to animus-based or statistical discrimination. In my view, the key to developing such a test is to determine the circumstances under which animus-based or statistical discrimination are most likely to arise. A test for animus-based discrimination, for example, would be to determine whether black employers are less likely than white employers to refuse to offer employment to black auditors. This approach is related to a question posed by H/S near the end of their chapter: "What, if anything, distinguishes firms that discriminate against blacks or Hispanics from those that discriminate against whites or do not discriminate at all?" The way to answer this question is to incorporate into their model more complete formulations of the causes of discrimination.

Third, employer prejudice and statistical information processing are not the only possible causes of discrimination. Employers may discriminate against minority applicants, for example, because their current white employees or their current white customers prefer not to deal with minorities. Another valuable extension of the model would be to incorporate a more comprehensive set of causes.

The main focus of the H/S model is on the role of applicant characteristics that an employer believes will influence that applicant's productivity and that are not controlled or matched in the audit design. This issue is, of course, at the heart of an audit study. An audit is a controlled experiment in the sense that it attempts to pair teammates that are identically qualified for a job, but the quality of the experiment is only as good as the quality of the pairing. If teammates are not matched on some important characteristic, inferences about differences in teammate treatment may not be valid.

This issue is well known, but H/S provide a more detailed analysis of the consequences of inadequate matching than any previous study. In the context of their behavioral model, they show how uncontrolled characteristics can lead researchers to over- or underestimate discrimination, even if the average value of these characteristics is the same for Anglo and minority auditors. These results should help researchers who conduct audit studies to understand, and one hopes to avoid, the potential problems from inadequate matching.

Because of the potential problems from uncontrolled characteristics, the complexity of hiring decisions, and doubts about the success of the matching process in the UI and Denver studies (based on the H/S homogenety tests), H/S appear somewhat skeptical about the results of these studies. They conclude, "If mismatching in characteristics occurs in half of the city/race sites despite the best efforts of the testers to prevent it, it would seem that our knowledge of the hiring process being audited is rife with uncertainty. One should be wary of assuming that much is known about how hiring decisions are actually made. The burden of proof that audit pairs are properly aligned must be assumed by audit pair analysts. More objective demonstrations of the matching methods actually used would increase the value of audit pair evidence."

No one could disagree with the conclusion that more audit evidence would be valuable. However, I am more confident about the results of the UI studies than H/S appear to be. These studies are by no means the last word on employment audits, but they were carefully and thoughtfully conducted. Moreover, the homogeneity tests support, in a phrase used by H/S, "the efficacy of the auditor matching and selection procedures" in three out of the four UI city/race sites, and H/S do not provide any specific examples of important auditor characteristics that were not considered in the matching process. In my judgment, therefore, the UI studies provide strong evidence of racial and ethnic discrimination in hiring. The case for the Denver study is less clear, both because, as H/S point out, its procedures are different enough from the UI procedures that the Denver and UI results are hard to compare, and because the H/S homogeneity tests do not support the efficacy of matching for either of the groups covered in the study.

This is not to say that the UI studies are immune from criticism on their matching procedures. Matching is central to the validity of any audit study and researchers should continue to refine it. Moreover, employment audits are relatively new and matching procedures can undoubtedly be improved. H/S have done a service by exploring the possible consequences of imperfect matching in some detail, but, in my judgment, it would be inappropriate to dismiss the results of the UI studies on the basis of their arguments.

Finally, H/S show that the choice of the productivity level at which auditors are matched can influence the results. This link arises for two reasons. The first reason, which was discussed extensively by the researchers involved in HDS, is that discrimination itself may vary by productivity level for some reason. If so, a study that focuses on one particular productivity level may yield an accurate measure of discrimination for that level but cannot be generalized to other skill levels or to workers on average. To obtain an overall estimate of discrimination, one must conduct audits at all skill levels.

The second reason, which H/S derive from their model, is that the impact of unobserved characteristics on outcomes may depend on the selected level of observed characteristics. Even if minority and majority auditors have the same average value of unobserved characteristics, for example, H/S show that the distribution of these characteristics could lead to an overestimate of discrimination when observed characteristics are standardized at a high level and to an underestimate when they are standardized at a low level—or vice versa. Although the practical importance of these results is not yet known, they are a useful contribution to our understanding of audits and reinforce the need for audit studies to standardize at a variety of different skill levels.

The limitation imposed by standardizing at one skill level is recognized by the Urban Institute researchers, who present their studies as "exploratory." But future employment audit studies, particularly those intended to obtain national measures of discrimination in hiring, should struggle with this issue, which is, of course, primarily an issue of the sampling frame. Auditors must be qualified for the sampled jobs, so to a large degree auditors' skill levels are determined by the sampling frame one selects. Overall, H/S argue, persuasively I believe, that a representative measure of discrimination requires a sampling frame that covers more jobs within a skill category than do newspaper advertisements and that covers more than one skill level. This is no small challenge for future audit studies, because jobs at higher skill levels will require more elaborate training and role-playing procedures.

CONCLUSIONS

Everyone interested in employment and housing audits should read this chapter. It shows how complex audits can be, provides careful analysis of many cases in which audits can go wrong, and offers several valuable new statistical tools for use in audit studies. Several of the authors' suggestions, such as testing for homogeneity across audit pairs and building careful behavioral models of discriminatory behavior, should become standard practices in employment audit research. The authors also raise a variety of important issues in study design. Although I believe that their discussion does not fully recognize the practical difficulties that arise in running an audit study, the issues they raise deserve consideration in future audit studies.

Their chapter enriches our understanding of the importance of audit matching procedures. Future audit studies should carefully consider their findings, such as the importance of standardizing observed characteristics at a variety of different skill levels. Although I am more confident than H/S appear to be about the accuracy of the UI audit results, I believe that they have raised a variety of issues concerning matching, such as the need to match at a range of skill levels, for audit researchers to address.

Finally, the H/S model of hiring behavior provides a valuable foundation on which future research can build. By extending this model, future audit studies should be able to specify and test a variety of hypotheses about the causes of discrimination in hiring. Moreover, this model may make it possible to develop alternative simple measures of discrimination and hypothesis tests that, unlike the simple measures now widely used, do not have to make untestable assumptions about the underlying behavior and that take full advantage of multivariate methods.

RESPONSE TO COMMENTS
BY JOHN YINGER

James J. Heckman and Peter Siegelman

Professor Yinger faults us for pointing out fundamental problems in audit studies of the labor market without solving them. It seems to us, however, that the burden is on those who design such studies to resolve these problems, either by changes in the audit methodology or by demonstrating that the problems are not important.

In an effort to clarify what we have written, both in this chapter and in our companion paper, it may be useful to summarize our argument briefly, and then go on to respond to Yinger's criticisms.

A SUMMARY OF OUR MAIN ARGUMENT

We have made the following points:

(1) Audit pair studies are a version of a statistical matching procedure. Matching is only effective if pairs are matched on "relevant" productivity variables. Since so little is known about the labor market, what worker characteristics are valued, and how firms trade them off, it strikes us as premature to dismiss concerns about the potentially serious consequences of unobserved variables. Those conducting audit studies owe their readers much more detailed documentation about *all* the characteristics used to make matches (including the "subjective" ones) and the way teams are chosen. Put another way, it seems unlikely to us that out of a total of 23 applicants for audit pair work in Washington 10 persons turned out to be perfectly matched with someone else. (In Chicago, there were 31 applicants, out of which 10 were "perfectly" matched.) If auditors "know" what characteristics firms really value, and how they trade these off, they should make this knowledge widely available.

An objective demonstration of the quality of the matches would go a long way toward making audit pairs credible.

(2) Experimenter effects are a nontrivial issue. Not only were the testers told about the problem of discrimination in the United States, they may have inadvertently been motivated to find it.

(3) The use of falsified credentials and college student audit pair members who are overqualified for the markets they are sampling (especially in the summertime when employers may be suspicious of hiring college students who will quit in the fall) poses interpretive problems. Any discrimination that may be found may not be typical of that experienced by usual participants in the markets being sampled. Similarly, use of newspaper advertisements to sample entry-level labor markets likely misses the bulk of the hiring action. Characteristics such as beards and accents that distinguish minority and majority applicants raise questions about some of the studies.

(4) A measure of discrimination that counts all errors by firms as discrimination (alternatively, that assumes that firms make no race-neutral errors in job hiring) requires much more defense than is given by Professor Yinger or the authors of UIBW. We favor a weaker measure—asymmetry of mean labor market outcomes by audit pair by race. That measure avoids certain technical problems in hypothesis testing that attend use of the stronger "gross" measure. If the weak hypothesis of symmetry in aggregate outcomes is rejected, the stronger gross hypothesis is also rejected. Thus on both technical and interpretive grounds, the hypothesis we advance is a natural starting point for any statistical investigation of discrimination.

(5) There is a tradeoff between homogeneity in the level of observed skills across audit pairs and heterogeneity. Homogeneous pairs can be pooled, thus simplifying statistical analyses and building effective sample size. Heterogeneous pairs cannot be so easily pooled but, taken as a whole, are likely to provide a more accurate description of the labor market. Evaluating discrimination at one skill level may provide a very misleading picture of overall discrimination. If majority and minority members differ in their distribution of unobserved (by us) relevant productivity characteristics, it is possible to prove no discrimination, discrimination in favor of minorities or discrimination against minorities by judiciously—or accidently—picking a single "standard" skill level for observed characteristics across audit pairs.

(6) Large sample statistical theory of the type used to design and analyze the UI studies when correctly interpreted in a small sample setting produces inferences biased toward finding discrimination. Exact small sample statistics show much less evidence of discrimination but they are very conservative. Conditional tests currently not utilized

by the Urban Institute support its contentions more strongly. Large sample theory also offers a poor guide to optimal sample design.

THE CRITIQUE OF OUR CRITIQUE OF THE STUDY DESIGN

The fact that the mass of jobs obtained by youth are not found by responding to newspaper ads indicates a severe limitation of the audit pair method. What is sampled is unlikely to be representative. Sending blacks into Polish bars in Chicago or Poles into black bars to hear about network-generated job leads is obviously fraught with difficulty. It is a fundamental defect of the audit method that it is not well suited for sampling real labor markets.

We understand the reasons for telling auditors what they are doing and why. However, this does not eliminate the possibility that auditors might have been motivated to find what they have been told.

NET VS. GROSS MEASURES AND THE VALUE OF A SECOND AUDIT PAIR MEMBER OF THE SAME DEMOGRAPHIC GROUP

The "gross" approach to measuring discrimination—counting any instance of disparate treatment of the two audit pair members as discrimination—is designed to find it. It is valid only if firms make no race-neutral errors in hiring and if the audit pairs are perfectly aligned for *all* firms they encounter. These requirements are unlikely ever to be met in any audit pair study.

Our discussion of the "net" approach resolves why it is a better starting point. First, it produces a statistical hypothesis that avoids the conceptual problem that plagues the UIBW study (testing for a zero probability). Second, rejection of the hypothesis $P_3 = P_4$ (i.e., evidence of asymmetry of treatment) implies rejection of the hypothesis $P_3 + P_4 = 0$ because the latter can only occur as a special case of the former ($P_3 + P_4 = 0$ implies and is implied by $P_3 = P_4 = 0$ which is a special case of the null hypothesis $P_3 = P_4$).

Finally, the use of a third tester of the same race/ethnicity as one of the other two illuminates the case for the gross measure and provides a better way to test for symmetric treatment. (Adding additional testers can only help in this regard by calibrating background noise for each race/ethnic group.) If the gross measure has validity as anything other than an overstated measure of discrimination, $P_3 = P_4 = 0$ should characterize the data for members of the same demographic group. $\hat{P}_3$ and $\hat{P}_4$ provide estimates of background noise. At a minimum, advocates of the "gross" approach should adjust $\hat{P}_3 + \hat{P}_4$ obtained from majority/majority pairs by subtracting $\hat{P}_3 + \hat{P}_4$ obtained from same race pairs. Estimates of $\hat{P}_3$ and $\hat{P}_4$ obtained from the same race pairs can also be used to construct a *band* of values of $P_3 - P_4$ within which $\hat{P}_3 - \hat{P}_4$ from opposite race pairs could lie and still be consistent with the symmetric treatment hypothesis (i.e., instead of testing $P_3 = P_4$, testing if $P_3 = P_4 \pm \epsilon$).

HOMOGENEITY

It is important to distinguish homogeneity within pairs from homogeneity across pairs. The latter does not necessarily imply the former. For example, majority and minority members may be equally misaligned within pairs at the same level without causing us to reject homogeneity across pairs.

A test of the alignment procedure to examine within pair homogeneity would be possible if there were two or more audit pair members from the same demographic group. Alignment would imply that $\hat{P}_3 = \hat{P}_4 = 0$.

As we argue above, and in our papers, homogeneity *across* pairs is not necessarily a virtue. Such homogeneity may produce a misleading picture of actual labor market discrimination. Rejecting homogeneity—far from limiting one's ability to make inferences about discrimination—may enhance one's ability to make such inferences.

BEHAVIORAL MODELS

Our model can distinguish between animus-based and statistical discrimination. (Both, of course, are illegal under current law.) Including an "intercept" or "constant term" in $\underset{\sim}{C}_0^{\mathrm{MAJ}}$ and $\underset{\sim}{C}_0^{\mathrm{MIN}}$ allows firms to differ in their treatment of minorities solely as a consequence of values of the intercepts ($\gamma_{00}^{\mathrm{MAJ}}$ and $\gamma_{00}^{\mathrm{MIN}}$ respectively) independent of skill levels. A special case of our model allows for firms to be so discriminatory that they will not hire minorities at any price ($\gamma_{oO}^{MIN} = -\infty$). That is a stronger form of animus-based discrimination than is envisaged by Becker's seminal book and most papers in the literature. There might also be discrimination on specific attributes.

Professor Yinger also reminds the reader of our point about the danger of using one observed skill level to make inferences about an entire market. The obvious thing to do is to sample many skill levels and we say that in our chapter. If audit pair sampling cannot be performed on the entire range of skills, that is a flaw in the methodology which should be acknowledged and not papered over.

Professor Yinger writes as if we exaggerate the importance of unobserved characteristics, but provides no proof of that claim. Analysts who have estimated earnings functions from company personnel records with very detailed data on personal characteristics, test scores, and company employment histories still report a big unexplained residual. (R^2 rarely get as high as .6.) Unobservables may turn out to be unimportant, but we would like to see evidence, rather than assertions, for such a claim. Only then can the audit pair methodology lay claim to scientific respectability.

Chapter Six

POLICY IMPLICATIONS FOR HISPANIC AND OTHER NATIONAL-ORIGIN GROUPS

Antonia Hernández and Birgit Seifert

IMPORTANCE OF AUDITING AND TESTING IN CIVIL RIGHTS ADVOCACY

Testing and auditing[1] for discrimination have become increasingly valuable tools in advancing a civil rights agenda. Although the power and effect of these methods are just beginning to be explored, several points have already become clear. The first is that auditing research studies, such as those recently conducted by The Urban Institute, generate striking information about the continued disparate treatment of minorities. This documentation, and the press attention it has received, play a critical role in educating legislators and the public about the need for securing and enforcing strong antidiscrimination laws. This educational function has become all the more important as some politicians seek to blame employment discrimination laws in general, and affirmative action remedies in particular, for the unemployment of working-class whites and to gain thereby a political advantage.

Second, auditing research and testing for civil rights enforcement are very useful now that discriminatory practices are being conducted in a more subtle fashion. As many civil rights practitioners know, for the most part, employers no longer discriminate in a blatant manner or leave "smoking-gun" evidence in accessible places. The lack of such evidence makes discriminatory conduct much harder to detect in the first place and much harder to prove even where it is suspected. This additional burden has unfortunately deterred many civil rights practitioners from taking on cases that have substantial merit and has contributed to the lack of representation faced by victims of discrimination. Auditing research can help identify segments of the labor market or the housing market worthy of more detailed investigation, while testing for litigation purposes can garner otherwise undiscoverable evidence.

Third, these studies are a particularly valuable tool for documenting the barriers faced by Hispanics and other communities that have historically been underrepresented in our civil rights enforcement efforts. Much documentation of the disparate treatment of minorities in the labor market has come from two sources: academic wage studies and information generated through litigation. Analysis of income levels has consistently shown that after controlling for differences in education, training, and age, discrimination on the basis of ethnicity accounts for a significant degree of the earning gap between Hispanics and whites.[2]

Unfortunately, the use of litigation as a method of documenting and highlighting employment discrimination has not been a readily available tool for the Hispanic community. While victims of employment discrimination across the board have found it unusually difficult to secure adequate legal representation, this problem is especially acute for Hispanics. In many parts of the country where Hispanics are concentrated, there are few, if any, attorneys willing to take discrimination cases. Aggravating this situation is the fact that the Equal Employment Opportunity Commission (EEOC) has historically underserved Hispanics.[3]

Although auditing research is often not designed to produce the specific type of information needed for proof of disparate treatment in court, it can call attention to the discrimination faced by historically underserved communities. From this standpoint, the 1989 hiring audit study by the Urban Institute, which compared the treatment of closely matched Anglo and Hispanic job applicants,[4] and the 1991 housing audit study, which for the first time documented housing discrimination against Hispanics on a national level,[5] are particularly important. Auditing may also prove useful in surveying particular segments of the labor market or particular employers within an industry to determine whether more detailed and expensive testing is warranted for purposes of enforcement. Given the scarce litigation resources of Hispanic and other minority communities, the use of auditing and testing techniques in tandem could become an essential aspect of a cost-efficient civil rights strategy.[6] Having addressed some of the benefits of auditing and testing for civil rights enforcement in general, and for the advancement of Latino civil rights in particular, I would like to discuss two particular concerns I have about the development and use of this methodology. The first involves the need to address the criticisms of auditing and testing, especially those that go to questions of accuracy. The second involves the need to audit the treatment faced by all groups protected under American civil rights laws.

ADDRESSING CRITICISMS OF AUDITING AND TESTING

Research auditing and testing for civil rights enforcement are powerful tools, and it is precisely because of this that the methodology has been subject to some criticism. Some have argued that testers who experience discrimination are not truly injured and therefore do not have standing to enforce civil rights violations, while others have argued that when testers pose as a particular type of employment or housing applicant, they engage in a form of unethical behavior that must be prohibited.[7] Still others have challenged the accuracy of the auditing studies, claiming that there was inadequate control for certain factors or that the studies overestimated the level of discrimination.

The first two criticisms have already been resolved in the courts in the context of housing and public accommodations cases. Courts have long held that testers who experience disparate treatment on the basis of race are injured and therefore have standing to pursue litigation.[8] Implicit in these holdings is the belief that the misrepresentation involved in testing is worth the unique benefit this practice can provide in uncovering discrimination and enforcing civil rights laws. If courts extend to the employment context the rationale of these decisions— and there is no reason they should not—the argument against testing in the labor market for lack of standing or for misrepresentation should be answered favorably. The fact that the Equal Employment Opportunity Commission recently issued a policy guidance stating that persons have standing under Title VII of the Civil Rights Act of 1964 when they test for and discover discriminatory employment practices will make this outcome more likely.[9]

Once the issue of standing is laid to rest, however, and this methodology—which to date has been most widely applied in the field of housing—is employed more regularly in the labor market and in other fields, the methodology is likely to come under more rigorous scrutiny. For this reason, unusual care must be taken to use a methodology that cannot be claimed to overestimate discrimination or to provide inadequate control for extraneous factors.[10] When studying Hispanic and other national-origin groups, determinations will have to be made as to which factors to control and which to test. Given the variety of factors involved in national-origin discrimination that go beyond skin color—including surname, accent, language use, birthplace, and citizenship—this determination will require some reflection. Complicating the determination is the fact that Hispanics and other national-origin groups have been accorded protection against employment discrimination under several different antidiscrimination laws, including the 1866 Civil Rights Act,[11] Title VII of the 1964 Civil Rights Act,[12] and the antidiscrimination provisions of the 1986 Immigration Reform and Control Act (IRCA),[13] each of which protects a slightly different aspect of national-origin discrimination and each of which provides a significantly different remedy.

A brief summary of these provisions might help illustrate the problem. The EEOC and the courts have construed the Title VII prohibition against "national-origin" discrimination to protect against discrimination on the basis of birthplace, ancestry, culture, or linguistic characteristics common to a specific national-origin group. Title VII does not, however, protect against discrimination on the basis solely of citizenship; it does not provide an unqualified damages remedy;[14] and it does not cover employers with fewer than 15 employees. The IRCA's antidiscrimination provisions, adopted in anticipation of the widespread discrimination that would result from the statute's employer sanctions provisions,[15] apply to employers with four or more employees and protect against employment discrimination on the basis of citizenship or immigration status. Like Title VII, IRCA does not provide a damages remedy. Finally, when victims of national-origin discrimination can demonstrate that they have been denied an employment opportunity on the basis of "ancestry or ethnic characteristics," they may proceed under Section 1981 of the Civil Rights Act of 1866, as interpreted by the Supreme Court decision in *Saint Francis College v. Al-Khazraji*,[16] and, if successful, recover punitive and compensatory damages.

It is against this backdrop of overlapping statutes, the policies behind each of these laws, and the various protections they accord that auditing and testing national-origin groups must be considered. For example, the Urban Institute study conducted in Chicago and San Diego paired Anglos with closely matched Hispanics who were "foreign looking" and "foreign sounding." Hispanics with a "foreign-sounding" accent were used because the study was designed to measure the discriminatory impact of IRCA's employer sanctions provisions on U.S. citizens who look or sound foreign and because linguistic characteristics are often an essential aspect of national origin or "foreign" identification.

The study did not purport to establish a rigid benchmark of discrimination against all Hispanics, although the evidence it contains bears heavily on this determination. Spanish language and accent have often played a greater role than skin color or birthplace in identifying Hispanics as belonging to a particular national-origin group, and yet these characteristics have been overlooked by many civil rights advocates and social scientists.[17] The fact that other studies have used Hispanic testers with less distinctive accents, as was apparently the case in a study conducted in Denver, and have produced a different record of discrimination against Hispanics does not mean that controlling for accent, as opposed to testing for it, will create a more representative sample of the discrimination faced by "Hispanics" as a whole.[18]

What the issue of accent highlights is how difficult it is to find a pure, representative, or definitive average of the discrimination faced by Hispanics and other national-origin groups. Individuals within the Hispanic community come from many different ethnic groups; they have different physical attributes; and they possess other distinguishing social and cultural features. Some are U.S. citizens, and others are not; some speak only Spanish, whereas some speak little or none; some have Hispanic surnames, and others do not. The same is true for other national-origin groups.

For purposes of auditing, the important thing is that any differences between paired Anglo and Hispanic testers be clearly identified and that the reasons for the tested factors be carefully explained. Only then can expected charges of overestimation of the amount of discrimination be forcefully answered. In the context of litigation for enforcement purposes, the criticism targeted at testing evidence will not be the aggregate documentation of national-origin discrimination, as it is in the auditing situation. Rather, the criticism will be addressed to the remedy for the type of national-origin discrimination alleged. The answer will involve tailoring tests so that, for example, citizenship discrimination can be distinguished from ancestry discrimination, and the appropriate remedy—under IRCA in the former case and Section 1981 in the latter—can be pursued for the type of discrimination documented. Given the overlapping nature of these claims, this goal will be challenging, as it is under current national-origin litigation, but it is achievable and may become easier over time.[19]

COMMITTING AUDITING AND TESTING RESOURCES TO ALL PROTECTED GROUPS

The debate on the Civil Rights Act of 1990 and of 1991 has taught us that efforts to improve civil rights laws will be hard-fought battles. It has also taught us that these battles will be won only if two conditions are met: first, that the need for strong civil rights laws is so obvious that it becomes a moral imperative that few can deny; and second, that we demonstrate the need for and advocate the passage of civil rights legislation that benefits a broad segment of American society.

As to the first point, the documentation by The Urban Institute of disparate treatment in hiring faced by Hispanics and African Americans was essential to countering the belief held by some that discrimination had become a thing of the past. This documentation also helped refocus the debate away from charges that the Civil Rights Act was a "quota bill" that would lead to reverse discrimination, and permitted civil rights advocates to discuss the merits of the legislation.

As to the second point, during the debate it became clear that there was a misperception among many members of the public that civil rights legislation in general, and the Civil Rights Act of 1990 and of 1991 in particular, involved simply a question of black and white. The manner in which the *Patterson* decision hurt Hispanics, Asian Americans, and women was often lost in the press and in the eyes of the public, as was the fact that the *Wards Cove* case involved mostly Filipinos and Alaskan natives.[20] Similarly, the consequences of the lack of a damages remedy for women, though often discussed by legislators, did not deeply penetrate the general population.

This misperception about the legislation was fueled by those opposed to the bill, and it worked to their advantage. It also occurred despite the efforts of civil rights organizations to explain the broad impact of the Supreme Court decisions. What this experience shows is that documentation of discrimination on behalf of all groups protected under our civil rights laws will be critical in furthering a jointly held civil rights agenda. For example, had hiring audit studies involving women, Asian Americans, and other protected groups been available, opponents would have been less successful in their efforts to stigmatize the legislation as a quota bill, and legislators would have been less able to support a limit on damages for intentional sex discrimination.

In conducting audits in the future, it would also be useful to study the interactive effects of race and gender on women of color. Despite the fact that black women, Latinas, and Asian-American women consistently earn less than white men, white women, or minority men, and despite the fact that studies on the "glass ceiling" show that women of color are almost completely absent from positions of mid- and upper-level management,[21] auditing studies have yet to be conducted on these groups. To be sure, the need for auditing and testing will always exceed the resources such studies require. At the same time, we must be careful not to overlook those individuals burdened by multiple forms of discrimination. In both research and civil rights enforcement, their needs must be considered.

Notes

1. Consistent with the terminology used by others, we use the term *auditing* to refer to studies documenting general patterns of discrimination and the term *testing* to refer to documentation used in civil rights enforcement activities.

2. For a discussion of the effect of discrimination on Latino incomes, see Carnoy et al. (1990), who found that for the years 1973–87, discrimination accounted for 10 to 16 percent of the earnings gap between Latino and white men and 30 to 40 percent of the earnings gap between Latino and white women; James (1984), who found that discrimination and labor market segmentation accounted for 18.1 percent of the earnings gap between Latino and white males in 1980; and Verdugo (1982), who found that 14 percent of the income disparity between white and Hispanic males and 29 percent of the disparity between white males and Hispanic females were due to ethnicity. See also U.S. Commission on Civil Rights (1982), concluding that discrimination continues to be a significant factor in the disparate rates of unemployment and underemployment for Hispanics and whites.

3. According to a study conducted by the Equal Employment Opportunity Commission (1983), the EEOC failed to establish any significant tie to and consequently underserved the Hispanic community. The study found that between the late 1970s and the early 1980s, the number of charges involving Hispanics actually dropped from an average of 7.5 percent to less than 5 percent, at a time when the EEOC had increased its caseload by 76.5 percent and the proportion of Hispanics in the labor force doubled, reaching 6 percent; that when charges by Hispanics were filed, they were more frequently closed without a remedy than were those of other groups; and that of the EEOC cases listed as significant between 1972 and 1982, no cases were listed in which Hispanics were the primary class represented. As a study by Gonzales and Lopez (1991) demonstrates, this lack of service has unfortunately not improved.

4. See Cross et al. (1990). Based on 360 hiring audits of closely matched young Hispanic and Anglo male job applicants in the summer of 1989, this study found that discrimination against foreign-looking and -sounding Hispanics in Chicago and San Diego was considerable. For example, Anglos received 33 percent more interviews and 52 percent more job offers than did Hispanics.

5. See Turner et al. (1991). This study found that in 8 percent of sales and 12 percent of rental audits, Hispanics were faced with a complete denial of information about the rental or sale. The incidence of unfavorable treatment in housing availability was 36 percent for Hispanic renters and 38 percent for Hispanic home buyers. With respect to completion of or contributions to a housing transaction, Hispanic renters faced a 42 percent rate of unfavorable treatment, Hispanic home buyers a 47 percent rate. On the basis of these figures, the researchers estimate that Hispanic home seekers experience some form of discrimination in at least half of their encounters with sales and rental agents.

6. This tandem use of auditing and testing would of course require that auditing studies not contain litigation restrictions.

7. The question of misrepresentation has worked its way into one civil rights proposal. See, for example, Section 10 of S. 478, the Civil Rights Amendments of 1991, introduced by Sen. Alan Simpson on February 22, 1991 (U.S. Senate 1991). This section, entitled "Prohibition on Fraud or Misrepresentation by Persons Testing the Existence of Employment Discrimination," would have amended Section 709 of the Civil Rights Act of 1964 to prohibit the use of testing procedures by the EEOC that involve "misrepresentation when presenting the education, experience or other qualifications of the prospective employee in an attempt to apply for a job." This section would also have required the EEOC to dismiss any claim involving such misrepresentation and would have required the chairman of the EEOC to take action against any EEOC officer or employee who pursued such charges.

8. For rulings recognizing the standing of testers in housing and public accommodations cases, see *Havens Realty Corp. v. Coleman*, 455 U.S. 363, 373 (1982) (tester is an "aggrieved person" under Title VIII when given incomplete information regarding housing); *Pierson v. Ray*, 368 U.S. 547 (1967) (conferring standing to black clergyman who entered a segregated bus terminal to test the legality of segregated public accommodations); *Evers v. Dwyer*, 358 U.S. 202 (1958) (conferring standing to black plaintiff who sat in the white section of a bus to test the legality of the state segregation laws); *Village of Bellwood v. Dwivedi*, 895 F.2d 1521 (7th Cir. 1990) (standing accorded to housing tester); *Watts v. Boyd Properties, Inc.*, 758 F.2d 1482 (11th Cir. 1985) (same); *Village of Bellwood v. Gorey & Assocs.*, 664 F. Supp. 320 (N.D. Ill. 1987) (same).

9. See U.S. Equal Employment Opportunity Commission (1990). The standing of organizations should likewise result in a favorable outcome. According to the Supreme Court, organizations that oversee housing testers can establish standing when significant resources are diverted from other programs to identify and counteract discriminatory practices. *Havens Realty Corp. v. Coleman*, 455 U.S. 363, 379 (1982). As the policy guidance recognizes (at n. 4), organizations may pursue claims on behalf of testers in the context of employment testing as well (pursuant to 29 C.F.R. § 1601.7(a), organizations have standing to file a charge on behalf of "a person claiming to be aggrieved").

10. With respect to all studies, this means that any tester effects must be carefully controlled and that compensation must be arranged so that it cannot be contended that testers were rewarded for reporting discriminatory conduct.

11. 42 U.S.C. § 1981.

12. 42 U.S.C. §§ 2000e et seq.

13. Immigration and Nationality Act, Section 274B, 8 U.S.C. § 1324b, as amended by the Immigration Act of 1990, Sections 531-39, Pub. L. No. 101-649, 101 Stat. 4978.

14. Section 102 of Public Law 102-166, the Civil Rights Act of 1991, codified at 42 U.S.C. § 1981a, provides for jury trials and limited amounts of damages for cases of intentional discrimination pursued under Title VII. Limits on compensatory and punitive damages are set at $50,000 for employers with 15-100 employees, $100,000 for

employers with 101-200 employees, $200,000 for employers with 201-500 employees, and $300,000 for employers with more than 500 employees.

15. IRCA prohibits any person or entity from hiring, recruiting, or referring for a fee any alien while knowing the alien is unauthorized to work in the United States. The statute also makes it illegal to hire any individual without complying with certain verification requirements. The adoption of IRCA was the first time federal law prohibited the hiring of undocumented workers and was the first time employers were required to enforce the immigrations laws of the United States under threat of sanction.

16. 481 U.S. 604 (1987).

17. It is in recognition of the relationship between cultural identity and one's primary tongue that the EEOC has promulgated guidelines regarding the unlawfulness of "speak English only" rules in the workplace. See 29 C.F.R. § 1606.7 (1987). See also Comment (1982).

18. Although it is unclear what the nature of the accents held by the Hispanic testers in the Denver study (James and DelCastillo 1991) was, it appears that their accents were not as strong as those held by testers in the Urban Institute study. As others have noted, there were also other differences between the studies.

19. Outside of citizen-only employment practices, which have been adopted by employers in their attempt to comply with the employer sanctions provisions of IRCA, situations involving "pure" citizenship discrimination that do not also involve national-origin discrimination are quite rare. Situations in which national-origin discrimination involves birthplace discrimination alone, and is therefore not protected under Section 1981, are likewise rare. Most often, discrimination on the basis of national origin involves a host of factors, and unless there is some need to proceed under IRCA, the complaining party generally alleges a cause of action under both Title VII and Section 1981. It is our hope that national-origin discrimination under Section 1981 will be interpreted in harmony with the national-origin discrimination provisions of Title VII and that some of these issues will be simplified in the future.

20. In *Patterson v. McLean Credit Union*, 491 U.S. 164 (1989), the Supreme Court held that the Civil Rights Act of 1866 did not protect against discriminatory conduct perpetrated after the initial formation of a contract. In the employment context, this meant that termination and failure to promote on the basis of race or national origin, as well as harassment on the basis of race or ethnicity, were no longer covered by this statute, and victims of such discrimination could no longer take advantage of the statutory provision of punitive and compensatory damages. In *Wards Cove Packing Co. v. Atonio*, 490 U.S. 642 (1989), the Supreme Court established new requirements for challenging "neutral" rules that have a discriminatory effect on minorities. No longer are employers required to prove that practices with an adverse effect on women or minorities are job related; instead they have only to articulate (but not prove) a legitimate employment goal served by the practice. The *Patterson* and *Wards Cove* cases were arguably the two most devastating decisions handed down by the Supreme Court in 1989. Both decisions were overturned by Public Law 102-166, the Civil Rights Act of 1991.

21. See U.S. Department of Labor (1991).

References

Carnoy, Martin, Hugh Daley, and Raul Hinajosa Ojeda. 1990. "Latinos in a Changing U.S. Economy: Comparative Perspectives on the Labor

Market Since 1939." New York: Inter-University Program for Latino Research, Research Foundation of the City University of New York.

Comment. 1982. "Language Discrimination Under Title VII: The Silent Right of National Origin Discrimination." *John Marshall Law Review*, 15: 667–691.

Cross, Harry, with Genevieve Kenney, Jane Mell, and Wendy Zimmerman. 1990. *Employer Hiring Practices: Differential Treatment of Hispanic and Anglo Job Seekers*. UI Report 90–4. Washington, D.C.: Urban Institute Press.

Gonzales, Claire, and Francisco Lopez. 1991. "The Empty Promise: Civil Rights Enforcement and Hispanics, Summary Report." Washington, D.C.: National Council of La Raza, July.

James, Franklin J. 1984. "The Lack of Hispanic Economic Progress During the 1970s: Preliminary Observations." Paper presented at a meeting of the Regional Science Association, November 9.

James, Franklin J., and Steve W. DelCastillo. 1991. "Measuring Job Discrimination by Private Employers Against Young Black and Hispanic Males Seeking Entry Level Work in the Denver Metropolitan Area." Unpublished report. Denver: University of Colorado, March.

Turner, Margery A., Raymond Struyk, and John Yinger. 1991. "Housing Discrimination Study." Washington, D.C.: The Urban Institute, August.

U.S. Commission on Civil Rights. 1982. "Unemployment and Underemployment Among Blacks, Hispanics and Women." Washington, D.C.: author, November.

U.S. Department of Labor. 1991. "A Report on the Glass Ceiling Initiative." Washington, D.C.: author, August.

U.S. Equal Employment Opportunity Commission. 1990. "Policy Guidance on whether "testers" have standing to file charges of employment discrimination against employers, employment agencies and/or labor organizations which have discriminated against them because of their race, color, religion, sex, or national origin." (Notice No. H-915-062) (November 20, 1990) *EEOC Compliance Manual* (BNA) N:6025-36.

U.S. Equal Employment Opportunity Commission's Task Force. 1983. "Equal Employment Opportunity and Hispanics: An Analysis of the Equal Employment Opportunity Commission's Service to Hispanics in the United States." Washington, D.C.: author, December 2.

Verdugo, Naomi. 1982. "The Effects of Discrimination on the Earnings of Hispanic Workers: Findings and Policy Implications." Washington, D.C.: National Council of La Raza, July.

Chapter Seven

USE OF TESTERS IN INVESTIGATING DISCRIMINATION IN MORTGAGE LENDING AND INSURANCE

George C. Galster

INTRODUCTION

The civil disorders of the 1960s metaphorically illuminated many of our urban ills under the harsh glare of searchlights and blazes set by arsonists. Among the panoply of inner-city problems cited by the Kerner Commission in investigating the source of the unrest was a dearth of lending for home purchase and improvement and underwriting for home insurance (National Advisory Commission on Civil Disorders 1968; President's National Advisory Panel 1968). The Kerner Commission report, buttressed by concerted lobbying by community activist groups, spawned several pieces of federal legislation that attempted to address the problems of urban credit and insurance: the Fair Housing Act of 1968, the Equal Credit Opportunity Act of 1975, the Home Mortgage Disclosure Act (HMDA) of 1975, and the Community Reinvestment Act (CRA) of 1977.

Despite these legislative efforts, and others at the state and local levels, claims of unfair lending and insuring practices continued during the ensuing decade (National Commission on Neighborhoods 1979; Midwestern Regional Advisory Committees 1979; U.S. Commission on Civil Rights 1983), supported for the first time by the statistical findings of many social scientists (e.g., Listokin and Casey 1980; Schafer and Ladd 1980; King 1980), most of whom analyzed data supplied under the auspices of the HMDA (e.g., Squires and Velez 1987a, 1987b; Shlay 1988).

Popular and congressional attention to the issue of lending and insurance practices more recently became crystallized by highly publicized journalistic reports published in Atlanta (Dedman 1988), Detroit (Blossom et al. 1988), and other cities, by the Federal Reserve Bank of Boston's studies (Bradbury et al. 1989; Munnell et al. 1992), and especially by the 1992 civil disorders in Los Angeles. Congressional hearings have been held at least annually on these topics since 1989, and among the provisions of the Financial Institutions Reform, Recovery and Enforcement Act of 1989 were extensions of the institutional scope and depth of data mandated under the HMDA and requirements that regulators' ratings of lenders' CRA performance be made public.

In spite of the spate of journalistic and scholarly studies, public outcries, and legislative pronouncements, many continue to argue that allegations of unfair lending and insuring practices were wildly exaggerated. Industry spokespersons claim that sound business practices—now more crucial than ever in a period of deregulated competition—require that all profitable opportunities be explored, and that discrimination makes no economic sense. Social scientists have pointed to technical shortcomings of statistical studies based on public data and have concluded that while results are consistent with unfair lending and insuring practices, they are not conclusive (e.g., Canner, n.d.). Federal financial institution regulatory agencies argue that their periodic examinations of lenders and their consumer surveys have failed to reveal any evidence of a major problem (Board of Governors 1991, 5–8).

It is within this context of sensationalized public allegations, scholarly debate, institutional skepticism, and overheated political discourse that the issue of testing arises. Testing is an investigative procedure in which a pair of individuals who are matched (either in fact or fictitiously) on a wide variety of characteristics, except the one being tested, pose as consumers of a particular service or product. Within a short period they individually approach an agent providing that service or product and attempt to obtain it or information about it. The behavior and information provided by the agent are recorded (separately) by both testers, and these records are analyzed by a third party, the test coordinator. The coordinator compares the teammates' records to assess whether the agent afforded them equal treatment. Continued, systematic differential treatment is adjudged to be discriminatory behavior.

Can such a testing procedure be used in the arena of mortgage lending and home insurance in such a way that it can clarify the current disagreement over the severity of unfair practices and thereby provide sound guidance to policymakers? What do we not know, or can we not find out by other means, that testing could help us discover? What legal, ethical, and practical issues confront testing in this area? Do we have any experience with lending and insurance testing and, if so, what can we learn from it? These are the questions that motivate this chapter and that I attempt to answer.

The chapter is organized as follows. The next section reviews the current state of knowledge about lending and insuring practices in the inner city and critiques the methodologies that have been employed to gain this knowledge, thereby establishing whether testing might in principle play a useful role in increasing our knowledge. The third and fourth sections discuss the legal and ethical issues, respectively, related to lending and insurance testing, in an attempt to evaluate the method's limits and propriety. The fifth section critically reviews the three extant pilot studies of lending that have used testers and the singular such study of home owners' insurance, with an eye toward gleaning hints as to the efficacy of the method and to practices of the lending and insurance industries. The sixth section analyzes the strengths and weaknesses of the testing method as applied to lenders and insurers and points up a variety of unresolved operational issues related to the method. Finally, the last section provides a summary evaluation of the testing method for investigating lending and insurance practices, suggests future directions in evaluating and improving the method, and draws policy implications for industry regulatory agencies.

I want to make clear at the outset that I try to give evenhanded treatment to all sides in the multifaceted debates surrounding the testing issue. I do not, however, shrink from providing my own judgments concerning the veracity of certain positions and my reasons for such judgments. Likewise, I do not refrain from speculation where that is appropriate, but make it clear when I do so. Finally, although the discussion is couched in terms of testing lending and insuring practices as they relate to race (of the applicant or neighborhood), virtually all of the analysis is applicable to testing for differential treatment on the basis of gender, age, marital or family status, and so on.

WHAT DO WE KNOW ABOUT MORTGAGE LENDING AND INSURANCE PATTERNS?

In this section I survey the current state of the art vis-à-vis statistical investigations of mortgage lending and insurance patterns. I critique studies of lending patterns using the original (pre-1990), publicly available HMDA data and then provide a prospective assessment of how the forthcoming, enriched HMDA data might be analyzed and what, if anything, they are likely to tell us. Finally, I similarly critique the few statistical studies of home owners' insurance practices.

Although I may steal my own thunder from the conclusion thereby, I give my assessment of all these studies at the outset. While valuable in describing patterns and identifying potential problems, none is capable of supporting any sort of statistical analyses that could conclusively confirm or deny the systematic practice of illegal lending or insurance practices. As such, they can serve only as highly circumspect guides to policymakers.

The original HMDA data were available only in geographically aggregated form, that is, loans were tallied by census tract. The new HMDA data may still be analyzed in aggregated form (though not necessarily so). Publicly accessible insurance data typically are similarly aggregated. Unfortunately, aggregate studies are inherently incapable of ascertaining unambiguously the absence or presence of discrimination because of the possibly confounding variations around the mean (or median) of the particular tract characteristic that is being analyzed. Aggregate studies can only show areas where loans or insurance policies of certain types are or are not being made, or even where loan and insurance applications are more often being rejected. They cannot by their very nature reveal anything about the circumstances surrounding particular decisions regarding individual applications (Galster 1991). This is the most common and most damaging shortcoming of all studies (HMDA or other) using aggregate data.

The new HMDA data will permit disaggregated analyses based on individual loan register entries, and this will offer some improvements. However, the new HMDA reporting forms omit crucial data that need to be employed as control variables. The unfortunate result is as before: Nothing definitive can be concluded about the causes of any potential racial disparities in rejection rates (Galster 1991). The upshot: Testing can potentially play a crucial role in resolving the current and prospective ambiguities in lending and insurance patterns.

Before proceeding I want to make clear that this critique of HMDA-based studies is not intended to disparage all their potential uses, but merely to caution against employing them to draw unfounded conclusions. Indeed, these studies provide the invaluable suggestion that certain neighborhoods may be starved for loans and insurance coverage. Whether due to illegal actions or not, such a condition is cause for public concern and intervention. Similarly, these studies may be powerful pieces of evidence in court proceedings against lenders or insurers because, when coupled with other sorts of evidence, they can help demonstrate the "preponderance of evidence" required to find for plaintiffs.

Lending Studies Using Original, Aggregate HMDA Data

The original (1977) HMDA reported the number and dollar value of both conventional and government-insured (VA, FHA) mortgage loans and home improvement loans provided by banks, savings and loans, and credit unions, by census tract.[1] Comparisons of these descriptive statistics with other data describing the tracts, which were available from decennial censuses, allowed for the testing of several hypotheses. The most frequent: Was there a relationship between lending volumes (or types) and the racial composition of the tract? Two methodologies have been commonly employed in testing this hypothesis: cross-tabulation and regression. I discuss both in turn.

CROSS-TABULATION STUDIES

Cross-tabulation tends to be the method chosen by journalists and less statistically trained analysts. Four recent examples are representative of this genre: the Kentucky Commission on Human Rights (1989), the *Atlanta Journal Constitution* (Dedman 1988), the *Detroit Free Press* (Blossom, et al. 1988), and the Center for Community Change (1989b).

The Kentucky investigation did the most elementary three-way cross-tabulation: loans (number and value) by racial composition by median income. It found 57 times more loans (32 times the value) in tracts having less than 10 percent black residents than in those having more than 50 percent. First and foremost, no attempt was made to control for demand for loans (Listokin and Casey 1980; Ostas 1985): The minority areas might have been fewer in number, have had more rental properties, have had lower home owner turnover rates, or have sought more loans from mortgage companies (which were not tabulated under the original HMDA). Second, income was "controlled for" only by limiting tracts to those with incomes between 80 percent and 120 percent of the Louisville MSA's median income. Clearly there is still a wide degree of income variation within this range, and it is likely that minority tracts are skewed more heavily toward the lower end of the range. Third, nothing else was revealed about these tracts: property values, age, abandonment, etc. Lack of control variables ran rampant (Shear and Yezer 1985). Fourth, no tests for statistical significance were provided.

The Center for Community Change (CCC) provided a modest methodological improvement by dividing savings and loan companies' data on number of loans per tract by the number of owner-occupied homes, and by classifying these data by four categories of tract median income. This established some control for demand, but the other aspects of demand remained uncontrolled. The CCC's 14-MSA sample of HMDA data for 1986–87 showed that, for low- and moderate-income classes of tracts, the number of mortgage loans on 1 to 4 family buildings per 1,000 owner-occupied dwellings was inversely related to the percentage of minorities in the tract, although this pattern was not evinced for middle- and upper-income tracts. All the other aforementioned criticisms still apply to the CCC analysis.

The Atlanta and Detroit studies did a better job of controlling for other aggregate features of the census tracts being compared. Tracts that had rapidly changing racial compositions, fewer than 500 single-family units, or dramatic changes in the number of single-family units were excluded from the middle-income tracts being analyzed.[2] The number of loans in "black tracts" (80 percent or more black) was then compared to that in "white tracts" (80 percent or more white). This comparison showed that the number of loans by banks and thrifts in "stable, middle-income white areas" was three (Detroit) to five (Atlanta) times higher than for comparable black areas.

These two studies' methodology has already been subjected to a withering critique by the staff at the Federal Reserve Board (Canner, n.d.), whose conclusions are similar to mine above. First, demand was not controlled for, and the rate of sales in middle-income white Atlanta neighborhoods was twice that in middle-income black neighborhoods. Second, mortgage flows will be understated by HMDA data because mortgage bankers (who did not report in the original HMDA) aggressively compete with depository institutions (who did report) in minority areas, and often benefit differentially from referrals from real estate agents. Third, income of tracts was not controlled for effectively. Within the "middle-income" classification the white tracts had a higher median income than the minority ones and 25 percent higher property values. In addition, as support for the point raised above about the problem of different variations around the means, only 19 percent of the homes in middle-income white areas had values under $30,000, while the comparable figure for middle-income minority areas was 38 percent. Finally, no tests of whether differences were statistically significant were provided. Thus, even the "best" of the cross-tabular studies are fraught with severe problems that confound an unambiguous interpretation of results.[3]

REGRESSION STUDIES

Regression studies generally do a superior job of controlling for non-racial characteristics of census tracts and testing for statistical significance than do cross-tabulation studies. The typical regression model has either the number or the value of conventional loans in a census tract during a particular period as the dependent variable, along with a host of (independent) control variables and (independent) variables measuring the tract's racial composition. The control variables attempt to serve as proxies for characteristics of both the population and the housing stock in the tract that are related to the supply of and demand for mortgage credit. Representative are the recent regression-based studies in Milwaukee (Squires and Velez 1987b), Baltimore (Shlay 1987), Cincinnati (Howe 1988), and Chicago (Shlay 1988).

The results of these studies are too lengthy to present here, but some consistent findings have emerged. The number of conventional loans in a tract proves to be negatively correlated (in a statistically significant fashion) with the percentage of black residents and (in Chicago) of Hispanic residents.[4] This relationship persists even when controlling for median incomes and property values, the percentages of married-couple families with children and those who lived in different dwellings in 1975, the percentages of single-unit structures and owner-occupied units, the vacancy rate, and the percentages of units built during various eras.

Thus, these regression studies have convincingly documented racial patterns to loan flows. Why these patterns exist, however, remains a key question that is beyond the scope of these studies, for several reasons. In spite of their multiple control variables, the aforementioned regression studies failed to adequately control for the demand for loans. The average age, income, prior mobility, and life-cycle stage of the population tell us something about likely mobility of the overall tract population, but not with perfect certainty. And whether these *average* characteristics accurately measure characteristics of *owner-occupants* is yet another matter. Furthermore, interpretation of the negative coefficient of the percent-black variable is problematic. It could simply indicate that since blacks are less likely to move than are comparable whites (Roistacher 1975; Boehm 1981), and/or there are fewer potential (white) buyers for units in predominantly black areas, there are fewer home sales in such areas. However, a researcher could obtain data from non-HMDA sources (e.g., county recorder's offices) about home sales in tracts and thus use conventional loans granted *per sale* as the dependent variable. Although to my knowledge this has never been done,[5] such an approach would, indeed, isolate the demand for some sort of financing, but not which sort. Thus, a negative coefficient for a percent-black variable in a regression on conventional loans per sale as the dependent variable could possibly indicate that black home buyers prefer FHA or VA loans, prefer the service that suppliers of such loans (primarily mortgage bankers) deliver, and/or are referred to such financing products more often by their real estate agents. In sum, even the most carefully specified regression models using aggregate HMDA data are incapable of controlling for the demand for a volume and type of financing instrument (Galster 1991). Because of this, they cannot ascertain whether illegal practices are the cause of the observed racial patterns.

Lending Studies Using New, Aggregate HMDA Data

The HMDA data that lenders have been gathering since January 1, 1990, will provide extra information not provided in the original HMDA data: the disposition of all applications for home purchase and home improvement loans, as well as the race or national origin, gender, and income of loan applicants.[6] These additional data will expand the options for statistical analysis by providing more potential variables to correlate with census tract racial composition. That is, for tracts one will know not only the number and value of various types of housing-related loans but also applications approved but not accepted, applications denied, applications withdrawn, and files closed for incompleteness.[7] One will know not only the median income of the tract but the median income of the applicants in the tract. These variables could be subjected to cross-tabular and/or regression analyses, just as the original HMDA data were.

In fact, the Federal Reserve Board will be providing (both by institution and aggregated for MSAs) some basic cross-tabulations of the above data as a regular feature of its annual HMDA reporting.[8] One table will provide for each type of purchase a two-way cross-tabulation of number (and value) of loans sold by racial composition of the census tract. Another will provide for each category of FHA, FMHA, and VA loan disposition a two-way cross-tabulation of loan number (and value) by racial composition of the census tract and a three-way cross-tabulation controlling for tract income as well. Other tables will do the same for conventional loans, home improvement loans, etc.

Such cross-tabulations will not be so interesting as one that could be easily created by dividing the above tabulations of applications denied by the tabulations of applications received, thereby deriving a tract loan rejection rate cross-tabulated by tract racial composition (and perhaps tract median income as well). This would offer an improvement over the original HMDA cross-tabulations, which could not control for the volume of demand for loans. It would still suffer, however, from the bevy of aforementioned shortcomings that any cross-tabulation based on *aggregate* data does.

Regression-based analyses of such new, aggregated HMDA data would (like rejection rates) similarly fare little better than their earlier counterparts that analyzed the original HMDA data. Even if a regression were to show conclusively that the average rejection rate of a tract was strongly correlated with the percentage of black residents, controlling for *all* the other average characteristics of the tract's population and housing stock that were available from the census, the result would not conclusively suggest discrimination. Crucial control variables would still be missing: the tract population's average indebtedness, credit histories, etc. Furthermore, the average characteristics of a tract's population may poorly approximate those who actually applied for mortgages; again, one has the classic pitfall of aggregate analyses of any sort.

To conclude, the new HMDA data will permit some interesting new variables (such as rejection rates) to be analyzed and provide better controls for loan demand. However, if data are aggregated by census tract, no sort of statistical method will be able to ascertain definitively whether any observed correlations with neighborhood racial composition are due to illegal or financially sound practices by lenders (Galster 1991).

Lending Studies Using New, Disaggregate HMDA Data

Analyses of new HMDA data can diverge in more important ways from analyses of original HMDA data if the potentially disaggregated nature of the former is exploited. That is, the new data will permit examination of the disposition of individuals' loan applications, not merely the geographic aggregations of such dispositions by census tract. This, of course, offers the important statistical advantage of avoiding confounding variation around the means of aggregate data.

The Fed will provide as part of its regular HMDA reports some cross-tabulation of these disaggregated data. For instance, one table will provide for each type of loan a three-way cross-tabulation of application disposition, by race and gender of applicant. Other tables will do the same, except race and income will be cross-tabulated. Unfortunately, these procedures do not control for all three aforementioned characteristics of the applicant simultaneously, and income is only crudely controlled for.[9] Furthermore, no characteristics of the dwelling or the neighborhood are considered. Thus, as before, the published Fed cross-tabulation—even when based on disaggregated data—will be unable to ascertain the causes for any observed racial patterns in, for example, loan rejection rates.

Researchers will not be limited to published Federal Reserve cross-tabulations, however. The Fed will make available the raw data from lenders' loan registers, with information identifying individual loan applicants deleted. These data could be merged with census data that describe aggregate characteristics of the population and housing stock to create a unified database. This would permit the application of more sophisticated regression and probability model approaches (Galster 1991). For example, one obvious probability model to estimate would be:

$$P = a + bB + cH + dA + fF + gI + h_i[POP_i] + n_k[HS_k] + e,$$

where a, b, c, d, f, g, h, and n are terms to be estimated by regression or other statistical procedures, e is a random error term, and all uppercase letters represent variables. Thus,

P   = 1 if the individual application was rejected, 0 if approved (or a logistic transformation);

B   = 1 if the applicant was black, 0 otherwise;

H   = 1 if the applicant was Hispanic, 0 otherwise;

A   = 1 if the applicant was Asian American, 0 otherwise;

F   = 1 if the applicant was female, 0 otherwise;

I   = income of applicant;

POP_i = a series of variables describing the population of the census tract in which the given property is located (e.g., median income, percentage of whites, percentage age 65 years or older); and

HS_k = a series of variables describing the housing stock in the census tract in which the given property is located (e.g., median value, percentage built before 1960, percentage owner occupied).

Should the coefficient b turn out to be significantly greater than zero, it would be supportive of (though not definitive proof of) a claim of differential treatment based on race of applicant. Should the coefficient h_i of the tract variable describing the percentage of white residents turn out to be significantly less than zero, it would be supportive of (though, again, not conclusive proof of) a claim of "racial redlining": rejections based on the racial composition of the *area* independent of the race of the applicant.

Such evidence, were it forthcoming, would be more convincing because it would have been produced by a method applied to a type of data that overcomes most of the shortcomings of the previous aggregate analyses. The primary shortcoming that would remain is lack of appropriate control variables. In spite of the wealth of possible control variables describing average characteristics of the *tract* in which the property was located, there would be no data about the *individual* property in question. There would be only three variables about the individual applicant in question—race, gender, and income. Clearly, lenders look at many property characteristics (condition, appraised value, etc.) and applicant characteristics (credit histories, indebtedness, down payment available, etc.) in disposing of a loan application that are not controlled for in the equation above. Yet it is likely that these omitted characteristics are correlated with the race of the applicant and the predominant race of the neighborhood in which the property is located. In such circumstances the coefficients of applicant racial variables and neighborhood racial variables in the equation would be erroneously calculated by the regression procedures. Put simply, if the estimate for b were to turn out as I posited above, we would not be able to tell whether that was due to discrimination by banks or to blacks having systematically poorer credit histories, more indebtedness, and less available for down payments than whites of the same sex and income (Galster 1991).

To conclude, it is safe to say that the new disaggregated HMDA data will permit some radically different and marginally more reliable studies of lending patterns. Indeed, such studies should overcome most of the methodological criticisms that can easily discredit the conventional studies that use census tracts as the unit of observation instead of individual applicants. Nevertheless, I must stress that these new studies will not—indeed cannot—be definitive about the causes of any racial patterns to loan dispositions. This is because they will not include crucial variables that control for applicant and property characteristics that banks assess as part of sound business practices. Thus, new HMDA studies will not be definitive, and they will tend to be biased toward an implication of lending discrimination. This conclusion is important enough to warrant elaboration. Remember that the sorts of information that are omitted from HMDA data are precisely those that, if statistically controlled for, would typically tend to narrow (if not completely eliminate) any differences in loan application dispositions between protected and nonprotected classes. This implies that results of forthcoming analyses will tend to portray the lending industry in an unfavorable light, whether it deserves to be so portrayed or not.

Insurance Studies

Although there are no federally mandated reporting requirements for the home insurance industry, several states have imposed HMDA-like mandates. In two cases, Chicago and Milwaukee, the data have been subjected to statistical analysis (Squires et al. 1979; Squires and Velez 1987a). In both instances, similar methods were employed. The number of privately issued home owners' policies and the number of publicly issued, "last-resort" policies in force (per 100 housing units) across zip code areas were employed as dependent variables. Corresponding census data on racial composition, percentage of housing built prior to 1940, median family income, residential turnover (in Milwaukee), and fires and thefts (in Chicago) were coded. Partial correlations between the dependent variables and percentage of minority residents in the area (controlling for one or two of the other control variables) revealed a statistically significant negative relationship for private policies issued and a positive relationship for public policies issued. The same correlations were evinced when median income or property age was related to the dependent variables.

Unfortunately, the limitations noted earlier regarding aggregate HMDA studies apply here as well. One does not know the characteristics either of the particular properties for which insurance was sought (e.g., structural condition and construction materials) or of the particular applicants (e.g., claims history, credit history, employment record). Appropriate control variables are not provided for the insurance loss histories in the different areas,[10] thus raising the possibility that sound financial reasons were responsible for the observed patterns. Even if discrimination were responsible, it would be impossible here to ascertain whether it was directed toward minority individuals or their neighborhoods.

Two additional methodological problems are noteworthy. First, in both studies the insurance policy data covered only 70 percent or less of the policies outstanding. If such omitted data were disproportionately concentrated in minority areas, the apparent pattern could merely be an artifact of sample selection bias. Second, the small sample sizes[11] exacerbated the usual intercorrelations among racial, economic, and housing variables employed as controls. Such putative high multicolinearity precluded a meaningful analysis that simultaneously controlled for all the nonracial correlates of insurance policies in force (Squires et al. 1979, n. 7). However, my inspection of the reported bivariate correlations does not lead me to conclude that multicolinearity necessarily would lead to misleading statistical tests in a multiple regression analysis. That such an analysis apparently did not reveal a strong racial correlation when all other controls were entered might, indeed, have been due to multicolinearity; it may also simply have indicated a truly insignificant racial effect.

To conclude, the studies of home owners' insurance find a putative pattern relating to neighborhood racial composition. There are reasons to believe, however, that this pattern may be a statistical artifact. Even if it is not, the aggregate nature of the data precludes a definitive determination of whether the patterns resulted from sound business decisions or discriminatory ones and, if the latter, whether the discrimination was based on individuals or areas.

The Current State of Ignorance

I have argued that although we have a good deal of descriptive statistics about racial differences in the flows of home loans and insurance policies, we know precious little about the origins of these differences. Primarily because of the aggregate nature of these data and/or the lack of appropriate statistical controls, past studies have failed to provide definitive evidence as to whether the differences are due to race per se (and thus are discriminatory) or to sound business decisions that only appear spuriously to be related to race. Unfortunately, the kinds of data needed to sort this out (e.g., employment, credit, and debt data for applicants, structural features of properties in question, claims and loss histories) are not publicly available.[12] Absent such data, we appear to be at an investigative cul-de-sac.

It is this context that provides the raison d'être for the testing discussion: the urgent need for an empirical method that obviates the shortcomings of past analysis and provides more definitive answers to the charges of illegal practices. In the next sections I probe whether testing is legal, ethical, and empirically robust, in an attempt to ascertain whether it is capable of clarifying the present empirical muddle.

LEGAL ISSUES IN LENDING AND INSURANCE TESTING

In this section I briefly review the law as it relates to prohibited lending and insurance practices and to the testing procedure for investigating such practices. I show that there appear to be no legal barriers to the use of testing in this field, at least up until the point at which the tester files an application; after that point serious barriers may exist.[13]

Legal Strictures against Discrimination in Lending and Insurance

Discrimination in connection with real-estate-related credit transactions on the basis of race, national origin, color, gender, and religion is prohibited by federal law under both the Equal Credit Opportunity Act (ECOA) and the Fair Housing Act.[14] The ECOA (and the Federal Reserve's implementing Regulation B) prohibits discrimination in any aspect of a credit transaction, including the discouraging of potential protected applicants from applying. The Fair Housing Act (both the 1968 act and its amended 1988 version) focuses on transactions related to the financing of residential property and prohibits discrimination in making available loans (or in loan terms and conditions) to purchase, construct, improve, repair, or maintain a dwelling.

At the federal level, legal strictures against discrimination in the provision of home owners' insurance have been the subject of more debate (DeWolfe et al. 1980). The Civil Rights Acts of 1866 and 1870 and that part of the act of 1871 sustained by the 13th Amendment provide guarantees to all persons to make and enforce contracts and to buy and sell real property.[15] Insurance can be seen as both a contract and a personal-property right. Thus, it could be argued that "insurance practices which affect property and contract rights of members of racial minorities lie within the scope of protections afforded by federal civil rights laws" (Midwestern Regional Advisory Committees 1979, 27). Similarly, if a refusal to issue insurance makes a particular dwelling effectively unavailable, the practice may be prohibited under the Fair Housing Act (Byrne 1980; Midwestern Regional Advisory Committees 1979, 27). Experience in federal court decisions regarding these claims currently appears to be mixed.[16] The less ambiguous legal prohibitions related to insurance practices typically involve state statutes, since state regulatory agencies have assumed primary monitoring responsibilities for this industry (Midwestern Regional Advisory Committees 1979, chap. 3; Squires and Velez 1987a).

None of the above statutes prohibits differential treatment of applicants when it is based on objective, financially sound and necessary underwriting standards and the pertinent elements of the applicants' creditworthiness or insurability. Such differential treatment becomes illegal discrimination (i.e., "intentional" disparate treatment) when it is based purely on a protected classification of the applicant (like race) or of the property in question (like neighborhood racial composition).[17] The central question here is whether evidence gathered from testing can provide probative evidence in establishing such unlawful disparate treatment.

Legal Precedents Related to Testing

There is ample legal precedent from federal courts that tester evidence is admissible in fair-housing cases.[18] Such evidence cannot be discounted merely because it is from a tester, indeed it may be more reliable because of that fact.[19] That testers have standing to sue and to claim damages in fair-housing cases has also been affirmed.[20] However, "the specific question of . . . whether testers may file lawsuits as aggrieved persons alleging violations of the ECOA, the Fair Housing Act, or other antidiscrimination laws in connection with housing finance . . . has not been litigated" (Board of Governors 1991, 17). To my knowledge, only one case involving property insurance discrimination has used the testimony of testers, and it is now pending appeal of its earlier dismissal on other grounds.[21]

A further issue arises as to whether testers may be liable for misrepresentation or fraud. Again, all cases that have addressed this issue involved fair-housing allegations. A Wisconsin statute that made testing unlawful on the above grounds was struck down after the Justice Department filed suit on the basis that the law conflicted with the Fair Housing Act.[22]

More problematic, however, may be the legal obstacles if testers go so far as submitting falsified applications to lenders or insurers. Section 1014 of Title 18 of the *United States Code* criminalizes certain misrepresentations made in connection with loan applications "for the purpose of influencing in any way the action of any [financial institutions]" (Board of Governors 1991, 20). What has yet to be litigated is whether testers possess the requisite "intent to influence" that would render them liable under this statute. Needless to say, these liability questions become moot if testers provide accurate information about themselves and their properties in their applications, even if they have no intention of accepting the loans or policies were they to be offered by the underwriter. Of course, such a testing procedure raises extremely thorny operational problems, which I discuss in a later section.

To summarize this section, there is little doubt from a legal perspective that testing has the potential for providing probative evidence in assessing whether lenders and insurers have engaged in prohibited discriminatory practices. Indeed, implicit support for this conclusion is provided by a host of recent governmental actions backing such testing. The Federal Trade Commission throughout the 1980s conducted phone tests of consumer credit companies and apparently did a few tests of mortgage lenders (Board of Governors 1991, 10). The Fair Housing Amendments Act of 1988 authorized funds for private fair-housing groups to test lenders for enforcement purposes. The Federal Reserve authorized in 1983 the use of testers by its district banks to investigate lenders suspected of illegal activities (Board of Governors 1991, 11–12). The major legal uncertainty remaining is whether testers are permitted to push the testing process to the point where they file a (possibly falsified) application for a loan or an insurance policy. Testing that stops short of making applications (or, if possible, uses correct information in making such applications) does not appear to confront any legal impediments.

ETHICAL ISSUES IN LENDING AND INSURANCE TESTING

The mention of testing in the lending and insurance industries inevitably elicits indignant responses from agents in those industries; phrases like "Orwellian tactics," "Gestapo-like," and "insult to the industry" are recent examples.[23] Here I consider the more reasoned ethical concerns that have been raised about entrapment, privacy, informed consent, and unfair harm, and contrast them with the social benefits that might follow from the application of testing.[24]

Concerns over Entrapment, Privacy, Deception, and Fairness

Some see testing as entrapment and argue that people should not be tricked or tempted into undertaking "illegal acts" that are, in fact, subterfuges initiated by law enforcement agents. I find little merit in this position because, unlike "sting" operations, testing provides no inducements for violating the law. Testers (whether they are enforcement agents or researchers) merely observe and record behaviors in a context in which normal, legal transactions are the norm and are presumed. Indeed, industry representatives argue that personal and institutional interests are served by not discriminating. Tests ascertain whether, in fact, differential treatment is occurring and do not provide incentives to agents one way or the other.[25]

A second concern deals with invasions of individual privacy. It could be argued that lending and insurance agents have a right to keep their behaviors in the workplace confidential, especially if information about such behaviors is to be transmitted to the government (Board of Governors 1991, 24–26). Others contend that such privacy rights are largely forfeited in the domain of public commerce. Presumably this latter view is recognized by the many retailers and lenders who hire "shoppers" to pose as customers in their own institutions to ascertain the way bona fide customers are being treated, company policies are being followed, and information is being transmitted.

Deception and "informed consent" represent a third ethical issue. Obviously, in order to gain unbiased observations testers must use deception and some degree of misrepresentation so that they appear to the agent to be bona fide customers. Since those being tested both are unaware that they are being studied and are given no opportunity to decline participation in the study, the principle of informed consent is violated (Board of Governors 1991, 23–24). Furthermore, some argue that lying per se is morally unacceptable and that its sanctioned use (especially by the government) undermines a citizen's trust of others and reinforces the notion of deception as an acceptable element of social intercourse. This argument has been extended to the case of institutions: If regulators of lending and insurance industries employ testing it will erode the mutual trust between them and those they regulate that is crucial for an effective oversight system.[26] To me the above arguments are based on totally unfounded empirical assumptions.

Finally, there is the concern that unfair harm will accrue to individuals and institutions being tested. Some worry that those tested may have their reputations tarnished and suffer financial losses, even if unlawful acts are not being committed (Board of Governors 1991, 26–27). This argument presumes that testing is an unreliable tool or one that is biased in favor of finding discrimination; both presumptions are unfounded, as I argue in a later section. Furthermore, it fails to recognize the reality of civil rights litigation: Given the difficulty in proving discrimination and the enormous expenses involved in initiating legal suits,[27] cases are unlikely to be filed unless the testing evidence is overwhelming.

A variant of this concern is the argument that organizations using testing will build cases solely to intimidate the accused into undertaking actions financially supportive of the testing organization. Testing by private organizations has been called "an invitation to legalized extortion."[28] This extreme view seems to overlook not only legal strictures against such extortion attempts but the fact that extortion is possible today whether testing is used or not. Indeed, both of the above concerns over unfair harms to those in the lending (and, to a lesser extent, the insurance) industry ignore the severe reputational and financial havoc that is now being wreaked by the methodologically flawed but widely publicized studies I cited in the second section. If anything, testing holds more promise than any other technique of verifying the innocence of those who might now be unfairly accused.

Comparing Harms and Benefits

I do not find the concerns over invasion of privacy, deception, and possible unfair harm to be convincing arguments against the use of testing, primarily because putative harms of testing are rarely compared with the likely benefits of testing or with the harms of not testing. Proponents of testing do not suggest that privacy rights should be ignored or that lying be the approved form of social intercourse; rather, they suggest that these not be held sacrosanct. Surely, one can easily think of situations in which a rigid adherence to privacy or to honesty would be to commit the greater immorality. If one accepts this fundamentally relativistic, situational view of ethics, then one must judge the relative harms and benefits of both testing and not testing.

To ascertain whether testing can be morally justified, one must assess many factors: (1) whether the information gathered is necessary (or merely desirable); (2) whether the individual agents tested must be identified publicly; (3) whether the invasion of privacy and the deception are being limited to the greatest extent possible consistent with an accurate test; (4) whether the test is conducted by trained professionals under controlled conditions; and (5) whether an overriding public interest favors the research and such interest has been recognized explicitly by the government (Board of Governors 1991, n. 38). Each factor seems to be fulfilled in the case of lending and insurance testing. For the first factor, I refer the reader to the analysis of our current state of ignorance in the second section and to the discussion of the prospective efficacy of the method in the sixth section.

How the second factor is assessed depends on whether the tests are done for research or enforcement purposes. If the former, there is no reason why the research coordinator could (indeed should) not keep the names of all tested agents and institutions confidential; if the latter, presumably there would have been prior suspicions of the agent(s) or institution(s) and their identities would be revealed only if subsequent tests were to reveal probable cause. Factors 3 and 4 are part and parcel of standard testing procedures and could be further enhanced by including industry practitioners on teams that design and interpret the tests. The last factor clearly has been satisfied (see the prior discussion of the spate of antidiscrimination statutes and approval of the testing method by a variety of public agencies and judicial decisions).

In contrast to its minimal harms, the benefits potentially derived from testing-based investigations of lending and insurance practices are likely to be sizable. If the investigations were to show that discrimination was absent, one could conclude that the racial patterns of loans and insurance policies described above reflected the application of sound financial principles. This, in turn, would lead one to ask different sorts of policy-related questions about why these principles lead to racial disparities and what might be done to alter the disparities (beside antidiscrimination actions). Incidentally, the industries also would benefit from such a finding, both in enhanced image and in resources saved in fighting unfounded accusations. On the other hand, if the investigations were to show discrimination, one could rationally focus (and perhaps strengthen) enforcement efforts on particular violators, thereby guaranteeing in the most resource-efficient means possible the socially desirable flow of loans and insurance policies into all neighborhoods.

Finally, one cannot overlook the comparative harms associated with not pursuing lending and insurance testing. Ignorance is bad public policy, and testing offers promise of removing current ignorance in a key area of concern. Furthermore, maintaining the status quo involves distinct potential moral harms. State and federal regulatory agencies may be violating the public trust and failing to uphold their legal mandates if discrimination is occurring unbeknownst to them. Conversely, individuals and lending and insurance companies may be unfairly stigmatized by accusations based on the biased HMDA data currently available (see the second section).

In sum, some of the ethical concerns raised here have validity; others do not. But the severity of the harm implicit in even the valid concerns pales in comparison with both the prospective benefits of pursuing insurance and lending testing and the harms of maintaining the status quo. In the words of a federal court:

> It is surely regrettable that testers must mislead . . . . Nonetheless, we have long recognized that this requirement . . . was a relatively small price to pay to defeat racial discrimination. The evidence provided by testers both benefits unbiased [agents] by quickly dispelling false claims of discrimination and is a major resource in society's continuing struggle to eliminate the subtle but deadly poison of racial discrimination.[29]

PREVIOUS TESTING PILOT STUDIES OF LENDERS AND INSURERS

To date only four testing pilot studies have been completed that, although preliminary and exploratory in nature, shed light on both testing methodology and the practices of lenders and insurers. Here I critically review these studies' methods and findings, with an eye toward assessing the strengths and weaknesses of testing in this vein. These pioneering studies have been invaluable in demonstrating the applicability of the testing methodology to the lending and insurance arenas.

Lending Pilot Studies

PONTIAC

Pursuant to a broad fair-housing contract with the city of Pontiac, Michigan, the Fair Housing Center of Metropolitan Detroit conducted what were, to my knowledge, the first experimental tests of lending institutions. Eight paired tests of two commercial banks and one savings and loan in Pontiac[30] were carried out from November 1984 through August 1985. From the written documentation it cannot be ascertained what characteristics of testers or properties were used. However, in four tests both teammates sought loans for specific properties (two pairs had signed purchase contracts[31]); in the other four only a general interest in buying a home in Pontiac was expressed by the testers. All walked into offices without appointments and requested conventional mortgages.

The report concluded that "none of the tests produced any significant differences in treatment. There were some differences . . . but nothing that would provide the basis for formal complaints" (Fair Housing Center of Metropolitan Detroit 1985, 3). In my reading of the test summaries, however, at least one test showed substantial differences in treatment. In that test, very little information about the application process was given to the black tester, who was then referred to a different office of the lender and to a different mortgage company. In three other tests the black tester was informed that no loan officer could see the tester at the time (this occurred only once to a white tester). Unfortunately, the effect on the tests of having signed an offer to purchase could not be observed clearly because of idiosyncratic events associated with both such tests.

The Pontiac effort was path-breaking. Unfortunately, as is common of reports not written for a research-oriented audience, unnecessary ambiguity clouds the project and its results. We know little about how sites were sampled, the demographic and economic profiles of testers, and the nature of the properties in question (when some were specifically used). No tests of statistical significance were provided. Finally, even the qualitative interpretation of the findings appears questionable: The summaries of at least one (if not more) of the eight paired tests suggested to me, at least, noteworthy differential treatment.

LOUISVILLE

The Kentucky Human Rights Commission, in conjunction with the CCC, conducted experimental tests of 10 Louisville lenders during the summer of 1988 (CCC 1989a). Two commercial banks, four thrifts, two mortgage companies affiliated with banks or bank holding companies, and two independent mortgage companies were sampled. These institutions were selected from the top 15 Louisville lenders on the basis of (1) maintaining a balance in types of institution; (2) including lenders who had little activity in minority neighborhoods as revealed by HMDA data; and (3) including lenders about whom complaints had been made or to whom suspicious activity had been attributed.

Five white and five black testers were hired by the commission and trained as testers. Each tester (whether male or female) represented a married couple with one child buying their first home, with a purchase contract on a "for sale by owner" home. All requested a conventional mortgage. The homes used were taken from expired listings in the Louisville multiple listing service.[32] Each pair of testers was assigned homes in a neighborhood of similar racial composition: predominantly black, integrated, or predominantly white. Both members of the team had similar loan- and debt-income ratios, adequate assets, and longevity on the job (CCC 1989a, vol. 1, chap. 5).[33]

Each tester phoned lenders to inquire about obtaining home financing. Attempts were made to have in-person interviews with all loan originators at specified times. In a few instances, black testers had difficulty obtaining such appointments, and in one case a black tester was discouraged from visiting after a cursory review of information provided over the phone. When lenders had branch offices, testers also visited unannounced to inquire about a mortgage. They were generally told to phone the central office; the one exception with branch loan originations proved to have such unreasonable and idiosyncratic procedures that it was deemed incompetent and not amenable to testing (CCC 1989a, vol. 1, p. 21).

Testers were instructed to begin each contact with: "I have a contract on a house in [neighborhood] and I want information about getting a mortgage." They were to obtain as much information as possible, short of signing a loan application. A test was completed once the appointment with the lender was finished and a debriefing occurred. A goal of five (paired) tests for each of the 10 lenders was established.

Partly because all tests were conducted over only 2½ weeks, only 10 lenders were tested, several testers were seen (by chance) by the same loan officers, and "for sale by owner" contracts are comparatively rare, suspicions were aroused during the test project. When, on consecutive days, testers were asked by lenders "if they were taking a real estate course," the decision was made to cancel further tests (CCC 1989a, vol. 1, p. 20). At least seven individual tester visits had been completed at each institution at that point; 85 visits (41 by blacks) were completed altogether (of which 76 were paired).

The findings indicated that (with one exception) testers did not know whether they were treated differently from their teammate. The superficial aspects of the appointments were virtually identical for all pairs: courtesies, time spent with tester, lender's rates and terms, provision of consumer brochures and guides (CCC 1989a, vol. 1, p. 21). In three areas differential treatment based on race did occur, however (CCC 1989a, vol. 3, pp. 6ff.).

The most prevalent difference was a comparative lack of interest on the part of the loan originator to obtain or provide meaningful information, to prequalify, and/or to encourage black applicants to return and formally apply. As specific examples, black testers were (CCC 1989a, vol. 1, pp. 16–17):

1. Told the lender does not interview for mortgages at the bank—that they should go to the lender's mortgage corporation; whereas whites who inquired about mortgages at that bank were told they were in the right place and were given information about conventional loans;
2. Urged to consider another lender. For example, minority testers were told they "might" qualify for a loan, "it is hard to tell," but were strongly urged to consider an FHA loan (which this lender did not make) because it is "so ideal" for a first time home buyer. The tester would then be given the name and phone number of a lender that did make FHA loans. On the other hand, FHA was not even mentioned to white borrowers; rather they were encouraged to apply right then and there for a conventional loan;
3. Told that the loan officer could not give them any indication as to whether or not they would qualify, because it takes too long, they have to submit a full application and payment, or it's a complicated process. White borrowers, in contrast, were told that they were likely to qualify in a matter of minutes without a full application, payment, or having to provide any additional information.

A second area of differential treatment involved withholding "how to qualify" information from black testers: helpful hints and "little secrets" that often can be the critical factor for marginally qualified applicants. In quantitative terms, black testers made 41 visits and received useful information about how they might qualify during 6 (15 percent) of them. Whites made 44 visits and received such information during 12 (27 percent) of them. For example, black testers were (CCC 1989a, vol. 1, pp. 16–17):

1. Told the rules, but not the exceptions. For example, minority testers were told that with a 10 percent downpayment, they need six mortgage payments in the bank after closing costs are paid. Whites were told the same thing, but they were also told that with an 11 percent downpayment they need only the cash equivalent of two—not six—mortgage payments in reserve.
2. Told they fell short of meeting the lender's underwriting standards, but not how to improve on their shortcomings. For example, minorities were told they had too little cash on hand or too many debts. Whites were told the same thing but were then told how to get around the problems, by getting "gift" letters from relatives or applying on payday when they would have the most money in the bank.

A third area appeared to be differential treatment in prequalifying (CCC 1989a, vol. 1, pp. 16–17). Black testers were:

1. Told their ratios were too high by computing them falsely. For example, utilities were included in computing monthly housing costs for a conventional loan for a black tester, but not for any white testers. Utility costs are included when calculating ratios for FHA loans, but not conventional loans. This particular lender did not make FHA loans, so it could not have been a simple mistake.
2. Told they did not qualify because their ratios were just over the limit, while a white applicant with the same ratios was told that they would qualify.

The final area of differential racial treatment was recommending FHA/VA loans more frequently to black testers, even though they requested conventional loans. In addition, black testers were sometimes directed to apply for loan types for which they would not qualify without the sorts of information described above (which was not supplied by the lender).

The study also attempted to draw some conclusions about whether certain types of institutions were more likely to discriminate and whether discrimination against particular sorts of neighborhoods was occurring. The study reported (CCC 1989a, vol. 3, p. 7) that the incidence of differential treatment was greatest at commercial banks (16 visits), next greatest at thrifts (38 visits), and lowest at mortgage companies (31 visits), although no statistics are presented to support these claims. The tests did not reveal any conclusive findings relative to the neighborhood issue (CCC 1989a, vol. 3, p. 12) because of inadequate subsample sizes.

As important as this pilot study is, its usefulness could have been greatly enhanced by reducing the ambiguity of its derivation and reporting of results. The analytical method apparently focused on each tester visit separately, instead of as a pair, raising a question as to why pairs were employed at all. What "integrated" neighborhoods were is unclear; apparently they were selected by "local experts" to match the "perceptions of lenders" (CCC 1989a, vol. 3, p. 11). There are no quantifications of results, save for the fraction of interviews in which "how to qualify" information was provided. Even then, however, what precisely constituted such information remains vague. The total number of paired tests in which (according to the CCC's criteria) blacks were treated differentially is not reported. Contrary to the report's assertion that because the results are "qualitative and subtle" they are "not amenable to statistical analysis" (CCC 1989a, vol. 3, p.

13), a simple binary variable indicating differential treatment (for a single variable or a paired test as a whole) is easily analyzed statistically (Yinger 1985; Galster 1990). Finally, when results from tests are described with phrases like "had to fight to get information out of the loan officer" and "a totally negative experience" (CCC 1989a, vol. 3, p. 7), one wonders whether added attention should have been given to devising variables to measure aspects of the experience in a more objective, less emotional manner.

Chicago

In the spring and summer of 1990 two banks, three savings and loans, and five mortgage banks were experimentally tested as part of a study conducted by the Chicago Area Fair Housing Alliance with the financial assistance of the John D. and Catherine T. MacArthur Foundation.[34] Like the Louisville study, this project was an experiment designed to see what sorts of information could be learned through testing of lenders and would have been conducted differently had its purpose been enforcement. Institutions selected for testing were located, for the most part, in or adjacent to neighborhoods undergoing racial transition, primarily in the western and southwestern parts of Chicago and nearby suburbs. They were also selected on the basis of high overall loan volume and of suspicions aroused by HMDA data and by claims of a former loan officer.

Eight female testers (four black, four white) between the ages of 28 and 41 were trained for the lender tests, although all had significant experience as real estate testers or test coordinators. These testers posed as first-time home buyers who were married with one or two children. All were marginally qualified, that is, had a mortgage payment/income ratio of just under 28 percent and a total debt payment/income ratio of just under 36 percent, although black testers were slightly better qualified. All had been employed three or more years and had 10 percent down payments. Testers all presented "for sale by owner" contracts. These contracts were for actual homes of friends, relatives, and fair-housing advocates, although none was currently on the market. Testers were instructed to go so far as completing (but not signing) an application if the lender desired, but in fact none was asked to do so at the interview with the loan originator. Testers were instructed to be naive about lending procedures but to be assertive in obtaining information.[35]

Approximately 40 visits were completed, with different numbers at different institutions. As in the Pontiac project, testers did not call to make advance appointments but walked in, whereupon they stated that they had a contract for a house in a particular neighborhood and wanted information about obtaining a loan. In an interesting methodological development, testers were not paired in the traditional way. Rather, since all eight had comparable characteristics, the experiences of black testers as a group were compared with those of white testers as a group. In some cases, only black testers went to an institution because the behavior of loan officers in these cases was judged by the test director as so discriminatory that further testing was suspended. Unlike in the Louisville study, which used a comparable test scenario but compressed the visits to 2½ weeks, there apparently were no concerns about detection by lenders in Chicago. To the surprise of testers, loan officers did not quiz them on their contracts or ask about the properties in question.

The study director claimed to find evidence of discriminatory behavior at 7 of the 10 institutions tested, at least three instances of which were serious enough to warrant formal complaints. There did not appear to be differential treatment in the types of loans recommended, in the terms or conditions of loans described, or in the courtesies offered. As in the Louisville pilot project, the most common difference was that some black testers found it difficult to get loan officers to take the time to provide much information or to prequalify them. Other black testers were more actively discouraged by being told that they needed to fill out an application (complete with its fee paid) before complete information would be provided or that the institution did not make loans to first-time home buyers or made no loans under $40,000.

Unfortunately, until a detailed final report is published, this provocative pilot study only raises questions. How often did the putative discrimination occur at the seven institutions so charged? Were all black testers at these institutions treated unfavorably, or just a few? Were white testers ever treated unfavorably, compared with either other whites or blacks? Can one be certain that the putative "severe" discrimination faced by black testers at certain institutions would not have been replicated had white testers followed up? Were the differences in the incidence of differential treatment (either at individual institutions or overall) statistically significant? What sorts of neighborhoods were tested properties in? Were they comparable? Since the study only tested lending offices in white communities adjacent to racially transitional areas, one cannot ascertain whether the results are generalizable. The findings are clearly not generalizable to the broader set of lending institutions, given that those tested were non-randomly selected on the basis of prior suspicions. Nevertheless, this study is valuable because it indicates that unambiguous evidence of differential treatment can be gained through testing that proceeds only through the preapplication phase, at least in some subset of institutions located in particular areas.

The Milwaukee Pilot Study of Insurance

At this writing the singular completed report of testers used to investigate property insurance practices is the Milwaukee study of Squires and Velez (1988).[36] In this study the area's three largest insurance companies (in terms of number of home owner policies sold in the Milwaukee area through their own agents) were contacted on the phone by testers posing as home owners requesting information about buying home owners' insurance. In some tests a trio of testers represented otherwise comparable applicants whose homes were located in a predominantly white, integrated, or predominantly minority neighborhood; in others a pair of testers with homes in a predominantly white and either of the other types of neighborhoods were involved.[37] All eight tester teams were trained and given matching scenarios in terms of income, occupational status, construction type and value of home, claims experience, and other personal, property, and neighborhood characteristics that affect insurability.[38] When characteristics were not identical, those that would reduce insurability were always assigned to the tester representing the home owner in the predominantly white area.

Phone tests were conducted from March through May of 1986. Twenty-four tests, involving a total of 60 observations (36 of testers posing as home owners in integrated and predominantly black areas), were completed successfully. The questionnaires completed by all tester-callers were analyzed to ascertain whether the insurance agents treated individuals differently on the basis of the racial composition of the area in which their property was located.

The reported results rarely revealed refusals to offer policies in particular neighborhoods or blatantly discriminatory action.[39] Squires and Velez did, however, find a pattern, which they interpreted thus: "Agents exhibited more eagerness to sell insurance policies to testers representing white neighborhoods and placed more hurdles in the paths of callers from integrated or minority areas" (1988, 66).

Although all callers were quizzed about the location of their property as well as frequently about other personal and property characteristics, there were other patterns of agent questions that indicated geographic differentials. First, agents had a 14 percentage-point lower incidence of asking the potential customer's name when the caller was from a nonwhite area;[40] see table 7.1. Second, callers from nonwhite areas were asked about their present policies at a 25 percentage-point lower incidence than their counterparts from white areas; see table 7.2. Squires and Velez conclude that the findings shown in table 7.2 represent a weaker effort on agents' part to pursue sales to home owners in nonwhite areas.

In addition, they found differential treatment related to home inspections. Fifty-eight percent of the testers representing home owners in predominantly white areas were offered policies over the phone without the need for inspections, while only 47 percent of their teammates were. Similarly, of those told that inspections were needed, detailed inspections were required of testers representing nonwhite areas at a 29 percentage-point higher incidence; see table 7.3. Inspections of any sort were not completed as part of this project, therefore it could not be discovered whether any refusals to underwrite policies would have been the eventual outcome after an inspection. Nevertheless, the authors conclude that such inspections at minimum provide a discouragement to applicants and could be a vehicle for the discriminatory denial of insurance to minority areas.

Table 7.1 INSURANCE AGENT REQUEST OF NAME BY AREA RACIAL COMPOSITION

	Not requested	Requested
White	8.4	91.6
	(2)	(22)
Nonwhite	22.2	77.8
	(8)	(28)

Source: Squires and Velez (1988, table 1).
Notes: Figures are percentages, with the number of observations shown in parentheses; t test = 1.41; one-tailed probability = .10.

Table 7.2 INSURANCE AGENT REQUEST OF CURRENT POLICY INFORMATION BY AREA RACIAL COMPOSITION

	Not requested	Requested
White	8.3	91.7
	(2)	(22)
Nonwhite	33.3	66.7
	(12)	(24)

Source: Squires and Velez (1988, table 2).
Notes: Figures are percentages, with the number of observations shown in parentheses; t test = 2.3; one-tailed probability = .025.

Table 7.3 TYPE OF INSPECTION REQUIRED BY AREA RACIAL COMPOSITION

	Drive-by	Detailed
White	44.4	55.6
	(4)	(5)
Nonwhite	15.8	84.2
	(3)	(16)

Source: Squires and Velez (1988, table 3).
Notes: Figures are percentages, with the number of observations shown in parentheses; t test $= 1.67$; one-tailed probability $= .10$.

This study suffers from two weaknesses. First, it is ambiguous and often omits key facts from its report, thereby harming its ability to be thoroughly evaluated and replicated. One is not told where the properties in the tests were located and thus cannot make city–suburb comparisons of precisely what the neighborhood racial categories mean or whether changing racial composition plays a role. Key facts of the testing method are not mentioned: timing between calls, whether the same agents were contacted, how many different offices were contacted, the locations of offices in comparison with properties, who actually owned the properties, etc. One does not know whether testers were matched by age, gender, or race; whether all homes were single-family ones in similarly zoned areas; which neighborhood characteristics were matched; and whether "neighborhood" was defined by block, tract, or zip code. Moreover, one does not know whether results were consistent across all three insurance companies tested.

Second, the study has apparent design flaws. Because testers indicated only a general desire to purchase home owners' insurance and did not ask for identical coverages and deductibles, prices quoted by agents typically involved different policies (Squires and Velez 1988, 70). This makes it impossible, unfortunately, to determine whether there was differential treatment in prices quoted for identical policies. In addition, because testers did not continue to express interest if inspections were required, there was no opportunity to ascertain whether a refusal to underwrite was forthcoming. If, as the authors speculate, such an inspection provides a justification for a discriminatory refusal, the testing procedure would have failed to uncover the primary locus of the phenomenon. Finally, because agents may have guessed the race of the tester-caller because of either voice patterns or racial composition of the area where the home was located, the tests could not clearly identify differential treatment based on the race of the tester or the area.

The four pilot studies reviewed in this section have been extremely valuable, path-breaking experiments and have served valiantly to advance the state of knowledge about testing in this field. In spite of their exploratory nature, several tentative conclusions can be drawn from these works. Testing apparently is a device that can elicit useful information, even if it is restricted to transactions prior to submitting an application. Instances of putative discrimination appear to occur in a small fraction of transactions, except perhaps when tests are conducted at institutions evincing prior suspicious behaviors. When differential treatment occurs it seems to involve (in lending) the provision of less information, less frequent prequalifying, and (in both lending and insurance) a lower degree of sales effort afforded to black testers. These conclusions must be taken with caution, however, since the test projects were experimental in nature. This, quite understandably, means that their reports, where they exist, fall short of social-scientific standards of clarity, replicability, and statistical validity.[41]

METHODOLOGICAL ISSUES IN LENDING AND INSURANCE TESTING

In this section I examine eight operational aspects of testing methodology and try, when possible, to draw conclusions about whether the particular concern raises a serious barrier to the effective implementation of the method in the lending and insurance venues.[42] Reasonably firm conclusions can be put forth regarding the first two issues—detecting subtle differential treatment and distinguishing random from systematic treatment. Few can regarding the other six. Conclusions related to these other issues—sample design, sample size, discovery, extent of testing into application process, test scenario, and analytical design—cannot be arrived at for any single one because appropriate parameters for one are so dependent on the parameters of others. For instance, larger numbers of tests in an institution or a metropolitan area increase the statistical power of the investigation but also increase the chances of discovery by those being tested. Specifications of tester identities affect chances of discovery as well as how far into the application process the test probes. Analytical designs that treat a pair of testers as the unit of observation versus those that treat each tester individually hold different implications for sample sizes and the feasible extent of the testing probe. Therefore, the key question I attempt to answer is whether there are some permutations of the above parameters that lead to an efficacious method of research.

The discussion here presumes that testing is used purely as a research tool. Its potential as an enforcement tool is explored in the next section. In addition, the issues I raise are typically apropos of both lending and insurance testing; where necessary I mention exceptions to the generalizations.

Detecting Subtle Differential Treatment

Some have raised concerns that the sorts of behaviors evinced by loan officers or insurance agents who might be trying to discriminate at the preapplication stage would likely be so subtle that tests would be unable to detect them (Board of Governors 1991, 33–37). One aspect of this concern is that the discouragement of an applicant might take place only through a series of interpersonal nuances that would not easily be amenable to debriefing on testers' descriptive forms, to an objective assessment by the test coordinator reading these forms, and/ or to rigorous quantification into a variable(s) suitable for analysis. It is certainly possible that some subtleties may be difficult to quantify. I believe that it is likely, however, that a series of objective questions posed on tester debriefing forms could capture such discouragement in unambiguous ways. A checklist of the sort of information provided by the loan officer or insurance agent is one example. Was the tester invited to fill out an application? Was the tester prequalified for the loan or policy? Was the tester given hints as to how to increase the chances of qualifying?[43]

A second aspect of this concern is that no single variable may be sufficient to suggest an overall pattern of discouragement. This probably is true, but there is no reason why a cluster of debriefing items from testers' records could not be statistically analyzed for such patterns. Indeed, factor analysis and canonical correlation analysis are but two statistical means of detecting clusters of responses that, after interpretation, might clearly be indicative of multidimensional discouragement.

Distinguishing Systematic from Random Differences

An often-heard objection to testing in general is that any human agent is incapable of treating everyone identically, even with no discriminatory intent. Such things as time of day, state of agent's health, or subtle differences in the personality or responses of testers can lead to differences in treatment of testers (Board of Governors 1991, 32–33). Indeed, test designs cannot eliminate such random differences, but various means can be explored to better quantify the role of random differences in treatment, such as tests involving testers of the same race or "sandwiches" in which a tester pair is followed by another matched tester of one or the other race. As explained in chapter 1, an estimate of random differences in treatment can be used to adjust the results of the test corresponding to the definition of discrimination being employed.

A related issue is the worry that tests are compromised if both teammates do not contact the same individual (Board of Governors 1991, 46–47). This, too, can be sorted out by statistical procedures. If, for example, the assignment of agents to testers is random, the treatment afforded testers will tend to favor whites as often as it favors blacks, even if all the loan officers or insurance agents do not behave identically. On the other hand, if black testers are systematically assigned to certain officers or agents as a vehicle of discrimination (because these individuals are prejudiced, more inflexible in their applications of company guidelines, or whatever), that should be counted as discrimination. And indeed, it will appear as a systematic racial correlation with particular treatments in a proper statistical analysis.

Sample Design

The key sample design question is how the researcher chooses to allocate a given number of tests over the mortgage lenders and home insurers in the metropolitan area under investigation. Given that 40 percent of metropolitan areas have fewer than 25 lenders and 70 percent have fewer than 40 (Board of Governors 1991, table 1), it is often feasible to test all institutions. Elsewhere, a subset might be selected. This selection might be random, or the probability of an institution's being selected could be proportional to its share of the market. The selection might also be purposive with, say, the top five lenders or insurers in each institutional category being selected. An alternative purposive sample would be to select only those institutions for which there existed a priori suspicions of wrongdoing, as was done in the Chicago study described above (Board of Governors 1991, 49–55).

The purposive strategy has the obvious weakness of an inability to generalize findings to any other institutions in the local market. On the other hand, the universal or the randomized sampling strategies can produce ambiguous results, especially if sample sizes are modest and few institutions are tested more than once. In such cases the (expected) low overall incidence of differential treatment will be unable to distinguish between whether all institutions discriminate though infrequently or a few discriminate always and the rest never. (This is true even if the results are statistically significant.)

Sample Size

As in any empirical work, expanding the size of the sample increases the power of the statistical tests to distinguish between random, chance results and systematic ones. This power is not constant, however, for any given sample size but varies according to the frequency of the behavior being observed and the interracial differences in the frequencies of such behaviors. For example, to reject (at a 5 percent significance level) the null hypothesis of no interracial differences when white testers are discouraged 45 percent of the time and black testers are discouraged 50 percent of the time requires 772 paired tests.[44] Respective white and black tester frequencies of 10 percent and 5 percent, on the other hand, imply only 213 paired tests. Respective frequencies of 30 percent and 50 percent necessitate only 46 paired tests.

Unfortunately, a priori one can estimate little about what incidences and interracial differences in treatment one is likely to find in lending and insurance tests. The Federal Reserve's best guess for the lending market as a whole is a difference in treatment of no more than 15 percentage points and a frequency of no more than 25 percent for black testers (Board of Governors 1991, 64–65). The results of the pilot studies described earlier give no reason to quibble with this estimate for lenders, although the Milwaukee insurance tests are suggestive of somewhat higher frequencies and larger interracial differences between them. This means that about 200 paired tests should be contemplated if one is to be confident in a general sample of lenders (i.e., not including only suspicious institutions) of detecting a difference in treatment of at least 5 percentage points at a 5 percent level of significance; the sample possibly could be smaller for a general sample of insurance companies.

Of course, these estimates may be wildly exaggerated if one's sample includes only institutions suspected of discriminatory behavior. The Chicago lending test suggested more dramatic differences in treatment, for example. Once again, these results have not been reported in a way, unfortunately, that permits tests of statistical significance.

Discovery

The validity of the test is compromised by the discovery (or even suspicion) of its existence. One has already seen how this possibility was actualized in the Louisville pilot study (Board of Governors 1991, 33–34). Discovery is more likely (1) the more the tests are repeated in the same institution; (2) the more similar and/or unusual the tester-pair scenarios are; (3) the smaller the institution is, in terms of loan or policy originations and number of officers or agents; (4) the more predominantly white the racial compositions of the area in question is; (5) the more fabricated the documents and histories the testers provide are (especially when they are subject to potential verification by the institution).

One can infer from the Louisville study that the combination of unusual, "for sale by owner" tester scenarios, 7 to 10 visits (sometimes to the same officers) at the same institutions, and a 2½-week testing frame exceeded the limits for nondetection. Beyond that, however, there is little empirical guidance.

More to the point, would, say, 200 paired tests of a wide-ranging sample of institutions be feasible without detection? I believe so, at least in the larger metropolitan areas.[45] A smaller group of institutions (say, the 10 largest) would, of course, increase the number of repeat tests needed at each. Given the increasing centralization of loan and policy originations, these repeat tests could arouse suspicion. The director of the Pontiac pilot study estimated, however, that 24 visits (12 pairs) could be made to larger institutions without detection.[46] In addition, the Federal Reserve has noted that 20 visits (10 pairs) per institution is a reasonable operational estimate for a pilot study, presumably without discovery (Board of Governors 1991, 71). Of course, if the sample design is to focus on presumed violators, a smaller number of repeat tests would achieve the requisite statistical power and thus provide even less chance of discovery.

Extent of the Test into the Application Process

The current consensus is that testing of home mortgage and insurance transactions can feasibly proceed only until the point of submitting an application (Squires and Velez 1988; CCC 1989a, 11; Board of Governors, 1991, 19–20). As noted above, there are serious legal questions concerning tester liability if false information is provided on loan applications and, perhaps, on insurance applications as well. There are also extremely thorny operational difficulties involved in fabricating tester credit and employment histories, current income and debts, etc.

The above concerns would become moot if the testers relied upon their own identities throughout the testing process. Presumably, testers "posing as themselves" could file applications for loans and insurance policies without legal worry and with only an application fee as a minor practical obstacle, even though they would have no intention of accepting the offer if the application were to be approved.

This method would have the advantage of exploring deeper into the lending and insurance underwriting process to ascertain whether other sorts of discrimination (delays in processing, "lowball" appraisals, more stringent mortgage insurance standards, or unfavorable underwriting judgments) were present (CCC 1989a). The disadvantage would be great difficulties in recruiting pairs of testers with substantially equivalent real identities and with identities that the testing agency wished to use in the test scenario, for example, the marginally qualified borrower. This disadvantage could be mitigated somewhat by revising the statistical analysis to treat testers as individual observations of behavior, instead of as an observation of a matched pair, as I discuss below. The upshot is that it would be premature to dismiss the possibility of employing testing to probe deeper into the application process.

Tester Scenario

There has been a good deal of discussion of and a modicum of empirical experimentation with how testers should approach loan and insurance originators (Board of Governors 1991, 47–49). One issue regarding lending tests involves whether a specific property is mentioned. (This cannot be avoided in insurance tests, of course.) Testers can approach loan originators by saying that they wish to know in general how much of a loan they might be able to qualify for, because they are considering buying a home (perhaps in a particular neighborhood) and wish to know what range of affordability they can search in. Alternatively, testers can posit a contract for a particular house and seek to obtain information about whether they could obtain a mortgage for it. A criticism of the former approach is that testers will not be treated seriously without a sales contract in hand and therefore only a limited, superficial behavior will be elicited that will be unlikely to mimic behavior toward "real" prospects. Unfortunately, the results of the Pontiac study, which employed this scenario, are not definitive in this regard.[47] Another criticism is that unless the geographic area of the intended purchase is clearly specified, the potential for eliciting "redlining"-based discriminatory responses is eliminated.

Another scenario issue is whether testers should begin with attempts to set up appointments over the phone (and manually or electronically record information conveyed at both phone and in-person interview stages) or merely walk in unannounced at offices. The Louisville lending study found that rarely did distinct differential treatment occur at the phone stage (undoubtedly because the race of the caller could not be ascertained with certainty by the loan officer). The Pontiac lending study often "wasted" tests in the sense that its walk-in scenarios frequently led to situations in which one or both testers could not speak with any loan officers because they had prior appointments, although this apparently was not as severe a problem in the Chicago study. The Milwaukee insurance tests used only the phone stage. Although much information was elicited, it was impossible to test for discrimination on the basis of race of the applicant. In my opinion, the two-step phone/personal interview test is preferable in both lending and insurance tests, inasmuch as it would catch those (perhaps rare) cases of discrimination at the first stage, maximize the productive use of testers' time at the second stage, and allow for the unambiguous identification of the testers' race by the officer or agent and, thereby, for the possibility of discrimination on that basis.

If the sales contract scenario is employed in lending tests, the issue arises as to whether the sale should be by the owner or through an agent. The former scenario is operationally simpler because it does not require the collaboration of real estate agents and can use homes that are not currently for sale.[48] Its shortcoming is that such transactions are rare in most markets and therefore the appearance of many such putative sales during the testing period might arouse suspicions. In addition, loan originator behavior vis-à-vis such transactions may be different than when real estate agents who are familiar to the organization are involved. On the other hand, recruiting real estate agents to participate in a study (by, e.g., signing dummy sales contracts on homes currently off the market) would be risky because it might increase the chances of the tests being discovered. Agents might be reluctant to participate, since their livelihood depends on a close working relationship with lenders, although providing guarantees of anonymity should assuage fears in this vein. Another strategy might be to set up a temporary dummy real estate company, complete with office space, yellow pages listing, and a staff who would answer the phone. This company would handle all (or some, if a few "for sale by owner" units were used as well) the testers' transactions and would be cited by testers if questioned by lenders. Such a plan would overcome the shortcomings above, but at considerable expense and operational complexity.

The above issues are considerably simplified in the case of insurance tests. Sales transactions need not be involved, merely the putative imminent expiration of a home owner's policy. Thus, testers could use their own homes, or those of others recruited as part of the study, with relative ease.

A final issue is whether information provided by the tester is fabricated. Fabricating identities makes it easier to obtain close teammate matches and explore a variety of scenarios with a limited number of testers. On the other hand, it limits how far the test can probe into the application process (as explained earlier). If testers use their real identities, they can apply at any given institution only once. This, combined with the desire to employ a wide variety of tester characteristics (especially financial characteristics and geographic locations) and perhaps a pair of each multidimensional set of characteristics, raises an immense problem of recruiting testers. The worry about pairing may be allayed by employing a different analysis design, however, as explained in the next section.

Analysis Design

The standard analytical approach in testing has been to consider the differences in treatment (if any) of the pair of testers as the unit of observation, where as many of the characteristics of the teammates are controlled as possible. Each pair can thus be scored (for individual items of treatment or for the test as a whole) as either "white favored," "black favored," or "neutral." Both the frequencies of these results and the amount of differences (in certain ratio-level variables such as length of interview, time of processing application, points charged, etc.) evinced can be tabulated, and paired differences-of-means tests performed (see Yinger 1985, 1991). One can go further and identify any systematic racial differences in the results by employing multivariate techniques that control not only for the interpair variation in tester characteristics but also for the inter- and intrapair variation in agents seen, time of day of test, etc. (Yinger 1991).

An alternative is to view each individual visit by a tester as a unit of observation (Board of Governors 1991, 56–61; CCC 1989a, 15). Here the nonracial controls of the experiment are provided not by careful matching of testers but by multivariate statistical analysis of the results. That is, each visit provides a unit of observation for a model where the dependent variable is a measure of behavior toward the individual tester (measured in discrete or continuous terms) and the dependent variables control for characteristics of the tester, the loan officer or insurance agent, the property in question, the circumstances of the test, etc.

Unlike the paired method, such a model cannot provide an estimate of the overall incidence of systematic discrimination in the sample or even of whether particular visits evinced disparate treatment—only whether across the tests race accounted for a different probability or amount of a particular treatment, ceteris paribus. In addition, a larger sample of tests is required in order to provide adequate degrees of freedom for the statistical procedures.

Nevertheless, the nonpaired method offers two advantages: Because it can accommodate a wider variation in tester characteristics and scenarios, it complements testing involving real tester identities (thereby permitting a deeper probe into the application process) or testing with strong concerns over discovery arising out of excessively similar tester pairs.

Few firm conclusions can be offered about the best methodologies until we have considerably more field experimentation with testing of lenders and insurers. Nevertheless, I am confident that clever design of tester questionnaires and debriefing procedures is capable of detecting objectively even subtle forms of discouragement, and that multivariate statistical procedures are developed sufficiently to provide identification of multidimensional, systematic discriminatory patterns. The limited evidence also suggests to me that there is an intersection of test scenarios and sample sizes such that researchers can be confident of detecting rather modest yet statistically significant differences in treatment in a wide-ranging sample of institutions without having the tests discovered. Whether this is the case for a single institution is problematic unless that institution is already suspected of questionable behaviors, an issue to be discussed in the context of enforcement below. Tests would seem to be more efficacious if they could involve both phone contacts and (attempts to obtain) personal interviews, and if (in lending tests) they could avoid reliance on "for sale by owner" contracts or merely "shopping around for a mortgage" with no particular home in mind. Neither of these operational requirements seems onerous.

OVERALL EVALUATION, POLICY IMPLICATIONS, AND FUTURE DIRECTIONS

In this final section I first provide a summary evaluation of the efficacy of the testing method by exploring the following questions. Can it successfully probe behaviors of mortgage loan and insurance policy originators at stages prior to filing applications? How valuable is the sort of information revealed thereby? Are there alternative investigative methods that could substitute for testing in these venues? I then consider the testing method from the standpoint of its enforcement potential when used by lending and insurance company regulators and by civil rights groups. Finally, I suggest three areas that I believe offer fertile ground for exploring variations in the lending and insurance testing method.

Evaluating the Method as a Research Tool

As I suggested in the previous section, there is nothing in the limited experience with lending and insurance testing that leads me to conclude that it cannot be effectively used to investigate even subtle behaviors at the preapplication stages of transactions. Considerable numbers of tests may be required before the predicted small and infrequent differences in treatment in the market as a whole can be adjudged statistically significant, but this need not lead to discovery. Neither the legal questions nor the ethical objections appear to be compelling constraints to such tests, as discussed earlier. On the contrary, ethical considerations suggest an urgency to rectify the current state of ignorance. Designing the tests may be complicated (at least in the case of lending tests), especially if the "for sale by owner" scenario is scrapped in favor of a more typical transaction involving a real estate agent, but not impractically so.

It is crucial to investigate lending and insurance practices at the preapplication stage. Academics and regulatory agency representatives have worried for over a decade that this part of the transaction process could involve a great deal of discrimination that heretofore had been undetected (see, e.g., Schafer and Ladd 1980; Canner 1982). Indeed, there is reason to suspect that discrimination may be more likely before an application is filed than after. If an institution wanted to discriminate, it clearly would be more likely to escape detection if it left no paper trail of the rejected applications of minorities. Even if the management of an institution did not want to discriminate, behavior of loan and insurance policy originators vis-à-vis prospective customers may be less closely monitored than the behavior of underwriters vis-à-vis written documents subject to supervisory review. Thus, there is more room for personal prejudices and motivation to save costs and time on presumably less qualified applicants at the preapplication stage, both rationales for discrimination going unchecked by management (Board of Governors 1991, 29–32).

Finally, there appear to be no close substitutes for obtaining information equivalent to that revealed by tests. As I explained in the second section, HMDA data are woefully inadequate indicators. There are complementary studies of, for example, advertising practices or office locations that might provide, like HMDA data, suggestive (but not definitive) indicators of discriminatory patterns. Certain carefully specified, multivariate statistical analyses of the treatment afforded completed applications (King 1980; Schafer and Ladd 1980) can unambiguously detect discrimination in underwriting practices.[49] However, no alternative type of evidence can provide unambiguous indications of discriminatory behavior at the preapplication stage. As argued above, evidence from studies of advertising, office location, and underwriting practices may greatly understate the severity of discrimination at the less visible preapplication stage. Testing at the preapplication stage cannot, however, examine discriminatory policies such as undue delays in loan processing or systematic underappraisal of properties. Whether this proves to be a serious omission cannot be ascertained at present, but below I propose a more extensive test scheme that could provide such knowledge. The bottom line is that testing likely would offer a huge advance over our present state of ignorance about lending and insurance practices.

Implications for Regulatory Enforcement

Federal (and in the case of insurance, state) regulatory agencies have legitimate concerns about whether testing can and should be used as a means of carrying out their mandate to ensure compliance with civil rights laws. There is little doubt that some regulators are increasingly moving toward an acceptance, even advocacy, of testing principles: Witness the Department of Housing and Urban Development's longtime sponsorship of housing testing studies, the Department of Justice's use of testing evidence in filing housing pattern-and-practice suits and its growing interest in employment testing, and the Equal

Employment Opportunity Commission's recent approval of testing in employment cases.[50] Moreover, Sen. Orrin Hatch has offered a bill that would fund Department of Justice tests not only of housing transactions but also of mortgage lending practices.[51]

Current regulatory procedures are incapable of detecting discrimination at the preapplication stages of transactions because periodic examinations focus only on written documentation and have no means of investigating conversations between loan originators and policy agents that create no documentation (Board of Governors 1991, 7–8).

Whether testing can effectively fill this gap is not clear, however. The answer depends on the pattern of discrimination across institutions and, if discrimination is concentrated in a few institutions, whether these institutions can be identified for targeted testing. If discrimination at the preapplication stage is rare (or nonexistent) at lending and insurance institutions, testing would be an ineffective regulatory tool. Every institution would need to be tested a large number of times to ensure statistically significant results, yet this would likely lead to discovery as well as unreasonably high operational costs. On the other hand, if only a few institutions discriminate but do so virulently, a modest amount of testing would hold more promise of detecting the discrimination. This presumes, of course, that the violating institutions could be identified by some criteria before targeted testing was conducted. Perhaps consumer complaints or patterns of HMDA data could provide these indicators;[52] the Chicago pilot study suggested that such targeting might be effective, although not necessarily fair or systematic. Another option (albeit more costly) would be to do a broad-based sample of tests, with each institution receiving several. Those with high incidences of differential treatment could be the focus of subsequent targeted tests.

Needless to say, no definitive answer can be given to the question of the cost-effectiveness of testing as a regulatory tool until more testing fieldwork is done to ascertain the scope and depth of discrimination at the preapplication stage and the costs of conducting such tests. Indeed, it was this point, combined with an assessment of weaknesses in the current examination procedures and the great promise of the testing technique, that led the Consumer Advisory Council of the Federal Reserve to recommend in June 1991 that the Fed sponsor a systematic, social-scientific study of testing at the preapplication stage of lending.[53] Unfortunately, the Fed rejected this recommendation in September 1991,[54] leaving it in the tenuous position of admitting to a gap in its oversight procedures yet refusing to experiment with a method for closing it. I hope that this unconscionable position is reversed quickly; ignorance is bad public policy.

Implications for Civil Rights Litigation

Regardless of whether testing is used as a tool by regulators, it could be employed by civil rights groups to obtain evidence pursuant to legal proceedings alleging lending or insurance discrimination. The potential usefulness of the method here may well be greater than in either the research or the regulatory applications. For example, researchers' concern for statistical significance may be less important than the "preponderance of evidence" adjudged by the court, thereby diminishing concerns about sample design, sample size, and risk of discovery. Similarly, regulators' interest in the cross-institutional pattern and severity of discrimination becomes irrelevant when one institution is targeted in litigation.

Having said that the value of testing for litigation purposes may be quite independent of its value for research and regulatory purposes, I do not mean to imply that those three efforts are anything but mutually complementary. Indeed, advances in the method spurred by research initiatives may have clear payoffs in regulatory and litigation arenas. A growing body of case law establishing evidentiary standards for lending and insurance testing may persuade relevant regulators to look more kindly upon the method. In sum, all advances in lending and insurance testing should be supported by interested researchers, regulators, and civil rights groups, regardless of the tests' particular application.

Suggested Future Directions

I close by suggesting three areas in the field of lending and insurance testing that appear ripe for development. The first involves devoting more effort to either gaining the cooperation of real estate agents or, alternatively, experimenting with the establishment of dummy real estate offices prior to conducting lending tests. Success in such efforts would permit a wider variety of test scenarios to be created, including more sales through agents instead of by owners. This, in turn, would not only reduce the risks of detection (especially with repeat tests at the same institutions) but also enhance the representativeness of the test results.

My second suggestion involves conducting pilot tests wherein testers use their real identities and push the test through the actual filing of an application. The main advantage would be to explore behaviors associated with application processing and underwriting decisions (plus actions regarding appraisal and mortgage insurance in the case of lending, and costs and coverages of policies offered in the case of insurance). Such tests also would finesse any concerns about legal liabilities. On the other hand, sales contracts for bona fide homes would be required for lending tests, necessitating the cooperation of a real estate agent or the establishment of a dummy real estate office. (An insurance test might simply involve the tester's own house.) Perfect matches between testers would be unlikely in this case, so the statistical methods for nonpaired tests (described earlier) would have to be employed to provide nonracial controls.

Finally, I suggest exploring the connections between real estate agents' "steering" of prospects toward particular lenders and subsequent lender behavior. The recently released Housing Discrimination Study (Yinger 1991) showed that a substantial fraction of agents suggested FHA/VA financing to black testers but conventional financing to similarly qualified white testers. Whether such differences imply steering toward or away from particular lending institutions because of real estate agents' personal connections with these institutions or their expectations of differential treatment of their customers is unknown. An intriguing investigation would thus start with tests of real estate sales and continue with lending tests.

Notes

I gratefully acknowledge the information and suggestions provided by Glenn Canner, Cathy Cloud, John Goering, Deborah Goldberg, Diane Houk, Karla Irvine, Gretchen Miller, Cliff Schrupp, Anne Shlay, Shanna Smith, Greg Squires, Carla Wertheim, and Ron Wienk, while retaining responsibility for any flaws in the work. Charlotte Wahl provided invaluable clerical support.

1. These institutions must have had assets of at least $10 million to be subject to the original HMDA requirements. Loans made through banks' wholly owned mortgage subsidiaries and by mortgage companies were not reported. This lack of information about significant segments of the mortgage market raises a fundamental question about the ability of the original HMDA data to indicate accurately the *total* flows of funds into various neighborhoods.

2. "Middle income" was a broad range of between 70 percent and 122 percent of median MSA income. The methods employed in Detroit and Atlanta were essentially the same and were developed by Charles Finn of the University of Minnesota.

3. The above selection of studies was not meant to imply that all cross-tabular studies have identified lending disparities. A study of HMDA records in St. Paul, Minnesota, from 1981 to 1987 showed no racial pattern in loans per 1,000 owner-occupied units, controlling for income (Smith and Craig 1990).

4. When conventional and FHA loans are aggregated, a curvilinear pattern emerges, with the maximum dollar value of loans per unit occurring in 10 percent black areas (Squires and Velez 1987b).

5. A simple, cross-tabular analysis using this variable was recently completed (Obermanns 1989).

6. See the Federal Financial Institutions Examination Council (FFIEC) press release, July 2, 1990, and accompanying *Federal Register* notice. It also requires data on the type of purchaser of housing-related loans that are sold and permits lenders to report reasons for denying home loans.

7. In principle one could also calculate from individual HMDA loan registers the numbers of various sorts of applicants (by race/gender/income) in each of these application–disposition categories for all census tracts. As I have argued, however, such an aggregation from individual data would be foolish. Direct analysis of the individual data would prove more definitive, as I explain later.

8. See the FFIEC press release, July 2, 1990, for more details.

9. The categories used will be less than 80 percent, 80 to 100 percent, 100 to 120 percent, and more than 120 percent of MSA median income; see FFIEC press release, July 2, 1990.

10. Thefts per 1,000 residents and fires per 100 housing units, the two proxies employed in the Chicago study (Squires 1979) were intended for this purpose. However, they provide only a crude measure of the dollars actually lost on the particular insured properties in the area.

11. The number of zip codes used was 47 in Chicago and 33 in Milwaukee.

12. King (1980) and Schafer and Ladd (1980) gained access to private lender data, under the auspices of bank regulators, and were thereby able to do the most definitive statistical studies to date.

13. In this section I draw heavily from Board of Governors (1991, 14–21).

14. The Civil Rights Acts of 1866 and 1870 also have been interpreted as prohibiting lending discrimination.

15. The legal citations are found in Midwestern Regional Advisory Committees (1979, 26–27).

16. Compare, for example, the acceptance of these positions in *Dunn v. Midwestern,* 427 F. Supp. 1106 (S.D. Ohio 1979), and their rejection in *NAACP v. American Family Mut. Insur. Co.* (E.D. Wis. 1990). Actions may also be illegal if, although applied even-handedly, they have an "adverse impact" on minorities.

17. For more on the concept of unlawful discrimination, see Board of Governors (1991, 15–16).

18. See, for example, *United States v. Youritan Constr. Co.,* 370 F. Supp. 643 (N.D. Cal. 1973), *modified,* 509 F.2d 623 (9th Cir. 1975), and *Zuch v. Hussey,* 394 F. Supp. 1028 (E.D. Mich. 1975).

19. *Richardson v. Howard,* 712 F.2d 319 (7th Cir. 1983).

20. *Havens Realty Corp. v. Coleman,* 455 U.S. 363 (1982).

21. In *NAACP v. American Family Mut. Ins. Co.* (E.D. Wis. 1990) the judge accepted the defendant's motion to dismiss in December 1990, on the grounds that the Fair

Housing Act did not pertain to insurers. An appeal decision from the Seventh Circuit ruled that the 1968 Fair Housing Act *did* cover home insurance. The U.S. Supreme Court declined to comment upon this ruling in 1993.

22. *United States v. Wisconsin,* 395 F. Supp. 732 (W.D. Wis. 1975).

23. Letters from Wm. Watson of Cross Keys Bank (June 5, 1991) and from Malcolm Martin and Joseph Roberts of Lakeside National Bank (June 10, 1991) to Ann Marie Bray, Division of Consumer and Community Affairs, Board of Governors of the Federal Reserve.

24. Here I draw heavily from Board of Governors (1991, 22–27).

25. For an analysis of the legal defense of entertainment in testing cases, see Board of Governors (1991, 20–21).

26. See the minutes of the Meeting of the Consumer Advisory Council of the Federal Reserve, June 20, 1991.

27. Among the expenses can be penalties for bringing frivolous suits.

28. William North, vice president of the National Association of Realtors, quoted in Tilove (1991).

29. *Richardson v. Howard,* 712 F.2d 319, 321 (7th Cir. 1983).

30. Pontiac is an outer ring northwest of Detroit.

31. How such contracts were provided for testers is unclear.

32. The one exception was one tester who used her own home.

33. The front-end and back-end ratios were chosen such that all testers were marginally qualified.

34. Since no final report of this project had been published as of this writing, this section is based on my personal correspondence with the study's director, Cathy Cloud (Aug. 6, 1991), and on my notes on Ms. Cloud's speech given at the Kansas City Federal Reserve Bank's Conference on Credit and the Economically Disadvantaged, Nov. 8, 1990.

35. Testers were paid $100 for the seven-hour training session and $50 per test. The expectation that lending tests would take longer than real estate tests was not borne out.

36. This was conducted under the auspices of the Metropolitan Milwaukee Fair Housing Council.

37. It is unclear whether all were located in the city.

38. The report is vague about precisely what these characteristics were.

39. In the 60 observations only one white tester and two black testers were refused policies.

40. There were no differences in the responses for integrated and black neighborhoods.

41. The one exception is the Milwaukee insurance study directed by Squires and Velez.

42. In this section I draw heavily from Board of Governors (1991, 33–73).

43. A fuller list is provided in Board of Governors (1991, attachment C).

44. See Board of Governors (1991, table 2). Note, however, that these estimates treated testers as uncorrelated individuals, with no covariances.

45. Sixty-one (17 percent) MSAs have 50 or more lending institutions (Board of Governors 1991, table 1); no data on insurers were available to me.

46. This number was suggested in a proposal to the Michigan Financial Institutions Bureau by Cliff Schrupp, director of the Fair Housing Center of Metropolitan Detroit, April 4, 1990.

47. The final report asserts that "walk-in initial testing is not likely to produce a great deal of evidence of unlawful treatment" (Fair Housing Center of Metropolitan Detroit 1985, 3), but personal correspondence from Cliff Schrupp states that "the report form shows that testers who are at the early stage of a mortgage transaction, without having first spoken with a real estate agent, can gain a lot of useful, comparative information" (letter of June 3, 1991).

48. This avoids the possibility that a bona fide buyer with a sales contract will apply for a loan at the same institution as the tester.

49. Remember, however, that such analyses require proprietary data of institutions that are not typically available to researchers.

50. See the U.S. Commission on Civil Rights (1991, 5).

51. See the Congressional Record, Oct. 31, 1989.

52. Board of Governors (1991, 51n) provides a fuller discussion of options.

53. For details of the resolution and guidelines for the proposed research, see Board of Governors (1991, 67–74).

54. Similar proposals failed to win FFIEC support in both 1979 and 1990. The Fed unanimously rejected this resolution on Sept. 25, 1991.

References

Blossom, Teresa, David Everett, and John Gallagher. 1988. "The Race for Money." Detroit Free Press, August.

Board of Governors of the Federal Reserve System. 1991. "A Feasibility Study on the Application of the Testing Methodology to the Detection of Discrimination in Mortgage Lending." Washington, D.C.: author.

Boehm, Thomas. 1981. "Tenure Choice and Expected Mobility." Journal of Urban Economics, 10: 375–89.

Bradbury, K., K. E. Case, and C. R. Dunham. 1989. "Geographic Patterns of Mortgage Lending in Boston, 1982–87." New England Economic Review (Sept./Oct.): 3–29.

Byrne, Kevin. 1980. "Application of Title VIII to Insurance Redlining." Northwestern University Law School Review, 75: 472–505.

Canner, Glenn. 1982. "Redlining: Research and Federal Legislative Response." Study No. 121. Washington, D.C.: Board of Governors of the Federal Reserve System.

————. n.d. "Federal Reserve Staff Analysis of Atlanta Constitution Study." Washington, D.C.: Board of Governors of the Federal Reserve System.

Center for Community Change. (CCC) 1989a. "Mortgage Lending Discrimination Testing Project." Washington, D.C.: U.S. Department of Housing and Urban Development.

————. 1989b. "New Research Shows Savingsand Loans Shun Lower Income and Minority Neighborhoods." Washington, D.C.: author, June 13.

Dedman, William. 1988. "The Color of Money." *Atlanta Journal Constitution*, May 1–4.

DeWolfe, Ruthanne, Gregory Squires, and Alan DeWolfe. 1980. "Civil Rights Implications of Insurance Redlining." *DePaul Law Review*, 29: 315–51.

Fair Housing Center of Metropolitan Detroit. 1985. "Fair Housing Services for the City of Pontiac: Final Report 8/1/84–11/30/85." Detroit, Mich.: author.

Galster, George. 1991. *CRA, HMDA and the Banking Industry.* Washington, D.C.: American Bankers Association.

————. 1990. "Racial Discrimination in Metropolitan Housing Markets during the 1980s: A Review of the Audit Evidence." *Journal of Planning Education and Research*, 9: 165–75.

Howe, Steven. 1988. "Residential Lending Patterns in Hamilton County, Ohio: 1981–1986." Cincinnati, Ohio: Housing Opportunities Made Equal.

Kentucky Commission on Human Rights. 1989. "Louisville Lenders Approve Few Home Mortgages in Predominantly Black and Desegregated Middle Income Census Tracts in 1987." Report No. 89–2. Frankfort, Ky.: author.

King, A. Thomas. 1980. "Discrimination in Mortgage Lending: A Study of Three Cities." Working Paper No. 91. Washington, D.C.: Federal Home Loan Bank Board.

Listokin, David, and Stephen Casey. 1980. *Mortgage Lending and Race.* New Brunswick, N.J.: Center for Urban Policy Research, Rutgers University.

Midwestern Regional Advisory Committees to the U.S. Commission on Civil Rights. 1979. *Insurance Redlining: Fact, Not Fiction.* Washington, D.C.: U.S. Government Printing Office.

Munnell, Alicia, Lynn Browne, James McEneaney, and Geoffrey Tootell. 1992. *Mortgage Lending in Boston: Interpreting the HMDA Data.* Boston: Federal Reserve Bank of Boston, Working Paper No. 92-7.

National Advisory Commission on Civil Disorders. 1968. *Report of the National Advisory Commission on Civil Disorders.* New York: Bantam.

National Commission on Neighborhoods. 1979. *People Building Neighborhoods.* Washington, D.C.: U.S. Government Printing Office.

Obermanns, Richard. 1989. *Race and Mortgage Lending in Cleveland, 1985.* Cleveland, Ohio: Cuyahoga Plan.

Ostas, James. 1985. "Reduced Form Coefficients, Structural Coefficients, and Mortgage Redlining." *Journal of the American Real Estate and Urban Economics Association*, 13: 81–92.

President's National Advisory Panel on Insurance in Riot-Affected Areas. 1968. *Meeting the Insurance Crisis of Our Cities.* Washington, D.C.: U.S. Government Printing Office.

Roistacher, Elizabeth. 1975. "Residential Mobility." In *Five Thousand American Families,* edited by Gregory Duncan and James Morgan. Vol. 3. Ann Arbor, Mich.: Institute of Survey Research, University of Michigan.

Schafer, Robert, and Helen Ladd. 1980. *Equal Credit Opportunity in Mortgage Lending.* Cambridge, Mass.: Joint Center for Urban Studies.

Shear, William, and Anthony Yezer. 1985. "Discrimination in Urban Housing Finance: An Empirical Study Across Cities." *Land Economics,* 61: 292–302.

————. 1988. "Not in That Neighborhood: The Effects of Population and Housing on the Distribution of Mortgage Finance Within the Chicago SMSA." *Social Science Research,* 17: 137–63.

Shlay, Anne. 1987. "Maintaining the Divided City." Baltimore, Md.: Maryland Alliance for Responsible Investment.

Smith, Frederick, and William Craig. 1990. "Discrimination in St. Paul's Financial Services." *CURA Reporter,* 20: 1–6.

Squires, Gregory, Ruthanne DeWolfe, and Alan DeWolfe. 1979. "Urban Decline or Disinvestment: Uneven Development, Redlining and the Role of the Insurance Industry." *Social Problems,* 27: 79–95.

————. 1988. "Insurance Redlining and the Process of Discrimination." *The Review of Black Political Economy,* 16: 63–75.

Squires, Gregory and William Velez. 1987a. "Insurance Redlining and the Transformation of an Urban Metropolis." *Urban Affairs Quarterly,* 23: 63–83.

————. 1987b. "Neighborhood Racial Composition and Mortgage Lending: City and Suburban Differences." *Journal of Urban Affairs,* 9: 217–32.

Tilove, Jonathan. 1991. "Testers Go Undercover to Expose Rights Bias." *Syracuse Herald-American,* March 24, pp. F1, F4.

U.S. Commission on Civil Rights. 1991. *Civil Rights Update,* March/April.

————. 1983. *A Sheltered Crisis: The State of Fair Housing in the Eighties.* Washington, D.C.: U.S. Government Printing Office.

Yinger, John. 1991. *Estimates of Discrimination Against Blacks and Hispanics and Analysis of Variation in Discrimination Study.* Washington, D.C.: Urban Institute/U.S. Department of Housing and Urban Development.

————. 1985. "Statistics for Fair Housing Audits." Washington, D.C.: U.S. Department of Housing and Urban Development.

THE FAIR-HOUSING MOVEMENT'S ALTERNATIVE STANDARD FOR MEASURING HOUSING DISCRIMINATION: COMMENTS

Shanna L. Smith

Fair-housing advocates recognize the importance and validity of social science research in the fair-housing field. Many private fair-housing organizations have sponsored such research to provide information about the nature and extent of housing and lending discrimination. This information is used to develop more sophisticated enforcement programs. The large majority of housing discrimination resources, however, are concentrated on programs to eliminate housing discrimination. Enforcement efforts have brought about the most comprehensive and meaningful changes in discriminatory housing and lending practices.

The concern of the fair-housing movement is that standards for social science research will inappropriately be applied to enforcement efforts of fair-housing agencies. This has dangerous implications, some of which have recently been witnessed:

1. The Board of Governors of the Federal Reserve voted unanimously *not* to conduct a mortgage lending testing program, even though it had been recommended by the board's own Consumer Advisory Council. One of the primary reasons the proposed program was declined was that it was structured to measure the extent of discrimination at a level and cost far beyond that necessary and far beyond the boundaries of evidence required for enforcement purposes.

2. The recent Kennedy fair-lending amendment was defeated in the House of Representatives primarily beause of the testing requirement. The most persuasive argument against the testing component was that it would be too costly. These costs, however, were based on the testing program proposed by the Fed. Representatives were told that testing lending institutions could run as high as $200,000 per institution.

The testing program proposed to the Board of Governors was developed primarily by social scientists who lack experience in and knowledge about fair-housing and fair-lending enforcement. While members of the National Fair Housing Alliance endeavored to explain to them that substantially fewer resources could be used in a testing program for fair-lending enforcement, the researchers prepared a proposal designed as a research instrument. It is not surprising that the Board of Governors was reluctant to fund such a proposal and that Congress was unwilling to expend resources at that level. This is why members of the alliance believe it is imperative that testing for lending discrimination be considered in the context of enforcement, with the express purpose of eliminating discriminatory behavior and policies. An insistence on evaluating testing projects as "studies" and holding them to social science standards detracts from efforts to bring about these important changes.

DIFFERING STANDARDS FOR MEASURING HOUSING DISCRIMINATION

Although in chapter 7 of this volume, George Galster acknowledges the importance of testing for litigation purposes, I believe he continues to advocate for a standard of proof of discrimination that is not required by the federal district courts. I am concerned that he leaves the impression that for lending discrimination to be detected and litigated, there must be numerous incidents. This is a great disservice to the lending industry because it misleads lending institutions into a belief that a single act of discrimination is not a violation of the law.

The fair-housing movement does not dispute Galster's statement that reports under the Home Mortgage Disclosure Act (HMDA) alone cannot conclusively prove lending discrimination. However, we disagree with his statement that HMDA data are "woefully inadequate indicators" of discriminatory behavior by lenders and that lending discrimination is difficult to prove without applying extreme statistical controls and extensive testing. In fact, HMDA reports are often the *first* "indicators" of discriminatory behavior. These reports are useful in Community Reinvestment Act challenges and litigation to show a pattern of disinvestment by a particular lender. In a review of HMDA reports about the lenders that were defendants in the 15 lawsuits filed between 1979 and 1990 in Toledo, Ohio, we found that the lenders had few, and in one case no, mortgage loans in minority and integrated census tracts. This was in spite of the fact that there was a demonstrated demand for mortgage money in those areas. A serious problem in Galster's argument, in my view, is the emphasis on quantity rather than quality of information to prove discriminatory lending practices.

Federal courts across the country have clearly established the standard of proof for lending/housing discrimination cases: One act of discrimination constitutes a violation of the federal Fair Housing Act. Federal judges in Indiana and Ohio have set the prima facie or "threshold" case standards for mortgage lending discrimination as follows:

A. **Applicant Discrimination**[1]
   1. The applicants are members of a protected class;
   2. They applied and were qualified for a loan from the defendant;
   3. The loan was rejected despite their qualifications; and
   4. The defendant continued to approve loans for applicants with qualifications similar to the applicants.

B. **Neighborhood Discrimination**[2]
   1. The housing sought to be secured is in a minority neighborhood;
   2. An application for a loan to purchase the housing located in a minority neighborhood was made;
   3. An independent appraisal concluded that the value of the housing equaled the sale price;
   4. The buyers were creditworthy; and
   5. The loan was rejected.

Galster states that the Fair Housing Act does not prohibit "differential treatment of applicants when it is based on objective, financially sound and necessary underwriting standards and the pertinent elements of the applicants' creditworthiness or insurability. Such differential treatment becomes illegal discrimination (i.e., 'intentional' disparate treatment) when it is based purely on a protected classification of the applicant (like race) or of the property in question (like neighborhood racial composition)." The Fair Housing Act does not require a showing of "intent" to prove disparate impact. Every federal circuit court that has addressed the issue has held that one need only show the disparate "effect" of a policy or practice to prove housing discrimination.[3] I have yet to meet a lender who believes his underwriting standards are not objective, necessary, or based on maintaining the financial soundness of the institution. However, in reviewing these underwriting guidelines, I have found standards and policies that clearly have a discriminatory impact on minority and women applicants and are not "necessary" for sound fiscal management. In spite of the clear legal standard, Galster makes a strong statement that undermines these legal principles. He argues the need to show intent to discriminate by lenders and fails to address the effect of lenders' policies and practices. Leading lenders to believe that discriminatory actions must be intentional to violate the law is wrong and could result in their facing legal claims under the Fair Housing Act.

For instance, some lenders have established minimum mortgage loan amounts. Others have tiered interest rates for mortgage loans under $30,000 that increase by .5 percent for increments of $5,000. Either practice can have a discriminatory impact on persons protected by the Fair Housing Act. The Toledo Fair Housing Center investigated complaints involving minimum loan amounts and found that this policy would effectively eliminate all mortgage loan activity in census tracts serving 72 percent of the African-American population and 78 percent of the Hispanic population. Tiered interest rates result in minority, women, and lower-income applicants paying more to borrow less. The increase in the interest rate can put some borrowers over the debt ratios set by lenders. Increasing the interest rate in this fashion results in unequal treatment of protected class members. Setting these policies may not prove conclusively that the lender intended to discriminate against low-income applicants, women, or minorities, but the effect of these policies is clearly discriminatory within the definition of the Fair Housing Act.

Some lenders say it is a "business necessity" to establish minimum loan amounts and tiered interest rates because they do not break even servicing lower-priced loans. Obviously, they are willing to renege on their Community Reinvestment Act promise to "meet the credit needs of low and moderate income persons," a promise that is made to secure access to the Fed's discount window.

LEGALITY OF TESTING

Galster rightly concludes that testing is accepted universally by the courts as a means to prove discrimination. He also concludes, and we concur, that lending testing at the preapplication stage should raise no legal or ethical concerns in the courts. He raises the same concern fair-housing advocates have raised about the legal uncertainty of conducting full application testing where the tester submits an application with false information. Full application testing has been done, but the tester(s) used truthful information. We believe that full application testing is absolutely necessary because discrimination can and does occur at various stages of the lending process.

"CURRENT STATE OF IGNORANCE"

Galster writes that there is a "state of ignorance" surrounding fair-lending issues and seems to believe that fair-lending advocates are guilty of such ignorance. Yet, I think Galster demonstrates a lack of knowledge about fair-lending issues in the following statement: "If the investigations [preapplication testing] were to show that discrimination was absent, one could conclude that the racial patterns of loans and insurance policies . . . reflected the application of sound financial principles." It is naive to conclude that segregated lending patterns are the result of the application of sound financial principles absent a showing of discrimination during the initial application inquiry. Galster should study the numerous lending lawsuits brought in Toledo, Ohio, in response to acts of discrimination that occurred after applications were submitted. His conclusion fails to consider the historical and current discriminatory practices of credit bureaus, appraisers, underwriters, private mortgage insurance and home owners' insurance companies, loan committees, and the secondary mortgage market.

Additionally, it is widely known that where strong and successful enforcement of the Fair Housing Act occurs, there is a significant reduction in discriminatory conduct at the application phase in rental housing. Fair-housing agencies report that they often must complete rental applications and pay security deposits to uncover the sophisticated practices employed to discourage and deny assistance to minority applicants. Thus, one must look beyond the preapplication stage before coming to a conclusion about the lack of discrimination.

Galster implies that the only person likely to discriminate at a lending institution is the loan officer. He states: "Indeed, there is reason to suspect that discrimination may be more likely before an application is filed than after." He believes the reason it may be more likely is that once the application is filed, there is a paper trail for bank examiners to follow that discourages discriminatory practices. A simple comparison between the number of discriminatory practices reported by bank examiners and the number of lawsuits filed in just the Midwest demonstrates that bank examiners rarely find discrimination even with complete access to all lending files. Employees or other participants in the loan process clearly have no reason to be concerned that any acts of discrimination will be detected.

STANDARDS OF PROOF IN ANALYZING LENDING TESTS

Galster calls into question the objectivity of fair-housing groups that analyze the results of lending testing and further states that tester reports "fall short of social-scientific standards of clarity, replicability, and statistical validity." Fair-housing staff are trained to structure testing to determine whether an allegation of housing discrimination is valid. Staff are skilled at reviewing and analyzing test reports to identify subtle acts of housing discrimination. It is our responsibility to ascertain the facts. It is in no one's interest to charge discrimination where none exists. In fact, doing so could result in the agency's or complainant's being sued for bringing a frivolous claim. I believe the success of private fair-housing agencies in the federal courts attests to the fact that fair-housing staff are highly qualified to determine whether discriminatory conduct has occurred.

Having reviewed and participated in more than 2,000 tests in my 16 years in fair housing, I can say that subjecting testing to standards of social science research only results in a lack of clarity in demonstrating the nature and extent of housing discrimination. The nuances and differences in treatment between white and minority testers are not easily placed on a "checkoff" list. The written narrative report of the tester is the document that best reveals the often subtle and sophisticated methods used to discourage or deny assistance to minority applicants who try to rent, buy, or insure housing. Attempting to apply social science formulas to acts of direct discrimination and discrimination by omission, at best, is burdensome and imperfect and, at worst, undermines the established and accepted legal standards of proof in housing/lending discrimination.

Early in his chapter, Galster proposes a probability model for a more sophisticated regression approach to analyzing lending discrimination.

I am deeply concerned that Galster is attempting to set a higher standard than is already accepted by the courts to demonstrate lending discrimination. I must emphasize this point. One act of discrimination is a violation of the Fair Housing Act. The legal standard that has been set is a "preponderance of the evidence." The courts explain this as the scales "tipping" in favor of the plaintiff or defendant. One is not required to demonstrate that discrimination occurred over and over again to prove a violation of the law. In fact, a pattern or practice case may require only one discriminatory policy or as few as three individual instances of discrimination.

Lending testing is a difficult subject to analyze absent a review and clear understanding of the lawsuits and administrative actions brought against lending institutions in Toledo, Ohio; Gary, Indiana; Atlanta, Georgia; Cincinnati, Ohio; Detroit, Michigan; and other cities throughout the United States. Lending discrimination can and does occur at so many different stages of the loan process that using the methodology proposed by Galster would require so many tests as to be infeasible.

Having been involved with more than 15 lawsuits against mortgage lending discrimination, I can report that no two cases are exactly alike. Through discovery, our attorneys found all the information necessary to demonstrate disparate treatment of minority loan applicants or disparate treatment of loan applications for homes in minority neighborhoods. These cases involved discriminatory use or application of credit bureau and appraisal reports, income-to-debt calculations, and underwriting guidelines of the lender, private mortgage insurer, and secondary mortgage market buyer.

SOCIAL SCIENCE STUDIES VS. ENFORCEMENT ACTIVITIES

Studies do not change behaviors; enforcement changes behavior. Lenders have been told for decades to stop disinvestment practices in the older urban neighborhoods of America. Study after study indicates differences in treatment of loan applications in these neighborhoods. Yet the slight change we have seen resulted from challenges by fair-housing agencies and neighborhood organizations or legal actions brought by victims.

For example, the lenders who established minimum loan amounts and tiered interest rates knew or should have known that these policies have a disparate impact on women and minorities living in older housing. Although in several instances this information was provided to lenders, the lenders did not eliminate the practice. In each instance it took the threat of a Community Reinvestment Act challenge or actual litigation to eliminate the policies and practices. The fourth largest private mortgage insurance company was charged with discrimination in a lawsuit that challenged minimum insurance amounts. Instead of looking at the impact of its policy, the company argued that insurance was not covered under the Fair Housing Act. A lawsuit challenging the policy was filed by the Toledo Fair Housing Center, the buyers, and the sellers of the property. To its credit, the U.S. Department of Justice filed an amicus brief for the plaintiffs when the company sought to have the case dismissed. Shortly after the government's brief was filed, the company decided to settle the case. The settlement resulted in the company's eliminating the minimum insurance policy nationwide and paying $47,000 in damages to the plaintiffs (*Briceno v. United Guar. Residential Ins. Co.*).

I believe it is a far better expenditure of resources and time for social scientists to assist attorneys and fair housing/civil rights groups in analyzing loan documents secured during litigation of lending cases. A second priority would be for them to assist neighborhood organizations in evaluating HMDA data for purposes of promoting compliance with the Community Reinvestment Act and exploring Fair Housing Act violations. Third, and equally important, lenders should consult with social scientists, fair-housing agencies, and neighborhood organizations concerning fair-lending issues. Lenders should seek reviews of their underwriting guidelines and other procedures to evaluate them for possible disparate impact.

FOUNDATIONS' RESPONSIBILITIES

Fair housing continues to be the stepchild of the civil rights movement when, in many respects, it should instead be the foundation for civil rights. If fair-housing laws were vigorously enforced, there would be considerably less segregation in housing patterns, which would translate to better integration in the public schools and more opportunities for employment in suburban communities.

The private fair-housing movement has not enjoyed the financial support from major foundations that other, more traditional civil rights groups enjoy. Yet, it has been this small contingent of nonprofit fair-housing centers that has pioneered litigation in this area. These groups have challenged the discriminatory practices of major rental management companies, real estate companies, lending institutions, newspapers, appraisal companies, the Department of Housing and Urban Development, and agencies responsible for administrating VA and FHA loans. Their hard work has resulted in:

☐ Millions of dollars in damages for victims of housing discrimination and accompanying affirmative relief;

☐ "Set-aside" of units for minority applicants, homeless persons, and low-income persons;

☐ Affirmative employment practices in rental, sales, and lending offices;

☐ Desegregation of public housing and site dispersal of Section 8 private developments;

☐ Establishment of sexual harassment in housing as a violation of the Fair Housing Act;

☐ Securing the right to sue for testers and fair-housing advocates and municipalities;

☐ Elimination of minimum insurance amounts by private mortgage insurers; and

☐ Establishment of "futile gesture" and "knowledgeable inaction" as claims under the Fair Housing Act.

What can foundations do to support fair housing/fair lending testing? Foundations should assist the fair-housing movement by providing financial support for its continuing efforts to identify the sophisticated methods used to deny housing and home loan opportunities to minority applicants. This would include funding for preapplication testing designed for enforcement purposes as well as educational and investigative training programs for fair-lending enforcement professionals. Support from foundations for fair housing/fair lending efforts would go far beyond the financial resources provided; it would also represent a commitment from the private sector to the rights and values inherent in equal opportunity. This support would be a recognition of the key role housing opportunity plays in the quality of life for individuals, families, neighborhoods, and entire cities.

Notes

1. *Thomas v. First Fed. Sav. Bank*, 653 F. Supp. 1130, 1338 (N.D. Ind. 1987).

2. *Old West End Assn. v. Buckeye Fed. Sav. & Loan*, 675 F. Supp. 1100, 1103 (N.D. Ohio 1987).

3. See cases cited in nn. 93–108 and accompanying text in R. Schwemm (1990), *Housing Discrimination: Law and Litigation*, sec. 10.4 (1).

4. *Id.* at sec. 26.2 (2), nn. 27–33 and accompanying text.

Chapter Eight

USE OF TESTING IN CIVIL RIGHTS ENFORCEMENT

Roderic V. O. Boggs, Joseph M. Sellers, and Marc Bendick, Jr.

INTRODUCTION

This chapter discusses the use of testing as a civil rights enforcement technique. It is based on the experience of the Washington Lawyers' Committee for Civil Rights Under Law over the past 20 years. The chapter is organized in three sections: (1) a brief review of the Washington Lawyers' Committee's overall litigation program and its experience with the use of testing; (2) a more detailed analysis of the application of testing methodology to employment discrimination; and (3) suggestions concerning future use of testing techniques for enforcement.

The Washington Lawyers' Committee's Experience with Enforcement-Oriented Testing

The Washington Lawyers' Committee for Civil Rights Under Law is a private, nonprofit organization established in 1968 by leaders of the private bar in the District of Columbia to address issues of discrimination and poverty. It is one of a number of local lawyers' committees formed in response to the publication of the report of the National Advisory Commission on Civil Disorders (1968). Over the past 24 years, the committee has mobilized hundreds of lawyers to provide legal services to thousands of civil rights claimants in both individual cases and class actions. While the committee's work has included cases in almost all areas of civil rights practice, its litigation has concentrated on discrimination in employment and housing.

More than 100 suits concerning discrimination in employment have been won at trial or settled on favorable terms. These cases have involved more than 30 federal agencies and dozens of private employers and labor unions. More than $50 million has been secured in back and front pay for thousands of minorities and women. Injunctive relief has opened employment opportunities for even more individuals. In addition, the committee operates a specialized Intake Program to assess the claims of individuals who believe they have confronted discrimination in their employment. Last year, the program responded to more than 900 requests for assistance.

In addition, for more than 15 years, the committee has provided assistance to individuals in the Washington, D.C., area who seek to challenge discrimination in residential housing. While most cases have involved discriminatory refusals to rent on the basis of race or sex, the committee has also handled landmark cases challenging discriminatory advertising practices and successfully challenged the conversion of a high-rise apartment in Silver Spring, Maryland, to an all-adult building.[1]

In 1978, the committee began to provide counsel to an organization based in Richmond, Virginia—Housing Opportunities Made Equal (HOME). Established in the early 1970s, HOME was among the first private fair-housing organizations to use testing techniques as part of a comprehensive fair-housing enforcement strategy. HOME has become a model program in providing housing counseling to minority home seekers and in using paired testers to audit general housing practices and investigate specific complaints of discrimination. Among the most significant cases that HOME initiated was *Havens Realty Corp. v. Coleman*,[2] in which the Supreme Court reached the landmark unanimous decision upholding the standing of testers and fair-housing organizations to bring suit under the 1968 Fair Housing Act.

Drawing on its experiences with HOME, the committee assisted a group of local clergy in establishing an analogous fair-housing organization in the Washington metropolitan area in 1983. Over the past nine years, this organization, the Fair Housing Council of Greater Washington (FHCGW), has developed an extensive program of community education, outreach, and complaint counseling. Among other things, the FHCGW has used testing techniques to conduct five major audits of rental practices throughout the Washington metropolitan area. The FHCGW has also been involved in more than 30 lawsuits using testers as plaintiffs, either alone or in combination with bona fide applicants, to challenge discriminatory housing practices.

The results of these cases clearly illustrate the enormous impact that testing can have in winning fair-housing cases and securing meaningful relief. The FHCGW's litigation record reflects a steady increase in the monetary value of settlements achieved in cases employing tester-generated evidence. In the mid-1970s, fair-housing case settlements involving a payment of several thousand dollars were generally considered substantial victories. But by 1990 the FHCGW had secured more than a dozen settlements or verdicts of over $20,000 each, and recoveries in several cases have exceeded $100,000. In the majority of these cases, tester evidence was a decisive factor in achieving a successful result. Tester evidence provided a level of proof almost never attainable in other cases. In addition, the ability of the FHCGW to initiate cases exclusively on the basis of testing evidence meant that enforcement was no longer dependent on receipt of complaints from individual victims. Cases could be initiated proactively.

The FHCGW has also used testing to monitor compliance with settlements in earlier cases. Perhaps just as important, testing undertaken by the FHCGW as part of an annual survey has been a means of keeping the issue of housing discrimination in the forefront of public debate. Over the past five years, each of the FHCGW's highly publicized annual reports has generated a supportive editorial response from the *Washington Post* and extensive coverage in the print and electronic media.

The Washington Lawyers' Committee has also worked closely with the National Fair Housing Alliance (NFHA), an organization that has made a vital contribution to the development of testing techniques in fair-housing enforcement. The alliance is a membership organization of more than 50 private fair-housing agencies around the country assembled to pool their experience and capabilities to promote equal housing opportunity. The committee has assisted the alliance in (1) securing general legal assistance, (2) providing legal training to the staff of member organizations, and (3) preparing and submitting briefs as an amicus curiae to support member organizations in cases presenting important legal issues.

Particularly through its effective communications network and its Washington office, the alliance serves an indispensable role in apprising fair-housing groups throughout the country of legal and policy developments of mutual interest. The NFHA has also worked closely with officials of the Department of Justice and the Department of Housing and Urban Development (HUD) who are charged with fair-housing enforcement. These agencies have shown increasing interest in and support of the use of testing as an enforcement technique.

During the summer of 1988, the Washington Lawyers' Committee worked with the Southeast Vicariate Cluster, a coalition of church groups in Southeast Washington, and a team of social scientists at Howard University to adapt testing methodology to the problem of discrimination in the provision of taxicab service in the District of Columbia. This work involved substantial research using paired teams to test for discrimination involving (1) the refusal of service because of a passenger's race and (2) the refusal to transport passengers to predominantly black neighborhoods. Over the course of 2½ months, 292 tests were conducted by trained, carefully matched teams of black and white testers. The results revealed statistically significant disparities in the rates at which black testers were passed by in comparison with whites and at which service was denied to testers seeking to travel to predominantly black areas in the city. For example, black testers were passed by by cabs in 20 percent of the tests, while white testers were passed by in only 3 percent of the tests.[3] Testers were also nearly twice as likely to be denied transportation to predominantly black areas of the District than to destinations of comparable distance in predominantly white areas.[4]

As a result of this testing program, litigation was undertaken against three cab companies whose practices reflected particularly high levels of discrimination. These suits were settled on the eve of trial, after the court denied several dispositive motions by the defendants. The settlement included a substantial monetary payment— nearly $50,000—and significant injunctive relief. Perhaps most significant, during the course of the litigation the court ruled for the first time in this country that cab companies could be held liable for the discriminatory conduct of their drivers.[5]

Early in 1990, the Washington Lawyers' Committee, after discussions with local attorneys who have substantial experience in the fields of employment and civil rights enforcement, moved to establish a new private organization that would utilize testing to address equal employment issues. Through the collective efforts of Peter Edelman, associate dean of Georgetown Law Center; Inez Smith Reid, former D.C. corporation counsel; William Robinson, dean of the District of Columbia School of Law; and Leroy Clark, a former general counsel of the Equal Employment Opportunity Commission (EEOC), a new organization was established named the Fair Employment Council of Greater Washington (Fair Employment Council). The Washington Lawyers' Committee and the firm of Arnold & Porter serve as general counsel to the Fair Employment Council.

As initially formulated by its board, the activities proposed for the Fair Employment Council to undertake included the following:

1. A comprehensive analysis of basic demographic and work force data concerning the Washington metropolitan area to identify any

occupations and industries in which minorities and women appear to be underrepresented.
2. Pursuit of testing audits to identify the extent to which discrimination influences hiring decisions in various sectors of the regional economy.
3. In appropriate circumstances, initiation of litigation and administrative actions to address discriminatory practices identified by the council's testing and research activities.
4. Provision of lawyer referral services to individuals who may have been affected by discriminatory practices disclosed through the council's testing and research.
5. Issuance of an annual report assessing the state of fair-employment practices and equal employment opportunity law enforcement efforts in the Washington metropolitan area.
6. Initiation of public education and outreach activities to acquaint community groups and public and private civil rights organizations with the council's programs.

Over the past year, the Fair Employment Council has made considerable progress in implementing these programs. Its activities have included adaptation of testing methods originally used by the Urban Institute in its research to the demands of enforcement-oriented testing; identification of an initial set of industries and occupations on which to concentrate testing activities; recruiting, training, and fielding a staff of black and white testers who have completed more than 200 tests; and initiation of two lawsuits based on testing results, along with preparation of additional suits. Of the two suits already filed, one alleges racial discrimination and one sex discrimination.

METHODOLOGICAL CONSIDERATIONS IN ENFORCEMENT-ORIENTED EMPLOYMENT TESTING

Of all the activities undertaken by the Fair Employment Council to establish testing as a major enforcement tool in employment discrimination, none is more important or more complex than the adaptation of testing methodology to the special needs of enforcement. The methodology used in research-oriented employment testing is described elsewhere in this volume.[6] The methodology for enforcement-oriented testing shares with it many common elements. Both can be defined as social science procedures that create laboratory-like controlled conditions for recording candid responses to human characteristics. As social science methodologies, both reflect a fundamental style that emphasizes objectivity rather than advocacy and a focus on promulgating facts rather than conclusions. In search of laboratory-like control, both rely on pairs of testers selected, trained, and equipped with credentials making them comparable in job-relevant respects and isolating the characteristic being tested.

Nevertheless, there are important ways in which procedures designed for research-oriented and enforcement-oriented testing should differ. We consider, in turn, nine specific ways in which these differences are manifested. They can be grouped into general categories relating to (1) the development of testing staff, (2) applications for jobs and records of test experiences, and (3) targeting of and follow-up from tests.

Development of Testing Staff

Several of the differences between research-oriented and enforcement-oriented testing methods relate to the development of the testing staff.

SELECTION OF TESTERS

The first of the adjustments to research-oriented testing methodology pertains to the selection of testers. Research-oriented testing imposes a number of requirements on the characteristics of persons selected to serve as testers. These requirements demand that the testers be objective, approaching their job as a research activity and without preconceptions of what they will find; that they be observant, alert to relevant details of job application procedures and their treatment during these procedures; that they be meticulous record keepers so that their experiences will be completely and accurately documented; that they follow directions punctiliously; and that they be able convincingly to portray a job applicant with the credentials they are assigned.

Enforcement-oriented testing also requires all these characteristics. In addition, however, enforcement-oriented testing may call upon testers to serve as plaintiffs and witnesses in litigation. Such roles impose at least three additional considerations in selecting testers. First, the personal backgrounds of testers must be free of any difficulties that might reduce their credibility as witnesses. Second, testers must be sufficiently articulate to present their experiences clearly in written statements and oral testimony. Third, because litigation may require several years for resolution, testers must be willing to remain in contact with the testing program and return occasionally to participate in legal proceedings over an extended period.

The location of capable, dedicated individuals to serve as testers requires considerable time and effort but, in our experience, is readily achievable. Often, several dozen candidates must be screened for each tester hired. For the Fair Employment Council, the search process generally has worked best when it has (1) hired students from local universities; (2) identified candidates through personal referrals rather than open advertisements; (3) described the position as that of a research assistant; (4) hired individuals who are at least 20 years of age; and (5) selected individuals who possess more education and skills than the applicant they will portray.

COMPARABILITY OF TESTERS

Another difference between research-oriented and enforcement-oriented testing concerns the attractiveness of each tester to potential employers. In a research study, the design typically specifies that the protected-class tester and non-protected-class tester should be equivalent in job-relevant characteristics. Where that is not possible, it is appropriate to alternate randomly which tester in the pair has the stronger credentials.

In an enforcement test, that approach would be acceptable, but it might leave ambiguity regarding the inferences to be drawn from differences in treatment of the testers. Giving the protected-class tester a slight edge, however, helps ensure that differences in treatment to the detriment of the protected-class tester create an inference of discrimination. Accordingly, in enforcement-oriented testing, the protected-class tester might apply for a job before the control tester and the record of his education and experience might be somewhat stronger than the background presented by the control tester.

TRAINING OF TESTERS

Differences also arise in the course of tester training. In both enforcement and research work, thorough training of testers is essential to the success of the program. Enforcement testers spend several days in classroom training, receiving instruction in the theory and context of testing, preparing resumes, being coached on how to be an effective job applicant, practicing the completion of application forms and participation in interviews, and becoming adept at procedures for recording data. During this time, testers who will be paired work closely with and observe each other, developing a sense of teamwork and fostering a convergence of their personal styles. This classroom training is followed by several days of practice tests conducted under close supervision. While this training is very similar to techniques used to prepare testers in research-oriented programs, enforcement-oriented training should cover additional areas. Additional topics include the use of testing results to enforce the civil rights laws and the nature of the legal processes in which testers may become involved.

COMPENSATION OF TESTERS

Differences may also arise between research-oriented and enforcement-oriented testing in the terms on which testers are retained. Since employment testing requires testers to make substantial commitments of time and effort, it is generally advisable to hire testers rather than to rely on the efforts of volunteers. This conclusion, however, does not end the inquiry.

In both the research and enforcement contexts, it is crucial that testers be compensated in ways that do not make their earnings contingent on the results they report. Data generated by tests must be free of any inference that testers were motivated to report discrimination to benefit personally. Therefore, in the Fair Employment Council's testing program, testers are paid a fixed salary regardless of how many tests they complete or what results they find. Additionally, those testers who become plaintiffs in litigation agree in advance that any damages awarded to them as a result of litigation will be assigned to the Fair Employment Council.

Recording Test Experiences

Once testers are trained, they are ready to begin applying for jobs and reporting their experiences. Differences in methodology also arise in this area.

DEGREE OF SUPERVISION

Differences arise between research-oriented and enforcement-oriented testing in the degree of supervision provided to testers during their fieldwork. In research-oriented testing, testers are typically in regular contact with their field supervisor to receive assignments. But during the course of each test, the supervisor is consulted primarily when unusual problems arise. The emphasis is on following a standardized procedure so that all pairs of tests reflect parallel experiences so that the results can be aggregated in a statistical analysis.

In enforcement-oriented testing, on the other hand, concern with the completeness and clarity of the record in each test predominates over interest in uniformity among all tests. In enforcement-oriented testing, each tester should be mindful of taking actions that are comparable to those likely to be undertaken by his partner while still following the natural flow of each job application process. As a result, for example, testers might call back an employer about a job opening once in one test and six times in another test; a research-oriented testing program might specify a standardized number of callbacks.

These multiple goals—tailoring tester conduct to the particular circumstances of each job application, maintaining a clear and complete record of the test experiences, and ensuring that each tester acts in ways comparable to his partner—sometimes make heavy demands on testers. It may be necessary for judgments to be made while tests are in process. Thus, enforcement-oriented testers are instructed to maintain regular contact with their field supervisor, calling at each step in the job application process for instructions on how to proceed. As a consequence of this closer supervision, enforcement tests are more time-consuming, complicated, and expensive than typical research-oriented tests.

RECORDING THE DATA GENERATED BY TESTS

Yet another difference involves the extent and nature of data recorded from tests. For both research-oriented and enforcement-oriented testing, of course, objectivity, accuracy, completeness, and contemporaneous recording of data are important. Furthermore, both types of testing typically expect testing partners to record their experiences independently and not discuss these experiences with each other until after they have been documented.

The different ways in which test results are used in research and enforcement testing require some different record-keeping techniques. Because the emphasis in research-oriented studies is often on statistical analyses of testing results, their data collection procedures often use structured questionnaires with objective, scalable questions. At the Fair Employment Council, tabulations of test results are performed. However, where data collection will be used for enforcement-oriented testing, the goals are, first, to develop a record from which determinations can be made whether to undertake litigation and, second, to create a clear and complete record that will support claims of discrimination pursued in litigation. In pursuit of these goals, enforcement-oriented testing may warrant the use of semistructured record forms and essaylike narrative witness statements.

TYPES OF INFORMATION RECORDED FROM TESTS

An issue related to the types of records created by the testers is which results or data from the job application process are worth measuring. In the research-oriented tests conducted by The Urban Institute, the focus of analysis was on the "bottom-line" question whether the tester was offered a job. Differences in treatment during the application process were not extensively recorded.[7] This emphasis on the bottom-line test result reflected both the practical consideration that when fewer variables are gathered, more tests can be accommodated within a limited budget, and the conceptual consideration that how a candidate is treated during the application process may be relatively unimportant if he eventually is offered a job.

When testing is used for enforcement purposes, however, the test experiences must be recorded in more detail. Litigation based on tester evidence usually rests on the legal theory of disparate treatment, alleging that the protected-class tester and the non-protected-class tester were treated differently for reasons unrelated to their fitness for employment. Disparities in the treatment of the testers throughout the application process, therefore, are legally relevant and should be thoroughly documented. Evidence of the ultimate disparity—that one tester was offered a job while the other was not—should be supplemented with a record as complete as possible concerning treatment during each phase of the application process that may have led to this outcome. The sorts of variables bearing on the treatment of testers that might be recorded include: what information is demanded of applicants (e.g., are references checked, what tests are required); how job interviews are conducted (e.g., the length of interviews, the characteristics of interviewers, what questions are asked); the flow of information (e.g., what information is provided spontaneously, what must be requested); how applicants are treated (e.g., how long must the tester wait, what hospitality is offered, what names are used); how jobs are described (e.g., to what extent are career advancement opportunities emphasized); and so forth.[8]

Targeting of and Follow-up from Tests

TARGETING OF TEST SUBJECTS

The manner in which the subjects to be tested are selected also differs between enforcement-oriented and research-oriented testing. In research studies, such as those conducted by the Urban Institute, the goal of identifying the existence and assessing the extent of discrimination in a population of job openings requires the use of a random sampling strategy to obtain a representative sample. Enforcement-oriented testing focuses on a different objective. The goal of eliminating discrimination that adversely affects protected classes suggests a more targeted sampling approach.

The Fair Employment Council, for example, often gives testing priority to industries or occupations in which two conditions coincide. The first condition is that a substantial number of valuable job opportunities are available in the sector. The second condition is that there is reason to suspect that discrimination will be encountered there. To apply the first of these criteria to the Washington area, data on wage rates, job prerequisites, levels of employment, and rates of growth in various industries are examined. To apply the second criterion, a variety of information is consulted, including records of past litigation, complaints, and tips concerning specific employers, as well as theoretical reasoning from the social and behavioral sciences. For example, it has been hypothesized that racial discrimination may be more prevalent at firms serving upper-class customers and in jobs involving public contact.

The principal benefit of such targeting is the efficient use of scarce testing resources. The use of targeting, however, may limit the extent to which conclusions can be drawn from test results about the extent of discrimination in the general population of job openings. For that reason, tests of random samples of job openings, such as those conducted by the Urban Institute, remain essential complements to enforcement-oriented efforts.

FOLLOW-UP TO TESTS

The different uses of test results drawn from enforcement-oriented and research-oriented testing may lead to different steps following the completion of those tests in which disparate treatment is observed. In research-oriented testing, the goal of testing a representative sample of jobs requires that each job vacancy be the subject of only one test. In enforcement-oriented testing, however, it is often appropriate to perform repeated tests of the same job vacancy, or at least of the same employer. The goal of repeated tests is to assess and document the nature and extent of the discrimination in anticipation of litigation, principally to determine whether the observed differences in treatment were isolated or reflect a pattern or practice of discriminatory behavior.

In short, enforcement-oriented testing is a methodological first cousin to research-oriented testing, not an identical twin. While maintaining an unwavering commitment to objectivity and rigor, enforcement-oriented testing requires a modified design to generate information necessary for its potential use in litigation.

USES OF TESTING TO CHALLENGE EMPLOYMENT DISCRIMINATION

Once developed, the techniques of testing can be used in a variety of ways to audit employment decision making. Each application of testing serves a different purpose. Together, the array of applications affords a broad, effective means of detecting and challenging discrimination in employment. Each application of testing warrants separate consideration.

Surveying the Work Force

Testing can be used to survey the work force of a community to determine the extent to which discrimination influences employment decisions. The results of such surveys can yield insights about the factors that affect employment selections in the entire, or a sector of the, business community. This, of course, is the role and effect of the Urban Institute studies discussed in other chapters in this volume.[9]

The results derived from these surveys can inform a variety of public deliberations. Enforcement agencies can use such results to measure the effectiveness of their efforts and to direct their resources to those segments of the community where disparities in treatment are most pronounced. Similarly, legislatures can rely on testing results to assess the effectiveness of discrimination prohibitions and the sufficiency of resources deployed to redress any discrimination that is detected.[10] As a highly controlled, objective means of collecting aggregate information concerning employer decision making, testing surveys afford an invaluable opportunity to explore the behaviors and prevailing mores of a community of employers.

Monitoring Compliance with Injunctive Relief

Employment discrimination litigation in which plaintiffs are successful often concludes with the issuance of orders, constituting injunctive relief, by the court or agency before which the case was heard. Such orders might direct the employer to refrain in the future from any discriminatory activity and might direct the employer to undertake steps to remedy the effects of past discriminatory conduct. These might include affirmative recruitment, special training programs, and hiring and promotions guided in part by goals and timetables. While these orders carry the force of law, compliance with them cannot always be assumed. Employers who find the path of discrimination appealing or convenient or who do not take measures required to curb discrimination may repeat the behavior that originally gave rise to litigation. Supervision of an employer's conduct to ensure compliance with injunctive provisions can both discourage a resurgence of unlawful conduct and detect discriminatory conduct when it recurs. Such supervision, known as monitoring, is essential to achieving the permanent elimination of discrimination from the workplace.[11]

Most monitoring entails a review of records maintained by the employers subject to the injunctive provisions. Typically, these records consist of counts of the number of employees or applicants subject to the decision making being monitored and their race, gender, or other basis on which discrimination was alleged to have occurred. Statistical measures can be applied to these numbers to compare the composition by protected characteristic of those actually selected with the composition of those who could be expected to have been selected. Differences between the composition of those selected and those whose selection could be expected can be measured to determine if they are statistically significant and therefore can be attributed to discrimination, or are attributable to chance and therefore of no legal consequence.[12] Thus, most monitoring relies on statistical measures of the results of a substantial number of decisions to determine whether the decision making at issue comports with injunctive provisions.

Such monitoring techniques suffer from several limitations. First, they depend on records that employers themselves generate and therefore are susceptible to distortion if the information collected is, by inadvertence or willfulness, inaccurate. Second, the information to be collected requires someone, often each employee or applicant, to identify his race, age, disability, or other characteristic for which monitoring is being conducted, invading the privacy of some and creating the impression for others that discriminatory practices are being committed. Third, such monitoring depends on an ability to detect discrimination from differences between actual and predicted results from an aggregate of selection decisions, allowing isolated incidents of discrimination affecting a small number of selections to evade detection. Thus, although traditional monitoring techniques are a powerful vehicle for the enforcement of injunctive provisions, they suffer from a number of significant limitations.

Testing affords a mechanism for monitoring compliance with injunctive relief that is less subject to these limitations.[13] First, it can be conducted by the parties engaged in monitoring the employer's conduct, reducing the employer's role and, therefore, the risk that the information collected could be inaccurate. Second, testing eliminates the need to identify the race, gender, or other protected characteristic of employees or applicants for employment. Instead, monitoring is conducted through the use of testers whose race, gender, or other characteristic is specified by the party conducting the monitoring. Third and most important, testing can detect differences in treatment in isolated occasions and discriminatory practices that affect only a small number of employment decisions. No statistical measures are necessary to evaluate the results of these tests. Rather, each test affords direct insight into the employer's conduct. Discrimination can be detected from individual selection decisions, and no aggregation of the results from multiple selection decisions is necessary.

Such testing, of course, will be largely limited to monitoring the selection of applicants for employment and other decisions pertaining to those who seek to enter an employer's work force. These include hiring decisions themselves, as well as decisions to refer applicants for employment and other activities that precede the decision to hire. Testing is not likely to be of use in monitoring compliance with injunctions regarding promotions, imposing discipline, discharging employees, or any other decision making involving incumbent employees.[14] But, within this range of employment decision making, testing offers a powerful means of monitoring compliance with injunctive provisions. It can be employed either in conjunction with or in place of conventional monitoring techniques.

The use of testing to monitor compliance can, but need not, be memorialized in the consent decree or other order in which the injunctive provisions are established. Disclosure to the employer and the court or agency of plans to use testing to monitor compliance has the advantage of putting the employer on notice and, perhaps, encouraging voluntary compliance. It also places the court or agency on notice that monitoring will be accomplished through testing and that, in the event noncompliance is detected, testing evidence may be used to support such an allegation. On the other hand, the use of testing to monitor compliance without advance disclosure to the employer and court or agency may increase the chance that the employer will furnish candid reactions to the testers. In either event, when testing is used as a means of monitoring compliance with injunctive provisions enforcing the civil rights laws, the costs of testing may be subject to reimbursement by the employer.[15]

Investigating Allegations of Employment Discrimination

When discrimination occurs today it is typically subtle and clandestine. Direct evidence of discrimination is rare and, where such direct evidence exists, corroboration is even more rare. As a result, applicants for employment who suspect they have been discriminated against are not likely, without the benefit of discovery, to be able to confirm the employer's discriminatory intent. Testing can be enormously helpful in the investigation and evaluation of allegations of hiring discrimination.

Detecting discrimination in hiring decisions has traditionally been very difficult, and even when discrimination is suspected, it is rarely challenged. Most applicants for employment never observe the treatment of other applicants, much less the treatment of other applicants who may have comparable credentials. Thus, unless the mistreatment is overt, applicants who have been subject to discriminatory treatment lack any means of determining that the treatment they received was unlawful. Moreover, when discrimination is suspected, most applicants lack the evidence with which to mount an effective challenge to the unlawful conduct. And even those who may have the necessary proof to support a claim of discrimination often are reluctant to shoulder the burdens of litigation, particularly when their first priority remains finding a job.[16] Accordingly, testing is a particularly important vehicle for detecting the existence of discrimination in hiring decisions.

Testing can be used to corroborate as well as dispel allegations of discrimination that have been leveled against an employer. The denial of employment for reasons suspected to be discriminatory can be investigated by deploying pairs of testers to determine whether they receive different treatment attributable to discrimination. Neither the denial nor the offer of employment to the tester with the same characteristic as the complainant, of course, is necessarily determinative of the merits of the original discrimination allegations. But the denial of employment to the protected-class tester and offer of employment to the non-protected-class tester may suggest a more extensive investigation. And when the testers experienced differences in treatment that mirror the allegations of discrimination, an inference of discrimination may be drawn.[17] Indeed, when differences in treatment of the testers resemble the allegations of discrimination, tester evidence is admissible in subsequent litigation to show the employer's habit of committing discrimination.[18]

The use of testing to investigate the possibility of employment discrimination has several other advantages. First, testing can be used to identify the specific points in the application or selection process where discrimination manifests itself. Testing affords opportunities to examine the minute, discrete components of the hiring process. For example, rather than accept unexamined the allegation that the interviewer was hostile to a minority candidate, testing permits a comparison of specific questions asked of minority and nonminority applicants. Testing also permits assessment of whether protected-class and non-protected-class applicants are scrutinized equally, such as in the thoroughness of background investigations or the administration of drug testing, and whether they are afforded the same opportunities to demonstrate job-related skills. With testing, therefore, allegations of discrimination can be framed with more specificity than otherwise, and employers can respond to such allegations with comparable precision.

Second, testing permits investigation of hiring practices of particular employers without the pendency of a claim of discrimination. Leads about the presence of discrimination, as well as allegations of discrimination leveled by persons without colorable claims, can be investigated thoroughly and accurately. Thus, testing can be targeted at an employer whose work force reflects a significant underrepresentation of minorities or women. Similarly, employers against whom multiple claims of discrimination have been lodged, even if none of the claims can be supported with admissible evidence, can still be tested. And governmental enforcement agencies can use testing as a component of their systemic investigations.[19] Because testing can detect discrimination in the hiring process without the initiation of formal legal proceedings or discovery, the technique is a particularly versatile enforcement device.

Third, and perhaps most important, employers may, and should, use testing to detect discrimination in their own organizations. Voluntary compliance with the Equal Employment Opportunity (EEO) laws, of course, is the preferred means of avoiding discrimination. Testing affords employers a means to scrutinize hiring decisions in their own organizations without the threat or the pendency of expensive and embarrassing litigation. The use of testing for such a purpose would by no means be a novel development. Retail companies routinely use testing techniques to monitor the service they provide to their customers. The same methods can be deployed inexpensively and discreetly to detect the presence of discrimination and rectify problems before they precipitate any litigation.

Challenging Hiring Discrimination

None of the applications of testing described above affords the opportunity to challenge discrimination directly where it is detected by the testing. But testing can be used for that purpose as well. Relying on legal principles well established in testing for discrimination in housing and public accommodations,[20] testers suffering discrimination during a test may themselves serve as plaintiffs in litigation challenging that discrimination. While this use of testing must be carefully conducted to survive the rigors of litigation, it provides a powerful weapon to combat discrimination and is probably the most economical means of enforcing the civil rights laws.

In this use of testing, testers initiate litigation when they have been subjected to disparate treatment creating the inference of discrimination and harming the protected-class tester. The testing techniques used here are largely the same as those employed in other adaptations of testing to the field of employment, except as noted earlier. However, two additional demands arise form the particular legal requirements that typically govern EEO claims.

First, whenever possible, each pair of testers should proceed with its tests until one tester is offered employment. Other uses of testing do not necessarily impose this requirement. Testers who bring claims in their own name as a result of their tests must have had a right infringed that is protected by the statutes invoked by their litigation. Therefore, before undertaking testing that may lead to litigation on behalf of testers, the laws on which litigation would rely should be consulted to ensure that the rights they protect will be implicated by the testing. Most often, those laws protect against the denial of employment opportunities on prohibited grounds, and, therefore, testers who might avail themselves of such laws should persist in their tests until at least one tester is offered employment.[21] Then, the tester disadvantaged by the differences in treatment can assert in the litigation that he was denied an offer of employment and suffered harm prohibited by law for which the law provides a remedy.

Second, for similar reasons, whenever possible testers should be supervised in their testing activities by someone other than the lawyers who would represent them in the litigation. Supervision can be furnished by a testing coordinator or even a separate organization, such as the Fair Employment Council. Otherwise, the lawyers representing the testers might be called upon to serve as witnesses in the litigation, a role incompatible with their service as counsel of record.

In 1990, the EEOC issued policy guidance to its regional offices, directing them to accept claims of employment discrimination brought by testers.[22] After examining the principle of standing to sue and the application of testing in the field of fair housing, the EEOC concluded that testers denied equal employment opportunities for a reason prohibited by EEO laws have been harmed and may challenge the discrimination themselves. This development constituted the first endorsement by a government agency of the use of EEO testing as an enforcement technique. The EEOC's interpretation of EEO laws is entitled to substantial deference by the courts when they are faced with cases brought by EEO testers.[23] Moreover, the only federal court to consider this issue endorsed the pursuit of claims by testers under Title VII of the Civil Rights Act of 1964.[24] Thus, there is reason to hope that courts will be receptive to EEO claims brought by testers.

In the wake of the EEOC's endorsement of testing, a handful of claims have been brought on behalf of EEO testers. The Fair Employment Council has brought the only two cases in the courts based on EEO testing evidence.[25] In addition, a number of charges have been filed with the EEOC.[26]

The first of the Fair Employment Council's cases was filed in May 1991 in the U.S. District Court for the District of Columbia against the Washington, D.C. franchise of a nationwide employment referral agency, Snelling & Snelling. Titled *Fair Employment Council v. BMC Marketing Corp.*,[27] the case relies on two tests conducted on consecutive days in December 1990. In both tests, the testers were male college students whose only material differences were their race. They had been selected and paired to present similar behavioral characteristics, and they had biographies designed for them that presented credentials similar in all respects relevant to the office-type jobs they sought. In each test, the black tester entered the test site first. In the first test, while the black tester was waiting to be interviewed, his white partner was offered a referral that ultimately led to a job offer. In the second test, the black tester was never even given the chance to submit an application for a job referral. Instead, he was told that there were no jobs available for candidates with his credentials. Minutes later, his white partner presented similar credentials and was offered a referral that led to a job offer. The litigation has been brought on behalf of the two black testers and the Fair Employment Council, invoking 42 U.S.C. § 1981, Title VII of the Civil Rights Act of 1964, and the D.C. Human Rights Act.

The second case was filed by the Fair Employment Council in June 1991 against another employment referral agency. This case, titled *Fair Employment Council v. Molovinsky*,[28] was filed in D.C. Superior Court. Here, the protected-class testers were females deployed in response to a complaint of sexual harassment brought to the EEO Intake Program of the Washington Lawyers' Committee. Two tests were conducted in which each team comprised a male and a female tester. The female testers were each approached, as the initial complainant had been, about engaging in a sexual relationship with the proprietor, and each was offered a waiver of a referral fee if she consented to the advance. Their paired male testers were simply asked to pay a fee for the referral. The case has been brought on behalf of the initial complainant, the two female testers, and the Fair Employment Council, invoking the D.C. Human Rights Act.

For the most part, testers who pursue claims of discrimination should be entitled to the same types of remedies as are normally available to victims of discrimination. Testers may suffer harm from being exposed to discrimination regardless of their ultimate intentions to decline any offer of employment extended to them. For example, if a tester is exposed to an unexpected racial epithet or, as actually occurred, confronted by unwanted sexual advances in the course of seeking employment, there should be no doubt that the tester has suffered harm. More subtle forms of discrimination, such as being asked to wait while a white partner with comparable credentials is offered a job referral or being denied the chance to apply for a referral while a white partner is welcomed and offered a job referral,[29] have the capacity to cause real and substantial harm.

Accordingly, EEO testers who pursue claims of discrimination should be entitled to declaratory relief, establishing that the conduct that led to the differential treatment was discriminatory. Similarly, testers may be entitled to injunctive relief to ensure that they are never again exposed to discrimination from the employer they tested.[30] An organization that is dedicated to promoting equal employment opportunity, such as the Fair Employment Council, and that oversees testing as part of its broader EEO program, should likewise have standing to obtain both declaratory and injunctive relief.[31] In addition, both EEO testers and an organization overseeing their activities should have standing to obtain damages for the harm caused by a tested employer's discriminatory conduct.[32] Where damages are available under civil rights laws, typically both compensatory and punitive damages may be sought. Compensatory damages afford relief for lost employment opportunities as well as for embarrassment and humiliation caused by the discrimination and have been awarded to testers and organizations overseeing their activities.[33] In contrast, punitive damages are intended to punish the discriminator and deter it and others from engaging in such conduct in the future. Entitlement to punitive damages is based largely on an assessment of the discriminator's conduct, and therefore the fact that the victim of the discrimination was a tester has little bearing on the availability of punitive damages.[34]

Equal employment laws that afford only equitable relief, however, may not provide for award of back pay for the denial of employment opportunities. Some statutes, such as Title VII, have in the past limited any monetary recovery to the job benefits actually lost as a result of the discrimination.[35] Such "make-whole relief," as it is often termed, may not permit the recovery of lost salary or other benefits if the applicant discriminatorily denied employment never intended to accept the employment offer. In the only reported case ever to consider this issue, the U.S. Court of Appeals for the Fourth Circuit reached this very conclusion.[36] The court nonetheless affirmed the award of declaratory and injunctive relief to the testers as well as the award of attorneys' fees.[37]

CHALLENGES TO THE USE OF TESTING AS AN ENFORCEMENT TOOL

Despite the power of testing as a basis to challenge discrimination, or perhaps because of that power, the use of the technique as a prelude to litigation has drawn considerable fire. These challenges largely consist of, first, assaults on the legal soundness of claims brought on behalf of testers and, second, suggestions that the use of testing generally, and especially as a basis for litigation, is improper and even unethical because it involves deception.

The legal challenges advanced to date have called into question the standing of testers and of any organization that supervises testers to recover relief under the civil rights laws.[38] Principally, these arguments contend (1) that the testers cannot have suffered harm because they were aware of the risks of discrimination when they undertook their tester positions; (2) that the testers' intention to decline offers of employment rendered the discriminatory denial of a job offer harmless; and (3) that the organization overseeing the testing program suffered no harm and therefore lacks standing as a plaintiff. Each argument and the response to it are discussed more fully below.

First, opponents of the pursuit of EEO claims by testers contend that testers voluntarily incur any injury they suffer and, therefore, that the testers and not the discriminating employer are actually the cause of the harm.[39] For more than 30 years, the U.S. Supreme Court has held otherwise. Beginning with *Evers v. Dwyer*,[40] the Supreme Court concluded that a black man who chose to sit in the white section of a segregated bus solely to test the lawfulness of the segregation policy suffered harm protected by the civil rights laws. A decade later in *Pierson v. Ray*,[41] the Supreme Court found that a black man had been harmed when he was arrested after entering the segregated section of a bus station with the purpose of testing the legality of the segregation policy. Then, in *Havens Realty Corp. v. Coleman*,[42] the Supreme Court once again found that black testers who inquired about housing to test for discriminatory practices were harmed by being misled about the availability of that housing. Together, these authorities establish that testers do not surrender their rights to be free from discrimination simply because they voluntarily approach test sites with the intention of testing for discrimination.[43]

Second, opponents argue that since testers have no intention of accepting an offer of employment, they have suffered no harm when a job offer is withheld, even for discriminatory reasons.[44] Once again, for good reason, the courts have held otherwise.[45] Testers have the same right as other applicants to be informed truthfully about the availability and nature of jobs and the same right to negotiate for employment as applicants who intend to accept job offers.[46] Regardless of testers' ultimate plans to decline offers of employment, the denial to them of referrals to potential employers constitutes an act of discrimination.[47]

Third, the standing of organizations such as the Fair Employment Council has been challenged on the grounds that even if their testers have suffered discrimination, the organizations have suffered no resulting harm.[48] In *Havens Realty Corp. v. Coleman*, however, the Supreme Court laid this challenge to rest by prescribing a blueprint for organizations that oversee testing to establish standing in their own right. So long as significant resources must be diverted from other program activities to "identify and counteract" the discriminatory practices, the Supreme Court concluded, the organization has suffered harm sufficient to confer standing.[49] Organizations such as the Fair Employment Council, whose programs encompass such activities as the delivery of services to the community, public education, and research, should readily enjoy standing when legal actions they initiate based on test results require a significant diversion of resources from other operations.[50]

In addition to these legal arguments, opponents of the use of EEO testing as an enforcement tool have contended that its use of deception renders it offensive to public policy and even unethical. This line of attack often compares testing to the use of entrapment in the criminal justice field. While raising a legitimate concern where testing is used irresponsibly, these broad attacks on civil rights testing do not withstand scrutiny.

In particular, the analogy to entrapment is in error. The entrapment defense is invariably used in criminal cases in which a defendant contends that the prosecution induced the commission of a crime by direct involvement in a criminal enterprise.[51] Civil rights enforcement testing, as employed by fair-housing groups for many years and in recent months by the Fair Employment Council, is different from most undercover law enforcement. In civil rights testing, testers are instructed *not* to suggest a discriminatory outcome of their test. When an intent to discriminate is expressed, it is initiated by the test subject.

Given this distinction, it is not surprising that courts have regularly approved the use of civil rights testing in cases extending back many years. The Supreme Court upheld tester claims in civil rights cases involving the right to travel on buses (*Evers v. Dwyer*), to enter bus stations (*Pierson v. Ray*), and to have equal access to housing (*Havens Realty Corp. v. Coleman*). Lower courts have reacted in similar fashion to arguments that tester evidence is tainted. For example, the Fifth Circuit allowed a challenge to the all-white admission's policy of a day camp by plaintiffs whose only purpose was to integrate the facility.[52] In the only reported case to address employment testing, the Fourth Circuit upheld a challenge to a company's hiring practices by women who sought employment only to detect and challenge discriminatory practices (*Lea v. Cone Mills Corp.*).

The acceptance of tester evidence by the courts is no doubt attributable in part to the strong national policy favoring vigorous enforcement of our civil rights laws. This position has been well expressed by the Seventh Circuit in a fair-housing rental case that relied on tester evidence. In endorsing the use of testers, the court stated:

> It is frequently difficult to develop proof in discrimination cases and the evidence provided by testers is frequently valuable, if not indispensable. It is surely regrettable that testers must mislead commercial land-

lords and homeowners as to their real intentions to rent or buy housing. Nonetheless, we have long recognized that this requirement of
deception was a relatively small price to pay to defeat racial discrimination. The evidence provided by testers both benefits unbiased landlords by quickly dispelling false claims of discrimination and is a major resource in society's continuing struggle to eliminate the subtle but
deadly poison of racial discrimination.[53]

FUTURE OF ENFORCEMENT-ORIENTED TESTING

On the basis of its experience with civil rights enforcement generally
and its specific work with programs using testing, the Washington
Lawyers' Committee offers several suggestions that may be helpful in
considering the future use of this technique by private and public
agencies.

First, with the obvious qualification that testing cannot supplant
other forms of complaint investigation and enforcement activity, we
strongly believe that testing can make—and indeed has already begun
to make—an enormous difference in the quality of civil rights enforcement in our country. As we have discussed above, this success has
been particularly evident in the field of fair housing. However, we also
have seen the great value of testing in tackling discrimination elsewhere, such as in the delivery of taxi service. While experience is
limited at this point, we are greatly encouraged by the progress made
in adapting testing techniques to employment hiring practices. We
foresee similar applications in public accommodations and other
areas where discrimination may continue to flourish.[54]

It is important to emphasize that testing has already proved helpful
in ways that go well beyond litigation. For example, the annual audits
conducted by groups such as the Fair Housing Council of Greater
Washington and the recent studies conducted by the Urban Institute
in the housing and employment areas have done a great deal to focus
public attention on the existence of civil rights denials quite apart
from any individual cases of discrimination. It is very important that
this type of research testing be continued.

By the same token, testing has proven an indispensable aid in monitoring compliance with previously negotiated settlements and court
orders in fair-housing cases. The Washington Lawyers' Committee
intends to make use of this technique in areas such as public accommodations, where a number of major cases have recently been con-

cluded. Similar opportunities will no doubt present themselves in the employment field.

As stated earlier, whether used as an enforcement strategy or as a research tool, testing is best conducted as part of a comprehensive approach to addressing civil rights issues. Apart from obvious concerns about the standing of organizations to pursue litigation if they exist solely to do enforcement testing, we are convinced that groups with multifaceted programs offer the best hope for addressing discriminatory practices and opening meaningful opportunities for full participation in our society. This is equally true whether the goal is equal employment, fair housing, access to public accommodations, or the vindication of other civil rights. We strongly support a combination of approaches in each of these areas, linking testing for enforcement and research purposes with community outreach, education, and client counseling. In the EEO field, we are particularly impressed by the potential for organizations like the Fair Employment Council to develop cooperative relationships with job counseling and vocational programs in the public schools. This work would likely couple the identification of areas in the job market that may be expanding with coaching potential applicants in effective job-seeking techniques.

Among the tasks that the Fair Employment Council would like to pursue, given sufficient funding, is refinement of its testing methodology. To date the organization's testing activities have concentrated on jobs for which the necessary hiring qualifications are relatively limited. As the council moves ahead with its program, there will be a need to consider more sophisticated forms of testing involving job categories with more elaborate qualifications. Testing should also be developed to detect discrimination against all people protected by the equal employment laws. And it will always be important continually to subject all aspects of the testing methodology to careful review and revision to reflect the lessons learned from additional testing.

It is also essential to emphasize the need for establishing effective mechanisms for regular communications between public and private agencies engaged in the use of testing techniques. In the field of fair housing, where the technique has been well accepted by the courts and many local groups are operating extensive testing programs, a national clearinghouse and training capability is particularly important. The National Fair Housing Alliance (NFHA) is a natural model for facilitating this type of exchange. This type of communication will be all the more significant as federal agencies such as HUD become more involved in financially supporting testing initiatives.

As testing techniques in the employment field are refined and standards subjected to review by the courts, the need for information exchanges and technical assistance will become more and more important. The very facts that the Rockefeller Foundation and the Urban Institute recently sponsored a conference on testing, and that the Fair Employment Council has received so many requests for information, confirm the need for these services. The Washington Lawyers' Committee and the Council stand ready to provide assistance in this area. The primary constraints on their ability to deliver these services have been limited resources and the need to give full attention to pending program commitments, including litigation of the test cases now before the courts.

Quite appropriately, HUD funding has become a primary source of support for testing efforts in the field of fair housing. We strongly support continued and increased funding of private housing testing programs.

In the area of EEO testing, we foresee a similarly important role for the federal government. As noted earlier, the EEOC has already issued helpful policy guidance, establishing that it will accept complaints from testors and tester organizations. The EEOC has also filed a brief as an amicus curiae in support of the claims of EEO testers in the first federal court litigation to use employment testing evidence. In addition, it is currently considering proposals to fund a program to train private and public agencies to utilize employment testing techniques. These are all extremely encouraging developments.

In addition to the vital role of the federal government in supporting development and expansion of civil rights enforcement testing, there are significant ways in which private foundations can contribute to the effective development and application of this strategy. Most important, foundations can help by providing general support to organizations such as the NFHA and the Fair Employment Council, which furnish research and technical assistance for local private agencies around the country. It is important that such groups secure sufficient general support to ensure that their programs are not restricted by categorical funding. Such restricted funding, while useful, generally does not allow for the flexibility necessary to address the range of responsibilities these groups must discharge. An acute example of this problem can be seen in the NFHA's current situation, in which virtually all its funding is derived from a HUD grant limited to education and outreach functions.

It is equally important that organizations such as the NFHA maintain a degree of financial independence, since, among other responsibilities, they must be capable of objectively evaluating the performance of federal enforcement agencies. Accordingly, private foundation funding is crucial to the preservation of this independent role. The same considerations apply to equal employment enforcement.

As testing gains acceptance as an enforcement technique, attention will increasingly focus on such questions as whether particular types of testing are best conducted by public or private agencies and, if the government does undertake testing, what roles federal, state, and local agencies should play. We hesitate to suggest any hard-and-fast rules in this area, but we believe that several basic considerations should be kept in mind.

It is not clear whether the opportunities for private testing groups to initiate complaints and litigation, which can lead to the award of damages and other forms of relief, are available through testing operated by the government. As a general rule, we believe there are advantages in pursuing civil rights claims in multiple forums, with public and private agencies working in concert. At the same time, there are likely to be occasions in which government agencies need to deploy testers on extremely short notice and therefore would benefit from retaining them on staff. Before these staffing decisions can be made, considerations of cost efficiency and the need to control the quality of testing also must be weighed. While the appropriate mix of private agency and government-directed testing needs further study, we are certain that there will be a major role for private groups in this field.

Apart from the long-term policy issues that must be considered, we can suggest several immediate steps that should greatly improve the ability of government enforcement agencies and private organizations to use enforcement testing to the best advantage.

Because testing is often most effective when employed in connection with the investigation of bona fide complaints, consideration should be given to ways in which individuals filing complaints of discrimination with HUD, the EEOC, or equivalent state and local agencies could be promptly informed of the availability of private organizations and attorneys to undertake appropriate testing procedures.

The importance of involving testing agencies and independent attorneys as soon as possible cannot be overemphasized. Most government enforcement agencies are required to inform respondents of pending complaints soon after they have been filed. Because knowledge of pending complaints may prompt a respondent to change its practices or destroy evidence of illegal conduct, it is essential, whenever possible, that testing take place before a respondent learns that it is the subject of an investigation. To the best of our knowledge, no federal or local agencies currently refer complainants to private organizations for counseling and testing before informing the respondent that a complaint has been filed.

Looking to the future use of testing, we strongly support the creation of a mechanism for regular meetings and discussions of testing issues among representatives of the principal private and public agencies that share an interest in this technique. While the list of organizations that should be included in this type of network is open to expansion, we suggest at a minimum the initial participation of representatives from federal agencies such as the EEOC, HUD, and the Department of Justice; private agencies such as the NFHA, the Fair Employment Council of Greater Washington, and the Washington Lawyers' Committee; and staff from state and local enforcement agencies and their national organization, the International Association of Official Human Rights Agencies.

Finally, we would like to emphasize that the development of testing as a civil rights enforcement technique must be accompanied by an assurance that responsible groups are available to provide high-quality technical assistance and coordination. The assurance of quality in the delivery of testing services is essential to minimize the possibility of adverse legal rulings and unprofessional conduct. Of course, it is impossible to predict with certainty the outcome of any legal challenges enforcement testing might face. Nonetheless, we are greatly encouraged by the progress that has been made to date in marshaling the legal arguments to support enforcement testing and in assembling the network of public and private agencies that is necessary to ensure that the potential for enforcement testing is fully realized.

Notes

1. See *Spann v. Colonial Village, Inc.,* 899 F.2d 24 (D.C. Cir. 1990); *Betsey v. Turtle Creek Assocs.,* 736 F.2d 983 (4th Cir. 1984). *Betsey* was one of the first applications to fair housing of the disparate impact theory developed under Title VII of the Civil Rights Act of 1964.

2. 455 U.S. 363 (1982).

3. See Ridley et al. (1989, 17).

4. Ridley et al. (1989, 21, 27).

5. See Floyd-Mayers v. American Cab Co., 732 F. Supp. 243 (D.D.C. 1990).

6. See chapter 1, as well as Bendick (1989) and Bendick et al. (1991).

7. For example, in the Urban Institute's most recent study of the hiring process (Turner et al. 1991), data on the treatment received by testers during the application process are found principally in an appendix to the report, as annex C, and there the main effort is to summarize numerous variables into a single numerical scale.

8. While this information may be essential to litigation that ensues, such detailed records also present a unique opportunity to conduct research of the behavioral manifestations of discrimination. See Essed (1991).

9. See chapter 1.

10. For example, with assistance from the Urban Institute, the U.S. General Accounting Office (1990, 29–31) conducted a study to test the extent to which employers' hiring decisions are influenced by the national origin of applicants. The test results, finding widespread discrimination, were subsequently relied on by Congress in its decision to extend the life of provisions of the Immigration Reform and Control Act prohibiting discrimination on the basis of citizenship.

11. See, for example, Northcross v. Board of Educ., 611 F.2d 624, 637 (6th Cir. 1979), cert. denied, 447 U.S. 911 (1980); Richmond Black Police Officers Ass'n v. City of Richmond, 548 F.2d 123 (4th Cir. 1977).

12. See Wards Cove Packing Co. v. Atonio, 490 U.S. 642, 650–52 (1989); Castaneda v. Partida, 430 U.S. 482, 496 n. 17 (1977); Palmer v. Shultz, 815 F.2d 84, 90–97 (D.C. Cir. 1987).

13. To ensure that testing is a useful monitoring technique, the consent decree or order should provide that the court or agency will retain jurisdiction to ensure compliance with its terms. See United Steelworkers v. Libby, McNeil & Libby, 895 F.2d 421 (7th Cir. 1990). Then, in the event testing yields results from which a violation of the decree or order can be detected, the plaintiffs can bring the matter to the attention of the court or agency immediately and request relief from violation of an order. See generally Local 28, Sheet Metal Workers v. EEOC, 478 U.S. 442–44 (1986).

14. Of course, discrimination in one set of employment decisions, such as denials of promotion, may be relevant in determining whether the same employer engaged in discrimination in another set of employment decisions.

15. See Brewster v. Dukakis, 786 F.2d 16, 18–19 (1st Cir. 1986); Willie M. v. Hunt, 732 F.2d 383, 387 (4th Cir. 1984). Where the use of testing is memorialized in the consent decree or order, provision for the employer to subsidize the program can also be reflected. See, for example, United States v. Cenvill Ill. Corp., No. 90-C-0644 (E.D. Ill. Feb. 12, 1990) (Department of Justice consent decree included a requirement that defendant pay $51,000 to a private fair-housing organization for training and monitoring); United States v. La Fonge Ass'n, No. 89-1729 (D.N.J. May 30, 1989) (Department of Justice consent decree included a requirement that defendant pay $50,000 to a private fair-housing organization for general enforcement).

16. The record of charges lodged with the EEOC is consistent with these observations. In 1986, for example, of 48,756 charges filed alleging race discrimination, only 4,147 involved refusals to hire. Nor has this ratio changed. In 1990, 47,394 charges were filed alleging race discrimination and only 3,714 involved refusals to hire. The Washington Lawyers' Committee's equal employment opportunity (EEO) Intake Program likewise has received only a paltry number of hiring claims. While the Intake Program reviewed in excess of 900 EEO claims last year, only about 50 claims involved in any way a challenge to a hiring decision.

17. See McDonnell Douglas Corp. v. Green, 411 U.S. 792 (1973); Lowe v. City of Monrovia, 775 F.2d 998 (9th Cir. 1985).

18. See rule 406 of the Federal Rules of Evidence.

19. Following the Washington Lawyers' Committee's administration of tests of taxicabs operating in the District of Columbia and the ensuing litigation against three companies that showed that race frequently affected the delivery of service, the District of Columbia Department of Human Rights inaugurated an ongoing program to test the delivery of taxi service and, where necessary, initiate charges against companies shown to discriminate. See Wheeler (1990).

20. See *Havens Realty Corp. v. Coleman*, 455 U.S. 363 (1982) (recognizing that testers denied housing may bring claims on behalf of themselves under the Fair Housing Act); *Pierson v. Ray*, 386 U.S. 547 (1967) (endorsing the use of testing to challenge a segregated bus station under 42 U.S.C. § 1983); *Evers v. Dwyer*, 358 U.S. 202 (1958) (approving claim brought by tester challenging segregated bus).

21. Mere differences in treatment during the application process, without one tester receiving an offer of employment, may leave the harm the other tester suffered somewhat speculative.

22. U.S. Equal Employment Opportunity Commission (1990).

23. Interpretation given statutes by the agencies charged with enforcing those laws are often entitled to deference. See *Griggs v. Duke Power Co.*, 401 U.S. 424, 433–34 (1971); *Udall v. Tallman*, 380 U.S. 1, 4 (1965).

24. See *Lea v. Cone Mills Corp.*, 438 F.2d 86 (4th Cir. 1971).

25. In addition to filing suits in these two cases, the Fair Employment Council filed charges with the EEOC alleging violations of Title VII, relying on the same tester evidence.

26. See "NAACP Uses 'Testers' " (1990).

27. No. 91–0989-NHJ (D.D.C. filed May 2, 1991).

28. No. 91–7202 (D.C. Super. Ct. June 7, 1991).

29. These are, of course, the circumstances of the two tests on which *Fair Employment Council v. BMC Marketing Corp.* is based.

30. For example, injunctive relief was awarded to three testers in *Lea v. Cone Mills Corp.*, 438 F.2d 86, 88 (4th Cir. 1971).

31. See, for example, *Havens Realty Corp. v. Coleman*, 455 U.S. 363 (1982).

32. The harm to the organization that warrants an award of compensatory damages stems from a different injury than the kind suffered by the testers themselves. See *Haven Realty Corp.*, 455 U.S. at 363; *Spann v. Colonial Village, Inc.*, 899 F.2d 24, 27–29 (D.C. Cir. 1990), *cert. denied*, 111 S. Ct. 508 (1990).

33. See, for example, *Bryant v. Kay Bros. Builders*, No. B-86-534 (D. Md. Feb. 18, 1988) (awarding compensatory damages to housing testers); *Davis v. Mansards*, 597 F. Supp. 334, 347 (N.D. Ind. 1984) (fact that plaintiff is tester "does not affect the measure of her actual damages . . . [i]n 1984, no one should have to toughen themselves to racial discrimination—a tester has no reason to expect mistreatment at the hands of ostensibly fair-minded businesspeople"); *Saunders v. General Servs. Corp.*, 659 F. Supp. 1042, 1060–61 (E.D. Va. 1987) (awarding damages to fair-housing organization for diversion of resources); *Davis v. Mansards*, 597 F.Supp. at 348 (same).

34. See *Smith v. Wade*, 461 U.S. 30, 54 (1983). Courts have endorsed the award of punitive damages to testers denied fair-housing opportunities. See, for example, *City of Chicago v. Matchmaker Real Estate Sales Center, Inc.* (Apr. 5, 1991), 1991 U.S. Dist. LEXIS 4435 No. 88-C-9695.

35. The Civil Rights Act of 1991 provides for the award of compensatory and punitive damages to persons claiming intentional discrimination under Title VII against private employers. 42 U.S.C. §1981A.

36. See Lea v. Cone Mills Corp., 301 F. Supp. 97, 102 (M.D. N.C. 1969), aff'd, 438 F.2d 86, 88 (4th Cir. 1971).

37. 438 F.2d at 88.

38. See Defendant BMC Marketing Corp.'s Motion to Dismiss Pursuant to Rule 12(b)(1) and 12(b) (6), Fair Employment Council v. BMC Marketing Corp., No. 91–0989-NHJ (D.D.C. filed July 9, 1991) ("BMC's Motion to Dismiss"); Brief of Amicus Curiae of the Equal Employment Advisory Council in Support of the Defendant's Motion to Dismiss, id. ("EEAC's Amicus Brief"); Answer, at 4, Fair Employment Council v. Molovinsky, No. 91–7202 (D.C. Super. Ct. June 26, 1991).

39. See BMC's Motion to Dismiss, at 5 n. 4, 22 n. 9; EEAC's Amicus Brief, at 26–27 (both cited in full in note 38 supra).

40. 358 U.S. 202 (1958).

41. 386 U.S. 547 (1967).

42. 455 U.S. 363 (1982).

43. This argument was advanced by the plaintiffs in Fair Employment Council v. BMC Marketing Corp., supra note 38. See Plaintiffs' Memorandum in Opposition to Defendant's Motion to Dismiss, at 13–14 ("Plaintiffs' Opposition"). In addition, the EEOC addressed this point in a powerful brief it filed as an amicus curiae in Fair Employment Council in opposition to the motion to dismiss. See Brief of the Equal Employment Opportunity Commission as Amicus Curiae in Opposition to the Motion, at 8–9 ("EEOC's Brief").

44. See BMC's Motion to Dismiss, at 19–21 (supra note 38).

45. See Watts v. Boyd Properties, Inc., 758 F.2d 1482, 1485 (11th Cir. 1985); Meyers v. Pennypack Woods Home Ownership Ass'n, 559 F.2d 894 (3d Cir. 1977); Coel v. Rose Tree Manor Apts., Inc., No. 84–1521 (E.D. Pa. Oct. 13, 1987), 1987 U.S. Dist. LEXIS 9212 ("testers have the same right to truthful information" about the availability of possible contracts under Section 1982 "as anyone else" and "the same right to negotiate" for such contracts); Village of Bellwood v. Gorey & Assocs., 664 F. Supp. 320, 324–26 (N.D. Ill. 1987) (testers denied housing opportunities under Section 1982 could seek relief for "direct and palpable injuries to their individual persons"); Biggus v. Southmark Management Corp., No. 83-C-4024 (N.D. Ill. June 13, 1985), 1985 Westlaw 1751 (testers had standing under Section 1981 although they had no intention of leasing an apartment); Sherman Park Community Ass'n v. Wauwatosa Realty Co., 486 F. Supp. 838, 842 (E.D. Wis. 1980) (testers had standing under Section 1981 even when they had no intention of renting apartment).

46. These arguments were advanced by the plaintiffs in Fair Employment Council v. BMC Marketing Corp., supra note 38 (see Plaintiffs' Opposition, at 15–19) and by the EEOC in the same case (see EEOC's Brief, at 10–13).

47. See Complaint for Declaratory Judgment, Permanent Injunctive Relief and Damages, paragraphs 7, 10–13, 20–22, 26–29, in Fair Employment Council v. BMC Marketing Corp., supra note 38; Complaint for Declaratory Judgment, Permanent Injunctive Relief and Damages, paragraphs 1, 8, 19, 24, 34, in Fair Employment Council v. Molovinsky, supra note 38.

48. See BMC's Motion to Dismiss, at 4–11; EEAC's Amicus Brief, at 10–15 (supra note 38).

49. 455 U.S. at 363, 379. See also *Spann v. Colonial Village, Inc.*, 899 F.2d 24, 28 (D.C. Cir. 1990), *cert. denied*, 111 S. Ct. 508 (1990); *Pacific Legal Found. v. Goyan*, 664 F.2d 1221, 1224 (4th Cir. 1981).

50. See Plaintiffs' Opposition, at 20–25 (*supra* note 38).

51. See *United States v. Russell*, 411 U.S. 423, 435 (1972); *Sherman v. United States*, 356 U.S. 369 (1958).

52. See *Smith v. Young Men's Christian Ass'n*, 462 F.2d 634 (5th Cir. 1972).

53. *Richardson v. Howard*, 712 F.2d 319, 321 (7th Cir. 1983).

54. For an interesting discussion of the use of testing to detect differences in treatment of automobile purchasers, see Ayres (1991).

References

Ayres, Ian. 1991. "Fair Driving: Gender and Race Discrimination in Retail Car Negotiations." *Harvard Law Review* 104(4): 817–72.

Bendick, Jr. 1989. *Auditing Race Discrimination in Hiring: A Research Design.* Washington, D.C.: Bendick and Egan Economic Consultants, Inc.

Bendick, Marc, Jr., Charles W. Jackson, Victor A. Reinoso, and Laura E. Hodges. 1991. "Discrimination Against Latinos: A Controlled Experiment." *Human Resource Management* 30 (Sept.).

Essed, P. 1991. *Understanding Everyday Racism.* Newberry Park, Calif.: Sage Publications.

"NAACP Uses 'Testers' as Basis of Bias Complaint Against Miami Store." 1990. Daily Labor Report (BNA), December 24, p. A5.

National Advisory Commission on Civil Disorders. 1968. *Report of the National Advisory Commission on Civil Disorders.* New York: Bantam.

Ridley, Stanley E., James A. Bayton, and Janice H. Outtz. 1989. "Taxi Service in the District of Columbia: Is It Influenced by the Patron's Race and Destination?" June. (Prepared for the Washington Lawyers' Committee).

Turner, Margery, Michael Fix, and Raymond Struyk. 1991. *Opportunities Denied, Opportunities Diminished: Racial Discrimination in Hiring.* UI Report 91–9. Washington, D.C.: Urban Institute Press.

U.S. Equal Opportunity Commission. 1990. "Policy Guidance on the Use of EEO Testers." *EEOC Compliance Manual* (BNA), Section 405 (November 20): 6951–58.

U.S. General Accounting Office. 1990. "Immigration Reform: Employer Sanctions and the Question of Discrimination." GAO/GGD 90–62. Washington, D.C.: author, March.

Wheeler, Linda. 1990. "Undercover Riders Gauge Prejudice of D.C. Cabbies." *The Washington Post*, July 17, p. D1.

Chapter Nine

IMPLICATIONS OF EMPIRICAL STUDIES ON RACE DISCRIMINATION

Christopher Edley, Jr.

The papers and comments collected for this volume promise to advance our nation's civil rights debate in two important respects. First, they highlight the considerable methodological value of audits or controlled experiments in detecting discrimination, notwithstanding the technical difficulties of any individual study. Second, these and related studies provide powerful evidence of continuing, substantial discrimination in a variety of settings. The results of the studies are summarized elsewhere in this volume;[1] it falls to me to suggest the broader implications for legal doctrine, public policy, and politics.

My subject is a fundamental one: Can social science evidence effectively shape our discussion of the color question against a background of long-standing national neurosis and controversy? Whatever can be said for the difficulty of using evidence and reason to shape the public policy choices made by political actors, surely the difficulties are pronounced in this setting. These difficulties, in summary, include:

☐ A deep, sharp, and confusing political battle to locate the "mainstream" in racial policy;

☐ An absence of candor and forthrightness on the part of many leaders (and, one might add, scholars) in discussing matters of race;

☐ The high political "magnetism" of subtle racial appeals—generating potent attraction for some voters and equally potent repulsion for others; intuitively, it seems likely that such a situation is ripe for demagoguery and threatening to responsible civic culture;

☐ As a consequence of the above factors, a public debate often untroubled by serious attention to evidence or logic;

☐ Like the confusion in locating the policy mainstream, an uncertainty about where to draw (and how to enforce) a line between polite self-interest and bigotry.

What difference will new evidence of discrimination make to the world, in light of these considerations?

RESEARCH BY TRICKERY?

One immediate objection raised against the use of the tester methodology is a moral critique. Alan Greenspan, chairman of the Board of Governors of the Federal Reserve, has objected to the use of audits because they involve "deception." Can it be fair, critics ask, to conduct social science research by lying?[2] Can it be fair to base civil enforcement litigation on information collected by deception? Is it fair to hold a defendant liable when the plaintiff had no bona fide interest in renting the apartment, purchasing the automobile, gaining employment, or borrowing money?

This ethical critique is less compelling than it may first appear. First, given that such "deception" is commonplace in law enforcement, on what ethical basis can one defend the refusal to apply comparable investigative methods to combat the social evil of discrimination? Second, the subtle forms of individual and institutional discrimination revealed by audits are all but impossible to detect using other means. The aggregate data produced by cross-sectional data and regression analysis typically suffer from serious methodological difficulties, and the conceptual complexity of the underlying models makes the resulting statistical inferences far less politically potent than audit or tester data.

It is far more in keeping with our policymaking and political practices if we eschew absolutism and instead put the ethical question of deception into a pragmatic, balancing framework. The comments in this volume of Michael Fix and Raymond Struyk[3] seem correct but understated in their praise for discrimination audits in comparison with traditional regression analyses. The newer methodology is very powerful. We can easily justify the use of testers in utilitarian terms, reasoning that the moral costs of deception are outweighed by the great benefit of developing a clearer understanding of the social disease. As Fix and Struyk observe, the balancing is even more decisive when testers are used for research purposes only, rather than to identify and penalize lawbreakers.

But what response can be made to a nonutilitarian? To those who reject the claim that our ends justify the means? True, these moral critics are unlikely to object to income tax audits by the IRS, to undercover police work by the Drug Enforcement Administration, or to "sting" operations designed to snare corrupt politicians. Our ready acceptance of testerlike devices in these and other arenas demonstrates that the ethical coherence of opponents to discrimination audits is a matter of doubt.

The ethical objection to research under false pretenses must be that the deception is somehow an insult or affront to personhood. That is, there is some implicit social theory of personality, expressed as a conception of rights and responsibilities. Concretely, it must be a personal right not only to harbor discriminatory animus but also to shield that animus from unwanted discovery. It thus seems that what is at stake is really a claim of privacy—the tester's trick has induced the landlord or banker to reveal a private discriminatory animus, and this intrusion is an unacceptable social claim on the individual's personhood.

Is this theory of personal rights and social obligations acceptable? Everyone knows it would be impermissible to bug the banker's dinner party to find out whether she uses racial epithets or boasts of profiting through redlining. And many would also object to using undercover agents at her health club to eavesdrop on locker room chat. But the privacy interest seems quite remote once the banker is at the office dealing with the public in commerce. It is difficult to see that any social theory of personality would protect such public behavior from exacting scrutiny of the sort at stake in discrimination audits. The ethical objection to testers thus seems rather obscure.

More likely, the objection is just based on a sense that discrimination audits are an intrusive kind of surveillance to be resisted as though they were an intrusive kind of regulation. Audits are just another hassle for businesses. One suspects that this is the basis for resistance to discrimination audits by the Board of Governors of the Federal Reserve System.

In general, therefore, the nonutilitarian assessment of this research and enforcement tool must depend on our understanding of the individual's responsibilities and rights as part of the community. This in turn depends on our evolving sense of what kind of society we have and how we want it to change. And that in turn suggests that by changing our understanding of the underlying social problem of discrimination we can alter our notions of individual rights and responsibilities—not in the technical sense of *legal* rights, but rather in the social sense of mutual duties and defenses.

In some sense, it is the results of discrimination studies that will make the empirical case for reconceiving social relations so as to make compellingly clear the ethical justification for extraordinary measures tailored to address the social harm.[4]

Support for this argument could be found in evidence that strong opposition to the use of discrimination testers is correlated with strong doubts about the existence of discrimination. In a world where discrimination and bias were rare, the ethical argument for making random individuals submit to undercover police work or secretive social science research would be a very weak one indeed. In the different world we inhabit, however, only a militant atomism would leave individuals completely free of any obligation to assist in rooting out the problems.

METHODS AND INFERENCE

There can be no doubt that the scientific use of testers constitutes a methodological breakthrough. The many reasons for this are detailed elsewhere in this volume. With regard to the likely impact on legal doctrine and political policymaking, however, the most important quality of this methodology is its narrative form. Because the very model of sending matched individuals to the employer, landlord, or banker resonates so clearly, one cannot help but be moved by the evidence. The methodology allows one to investigate discrimination and bias in their subtle forms. The difficulties of gross comparisons with aggregate data are substantially avoided. And one can test directly for bias rather than imputing bias from regression analyses.

Certainly technical difficulties remain. As the chapters by John Yinger and by James Heckman and Pete Siegelman illustrate, even after 20 years there are important and interesting methodological questions in the field of housing discrimination audits.[5] One presumes that in the comparatively less developed arenas of employment, credit, and retail sales the difficulties are somewhat greater. One such problem not addressed in the literature thus far, but familiar to social psychologists, is the so-called Pygmalion phenomenon. Even in highly quantitative experiments involving laboratory animals, researchers have demonstrated that biases rooted in the subjective expectations of the experimenter (say, doctoral students timing mice in a maze) can be quite significant.[6] So long as testers have an inkling of the purpose of a study, there may well be some bias in their reports. This is not to suggest that the direction and general magnitude of the study results will be incorrect, but merely that uncertainties and questions will remain.

For example, the pilot study of employment discrimination reported in this volume by Ronald B. Mincy offers compelling evidence.[7] But this example raises a difficult question. In view of the remaining methodological uncertainties, are these results sufficient bases upon which to make public policy decisions? Here we face the stark difference between notions of proof and evidence in social science research and in public decision making. Considered closely, there are at least five layers to this problem:

- ☐ Statistical confidence levels;
- ☐ False negatives versus false positives, or type I and type II error;
- ☐ Combining intuitive or experience-based prior views with new research results (the Bayesian problem);
- ☐ Combining results (especially if conflicting) from several studies—perhaps studies using different methods or analyzing different populations;
- ☐ Deciding when enough is known about a problem to finally legislate a response.

(An additional set of questions concerns bureaucratic factors affecting the weight we can expect research to be accorded by policymakers or other audiences. Part of the answer depends on differences in the nature of the research, such as qualitative versus quantitative or "counting" versus complex inferences and predictions. These issues are considered in a later section about modeling the impact of research on policymaking.)

Confidence Levels

Social scientists typically consider that a 95 percent or 98 percent confidence level is required to reject a null hypothesis—generally speaking, this is the likelihood that the observed result occurred as a result of systematic factors rather than at random. Think of this as proof beyond a reasonable doubt: To reject the "null" hypothesis of innocence, one wants a very high level of assurance that the incriminating evidence has not appeared by chance. No such high degree of confidence is required when judges or juries make their decisions in an ordinary civil matter, however—like a contract dispute or a civil suit for employment discrimination. In such cases the test is "more likely than not" or a "preponderance of the evidence." Loosely speaking, both inquiries are directed toward finding "truth," but in the criminal context one wants to be about as certain as practical considerations and human fallibility permit.[8] The latter standard seems also to be the culture of scientists in search of provable truth.

Now consider the problem of public policy choice. There is never perfect information—or anything approaching perfection. Does the reluctance of social scientists to declare that a proposition is proven mean that the evidence should not be used by official decision makers, understanding that these officials are less pure? The answer must be no. Science and policymaking are different. The calculation of how to launch a satellite proceeds along different standards of accuracy and rigorous certainty than does the policy calculation of whether the satellite mission is a good idea, or a comparatively wise use of resources, or unacceptably dangerous in today's weather. The policy analysis can certainly be rigorous (and even quantitative in significant respects), but "truth" and "proof" have contingent, elusive content in the realm of policy choice.

There is an inclination among policy analysts, especially those of a more academic bent, to heap skepticism on findings that do not "measure up" to the scientific rigor to which we aspire. A certain amount of this is desirable if only to constantly remind everyone of the importance of rigor and, indeed, truth. On the other hand, skepticism and disbelief are often used in politically or ideologically motivated efforts to exclude imperfect research from being considered at all. A fair-minded policy process must be balanced in its assessment of methodology, and the work in this volume provides ample demonstration that the audit or tester methodology provides probative evidence that deserves attention and weight.

Type I and II Errors

In public policy contexts, it seems that the relative importance of false positives and false negatives will vary depending on many factors. In some circumstances official action disturbs subtle expectations or imposes high transactions costs. Or there may be especially egregious consequences to the unexpected side effects of legislative action— side effects we would like to avoid. There may be more uncertainty about the benefits of a proposed measure, while the costs may be quite clear. The various forms of error may fall on different populations and therefore be weighted differently in accordance with our redistributive norms.

In the present context, there are obvious differences in the distributional consequences of adopting policies based on the false belief in the existence of discrimination, in comparison with the consequences of policies adopted in the false belief that discrimination is gone. The second form of error—such as premature dismantling of affirmative action or reduction in civil rights enforcement activity— would obviously have a greater cost to minorities, who are disproportionately disadvantaged. Thus, if we demand ever higher standards of proof before we accept an empirical finding of discrimination, we run the risk of pursuing weak civil rights policies in the erroneous belief that there is no longer a problem, and this kind of error has worse distributional effects than the opposite error.

All of this suggests that notwithstanding fine points of methodological imperfection, it is important to give studies the benefit of the doubt when erroneous disbelief would be unacceptably costly.

Revising Prejudices

Another complication is that on most policy matters, officials begin the debate with some predispositions based on experience. These a priori probability estimates of benefits, costs, likely truths about the world, and so forth cannot be suddenly abandoned because one social scientist appears at a hearing with an econometric study.

This is more than a psychological observation. It is a principle of rational statistical decision theory. As a technical matter, it seems impossible to prescribe a formal method for revising a subjective estimate of rates of discrimination in light of new scientific evidence. Without a reliable sense of the underlying probabilistic structure of discrimination and audit experiments, statistical theory gives us little to go on.

Nevertheless, the policymaker's prior experiences and intuitions count for something. Even if one piece of scientific evidence happened to represent "truth," it would not be strictly rational to assume so. On the other hand, dismissing or ignoring valid research results is a familiar and unscientific response when prejudices are challenged.

In the race relations arena, prejudices and a priori judgments are especially problematic. As a society so divided by class and color, our intuitions about the experiences of other groups are quite likely inaccurate and are susceptible to purposeful and even demagogic manipulation.

Combining Disparate Research Results

Of course, not all prior knowledge is subjective and unscientific. There may be competing studies, using disparate methodologies. The pooling of experimental results is an area of vigorous but inconclusive current research.

Analytically, the relative weight accorded different research findings should depend on the quality of the methodology as well as the reported statistical confidence. The assessment of methodological rigor, however, is itself less than scientific. Experts will differ, and the lay consumer will have to decide which experts to believe. The risk is especially great, therefore, that partisan expert shopping will yield not only a range of research results but also a range of opinions on methodological strength.

Specifically, the results of discrimination audits will be subject to both legitimate and partisan attacks on methodological grounds, and the latter critiques will be subject to partisan manipulation. The comparative novelty of the research method makes tester studies more vulnerable, in this political sense, than long-established methods. But perhaps this vulnerability is offset by the (nonrational) weight generated by the narrative power of audits.

Knowing Enough

Finally, we must consider the question of how much research is enough. There is undoubted academic and intellectual value in perfecting methodology and replicating results. As a scientific matter, however, we can evaluate whether additional research is desirable based on estimates of the likely results and the possible consequences for the decision to be made. (Put analytically, this entails comparing the expected marginal costs of the new information with the expected marginal benefits; it is often a difficult undertaking if rigor is demanded.)

In a policy context, of course, the consequences of research for the decision are in large measure dependent on political factors. Evidence may be superfluous or redundant in the analytical sense, and hence a waste of money, but valuable in the political sense if decision makers appraise the evidence by crudely balancing the volume of testimony rather than assessing the reliability and force of competing empirical propositions. Recent studies suggest that such crude, semirational decision-making methods are commonplace.[9] We should expect no better from public policy officials, even as we hope to be surprised.

For example, the studies in this volume, together with previous research, would seem to many to be a completely compelling case that discrimination continues to exist in several settings. Is it worthwhile to spend additional money in hopes of documenting with greater precision the frequency of discrimination in particular labor markets or for particular job categories? Analytically, it looks like a waste of money because the chances are overwhelming that the currently available results will essentially be confirmed, and the increased precision will not affect the analysis of appropriate policy responses.

On the other hand, for many decision makers the finding of persistent discrimination is counterintuitive, "politically incorrect," or both. There is and will be nonrational resistance to the findings and their implications.

Nor, in this understanding of things, is it obvious that replication of the studies is the most cost-effective way to change the attitudes of these resistant decision makers or of the public. At any given moment in the history of a policy problem, we must ask whether there would be a greater return from investing in additional research or from improved dissemination of the existing body of results. In this broader framework, the question of "how much is enough" is more properly understood as a two-sided problem: the decision maker's calculation of how to act under conditions of uncertainty and the advocate's calculation of expected benefits from alternative investments in research and dissemination.

STATUS OF TESTER LITIGATION

Another important dimension we must evaluate as a preliminary matter in estimating the likely impact of race discrimination studies concerns the history and status of tester litigation. These cases have involved civil suits brought by private plaintiffs who, while serving as testers, uncovered the alleged discriminatory behavior of the defendant—say, a landlord or employment agency.

The issue is not the admissibility or credibility of evidence (are the tester's allegations believable?) so much as it is the standing of plaintiff-testers.[10] While standing doctrine is rather complex, at an intuitive level the inquiry is whether the plaintiff is the kind of person we think ought to be given the power to drag the defendant, involuntarily, into court and call the defendant to account. In some situations, the plaintiff simply seems too far removed from actual injury or too tenuously linked to the policy at stake in the legal issue posed.[11]

The central precedent for testers is the Supreme Court's decision in *Havens Realty Corp. v. Coleman.*[12] That 1982 case, however, is narrowly drawn. The court held that housing testers could maintain an action under the federal Fair Housing Act based on that statute's language creating an interest in nondiscriminatory information about housing opportunities.

No comparable language exists in employment or credit discrimination legislation, or in the basic nineteenth-century civil rights statute barring discrimination in the formation of contracts.[13] The latter statute, called Section 1981, was at issue in several cases in which plaintiff-testers have been accorded standing or in which exercises in civil disobedience form the basis for civil rights actions. These precedents, however, probably have little continuing force in light of the recent Supreme Court decision in *Patterson v. McLean Credit Union*,[14] in which the court narrowly construed Section 1981 to be inapplicable to alleged sexual harassment on the job because such harassment was unrelated to the actual formation of a contract. Arguably, this same trend in narrow interpretation could apply if plaintiffs sought to use Section 1981 as the basis for claiming injury in the form of insult, emotional distress, or misinformation occurring as a result of tester encounters with bias.

More broadly, the Supreme Court in recent years has demonstrated an inclination to construe civil rights statutes quite narrowly. The Civil Rights Act of 1991, the Civil Rights Restoration Act of 1988, and the effects-test provisions of the Voting Rights Act Amendments of 1982 are only the three most prominent such examples. As Professor William Eskridge (1991) has noted, the pattern is actually far broader and quite dramatic. Beginning in the early 1970s, the Supreme Court and the administration moved steadily to the right of the Congress. Among the legislative reversals of the Supreme Court he analyzes are:[15]

☐ Civil rights attorney's fees statutes enacted to overturn the restrictive 1975 case of *Alyeska Pipeline Service Co. v. Wilderness Society*;[16]

☐ The Age Discrimination in Employment Amendments of 1978, overturning *United States v. McMann*[17] ("bona fide plan" exception in the statute is broad; mandatory retirement plans are not necessarily banned);

☐ The Pregnancy Discrimination Act Amendments of 1978, overturning *General Electric Co. v. Gilbert*[18] (refusing to apply the statute to require that employer's temporary-disability plan includes pregnancy leave);

☐ The Voting Rights Act of 1982, overturning *City of Mobile v. Bolden*[19] (suggesting that plaintiffs must prove discriminatory intent, not mere effect, in adoption of an electoral mechanism);

☐ The Rehabilitation Act Amendments of 1986, overturning *Atascad-ero State Hospital v. Scanlon*[20] (holding that Congress had not abrogated the Eleventh Amendment's sovereign immunity of states to suits for damages);
☐ The Civil Rights Restoration Act of 1988, overturning *Grove City College v. Bell*[21] (narrowly interpreting "program or activity" language to erode antidiscrimination requirement in federal grant statute);
☐ The Older Workers Benefit Protection Act of 1990, overturning *Public Employees Retirement System v. Betts*[22] (permitting denial of disability benefits because of age).

There is little likelihood that this guerrilla warfare between the legislative and judicial branches will ease in the years immediately ahead. As a consequence, the legal uncertainty surrounding tester litigation outside of housing—that is, whether there is an underlying statutory cause of action and the question of who may be permitted to bring the action—will probably not be resolved through generous statutory construction in today's courts.

But while the climate of retrenchment in civil rights policy and doctrine makes it generally unlikely that courts will embrace an aggressive program of audit-inspired private litigation, three points are worth noting. First, the narrative evidence provided by audit data is qualitatively different from the claims made by proponents of effects-based indicia of discrimination, and it thus provides a more powerful factual predicate for affirmative action, flexible goals, and other remedial measures. Second, retrenchment by the increasingly conservative federal judiciary is not mirrored in all of the state court systems, so that litigation in those courts based on state statutes (and state requirements for plaintiff standing) may be an increasingly useful avenue for tester-plaintiffs. This possibility deserves further analysis and test litigation.[23] Third, in both federal and state courts, government-employed testers may be more welcome than private plaintiffs. That is, one might craft an argument that private enforcement "under color of agency authority," while not identical to agency enforcement, is distinguishable from free-lance private litigation for purposes of standing analysis.

In summary, the impact of discrimination audits on litigation may be significantly limited by conservative judicial decisions. Any such difficulties and uncertainties could be substantially ameliorated through legislation to resolve the statutory and standing questions.

How feasible is such a statutory clarification? A legislative effort to support the use of testers as an enforcement tool may appear politically less controversial than efforts to strengthen the underlying substantive antidiscrimination protections or to recast the sweep of remedial measures. Here again, the analogy to police undercover work seems persuasive, especially in light of the several existing studies, including those in this volume, that demonstrate the persistence of the social pathology.

THE HOUSING DISCRIMINATION PRECEDENT

To what extent can we predict the impact of tester studies by looking to the role research played in recent housing legislation? As the authors of chapter 1 observe, there was essentially no debate about the existence of housing discrimination during debate over the 1988 Fair Housing Amendments Act. There was massive evidence of discrimination at that time, and now there is even more such evidence. Because most of the evidence was the product of government-sponsored research, the findings were perhaps endowed with a certain credibility in the eyes of government officials.

But even more important, the conceptual context for the fair-housing amendments was radically different from the context of current policy battles. The 1988 amendments were framed primarily in the language and sentiment of a pure anti-discrimination norm. Today, the public debate is framed by many political leaders in terms of affirmative action, reverse discrimination, and racial preferences. In the 1988 housing debate there was no question about the continued existence of discrimination; today there is a strong undercurrent of political sentiment that "we have done enough" to help "those people."

As a result of these factors it seems clear that political leaders can readily embrace antidiscrimination measures such as the Fair Housing Act but feel no compunction about opposing antibias and remedial measures in other contexts. We cannot be sanguine about extrapolating the 1988 successes: The world is different; the problems are different. Even though increasingly solid, the research consensus about continuing discrimination will not so easily be translated into legislative momentum when the policy problems are—rightly or wrongly—framed in something other than the antidiscrimination norm.

CHALLENGES IN AN UPSIDE-DOWN WORLD

Ultimately, of course, the fundamental question before us is this: What difference do ideas make? The answer will inform the research agenda as well as the strategic choices of political movements. This is especially true for the civil rights movement, which stands at a crucial crossroads.

In answering the question, however, there is more to examine than the seeming impenetrability of policymaking bureaucracies to evidence about social reality. It may be that many of us in the civil rights policy community grew accustomed over the years to understanding government as a natural ally in efforts to shape social policy. We have an expectation that policymakers will eagerly digest and respond to research of the sort presented in this volume. We have an expectation that we will be aides to, if not actors in, the government's decision making. The world in these respects may now be upside-down. Our expectations of receptivity on the part of policymakers must be revised in light of recent evidence and continuing trends.

In this new world, the role of civil rights research is quite different. Perhaps paramount is the value to be found in its contribution to the defense of past gains and initiatives. And rather than gently laying research before decision makers, we may now be called upon to develop aggressive marketing strategies for ideas and insights that seem to us self-evident and compelling.

It may be that increasingly compelling, narrative research on the continuing power of discrimination will help shift the ideological debate by reinforcing the need for powerful remedies. We cannot avoid the fact, however, that there is a growing confusion and political polarization around the formulation of remedies. More research on alternative responses to unequal opportunity, including careful analyses of the many designs for affirmative action, may help.

Understanding the new role of ideas and research in the dramatically changed streams of politics, policy, and problems poses an interesting challenge to the research community. It is not unlike the challenges facing the civil rights community as a whole. It makes sense, after all, that social policy research should be so exceptionally difficult when it is focused on this most difficult and persistent of social problems.

Notes

1. See chapters 1 through 4 and 7.

2. See Bok (1979).

3. See chapter 1.

4. Is this recursiveness in fact a fatal circularity? Perhaps not. As a conceptual matter, one might ask whether an "experimental" exercise should be permitted in order to explore the condition of society and hence the desirable character of social relations. Using this variant of the Rawlsian "original position behind the veil" construct, one can grant an ethical principle against deception but agree a priori to experiments narrowly tailored to assist the process of community and individual growth. A related analysis seems at play when medical patients agree at the start of an experimental protocol (the initial position) to accept the possibility of receiving a "deceptive" placebo rather than the drug being researched.

5. See chapters 2 and 5.

6. In one famous example, graduate student researchers were asked to test the intelligence of rats by timing their attempts to learn a maze. The rats were divided randomly into two pools. One group of graduate students was told that the first pool had been bred to be intelligent at learning mazes, while the other researchers were told that their rats had been bred to be stupid. There was a strong and systematic bias in the results reported by the two groups of researchers, indicating that their a priori expectations somehow influenced the quantitative experimental results.

7. See chapter 4.

8. See Tribe (1971).

9. See, for example, Tversky and Kahneman (1988).

10. It is clear that both admissibility and credibility of tester evidence in discrimination cases are well settled. With no contrary precedent, early tester cases resolved the admissibility question. *United States v. Youritan Constr. Co.*, 370 F. Supp. 643 (N.D. Cal. 1973), *modified*, 509 F.2d 623 (9th Cir. 1975), and *Zuch v. Hussey*, 394 F. Supp. 1028 (E.D. Mich. 1975), both found tester evidence to be perfectly valid, even where tester evidence is the foundation for the whole lawsuit. Regarding credibility, there is minimal dissent from the view that tester evidence is favored. While some courts have suggested that testers, by nature of their jobs, may be biased against white landlords or realtors, *Village of Bellwood v. Dwayne Realty*, 482 F. Supp. 1321, 1331 (N.D. Ill. 1979), the rule in that circuit, and apparently nationwide, is the opposite: Tester evidence is fully credible and any evidentiary undervaluation of such proof constitutes reversible error. *Richardson v. Howard*, 712 F.2d 319 (7th Cir. 1983). Standing, on the other hand, is in question in contexts other than housing. Opponents of tester standing argue that since the harm of discrimination is invited by the tester, and since the tester has no real desire to get the job, home, or credit applied for, there is no actionable injury. In the context of housing, the Supreme Court has unanimously disagreed with this view. *Havens Realty Corp. v. Coleman*, 455 U.S. 363 (1982). Holding that the Fair Housing Act creates a statutory right for every citizen to accurate information from a landlord or real estate agent, misinformation on the basis of race is a statutory violation that constitutes actual injury and satisfies standing requirements. Such a statutory right of action is apparently unavailable for testers in the context of employment or credit discrimination, and, as a consequence, the standing of testers in those areas remains arguable. See, for example, *Fair Employment Council v. BMC Marketing Corp.*, No. 91-0989-NHJ (D.D.C. filed May 2, 1991).

11. In most private suits, standing is so obvious that it never becomes an issue. For example, corporations P and D had a contract, and P seeks damages, claiming that D

violated the terms; P certainly has standing. But what about an individual who owns stock in P? Or one of P's creditors? The issue is murkier still in "public law" litigation, where a public interest in, say, environmental quality or sanctions against South Africa is at stake.

12. 455 U.S. 363 (1982).

13. 42 U.S.C. §1981.

14. 491 U.S. 164 (1989).

15. Eskridge (1991, 623).

16. 421 U.S. 240 (1975).

17. 434 U.S. 192 (1977).

18. 429 U.S. 484 (1974).

19. 446 U.S. 55 (1980).

20. 473 U.S. 234 (1985).

21. 465 U.S. 555 (1984).

22. 109 S. Ct. 2854 (1989).

23. This leaves open the question of discrimination litigation based on state law. For example, New York's Human Rights Law provides that the equal opportunity to obtain employment is a civil right, a protection slightly broader than the right to make contracts without discrimination; a right to equal opportunity does not require, as the right to make contracts might, any desire on the part of the deprived to consummate an employment inquiry in order to prove statutory injury as under *Havens*. See also Gelb and Frankfurt (1983) (arguing that California's employment discrimination laws provide more sweeping protections than federal statutes). The absence of federal statutory support for private enforcement litigation by testers does not necessarily preclude such enforcement under state law.

References

Bok, Sissela. 1979. *Lying: Moral Choice in Public and Private Life.* New York: Vintage.

Eskridge, William. 1991. "Reneging on History? Playing the Court/Congress/President Civil Rights Game." *California Law Review* 79: 623.

Gelb, Marjorie, and Joanne Frankfurt. 1983. "California's Fair Employment and Housing Act: A Viable State Remedy for Employment Discrimination." *Hastings Law Journal* 34: 1055.

Tribe, Laurence H. 1971. "Trial by Mathematics: Precision and Ritual in The Legal Process." *Harvard Law Review* 84: 1329.

Tversky, Amos, and Daniel Kahneman. 1988. "Rational Choice and the Framing of Decisions." In *Decisionmaking: Descriptive, Normative, and Prescriptive Interactions*, D.E. Bell, H. Raiffa, and A. Tversky, eds. Cambridge: Cambridge University Press.

THE NEED FOR TESTING ENDURES AFTER TWO DECADES: COMMENTS

Robert G. Schwemm

Without a particular chapter to respond to, I limit my remarks to a brief discussion of four simple, but important, themes about testing. These are (1) the degree to which testing has come to be accepted over the years; (2) why it has been accepted; (3) the fact that there are multiple ways to do testing, depending on what one's goals are; and (4) the differences between testing done for an academic (or "scientific") study of discrimination and testing done for the purpose of law enforcement.

Let me begin with the acceptance of testing over the years. Twenty-one years ago—in September 1972—I was a lawyer with the Leadership Council for Metropolitan Open Communities, a fair-housing organization in Chicago, and we were asked to conduct a seminar on fair-housing litigation. My assignment was to discuss testing. This subject was considered somewhat controversial at that time. In fact, the senior lawyers at the Leadership Council told me that I could not even use the words "test" or "testing." I had to use a word like "investigation"—as in, "We sent out some investigators." So I had to give the kind of speech in which one part of your brain is talking to the audience while another part of it is talking to yourself: "Do not use the word 'testers.'"

By way of contrast, recently I attended various sessions of the National Fair Housing Alliance convention dealing with testing, a gathering at the Department of Justice on this subject, and the September 1991 conference sponsored by the Rockefeller Foundation and the Urban Institute. One of the wonderful things about these events for me was to contrast today's attitudes about testing with my experience back in 1972. Testing is out of the closet. It is being talked about openly; its methodology is being analyzed. As a technique for demonstrating discrimination, it has been accepted.

Testing has come to be accepted for a number of reasons. Among these are that testing can generate extremely powerful evidence; that often there is no other way to produce the kind of evidence that can be produced by testing; that testing is fair; and that testing can actually be helpful to a target of testing if the target is a law-abiding citizen.

Testing is a valuable—and, indeed, an essential—method of enforcing the Fair Housing Act. By eliminating other variables, testing provides a quick, relatively inexpensive, and generally definitive answer to the question of whether discrimination is taking place. It thus burdens a provider of housing far less than other ways of investigating a complaint of housing discrimination. Testing therefore benefits not only the victims of discrimination but also those who are mistakenly accused of discriminating and who might otherwise be called on to submit to inspection of their records, interviews with their employees and agents, and the like.

I have had occasion recently to look at some of the early fair-housing decisions from the late 1960s and early 1970s that involved testing evidence. The testing techniques used in those early cases often were quite simple, but the power of the evidence produced—the stark contrast shown between the treatment accorded the black plaintiff and that accorded the white tester—cannot be denied. In many of these cases, the judges did not even comment on how the testing was done; they just said, "Here are the results of the test. Therefore, the plaintiff wins."

Occasionally, defendants in these early cases challenged testing by arguing that it was deceitful, unfair, a form of entrapment, or what have you. For the most part, trial courts rejected these arguments. A few judges did agree with some of these criticisms of testing, but invariably their opinions were reversed on appeal. By the late 1970s, testing had become totally accepted by the federal courts as a legitimate means of producing evidence of unlawful housing discrimination.

In Chicago, for example, the federal judges came to understand— and the judges in Chicago were not known as an unusually liberal group—that testing was *the* way to prove a fair-housing case. Why? Because they became experienced in hearing testing evidence in this type of case. Some of them might not have cared for testing the first time they heard about it. Maybe they were a little skeptical the second time. By the fifth or sixth time, however, they were totally accepting of it.

By the time *Havens Realty Corp. v. Coleman*[1] reached the Supreme Court in 1982, there was a 14-year history of litigation under the 1968 Fair Housing Act, with numerous lower court decisions relying on and endorsing testing. Without this background, perhaps the Supreme Court would not have been as receptive as it was to the tester's claim in *Havens*. I think this slow evolution of tester-based fair-housing cases had a lot to do with the way *Havens* was decided.

The bad news is that one has to keep reinventing the wheel. If one goes to an area of the country that does not have a well-established fair-housing organization—and therefore does not have a tradition of active litigation in fair housing—one will find judges who are surprised and maybe even upset and a little shocked by this technique. In jury trials, one will almost always find, even in areas that are used to fair-housing enforcement, some jurors who are surprised by and somewhat skeptical about testing. To counteract these attitudes, many experienced fair-housing organizations call as a witness in these cases a professional testing coordinator to explain how and why testing is done, so that the fact finder will understand the appropriateness of this technique.

So we have not won the battle; we have to keep fighting it over and over again. But it is clear to me that the more knowledgeable people become about testing, the more they appreciate how appropriate and how necessary it is. And this is true not only for people in the civil rights community but also for judges and others.

The varying degree of familiarity with testing may be one of the explanations for the difference between the Department of Housing and Urban Development (HUD) and the Federal Reserve Board in their attitudes toward testing. HUD appears to be a leader in its acceptance and endorsement of testing. It has a lot of knowledge about testing, derived from its experience with fair-housing litigation and with funding fair-housing organizations that do testing and from conducting the path-breaking Housing Market Practices Survey in the late 1970s. The Federal Reserve Board, by contrast, just does not have the kind of experience that can lead to acceptance and endorsement of testing. Yet, how can it get comfortable with the concept of testing if it will not try even one pilot program?

Thus, one of the themes I want to emphasize is that more testing is better—every kind of testing. The Department of Justice is considering doing testing, and some people are skeptical about it. But I believe Justice should do it. The Federal Reserve should also do it. New fair-housing groups should be set up in areas of the country that have heretofore been without them, and they should do testing. The more testing there is, the more people will understand it and accept it and be moved by the power of the stories it can tell, as Christopher Edley has said (see chapter 9).

Another theme I want to mention is that testing can be done in a variety of ways. There is no single right way to do testing. A huge range of techniques exists, all of which may be appropriate depending on the particular objectives involved. The technique used in most of the studies discussed in this volume is auditing, which entails a large number of paired tests directed against randomly selected targets. Auditing is perfectly fine for a study designed to measure the overall incidence of discrimination. But it is not the only way to demonstrate discrimination.

For example, the early fair-housing cases I have mentioned rarely used paired testers. Almost all of these cases were based on a single white tester dealing with a housing provider that had rejected a minority home seeker, and almost all of these tests were considered so persuasive that the plaintiff won the case. Other testing techniques used in fair-housing litigation include the "sandwich" (or "wrap-around") test, in which a minority tester or complainant approaches the housing provider in between two white testers. There is also something called "decoy" testing, in which the white tester makes his visit immediately before the complainant's so that no third party can possibly rent the unit in between these visits. "Home seller" testing uses neighborhood residents to find out how real estate agents market homes to test for steering and blockbusting. Other types of testing exist as well.

Most of these techniques were invented and refined over the years by private fair-housing groups in response to specific complaints from individual home seekers and with an eye toward possible litigation. This type of complaint-based testing is different in crucial ways from the random audits used in most of the academic studies of discrimination. One obvious difference is that the targets of complaint-based testing are not randomly selected. Testing for enforcement purposes, even if it is not complaint based, usually focuses on certain potential defendants who have been selected for testing for the very reason that they seem more likely to discriminate than do randomly selected targets. To do otherwise would be to waste precious and limited enforcement resources. Multiple or follow-up testing of a particular target is also commonly done in enforcement work, which is another difference between testing for this purpose and auditing for measurement purposes.

This is not to say that those who do enforcement testing and those who do academic testing are or should be at war with each other. On the contrary, I believe that each group can learn from the other. The academic studies have used the basic idea of the early fair-housing enforcement tests and adapted it to their needs. The rigor required in academic testing may not always be necessary in enforcement testing, but it does serve to remind those in enforcement that they, too, must strive to eliminate all extraneous variables in order to be as persuasive as possible. Bad testing is obviously in no one's interest.

Some final thoughts. Some types of discrimination are inherently harder to test for than others. The easiest in housing has always been a rental agent's claim to a minority home seeker that no units are available. However, if a minority applicant is permitted to apply for housing, but is turned down later, say, for having poor credit, that is a harder situation to test. Cases involving sales are usually harder to test than those involving rentals. Financial discrimination is even tougher to test for. And how does one test for discrimination in an eviction case? It is not easy, but with some creativity it can be done. Sexual harassment is difficult, if not downright dangerous, to test for. Indeed, some people have suggested that no one, except perhaps undercover police, should even be asked to test for sexual harassment.

One of my concerns is that testing might just push discriminators to be more subtle. The fact that certain types of discrimination can be easily discovered through testing might lead housing providers to discriminate in other ways. For example, the recently completed Housing Discrimination Study found fairly low levels of discrimination in the form of outright refusals to rent or sell and outright denials of housing availability but found a great deal of discrimination at the later stages of housing transactions, which are more difficult to test. It may be that as testing for discrimination at the preapplication stages becomes more widespread, housing providers will tend to do their discriminating at later stages. Thus, testing may create its own problems over time. This means that the search for new and more sophisticated testing techniques must be an ongoing process.

Finally, I should mention the idea that testing may serve a third purpose in addition to the purposes of measuring discrimination and providing evidence for litigation, namely deterrence. When I was a member of the Kentucky Human Rights Commission, whenever we announced that we were conducting a testing program, every real estate agent in the state thought he was being tested. Agents often would come up to me and say, "I know you tested our office." And I knew that we had not. It seems to me there may be some value in having an industry think that it is being tested, for a great deal of voluntary compliance is likely to result. This underscores the theme that not all testing needs to be done the same way. It is usually very important *not* to reveal in advance that testing is being done if one's goal is to get an accurate picture of how those being tested are behaving. On the other hand, if one of the goals is to bring more people into compliance with the law, announcing in advance that a testing program is being conducted might be worthwhile, at least if the geographic area to be tested is large enough that an advance announcement will not ruin the results of the program.

Note

1. 455 U.S. 363, 373–75 (1982) (holding that testers who are falsely told that housing is unavailable because of their race have standing to sue under the Fair Housing Act).

EXTENDING THE REACH OF THE AUDIT METHODOLOGY: COMMENTS

John Charles Boger

One important measure of the vitality of an idea is its power to generate other good ideas. Measured by that standard, testing for discrimination is a very good idea indeed. The development of this new research methodology—a creative modification of methods used in fair-housing cases more than a decade ago—and its extension to research on employment and credit markets are positive contributions to the field of civil rights research. The elaboration of discrimination measures that can capture both opportunity "denial" and opportunity "diminishment" during the hiring or sales/rental process is an especially useful innovation. These new measures substantiate and clarify the adverse "head winds" often reported even by minority applicants who ultimately succeed in obtaining employment, housing, or credit after an intensive application process.

The extensive research findings generated by these new methods—which document widespread housing discrimination in cities throughout the country and a pattern of employment discrimination in three of the four metropolitan areas studied—have independent importance. They underline both the need for intensified civil rights enforcement and the importance of further research on discrimination.

The audit methodology has allowed researchers to explore possible discrimination in new markets and at previously unexamined decision points. The study by the Washington Lawyers' Committee for Civil Rights Under Law of taxicab discrimination in the District of Columbia is one example of such an inquiry.[1] It employed audit methodology to confirm, scientifically, the persistent suspicion of African Americans that they are often victims of racial discrimination by taxicab drivers. Ian Ayres's (1991) study of race and gender discrimination in the automobile sales market represents an additional step. Ayres has documented discriminatory treatment of blacks and women in a market in which many victims doubtless never suspected the price discrimination to which they were subjected.

My own area of interest is lower-income minority communities. Reviewing the research presented in this volume, I found myself wondering about the extension of audit methods beyond the sales and rental market to examine decisions about the allocation of public and subsidized housing assets by governmental actors. There is a long history of racial discrimination by federal, state, and local government actors in the provision of access to public housing,[2] a history that stretches back to the beginnings of the program in the mid-1930s. There are reasons to believe that some state and local housing authorities continue to practice such racial, ethnic, and gender discrimination.[3] Thus, it would be useful to employ the audit methodology to examine such "below-market" issues as:

☐ Whether local public-housing authorities continue to "steer" racial or ethnic minorities to specific housing projects;[4]
☐ Whether public authorities steer applicants by race, ethnicity, gender, family status, or age to conventional public housing, on the one hand, or to dispersed forms of subsidized housing, such as Section 8 programs, on the other;[5] and
☐ Whether racial, ethnic, gender, or other forms of prohibited discrimination continue to plague a wide range of federal housing programs carried out by the Department of Housing and Urban Development and the Farmers Home Administration, among others.

Audit methodology should also be extended to explore allegations of discrimination in the administration of other governmental programs. There are widespread indications of racial and ethnic discrimination in access to services such as health care. How frequently are minorities the victims of discrimination in hospital admissions, nursing home admissions, or Medicaid treatment by private physicians?[6] Some have suggested that employment training programs, such as the federally supported Jobs Training Partnership Act, sometimes steer otherwise eligible white and minority youth to different sites within the same city—whites to the more promising job training programs, blacks to low-income or dead-end training assignments.[7] Anecdotal evidence and unresolved suspicions in these areas can now give way to more systematic measurement via audits.

This brief catalog of additional research targets needs expansion. I suggest a series of working sessions involving (1) federal and state governmental lawyers responsible for civil rights enforcement, (2) civil rights and civil liberties groups (especially representatives of race, ethnic, gender, age, and disability groups), and (3) community advocates experienced in civil rights issues. The purpose of these working sessions would be twofold: (1) to introduce the audit methodology to these important civil rights actors and (2) to solicit information about additional areas where audit methods might uncover prohibited discrimination.

Audit methodology obviously has additional uses beyond litigation and formal enforcement activities. It offers great potential for institutional self-scrutiny. Outside the glare of public attention, governmental and corporate entities—the Department of the Navy, General Motors, state and municipal governments, and local real estate agents' associations, for example—might use audits as a method of "quality control" to test internally for discriminatory conduct that violates organizational policy.

Audit methodology can also make major contributions to the national debate on racial and gender discrimination, which often fails to move beyond rhetorical charges and countercharges. Empirical studies such as those presented in this volume—the 1989 Housing Discrimination Study (see chapter 2), the Urban Institute's various housing and hiring studies,[8] and George Galster's preliminary analysis of mortgage lending (see chapter 7), among others—promise to enrich the national debate by providing reliable measures of the incidence of discrimination. One can hope that policymakers, when reliably informed about the true dimensions of the problem, will be able to make wiser choices about future public policy.

Consider, as an example, the ongoing judicial and legislative debate on who—the employer or the employee—ought to bear the burden of proof in explaining disparate racial effects in employment discrimination cases brought under Title VII of the Civil Rights Act of 1964.[9] The damning evidence of persistent, though subtle, employment discrimination reported by the Urban Institute studies makes an important empirical contribution to that debate.

Despite my enthusiasm for this newly modified methodology, I must express a few apprehensions about its future. To begin, I share Christopher Edley's concern that the legal standing of testers to bring federal lawsuits challenging discrimination in employment or other contexts needs a firmer legislative foundation. I wish the Fair Employment Council of Greater Washington well in its ground-breaking tester litigation in the employment area,[10] and I believe that the chief legal precedent on which plaintiffs rely—the Supreme Court's decision accepting tester standing in *Havens Realty Corp. v. Coleman*,[11] a fair-housing case—can plausibly be extended to the employment context. However, the present Supreme Court has exhibited general hostility toward civil rights statutes and a marked tendency to narrow procedural avenues for their enforcement. During the past decade, the court has construed at least nine major civil rights statutes adversely to civil rights claimants, each time in a fashion later repudiated by Congress.[12]

Since testers' standing to sue is the key to the use of audit methodology in litigation, that standing should not be hostage to future judicial decisions—and need not be. Congress has ample authority to pass federal legislation that would put standing issues to rest. Such legislation, I suggest, should affirmatively guarantee the standing both of testers themselves and of the testing organizations that recruit and employ them. Congress should explicitly reaffirm the propriety of tester standing in the fair-housing context and express its intent to extend tester standing to all contexts in which federal or state law prohibits discrimination. The legislation should also affirm that evidence of substantial discrimination, uncovered through audits undertaken according to acceptable standards, will constitute prima facie proof of discrimination.

Others more knowledgeable in the ways of Washington can address the present political viability of such legislation.[13] Surely the research results provide a substantial empirical basis to justify its passage. Housing discrimination and employment discrimination, the research has demonstrated, remain widespread national problems; lawbreakers are now simply more careful not to reveal their biases openly. No reasons exist to tolerate this unlawful conduct or to deprive the nation of the necessary means—audit methodology—to uncover and uproot it. However, the political case for enactment of tester standing surely would not become easier in future Congresses if the current Supreme Court, as seems possible, were to interpret Title VII or 42 U.S.C. §§ 1981 and 1982 to forbid tester standing, or were to revisit *Havens Realty* in order to limit tester standing even in the fair-housing context.[14]

Once tester standing is secure, I agree with the authors of chapters 5, 7, and 8 that another high priority should be to impress testing organizations with the need for scrupulous adherence to scientifically valid testing procedures. Both enforcement audits and empirical research are destined for controversial uses, whether in assessing liability in specific lawsuits or in shaping national policy on civil rights issues. Studies that suffer from serious methodological deficiencies risk more than the dismissal of their research conclusions; badly conducted audits could eventually undermine acceptance of the methodology itself in the mind of courts, policymakers, and the public. Antonia Hernández (see chapter 6) warned participants at the September 1991 Rockefeller Foundation/Urban Institute conference that findings of discrimination are typically an unwelcome message that many seek to evade. Careful attention to methodology should ensure that public debate turns on the implications of audit findings—widespread, continuing discrimination—rather than on collateral issues of internal methodological validity.

In that regard, I support the proposal of Roderic Boggs, Joseph Sellers, and Marc Bendick (see chapter 8) for a national center to provide technical assistance and advice on audit methodology. Such a center could provide assistance in research and instrument design, tester training, and perhaps data analysis. One special reason for centralized expertise on audit methodology, I am told, is that good testing often is best accomplished by local actors familiar with the nuances of a local housing or employment market. A need to decentralize the actual testing process makes it especially important to create and fund a nationally recognized link that would provide local testers with centralized expertise on research design and execution.

Having applauded the extension of fair-housing audits to the credit, employment, and other markets—indeed, having urged a far greater expansion of this useful methodology for civil rights research, enforcement, and internal self-regulation—I must state a few reservations about audits. Within the employment market, as others have noted, audits work best in evaluating entry-level hiring decisions, not decisions on promotion and termination. Even in hiring, audits can address only that portion of the entry-level market for which employers circulate information about job availability. Similarly, audits are reliable only for that fraction of the housing market for which availability is publicly advertised in news media by sellers and landlords. To point out these limits is merely to acknowledge that the audit methodology is but one of a number of complementary civil rights research and enforcement techniques. Audits can perform some very useful tasks. But they should not supplant other techniques, such as retrospective statistical research involving aggregate data, that are also very useful in documenting patterns of discrimination in employment, housing, credit, and other markets. Funders and researchers should not abandon the use of other research methods, and courts should not be encouraged to view audits as the only reliable (or even the most reliable) form of evidence of discrimination in all circumstances.[15]

Still, audits have great intuitive power to suggest or substantiate other evidence of discrimination. Audit evidence of entry-level job discrimination by a corporation, for example, could provide strong complementary evidence to support an inference that statistical disparities in aggregate promotion or discharge data—data obtained via normal retrospective analysis of company employee files—are the likely product of continuing discriminatory actions by corporate personnel officers. Toward this end, audit methodology could be more widely employed as a supplement even by those who rely primarily on other methods to test for discrimination in America.

Notes

1. See chapter 8 of this volume, citing Ridley et al. (1989).

2. See, for example, Kushner (1979).

3. See, for example, U.S. House of Representatives (1987); Julian and Daniel (1989).

4. See, for example, *Young v. Pierce*, 628 F. Supp. 1037 (E.D. Tex. 1985) (racial discrimination in assignment to public-housing projects); *Comer v. Kemp*, No. 89-1556 (W.D.N.Y. filed Dec. 4, 1989).

5. See, for example, *Comer v. Kemp*, No. 89-1556 (W.D.N.Y. filed Dec. 4, 1989) (complaint alleges steering of blacks to public-housing programs, of whites to Section 8 programs); *Young v. Pierce*, No. P-80-8-CA (E.D. Tex. Mar. 3, 1988) (noting that Section 8 programs in East Texas are predominantly white, while public-housing programs are disproportionately black).

6. See, for example, *Cook v. Ochsner*, No. 70-1969 (E.D. La. June 13, 1989) (settlement of federal litigation with findings of racial discrimination in hospital admissions); *Linton v. Comm'r of Health & Env't*, No. 3-87-0941 (M.D. Tenn. April 20, 1990) (settlement of federal litigation with findings of racial discrimination in nursing home admissions).

7. See generally Orfield and Ashkinaze (1991).

8. See Cross et al. (1990); Turner et al. (1991a, 1991b); and chapters 1 and 3 of this volume.

9. Compare *Wards Cove Packing Co. v. Atonio*, 490 U.S. 642, (1989), with *Griggs v. Duke Power Co.*, 401 U.S. 424 (1971); see Note (1990).

10. *Fair Employment Council v. Molovinsky*, No. 91-7202 (D.C. Super. Ct. filed June 7, 1991).

11. 455 U.S. 363 (1982).

12. See Greenberger (1991).

13. The Civil Rights Bill of 1990, approved by both houses of Congress, was vetoed by President Bush on Oct. 22, 1990. A successor bill was approved by Congress and signed by the President on November 21, 1991. Civil Rights Act of 1991, Pub. L. No. 102-166, 1991 U.S.C.C.A.N. (105 Stat.)1071.

14. Chief Justice William Rehnquist, in a June 27, 1991, opinion overturning an earlier Supreme Court precedent barely four years old, addressed the Supreme Court's present judicial attitude toward the *stare decisis* of its prior cases: "[W]hen governing decisions are unworkable or are badly reasoned, 'this Court has never felt constrained to follow precedent.' . . . *Stare decisis* is not an inexorable command." *Payne v. Tennessee*, 111 S. Ct. 2597, 2609 (1991). The chief justice added that judicial respect for precedent should be at its "acme in cases involving property and contract rights, where reliance interests are involved, . . . [while] the opposite is true in cases . . . involving procedural and evidentiary rules." *Id.* at 2610.

It is conceivable that a current majority of the court might someday view the standing of testers or testing organizations, even in fair-housing cases, as presenting a "procedural" or "evidentiary" issue—subject to judicial reconsideration.

15. Federal courts, for example, should not be induced, because of the availability of audit methods, to devalue the independent legal significance or vitality of federal claims resting on proof of discriminatory impact or effect; see, for example, *Betsey v. Turtle Creek Assocs.*, 736 F.2d 983 (4th Cir. 1984).

References

Ayres, Ian. 1991. "Fair Driving: Gender and Race Discrimination in Retail Car Negotiations." *Harvard Law Review*, 104 (4): 817–72.

Cross, Harry, Genevieve Kenney, Jane Mell, and Wendy Zimmerman. 1990. *Employer Hiring Practices: Differential Treatment of Hispanic and Anglo Job Seekers*. Washington, D.C.: Urban Institute Press.

Greenberger, Steven R. 1991. "Civil Rights and the Politics of Statutory Interpretation." *University of Colorado Law Review*, 62: 37–78.

Julian, Elizabeth K., and Michael M. Daniel. 1989. "Separate and Unequal: The Root and Branch of Public Housing Segregation in the United States." *Clearinghouse Review*, 23: 666–676.

Kushner, James A. 1979. "Apartheid in America: An Historical and Legal Analysis of Contemporary Racial Residential Segregation in the United States." *Howard Law Journal*, 22: 547–685.

Note. 1990. "Reconstruction, Deconstruction and Legislative Response: The 1988 Supreme Court Term and the Civil Rights Act of 1990." *Harvard Civil Rights-Civil Liberties Law Review*, 25: 475–590.

Orfield, Gary, and Carole Ashkinaze. 1991. *The Closing Door: Conservative Policy and Black Opportunity*. Chicago, Ill.: Univ. of Chicago Press.

Stanley E. Ridley, James A. Bayton, and Janice Hamilton Outtz. 1989. "Taxi Service in the District of Columbia: Is It Influenced by the Patron's Race and Destination?" (June 1989).

Turner, Margery, Raymond Struyk, and John Yinger. 1991a. "Housing Discrimination Study." Washington, D.C.: Urban Institute, August.

Turner, Margery, Michael Fix, and Raymond Struyk. 1991b. *Opportunities Denied, Opportunities Diminished: Racial Discrimination in Hiring.* UI Report 91–9. Washington, D.C.: Urban Institute Press.

U.S. House of Representatives, Subcommittee on Housing and Community Development. 1987. Hearings on "Discrimination in Federally Assisted Housing Programs." (99th Cong., 1st & 2d Sess.) Serial No. 99-83&84; Nov. 21, 1985; Jan. 30, Feb. 27, May 6, May 13, 1986.

Wendy Zimmermann

SUMMARY OF THE URBAN INSTITUTE'S AND THE UNIVERSITY OF COLORADO'S HIRING AUDITS

Urban Institute Hiring Audits

The Urban Institute has conducted two hiring audits, one that compared the experiences of Hispanic and Anglo young male jobseekers and a parallel one that used black and white jobseekers. In a hiring audit, a minority group tester is matched with a majority group tester on all attributes relevant to the hiring decision. Openings for entry-level jobs are randomly selected from major city newspapers and each tester separately attempts to inquire about the position, fill out an application, obtain a job interview, and receive a job offer. Throughout the process the testers exhibit the same level of interest and enthusiasm in getting the job by, for example, coordinating the number of phone calls they make to the employer and answering interview questions similarly. At each step in the audit, the testers record their progress and treatment on data collection instruments. Differential treatment is determined by comparing the experiences and outcomes for the two testers.

The Hispanic/Anglo audit, conducted in the summer of 1989, was funded by the U.S. General Accounting Office (GAO) and was part of the agency's effort to determine whether the employer sanctions provisions of the 1986 Immigration Reform and Control Act resulted in increased discrimination against foreign-looking, foreign-sounding, legally authorized job applicants. Employer sanctions were designed to curb illegal immigration by imposing fines on employers for hiring unauthorized immigrant workers. The study was conducted in Chicago and San Diego and the four pairs of testers in each city completed a total of 360 audits.

The black/white study, conducted the following summer in 1990, was funded by the Rockefeller Foundation and used the same basic methodology. This study also collected data on steering—when an applicant applies for one job but is considered for another—and on other actions taken by the employer to discourage or encourage the applicants in any way during the hiring process. The study was conducted in Chicago and Washington, D.C., and a total of 476 audits were completed by the five pairs of testers in each city.

RECRUITMENT, MATCHING, AND TRAINING

For both studies testers were recruited at local colleges and universities. Between 20 and 40 applicants were interviewed at each site for the eight or ten positions available. All of the testers ranged in age from 19 to 24 years old. Reflecting the characteristics of the pool of Hispanic applicants, six out of the eight Hispanic testers hired had light moustaches, and one had a light moustache and small beard on the chin. None of the testers had full beards. Because the Hispanic-Anglo study was designed to test for discrimination against foreign-looking and foreign-sounding job applicants, all of the Hispanic testers had accents but spoke fluently and comprehensibly. Selection criteria included their credibility as an average jobseeker, reliability, organizational skills, and most importantly, potential to be matched to another tester. Testers were matched according to objective criteria such as age, weight, height, work experience, and education, and subjective criteria such as enthusiasm, articulateness, and demeanor. To ensure good matches, two or three members of the research team participated in the preliminary pairings of the testers and additional project staff participated in finalizing the matches during training.

The testers were trained for two and a half days in the Hispanic-Anglo study and for five days in the black-white study. During the training the testers and the project staff created the former's fictitious biographies. These biographies typically specified that each member of the team of testers had attended a community college for a few semesters and had worked at two or three jobs as a busboy, cashier, file clerk, or parking lot attendant, for example. The biographies were carefully designed to give each member of the pair equivalent levels of education and work experience. Testers also participated in simulated audits, in which they practiced filling out applications, conducting interviews, and completing the data collection instruments. The mock interviews gave the testers the opportunity to observe their partner's interview style and practice giving similar responses to typical questions. The testers also conducted practice audits where they made phone calls to real employers and filled out applications, giving them a chance to interact with employers.

A key element of both Urban Institute studies was the close supervision of the testers. The full-time field manager in each site closely monitored the testers' activities and tracked each audit as it progressed. Testers visited the site office daily to meet with the manager and called in an average of three times a day. This close communication and supervision allowed the managers to frequently review the data collection instruments, helped ensure the pairs made equal efforts at each stage of the audit, and reduced the possibility of testers fabricating data.

The site managers also ensured that testers alternated being the first to contact the employer and monitored whether the testers were contacting the employers within the required time frame. No more than half an hour passed between the time the two testers called an employer to inquire about a job opening. If an advertisement required that the application be made in person, no more than one or two hours could pass. The manager also helped ensure that the testers made the same number of follow-up calls for every audit. Testers were required to make follow-up calls within a two-day period unless the employer specified otherwise.

Testers were paid a fixed sum for the entire period of the study, including an allowance for travel costs. They were not paid according to how far they advanced in the hiring process so that they would not have incentive to fabricate data.

University of Colorado Audit

Concurrent with the Urban Institute's black-white study, researchers at the University of Colorado conducted a hiring audit using both black-white and Hispanic-Anglo pairs. The Hispanic and Anglo testers conducted 140 audits and the black and white testers conducted 145. The methodology they employed differed from The Urban Institute's in several ways.

Unlike The Urban Institute, the University of Colorado did not recruit all of its testers from colleges and universities. Most of the white testers were recruited through community or state colleges and most of the Hispanic and black testers were recruited through community-based organizations operating summer placement programs. Several testers did not have any college education.

Another important difference is that the hiring of the testers did not take into account whether a match could be found for them, as was the case in the Urban Institute studies. In the University of Colorado study, matches were not formed until the training, indicating that physical appearance, personality, and articulateness could not have been as important to the matching process as they were in the Urban Institute studies.

Because the University of Colorado researchers wanted their Hispanic testers to reflect the native-born Hispanic population in Denver, the Hispanic testers did not have Spanish accents, as did the testers in the Urban Institute study. They did, however, have Hispanic last names and were "Hispanic-looking." This difference greatly reduces the comparability of the two studies.

One of the most important differences between the University of Colorado and the Urban Institute studies was the way in which they were managed. While one full-time manager supervised four or, at most, five teams in the Urban Institute studies, in the Denver study one full-time manager supervised nine teams. The Denver manager met with the testers twice a week, rather than daily. It is unclear if there was any phone communication between the manager and the testers. Since the testers were not as closely monitored, the manager could not ensure that both members of a pair made equal efforts at all points in the hiring process. As a result, several minority testers made more follow-up calls in Denver than did their white counterparts.

To provide an incentive to the testers to proceed as far as possible through the application process, each team was paid for each stage reached in the process by at least one of the testers. This method of payment, however, may have given the testers an incentive to fabricate data, since their pay was based on their progress. Additionally, using the incentive theory, once one member of the pair reached the interview stage, for example, the other member of the pair would have no incentive to reach that stage since he would already be assured the additional pay.

The definition of an audit also differed in the two studies. The Denver study defined a valid audit as one in which both testers were able to *request* a job application. This was broader than the Urban Institute definition, in which an audit was valid if one or both testers actually *applied* for a job.

Results

All three studies focused their analysis on how far the testers proceeded through the hiring process from application, to interview, to job offer. In both of the Urban Institute studies, the black and Hispanic testers faced greater chances of receiving unfavorable treatment—not progressing as far in the hiring process—than did their white/Anglo counterparts. Overall, in 20 percent of the audits conducted in the black-white study, the white applicant advanced farther in the hiring process than his black counterpart, while in 7 percent of the audits the black advanced farther. Hispanics faced even greater unfavorable treatment: in 31 percent of the audits the white applicant advanced farther, while in 11 percent the Hispanic applicant did.

Higher levels of discrimination against Hispanics were found in Chicago than in San Diego, while blacks fared worse in Washington than in Chicago. In Chicago, Anglos advanced farther in 33 percent of the audits and Hispanics in 8 percent, while in San Diego Anglos advanced farther in 29 percent of the audits and Hispanics in 13. In the black-white study, the whites in Chicago were favored in 17 percent of the audits and blacks in 8 percent. In Washington, whites were favored in 23 percent of the audits and blacks in 7 percent.

In the University of Colorado study, the findings were substantially different, with the minority applicants receiving slightly more favorable treatment than their majority counterparts. Blacks advanced farther in 15 percent of the audits and whites in 17 percent. Hispanics advanced farther in 36 percent of the audits while their Anglo counterparts advanced farther in only 26 percent of the audits (table A.1).

In the Urban Institute black-white study, there was significant variation by industry and occupation. However, results varied widely

Table A.1 RESULTS FROM EMPLOYMENT AUDIT STUDIES: WHO ADVANCED FURTHER? (Percentage of All Audits Completed)

	Majority favored	Minority favored
University of Colorado		
Hispanic-Anglo	26	36
Black-White	17	15
Urban Institute		
Overall		
Hispanic-Anglo	31	11
Black-White	20	7
Hispanic-Anglo		
Chicago	33	8
San Diego	29	13
Black-White		
Chicago	17	8
Washington, D.C.	23	7

between the two sites, Chicago and Washington, D.C. Overall, blacks were much more likely to encounter unfavorable treatment in higher paying, higher status jobs and in jobs that involve substantial customer contact. In the Hispanic-Anglo audit, differences in treatment by occupation varied little from overall averages with the exception of management and office jobs, where Hispanics fared significantly worse than in other occupations. The industries with the highest level of unfavorable treatment toward Hispanics were manufacturing and construction. Additional research found little relationship between the extent of client contact and the probability of differential treatment in obtaining interviews or job offers.

The University of Colorado study found no major differences in the treatment of Hispanics and Anglos or blacks and whites in the major industries they examined or in the occupation groups they analyzed.

Analysis of the data from the Urban Institute black-white study shows that the race of the interviewer did not have an effect on outcomes. Surprisingly, in the Hispanic-Anglo study Anglos were more likely to receive a job offer from non-white interviewers. Additionally, Hispanic testers fared worse when facing a male interviewer than when facing a female. The University of Colorado study did not analyze the effect of the race or sex of the interviewer on outcomes.

Whether a tester was steered to a better or worse job was analyzed in the Urban Institute's black-white study and in the Denver study. In the Institute's study, employers steered blacks to less desirable jobs—in terms of wages, hours, and status—than their white counterparts in a small but significant share of all audits. In 5 percent of the audits, blacks were considered for a less desirable position and in 3 percent of the audits blacks were considered for more desirable positions. In the University of Colorado study, the number of audits in which both testers were offered jobs was too low to draw conclusions about the extent of steering at that stage. The researchers did not examine steering at the earlier application and interview stages.

The Urban Institute black-white study also examined "opportunity diminishing" behavior on the part of employers. For example, although the tester might have been able to proceed from one stage to the next he might have had to request an application several times while his partner was able to obtain one right away. Or an employer may have made positive, encouraging remarks to one tester and not to the other. Results of this type of analysis differed greatly by site. In Washington black applicants were treated worse than their white partners in 8 percent of the audits and in 6 percent of the audits the white partner fared worse. In Chicago, however, blacks were given more encouragement in 14 percent of the audits while whites were treated more favorably in 9 percent.

At the interview stage a composite index that takes into account waiting time, length of interview, number of interviewers, and positive comments indicates that, overall, whites were favored 50 percent of the time and blacks 27 percent of the time. However, results again varied by site and in Chicago blacks were actually favored slightly more often than whites.

Although the Urban Institute Hispanic-Anglo study did not collect data systematically on this type of unfavorable treatment, it did find anecdotal evidence of Hispanics receiving more discouraging treatment than their white counterparts. The University of Colorado study, using similar measures, found that both the Hispanic and black applicants were more likely to deal with lower level staff in the initial personal visits than their majority counterparts. However, at the interview stage, no significant differences were found in terms of length or content of interview or courtesy of the interviewer.

For further information on these studies see:

Cross, Harry, with Genevieve Kenney, Jane Mell, and Wendy Zimmermann. 1990. *Employer Hiring Practices: Differential Treatment of Hispanic and Anglo Job Seekers.* Urban Institute Report 90-4. Washington, D.C.: Urban Institute Press.

Turner, Margery, Michael Fix, and Raymond J. Struyk. 1991. *Opportunities Denied, Opportunities Diminished: Racial Discrimination in Hiring.* Urban Institute Report 91-9. Washington, D.C.: Urban Institute Press.

Kenney, Genevieve M., and Douglas A. Wissoker. 1991. "An Analysis of the Correlates of Discrimination facing Young, Hispanic Jobseekers." Washington, D.C.: The Urban Institute.

James, Franklin J., and Steve W. DelCastillo. 1992. "We May Be Making Progress Toward Equal Access to Jobs: Evidence from Recent Audits." Denver: University of Colorado.

ABOUT THE EDITORS

Michael Fix directs the Institute's Immigrant Policy Program. Recent works include: *Educating Immigrant Children: Chapter 1 in the Changing City* (with Wendy Zimmermann), *The Paper Curtain: Employer Sanctions' Implementation, Impact, and Reform* (editor); and *Opportunities Denied, Opportunities Diminished: Racial Discrimination in Hiring* (with Margery A. Turner and Raymond J. Struyk).

Raymond J. Struyk is a Senior Fellow at the Urban Institute, working for the Institute's Center for International Activities. His recent publications include *Housing Discrimination Study: Synthesis* (with Margery Turner and John Yinger) and *Housing Finance in LDCs: India's National Housing Bank as a Model?* (with Marisol Ravicz). He is currently living in Moscow where he is directing the Urban Institute-USAID technical cooperation program in the shelter sector in Russia.

ABOUT THE CONTRIBUTORS

Marc Bendick, Jr. is a labor economist and a principal of Bendick and Egan Economic Consultants, Inc. in Washington, D.C. He has been involved in the development of methodology for employment testing since 1987 as a consultant to both the Urban Institute and the Fair Employment Council of Greater Washington, Inc.

John Charles Boger is an associate professor of law at the University of North Carolina. He spent over a decade with the NAACP Legal Defense and Educational Fund, most recently as Director of the Poverty and Justice Project, where he initiated a new program on race and poverty law that concentrates on housing and education issues. He currently chairs the Poverty and Race Research Action Council.

Roderic V. O. Boggs is the executive director of the Washington Lawyers' Commitee for Civil Rights. He has been actively involved in the development of civil rights enforcement testing for over ten years as counsel to both the Fair Housing and Fair Employment Councils of Greater Washington.

Robert D. Butters is a member of the law firm Cichocki and Armstrong, Ltd. He is the former deputy general counsel of the National Association of Realtors®. Mr. Butters has served as a faculty member of the U.S. Housing and Urban Development seminars on Fair Housing and Fair Lending, and is an adjunct faculty member of the IIT/Chicago-Kent College of Law.

Christopher Edley, Jr. is associate director, Office of Management and Budget. Formerly, he was a professor at Harvard Law School. He has served as assistant director, White House domestic policy staff, 1978-79; special assistant, Secretary of Health, Education and Welfare, 1978-80; associate assistant to the President, White House, Office of the Chief of Staff, 1980; editorial page staff, *The Washington Post*,

1982-84 (part-time while teaching); and National Issues Director, Dukakis for President 1987-88. Professor Edley's board memberships include: Swarthmore College; Congressional Black Caucus Foundation; Center for Social Welfare Policy and Law; Boston Lawyers' Committee for Civil Rights Under Law; People for the American Way; Neiman Foundation Advisory Board.

George C. Galster is a senior research associate at the Urban Institute, and was formerly professor of economics and chairperson of the Urban Studies Program at The College of Wooster. He has published widely on the topics of racial discrimination and segregation, neighborhood dynamics, housing upkeep, community lending patterns, and residential satisfaction. His latest books are *The Maze of Urban Housing Markets* and *The Metropolis in Black and White*.

James J. Heckman is the Henry Schultz Professor, department of economics, and director of the Center for Social Program Evaluation, Harris Graduate School of Public Policy Studies at the University of Chicago, and a senior research fellow at the American Bar Foundation. He has published widely in econometric theory, labor economics, and the econometrics of program evaluation.

Antonia Hernández is the president and general counsel of the Mexican American Legal Defense and Educational Fund (MALDEF), a national Latino civil rights organization headquartered in Los Angeles. Prior to joining MALDEF, Ms. Hernández served as staff counsel to the U.S. Senate Committee on the Judiciary where she specialized in civil rights and immigration legislation. She also is a nationally-recognized expert on issues pertaining to education, employment, and voting rights within the Latino community in the United States.

Ronald B. Mincy is a senior research associate at the Urban Institute, where his principal areas of expertise are poverty, the underclass, and the effects of minimum wage. His career has combined teaching and policy oriented research in government, academic, and research institutions. Recent publications include "A Mentor, Peer Group, Incentive Model for Helping Underclass Youth" (coauthored with Susan Wiener).

Robert G. Schwemm is the Wendell H. Ford Professor at the University of Kentucky College of Law where he has taught since 1975. From 1986 to 1990 he was Vice-Chair of the Kentucky Commission on Human Rights. In 1991 he served as a special attorney and scholar-in-residence with the Housing and Civil Enforcement Section of the U.S. Department of Justice's Civil Rights Division. He has authored numerous articles and books on fair housing law including: *Housing Discrimination: Law and Litigation.*

Birgit Seifert is currently a Bosch Foundation Fellow, and was formerly staff attorney with the Mexican American Legal Defense and Educational Fund in Los Angeles, where she specialized in equal employment opportunity policy and litigation. Prior to joining MALDEF, she served as a law clerk to Judge Harold Greene of the U.S. District Court for the District of Columbia.

Joseph M. Sellers is the director of the Equal Employment Opportunity Program of the Washington Lawyers' Committee for Civil Rights Under Law. He has served as legal counsel to two civil rights testing programs: the first testing the delivery of taxi service in the District of Columbia, the second the Equal Employment Testing Program.

Shanna L. Smith is director of programs at the National Fair Housing Alliance. She has worked with the Alliance to bring together national civil rights organizations to launch a unified campaign designed to educate people about the subtleties of housing discrimination. Ms. Smith has testified before the Senate Banking Subcommittees on Urban and Consumer Affairs on issues ranging from fair housing provisions to the secondary mortgage market and has conducted hundreds of fair-housing training workshops for the housing and lending industry as well as federal, state, and private enforcement personnel.

Peter Siegelman is an economist and research fellow at the American Bar Foundation. His prior work has focused on employment discrimination litigation and on discrimination in the sale of new cars.

William R. Tisdale is executive director of the Metropolitan Milwaukee Fair Housing Council, Inc., where he has been employed since 1978. He is a member of numerous boards and committees and has served as President of the National Fair Housing Alliance since 1987.

Margery Austin Turner is the director of housing research at the Urban Institute, where she conducted the analysis of racial and ethnic steering as part of the national Housing Discrimination Study. In addition to her work on housing discrimination and segregation, Ms. Turner has published extensively on issues relating to housing market operations, housing needs and problems, and public sector housing programs. She is the author of *Housing Market Impacts of Rent Control: The Washington D.C. Experience* and coauthor of *Future U.S. Housing Policy: Meeting the Demographic Challenge.*

John Yinger is professor of economics and public administration and senior research associate at the Metropolitan Studies Program, the Maxwell School, Syracuse University. He has also taught at Harvard University, the University of Michigan, and the University of Wisconsin. He has published numerous articles on state and local public finance, racial and ethnic discrimination in housing, urban economics, and has coauthored two recent books: *America's Ailing Cities* and *Property Taxes and Housing Values.*

Wendy Zimmermann is a research associate at the Urban Institute. She has worked on both of the Institute's employment discrimination studies, or hiring audits, and has conducted research on immigration and immigrant policy. Her recent publications include: "Paired Role-Playing: Evaluating Service Delivery and Treatment" (with Margery A. Turner) in *Handbook on Practical Program Evaluation* (Harry P. Hatry, Joe Wholey, and Katheryn Newcomer, eds.) and "After Arrival: An Overview of Immigrant Policy in the United States" (with Michael Fix) in *Immigration and Ethnicity: The Integration of America's Newest Immigrants* (Jeffrey S. Passel and Barry Edmonston, eds.).